Photo Recon
Became Fighter Duty

Photo Recon Became Fighter Duty

Marine Observation Squadron 251 in World War II

STEVEN K. DIXON

McFarland & Company, Inc., Publishers
Jefferson, North Carolina

LIBRARY OF CONGRESS CATALOGUING-IN-PUBLICATION DATA

Names: Dixon, Steven K., author.
Title: Photo recon became fighter duty : Marine Observation Squadron 251 in World War II / Steven K. Dixon.
Other titles: Marine Observation Squadron 251 in World War II
Description: Jefferson, North Carolina : McFarland & Company, Inc., Publishers, 2016 | Includes bibliographical references and index.
Identifiers: LCCN 2016011280 | ISBN 9780786497980 (softcover : acid free paper) ∞
Subjects: LCSH: United States. Marine Observation Squadron 251. | World War, 1939–1945—Aerial operations, American. | World War, 1939–1945—Campaigns—Pacific Area. | World War, 1939–1945—Reconnaissance operations, American. | World War, 1939–1945—Regimental histories, American.
Classification: LCC D790.473 251st .D59 2016 | DDC 940.54/5973—dc23
LC record available at http://lccn.loc.gov/2016011280

BRITISH LIBRARY CATALOGUING DATA ARE AVAILABLE

ISBN (print) 978-0-7864-9798-0
ISBN (ebook) 978-1-4766-2497-6

© 2016 Steven K. Dixon. All rights reserved

No part of this book may be reproduced or transmitted in any form or by any means, electronic or mechanical, including photocopying or recording, or by any information storage and retrieval system, without permission in writing from the publisher.

Front cover—background: Guiuan Airfield, Samar, Philippine Islands, March 1945 (National Archives); inset: the original insignia designed by Eldon "Duke" Railsback (author's collection). Back cover—left: insignia after the squadron obtained F4U Corsairs; the gold wings of the original design have been replaced by the bent wings of the Corsair (courtesy of John W. Irwin); right: squadron insignia (designed by 2Lt. Danny Johnson) after the squadron was redesignated as VMF-251; they became known as "Lucifer's Messengers" (author's collection)

Printed in the United States of America

McFarland & Company, Inc., Publishers
Box 611, Jefferson, North Carolina 28640
www.mcfarlandpub.com

To all Marines of 251—
past, present and future

Acknowledgments

There are many people to thank for their help during the course of completing this book. First, I would like to thank authors John Lundstrom, Dennis Letourneau, Barrett Tillman and Gordon Rottman for answering my questions during the early stages of the book. I am especially indebted to Lundstrom's book *The First Team* and Letourneau's book, written with his father Roger, *Operation Ke*. I have relied heavily on these two works to piece together the squadron's operations during the Guadalcanal operation. Along with Frank Olynyk's *USMC Credits for the Destruction of Enemy Aircraft in Air-to-Air Combat World War 2*, some of the gaps of the squadron's early days of combat have been filled.

A special thanks to the Marine Corps Heritage Foundation for awarding me a grant to complete this book; the staff at the National Archives in helping this first time visitor find the documents pertaining to the squadron; and the staff at the USMC History Division for their help and quick answers to my emails.

I would also like to thank Kristine Krueger of the National Film Information Service, Margaret Herrick Library, of the Academy of Motion Picture Arts and Sciences for her help in obtaining documents pertaining to the filming of Wake Island.

Lt. Col. Jim Irwin, USMCR, Kristian Whitten, Briana Madden, Roy Spurlock, Jr., David Garton, Mary Timmons, and Brenda Lorch Putoff deserve special thanks. They graciously supplied me items pertaining to their relative's service with VMO/VMF-251. Briana also put me in touch with VMO-251 veteran Albert Hoffman. I was unable to speak with Hoffman, who passed away in 2015, but he did leave an oral history with the Command Museum at MCRD San Diego. A transcript was sent to me by historian Ellen Guillemette.

My thanks also go to Vito Murgolo and Hugh "Yogi" Irwin. Both answered my many questions and provided their recollections with the squadron. Along with Albert Hoffman, they were the only World War II veterans that served with the squadron that I could track down.

Thanks to the people at McFarland, who expressed early interest in the project and ultimately decided to publish the book.

Finally, many thanks to my friends and family: Paul and Amy Houston for housing and feeding me during my visits to the National Archives and the USMC History Division at Quantico; to my parents, uncle, sisters and brother for their generous support; to my wife Lisa, my daughters Sarah and Deanna, and my son Brian, all of whom had to put up with my many days in front of the computer screen.

For those I have failed to recognize, please forgive me. Your contributions are greatly appreciated.

Table of Contents

Acknowledgments — vi
Preface — 1

One. The Beginning — 5
Two. New Caledonia — 14
Three. Espiritu Santo and Guadalcanal — 32
Four. Home and Transition — 68
Five. Espiritu Santo, Green Island and Bougainville — 79
Six. Guiuan Field, Samar, Philippine Islands, and Deactivation — 156

Epilogue — 201

Appendices:
   1. Commanding Officers — 203
   2. Assignments, 1941–1945 — 203
   3. Casualties, 1 December 1941–1 June 1945 — 204
   4. Roster of Personnel, August 1942 — 206
   5. Roster of Personnel, March 1945 — 212
   6. Number of Japanese Planes Shot Down per 251 Pilot — 219
   7. Aircraft Markings — 221
   8. World War II Squadron Awards — 221
   9. Citations for Recommended Awards — 222

Chapter Notes — 224
Bibliography — 232
Index — 235

Preface

This book is an attempt to put to paper the World War II history of VMFA-251, currently home-based at MCAS Beaufort, South Carolina. I served with the squadron from 1976–1979. At the time, I was unaware of the squadron's involvement during the war. My interest was in the European Theater where my grandfather fought, and where my mother lived her childhood in Nazi occupied France.

Several years ago, I set up a website for squadron veterans. I soon began getting emails from family members who had fathers or grandfathers serve with the squadron during World War II. The pictures they provided piqued my interest and I soon began research into the squadron's history. Little did I know of the difficulties that I would soon face.

Trying to put together the World War II history of the squadron proved to be a puzzle: the pieces were there but locating them proved to be a challenge. Research led me to a historical society in Vermont, to the Academy of Motion Picture Arts and Sciences in Los Angeles, countless hours going through official documents at the National Archives and the website www.fold3.com, and a host of other avenues. Unfortunately with the poor recordkeeping by many of the units that participated in the Guadalcanal campaign, including VMO-251, a complete picture of the squadron's operations in 1942–1943 could not be made. Entries like "Routine combat operations" do not reveal any details and begs the question: what were routine combat operations? As I covered the days, months and years, what I had hoped would be a comprehensive history became a diary of the squadron's accomplishments during the war.

Marine aviation underwent a rapid expansion during the Second World War, one that is likely never to be experienced again. One of the squadrons born during that expansion was VMO-251. Within six months of its activation, it was sent to the South Pacific and ended up playing a unique role during the Guadalcanal campaign.

The squadron is certainly unique in the annals of Marine aviation. Formed in December 1941, it was designated as an observation squadron but the squadron—except for a lone F4F-7 attached to MAG-23—never flew a photo reconnaissance mission during the war. Events dictated that it serve as a fighter squadron and perform a host of other duties, doing so with distinction throughout the war. While performing combat air patrols, strike missions and close air support missions, the squadron retained its VMO designation. It wasn't until 1945 that it finally was re-designated as a fighter squadron.

The pilots flew long hours, often flying two or three times a day to complete missions. To keep up with the torrid pace of operations, the planes had to be maintained. That responsibility belonged to the mechanics. Their hours were even longer; often lasting 16 hours: inspections, repairs, fueling, loading ordnance, bore-sighting guns, changing out engines were just a few of the many duties they had to perform. Former squadron pilot Hugh "Yogi" Irwin echoed the sentiments of many pilots when he wrote that he "felt our ground crew was most efficient in keeping the aircraft in the best flying condition."[1]

The way in which the squadron was sent overseas in 1942 had a detrimental effect on how it could accomplish the missions assigned to it. That it was able to do so is a testament to the officers and men of the squadron and their ability to do the job with what was available.

The squadron's executive officer at the time, Major Charles "Fog" Hayes, who later became Assistant Commandant of the Marine Corps, was extremely critical of the way in which the squadron was deployed. In 1943, Hayes wrote a letter to the Commanding General, Marine Aircraft Wings, Pacific, stating in part that "much of the current comment on organization is based on the Task Force principle, or the grouping of component specialized units into a force especially designed and balanced for a specific operation. This principle is of proven value in flexibility and effects some economy of personnel by eliminating as excess baggage those parts of a standard organization which will not be required for a certain mission. However, such a force can be effective only if it is composed of complete, organized [*underline in original*] units. In my opinion there is a danger of losing sight of this requirement in the current mania for streamlining, pooling and hasty regrouping."[2]

Hayes did preface his comments by saying that some of the deficiencies expressed in his letter may have been corrected. Some were, but supply was always a nagging issue. Despite a huge logistical network for the movement of supplies to combat areas, bombs and .50 caliber ammunition, at times, became scarce during the squadron's second tour of combat.

Despite the setbacks, the squadron successfully performed the missions it was ordered to perform. It earned several streamers, including the Presidential Unit Citation and the Philippine Distinguished Unit Citation. It was also recommended for the Navy's Unit Commendation as well as the Army's Distinguished Unit Badge.

One can only imagine what the squadron's record may have been if it had all it needed from the start to get the job done.

For those unfamiliar with military aviation a few terms need to be defined. A squadron contained anywhere from 16 to 25 aircraft. During the Guadalcanal campaign, VMO-251 had 16 to 18 aircraft, excluding its utility aircraft. When the squadron began serving its second combat tour in 1944, it had 18 to 22 aircraft. In both cases, the numbers fluctuated due to combat, operational losses, and the availability of replacement aircraft. The squadrons were usually divided into four-plane divisions, each division containing two two-plane sections. A flight could be any number of divisions or sections. One pilot was given overall command of all planes on a mission, with other pilots designated as division and section leaders.

Since the end of World War II, geographic names have changed for many locations in the South Pacific. Because of this it was extremely difficult, in some cases, to find target locations. With the help of period maps, I was able to find the location of most of the primary targets. In order to avoid confusion, I decided to keep names as written in the diaries and aircraft action reports.

Speaking of the war diaries and aircraft action reports—in some cases I found the reports contradictory, often mistaking bomb loads, primary target locations and names of pilots. Where this happened, I used my best judgment to straighten out the discrepancies based on the available documentation.

All documents accessed during the course of research for this book have been declassified. Markings on documents used as illustrations are no longer in effect.

Semper Fidelis. Steven K. Dixon, Sgt., USMC, VMFA-251 1976–1979

ONE

The Beginning

By late November 1941, Japan had been at war for ten years. Korea and Manchuria were under Japanese rule. Japan launched an attack on China in 1937 and quickly found the ancient country would not give up so easily. The conflict tied up over a million Japanese troops by 1941. Under the guise of the Greater East Asia Co-Prosperity Sphere, the island nation sought to free Asia of colonial rule—Asia for Asians. For those nations, they soon found out that Asia for Asians came with a price—a brutal, totalitarian rule by Japan.

The United States sought to curtail Japanese expansion with economic sanctions, and eventually oil exports to Japan ceased. Japan was dependent on U.S. oil, and her strategic reserve would not support a prolonged war. If she was to bring Asia under Japanese rule, the country needed oil. The Dutch East Indies oil fields were the perfect target.

Plans were made to capture the oil fields, as well as the Philippines, Malaysia, French Indo-China, and numerous island chains in the vast expanse of the south Pacific. The United States Navy was perceived as the main threat to this large operation. It had to be neutralized to protect the flank and that meant attacking the fleet at its main anchorage—Pearl Harbor, Territory of Hawaii.

The Commander in Chief of the Japanese Combined Fleet, Admiral Isoroku Yamamoto, proposed to attack the base with planes provided by aircraft carriers. The plan was not accepted by the General Staff. Yamamoto, a popular officer in the Navy, threatened to resign should the plan not be accepted. Not risking a controversy within the military, the General Staff backed down and accepted the plan.

On 1 December 1941, the Japanese naval attack force was five days out of Hitokappu Bay. To accomplish the task of eliminating the threat from the U.S. Navy, Admiral Chuichi Nagumo, commander of the Pearl Harbor Attack Force, had under his command six aircraft carriers, three cruisers, two battleships, nine destroyers, nine tankers and several other vessels. The six carriers carried more than 400 aircraft, nearly double the entire inventory of aircraft of the United States Marine Corps at that time.

On the same day, at Naval Air Station (NAS) San Diego, California, authorization to activate Marine Observation Squadron 251 (VMO-251) came via a confidential mailgram. Captain Elliott E. Bard was named the commanding officer. Except for a photographic section and a radar section, it was a near duplicate of a 1941 USMC fighter squadron. Temporary housing for squadron Marines was on North Island.

When the squadron formed, it consisted of a cadre of five to seven officers and perhaps 25 to 50 enlisted men. No barracks were available at North Island so they

U. S. NAVAL COMMUNICATION SERVICE
MAILGRAM

VMO-251
Dec '41

DELIVER THIS MAILGRAM TO COMMUNICATION SYSTEM IMMEDIATELY UPON RECEIPT FOR DISTRIBUTION AND HANDLING AS A REGULAR DISPATCH

FROM: COMARAIRWING TWO
DATE: 1 DECEMBER 1941
Mailed at: SAN DIEGO, CALIF. 2230

ACTION TO: OPNAV (AIRMAIL)
MAJOR GENERAL COMDT (AIRMAIL)

INFORMATION TO: BUAER – CINCUS – COMBATFOR – COMAIRBATFOR – COMCARDIV ONE – NAVAIRSTA SANDIEGO – COMARAIRGROUP 21 – COMDG GEN 2ND FMF

Classification: Plain / *Restricted / Restricted *Officers only / *Confidential

Special Instructions: CONFIDENTIAL Ø12230 CONFIDENTIAL

*If not encrypted by originator do not retransmit by radio without thorough paraphrasing and encrypting.

RELEASE

MARINE OBSERVATION SQUADRON TWO FIFTY ONE ORGANIZED THIS DATE AT NAVAL AIR STATION SAN DIEGO CALIFORNIA

Return to HISTORICAL DIVISION HQ., USMC, Room 3235 ARLINGTON ANNEX

11232
RECEIVED
DEC 4 1941
WAR PLANS SECTION
MARINE CORPS

FILE

Authenticated: W. H. DORISS, ENS., USNR.
Signature, name and rank.

Order authorizing the organization of VMO-251 (National Archives).

were issued cots and housed in a large, empty hangar on the west side of North Island. They lived with what they had in their sea bags and footlockers.[1] The winter weather wasn't hospitable. In order to ward off drafts of cold air, personnel in the hangar used newspapers as insulation as they tried to sleep in their cots.[2]

The Marines who filled the ranks of the squadron came from all across the United States—from Washington to New York. Some were college graduates; some did not get past high school. Some were transferred out of other squadrons and sent to 251. Still others were fresh out of boot camp or aviation schools and assigned to VMO-251.

Technical Sergeant Wendell P. Garton and Staff Sergeant John W. Irwin left Hawaii on November 26 onboard the USS *Tippecanoe* (AO-21), a Patoka class fleet oiler.[3] Following a 10 day cruise, the *Tippecanoe* arrived in California on 6 December. Irwin was immediately assigned to VMO-251 upon his arrival while Garton joined the squadron a week later.

Garton was an enlisted pilot with VMSB-231 and a six-year Marine veteran. Irwin was a three-year veteran of the Marine Corps and serving with VMJ-2 as an aircraft mechanic when he received his orders. When Garton was assigned to VMO-251, he became the squadron's first enlisted pilot. Irwin would end up as the squadron's Aircraft Maintenance Officer by the end of the war.

Native New Yorker Vito Murgolo volunteered for the Marine Corps in 1940. When assigned to the squadron in December 1941, he was already an experienced engine mechanic. But without any planes, there wasn't much for him to do.

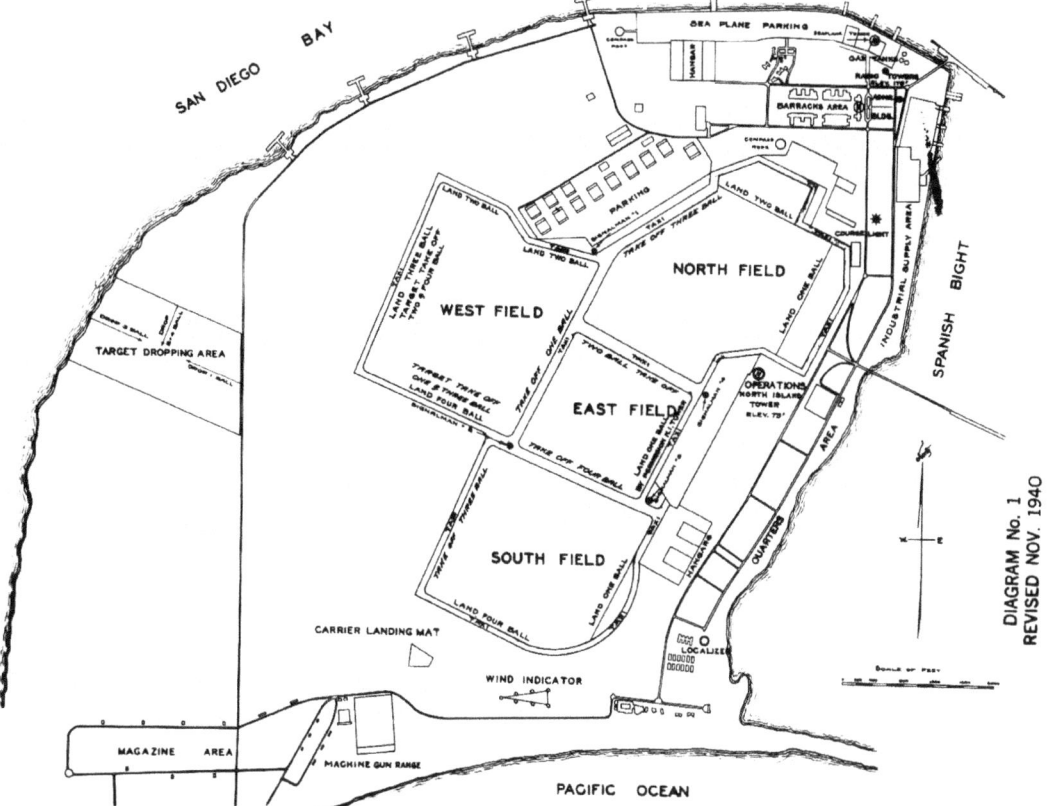

NAS North Island, November 1941 (courtesy Garton family).

Kansas native Dan Abrams was five years old when his family moved to Oklahoma. He dropped out of high school while a sophomore and ended up joining the Marine Corps in September 1941 at the age of 18. Having experience on farm equipment, after boot camp he found himself driving a jeep. When he was assigned to VMO-251, he became a truck driver.

"They wanted something for me to do because I wasn't a pilot, or wasn't going to be one, and at that time, and so they were just trying to place us where we were going to be the most good. At that time, whatever there was to do, well you did it," said Abrams.[4]

By 7 December 1941, the day the Japanese force attacked Pearl Harbor, Bard's command remained small and he still had no aircraft assigned to his squadron. Four days after the Pearl Harbor attack, he was relieved of command and became the commanding officer of VMD-154. Major John N. Hart—a 1925 graduate of the U.S. Naval Academy—took the reins of command from Bard and would eventually lead the squadron into combat. Hart was already a seasoned Marine combat aviator, having earned the Distinguished Flying Cross for actions while flying missions near Jicote Mountain and Saraguasa Mountain in Nicaragua.[5]

The squadron wasn't immediately assigned aircraft. In fact, it would not receive its aircraft until the spring of 1942. Those pilots who were eventually assigned to VMO-251 had to get their flight time and carrier landing qualification completed in any way they could: getting those hours wasn't easy. By the time the squadron departed for the South Pacific in June of 1942, very few of its pilots were carrier qualified. The lack of carrier-qualified pilots would have an adverse effect in the squadron's assignment when it arrived in the South Pacific.

While the squadron waited to get its primary aircraft, several secondary types were either loaned or assigned to it so that the pilots could get their flight hours and maintenance men could maintain their proficiency. These planes included two OS2U-3 Kingfishers, one J2F-4 Duck and three SNJ-3s.

The Kingfishers didn't stay with the squadron long. They were reassigned and the squadron received another SNJ to replace them. Garton then drew the assignment of training several of the enlisted men in the fine art of taxiing using the SNJs. The enlisted men apparently passed with flying colors and were signed-off as "approved taxi pilots."[6]

Second Lieutenant Roy Spurlock, fresh out of flight school, was at NAS North Island when the Japanese attacked Pearl Harbor. He was with a group of pilots assigned to the Advanced Carrier Training Group (ACTG) for training with current naval fleet aircraft. After the Japanese attacked, some of the new pilots flew anti-submarine patrols along the west coast. This continued until the threat of an attack on California died down. The pilots then continued with their training.

After a short time, the pilots were assigned to the USS *Hornet*, where they were to make five arrested landings aboard the carrier. The *Hornet* put out to sea for three days, at which time the Marine pilots received their carrier landing qualification.

Once the carrier returned to port, Navy and Marine pilots were ordered to report at a location in San Diego. A select number of these pilots were sent to Pearl Harbor, with the Marine pilots making it to Midway. Spurlock was not selected as part of this group. Instead, he was assigned to VMO-251 in early 1942.[7] During the June 1942 Battle at Midway, some of these Marine pilots lost their lives.

It was up to the Navy to decide which type of plane the squadron would use for its primary mission—photographic observation and reconnaissance. Float planes were considered, as well as the PBY Catalina and the Navy version of the B-24 Liberator—the PB4Y-1.[8] It wasn't until March 1942 that the Navy decided to assign the SBD Dauntless dive bomber to the squadron. The Marines objected to the idea, giving two reasons. They feared the squadron would end up as a dive bombing squadron operating off aircraft carriers, and based on British experiences in North Africa "they felt that a high-speed airplane with remote controlled camera installation would provide the best type of observation airplane."[9] The Marines fired back with their own proposal. They wanted the Grumman F4F-3 Wildcat.

In 1935, the Navy began seeking a replacement for its F3F biplane fighter. Brewster Aircraft Corporation and Grumman Aircraft were awarded contracts to develop the replacement. Brewster submitted the XF2A-1, a single wing aircraft made entirely of metal. Grumman submitted another biplane design, designated as the XF4F-1. However, at the suggestion of Grumman, the Navy asked Grumman to stop work on the XF4F-1. The Navy eventually awarded the contract to Brewster in 1938. Thus the Brewster Buffalo was born.[10]

All was not lost for Grumman. The Navy offered the company another contract, and with the lessons learned from its other submissions, developed the XF4F-3. Grumman's hard work paid off and the Navy ordered 54 F4F-3 Wildcats in August 1939.[11] By 1945, over 7,000 of all models of the Wildcat were produced.[12]

The F4F-3 was powered by a Pratt & Whitney R-1830 radial engine providing 1,200 horsepower. Its rate of climb was slow, only 2,303 feet per minute. The F4F-3 carried four .50 Browning machine guns with 450 rounds per gun.[13] With its 147 gallon fuel capacity, the plane had a range of about 845 miles. By the time the squadron departed for the South Pacific, officials knew it was no match for the Japanese Zero. Losses at Wake Island and later at Midway proved that fact. However, American pilots adapted to the shortcomings of the Wildcat, and developed a tactic to counter the superiority of the Zero known as the Thatch Weave.

Major Joseph N. Renner, who would take over as squadron commander in December 1942, described the tactic in an interview conducted by the Bureau of Aeronautics in Washington, D.C., on 17 July 1943.

> Against the Zero, because of its maneuverability and climb, we used tactics developed by Foss, Bauer, and Smith. In order to knock Zeroes down the Grummans stuck together, and each pilot paid less attention to the man on his tail than to the Zero on somebody else's tail. The Grumman fighters tried to stay in the same air, as we called it; once the dogfight started, we all revolved about in the same area. If a Zero dived out from the dogfight, our instructions were not to follow him but to swing back into the middle of the merry-go-round. In swinging back, you look for a Zero on some other Grumman's tail. This tactic worked out because a Zero can't take two seconds' fire from a Grumman and a Grumman can take sometimes as high as fifteen minutes' fire from a Zero. If you can summon up the courage in yourself to quit worrying about the guy peppering at you from behind and go after the Zero peppering your wing man from behind, gradually the Zeroes all disappear from the fight; and only the Grummans are left. Now it's damn hard to instill in a pilot the idea that even though there is somebody on his tail he's got to work on the guy that's on another's tail. That's exactly what we did, however, and it worked out very successfully.
>
> Naturally, the characteristics of the plane determine the tactics. The Zero could outmaneuver, out climb, out speed us. One Zero against one Grumman is not an even fight, but with mutual support two Grummans are worth between four and five Zeroes, and so on up.[14]

The Navy accepted the Marine Corps' proposal and by 15 April 1942 the squadron had in its possession at least 12 used Wildcats from the Navy.[15] The squadron may have had their Wildcats, but they were not ready to perform their primary mission. The planes needed cameras, and all were seriously in need of an overhaul.

Half the planes were sent to a modification station at North Island to have cameras installed and operational maintenance performed. The camera was added by replacing the reserve fuel tank behind the pilot and installing a Fairchild F-56 aerial reconnaissance camera in the lower part of the fuselage just behind the main fuel tank. The camera took pictures through an opening under the fuselage. A small, powered cover protected the lens when not in use. The pilot controlled the camera with a series of switches in the cockpit. By removing the reserve fuel tank, the fuel capacity was reduced from 147 gallons to 117 gallons. The loss in fuel shortened the operational range of the aircraft.[16]

Despite the fact the modified Grummans were expected to perform photo reconnaissance missions, the Wildcat's armament of four .50 caliber machine guns was not removed.[17] The Navy gave the modified Wildcats the designation F4F-3P.

As the squadron acquired its planes, pilots scrambled to get checked out in the Wildcat. First Lieutenant Pat Weiland, who joined the squadron on 22 April 1942, noted the Wildcat had a few quirks. The landing gear of the plane had a narrow track and if the pilot wasn't careful, the wings had a tendency to dip and scrape the ground on takeoff, leading to an unwanted accident. Pilots also had to struggle with cranking the landing gear up or down. The crank was located near the pilot's right leg, and it took 29 turns to complete the task. If a malfunction occurred during flight, the fast spinning handle often slammed against the pilot's leg, leaving it badly bruised.[18]

As the squadron was assigned its Wildcats, Hart received orders to send two officers to navigation school at Annapolis, the class being conducted by Lieutenant Commander Philip Van Horn Weems, a pioneer in the art of celestial navigation. Hart replied he could not spare two officers. Instead, he asked if he could send one officer and an enlisted pilot. He was given permission to do so. Captain W. H. Stiles and Garton were assigned to the class. Stiles, his wife and Garton left by train from California for Annapolis. Stiles and Garton did not return to the squadron until late May. Upon arrival, Stiles was transferred out of the squadron and Garton was designated the squadron's navigation officer despite his enlisted rank.[19]

During the modification and overhaul period, VMO-251 became involved in the 1942 Hollywood movie production of *Wake*

Pat Weiland, Espiritu Santo, New Hebrides, August 1942 (courtesy Robert T. Whitten).

One. The Beginning

Island. The film is considered the first of the World War II genre of films. In the movie, the heroic stand made at Wake Island during December 1941 was depicted as a fight to the last man, when in fact the defenders were overwhelmed and forced to surrender. Not much was known to the public as to what really happened on the island bastion, so the writers can't be faulted for taking liberties with the characters in the film, and adding additional plot items to the story.

Paramount Pictures sought the help of the Marine Corps to get the picture made. The Commandant of The Marine Corps authorized the cooperation and a team of five Marines was formed. Named to the team were Major General Ross E. Rowell, Supervising Officer; Lieutenant Colonel Francis E. Pierce, Technical Director; Lieutenant Colonel W. G. Farrell, Liaison Officer; Lieutenant Colonel John Hart, VMO-251 Squadron Commander; and Lieutenant Nicholas Presecans, Special Weapons Detail.[20] The help came with a few stipulations.

A Marine had to be present to supervise during the production of the film. Pierce was designated as the supervising officer on set and he instructed Paramount Pictures that no reference in their publicity was to be made "to the Marine Corps' cooperation, nor its lending physical assistance to the production by permitting our use of planes, equipment and material."[21] No reason is given for this request. It is possible that the USMC wanted to control the publicity concerning its involvement. In any case, Paramount Pictures honored the request.

Hart and several other pilots from the squadron spent at least two weeks flying their Wildcats over an improvised airstrip at Salton Sea in California and near Salt Lake City, Utah. They flew with the markings of VMF-211, which provided the air defense for Wake Island during the Japanese attempts to capture the island.

What led to VMO-251 being selected to participate in the film is not clear. Several squadrons with Wildcats were in the San Diego area, VMO-251 among them, at the time the film began production. However, lead actor Brian Donlevy and Hart may have known each other from their Naval Academy days in the 1920s. This friendship may have played a part in the squadron getting the Hollywood exposure.

While the 251 pilots were getting some much needed flying time during the production of the film, events were transpiring that would send the squadron to the South Pacific. VMO-251 would soon be involved in the capture and defense of an obscure piece of land in the Solomon Islands—Guadalcanal (code name Bevy).[22]

In March of 1942, Japanese forces invaded New Guinea, as well as entering the Solomon Islands. It was all part of a much larger plan to cut off and invade Australia. With what meager forces the Allies had available, they retaliated with airstrikes. If they hoped to slow the Japanese down, they were sadly mistaken. More forces were needed in the area if the allies were to halt the Japanese expansion.

On 22 April 1942, Rear Admiral Richmond K. Turner, then Assistant Chief of Staff of the Planning Division for the Commander in Chief, United States Fleet, sought approval from the Director, Division Plan and Policies at Headquarters, Marine Corps, to have VMO-251 assigned in direct support of the 1st Marine Division, currently packing up for a move from the United States to New Zealand.

Headquarters Marine Corps wasted no time in its answer. The following day, they gave their approval.

Despite Japanese setbacks during the battle of Coral Sea in May 1942 and at Midway in June of 1942, they continued to advance in the South Pacific. New Guinea and the

VMO-251 Marines involved in the production of the 1942 Paramount film, "Wake Island." Names—*standing left to right:* Murgolo, Irons, Adams, Waggoner, Myers, Gilmore, Siep, DeJong, Knight, Statchura, Holmes, Kiseliwiski, Cignotti. *Sitting left to right:* Straine, Spurlock, Kirk, Yeaman, Hart (Commanding Officer of VMO-251), Hayes (Executive Officer of VMO-251), Longley, McGothlin, Baesler (courtesy Vito L. Murgolo).

Solomon Islands soon saw increased activity by Japanese forces. Of special concern to the Allies was the airfield being constructed south and east of Lunga Point on the north coast of Guadalcanal. Japanese bombers flying out of this field could isolate Australia by interdicting the vital supply lanes between the United States and the island continent.

Plans were quickly drawn up and the invasion of Guadalcanal—code named Operation Watchtower—was set for early August 1942.

VMO-251 received its moving orders on 18 May 1942 and was set to depart San Diego the following month on board the USS *Heywood*, AP-12. Sailing with the personnel of 251 would be elements of the 1st Marine Raider Battalion and a battalion of the 22nd Marines.

Before the *Heywood* set sail for the South Pacific, Headquarters Marine Corps, Department of the Pacific, First Marine Amphibious Corps, Eleventh Navy District, Second Marine Aircraft Wing, Naval Air Station San Diego and the commanding officers of the ships involved coordinated the loading.[23] In reality, the squadron loading officer, along with several other 251 Marines, boarded the Heywood to take measurements of all holding spaces in order to pack the planes they had on hand, along with all necessary equipment to fulfill their job in supporting the 1st Marine Division. The disassembly of the planes for loading was handled by NAS North Island Assembly and Repair Section. With the help of the ship's boatswain, all necessary equipment and supplies to make the squadron self-supporting for several months were loaded aboard the *Heywood*.

The number of planes the squadron had when it departed cannot be known with any certainty, but it appears it may have been 16 or 18 Wildcats—most likely all F4F-3Ps. Official U.S. Navy documents show 16 Wildcats as of 25 June 1942.[24] Squadron records seem to indicate 18 Wildcats, as does Garton in his papers. Garton does say he could be mistaken on the number and in other documents he does mention 16. Sherrod's *History of Marine Corps Aviation in World War 2* also says 16 Wildcats. Along with the Wildcats were at least three SNJs and a Duck.[25]

A small detachment of VMO-251 personnel, as well as additional supplies and secondary items deemed not immediately needed by the squadron, found their way onboard another ship.[26] The loaded vessel departed two days before the *Heywood* to begin its long journey to New Zealand. These supplies would not reach the squadron until a month after the *Heywood* anchored at New Caledonia.[27] Unfortunately, no external fuel tanks for the Wildcats were loaded onboard the transport ships. The Navy had yet to send them, and their absence would be felt. It would be several months before these critical items would be received by the squadron.

The *Heywood* departed on 17 June 1942. Nearly 300 officers and men of VMO-251 were on their way to help the 1st Marine Division to capture Guadalcanal—or so they thought. Events were about to transpire that ensured that squadron planes would never fly a photo reconnaissance mission for the duration of the war.

Two

New Caledonia[1]

The USS *Heywood* made slow but steady progress as it zigzagged along its base course that would eventually take it to New Zealand.[2] Marines aboard the ship had little to do, but a routine was developed to keep them somewhat busy: early morning inspections and afternoon lectures.

To escape the unbearable heat below decks, many slept topside on the *Heywood* to take full advantage of the ever present breeze across the ship's deck as well the view of the setting sun across the expanse of the Pacific. But in nature, there is always a tradeoff. While they may have escaped the oppressive heat, they were soaked as the ship made its way through rain squalls.

While the war brought a temporary halt to the normal lives of the men onboard the *Heywood*, it certainly did not stop Navy tradition. As the ship neared the equator, those who had never crossed it—called pollywogs—were to be initiated into the domain of King Neptune. Beginning on 25 June, these pollywogs had to endure three days of physical and mental hardship. At the end of the rites, they became "Shellbacks" and forever known as sons of King Neptune.[3]

The ship's first stop was Samoa, and it was here that VMO-251 Marines learned that their assignment had changed. The squadron would not be going to New Zealand to support the 1st Marine Division. Instead they would be dropped off at Noumea (code name White Poppy) in New Caledonia (code name Cheekstrap, later Iret). After a brief layover at Samoa, the *Heywood* continued its voyage to New Zealand. Along the way it pulled into the harbor at Noumea on July 10. The Marines of VMO-251 began to disembark the ship, unload its equipment and await further orders. Apparently VMO-251 suffered its first casualty at this time when PVT. Richard Baird was wounded by a bullet in the left instep.[4]

New Caledonia was discovered by English Captain James Cook in 1774, but it was the French who laid claim to the island in 1853. Situated 1,224 miles to the east of Townsville on Australia's east coast, New Caledonia is a long, slender island running 248 miles in a northwest to southeast direction. The Solomon Islands lay to the northwest, 800 miles away. Due north 400 miles sits Espiritu Santo in the New Hebrides. The island's moderate weather made living there somewhat comfortable, and malaria was not an issue. The island was well developed with an adequate road system, and recognized by the United States as a critical air stop for aircraft servicing the route from the U.S. and Australia. By 1942, the U.S. Army had a sizeable force defending the island.[5]

Hart reported to Vice Admiral John McCain, Commander, Aircraft, South Pacific (COMAIRSOPAC) onboard the USS *Curtiss* (AV-4), also anchored in Noumea Harbor.

McCain directed Hart to set up his planes at Tontouta Airfield, located north and west of Noumea and await further orders. Squadron personnel would be camped five miles north of Tontouta. Within a few weeks after the squadron established itself at Tontouta, a contingent of VMO-251 personnel was sent to the airfield at Plaines des Gaiacs at the northwest end of the island near the town Pouembout to assist the 11th Bombardment Group.[6]

Unloading the squadron's equipment and getting it to the right location proved to be a problem. The *Heywood* could not linger long; the Army furnished much of the transportation to unload the ship but had orders to clear the dock as soon as possible, leaving little time for proper offloading. Squadron personnel, along with some natives of New Caledonia, worked nearly 24 hours straight to get the gear unloaded. Very

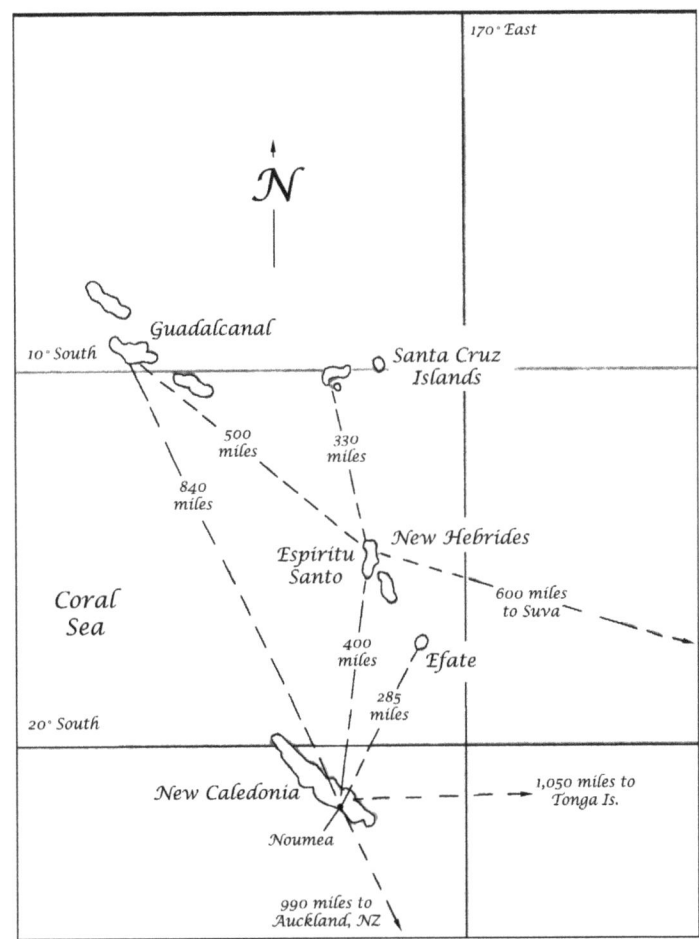

Distances from New Caledonia and New Hebrides (map adapted from The Big L—American Logistics in World War II, p. 327. http://www.ibiblio.org/hyperwar/USA/BigL/BigL-6.html).

few 251 vehicles were transported on the *Heywood*. While the number transported—three small tractors for towing aircraft and four jeeps may have been adequate to keep the squadron in operation as originally planned, they proved to be useless in moving gear to the camps. During the unloading process, one of the tractors ended up missing when squadron personnel accidently took one of the 1st Marine Raider Battalion's rubber landing rafts. Captain William R. "Soupy" Campbell drove to the raider camp and worked out a deal for the return of the tractor—the rubber raft was swapped for the tractor.[7]

As a result, items intended for the airfield wound up at the personnel camp and items for personnel ended up at the airfield. It took nearly five days to get the equipment situation straightened out. Once the equipment snafu was corrected, work began on putting the disassembled Wildcats back together again.

The airfield at Tontouta had no maintenance facilities, making it extremely difficult to get the planes reassembled. Compounding the problem, it was discovered during unpacking of the wing crates that many of the bolts needed to reattach the wings to the

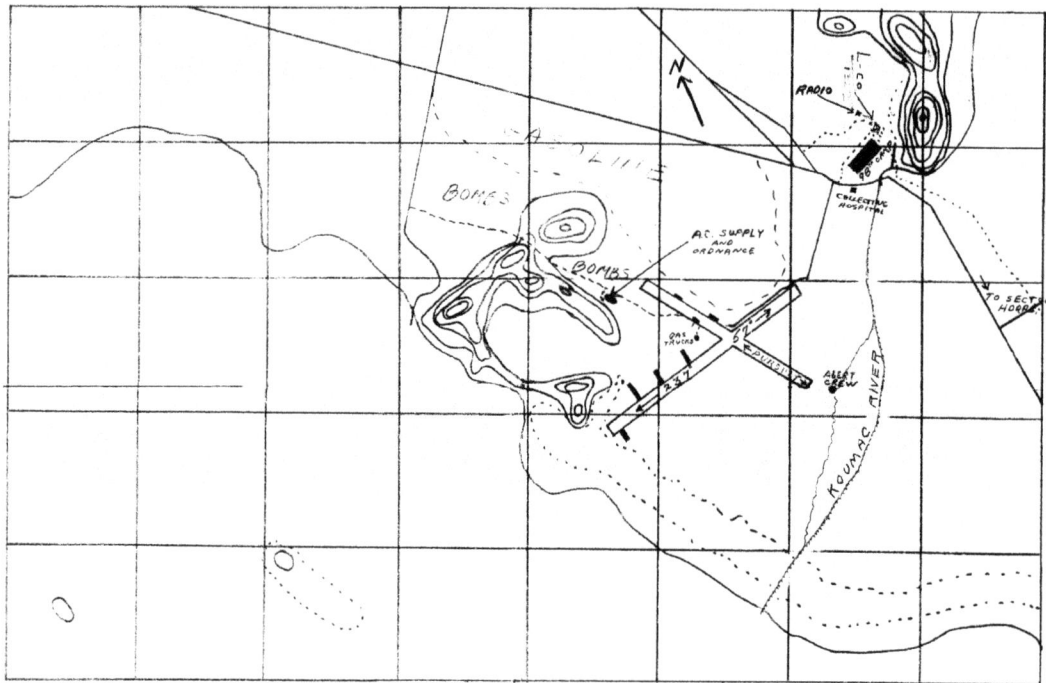

Diagram of field near Plaines des Gaiacs, New Caledonia (11th BG Records, Dec 1 1941–Aug 1 1945, Call #GP-11-SU-PH, IRIS #1096899, USAF Collection, AFHRA, Maxwell AFB AL).

body of the Wildcats were missing. In a stroke of luck, some machine tools were discovered on the island and new wing bolts were made to replace the missing bolts.

As the unpacking continued, more items were discovered missing giving rise to "a suspicion of sabotage."[8] A letter was sent to the commanding officer of the Assembly and Repair Section at North Island detailing the missing items. There is no evidence in 251 records of a response by the repair section commanding officer.

Maintenance personnel worked feverishly to rebuild their Wildcats to bring the squadron into operational readiness. As the days went by, the number of Wildcats that became operational slowly began to rise. The pilots now had a chance to get some flying time. However, 1LT Joe H. McGlothlin discovered that the magnetic declination was not the same as it was in San Diego. All the magnetic compasses in the Wildcats had to be recalibrated.

Garton was given the assignment. He enlisted the help of a nearby army engineering unit to lay out a compass rose. Garton then took each Wildcat and swung the compasses, making out new compass calibration cards for each plane during the process. Garton received no help from any of the squadron officers present.[9]

As the pilots began flying their Wildcats, mishaps occurred. On 22 July, 2Lt. George S. Kobler ground looped his F4F-3 while attempting to land. The plane was severely damaged, suffering the loss of one of its main landing wheels, a bent prop, bent wingtip and a destroyed tail wheel. After an assessment by maintenance personnel, the plane was written off and stripped for parts. Kobler was unhurt.[10]

Six days later Captain Ralph Yeaman was next to ground loop his Wildcat. Fortunately

2Lt. George Kobler's Wildcat following his accident at Tontouta Airfield on New Caledonia (courtesy Tailhook Association).

the damage was not as severe as Kobler's plane. The only damage to Yeaman's plane was a bent prop. A replacement prop was obtained from the USS *Curtiss* and the plane was quickly repaired.

Despite the lack of facilities and support, it is a testament to the excellent performance of the maintenance crews that they were able to get 13 of their Wildcats into operation by 30 July.[11] Morale remained high despite the heavy workload, and some Marines found time to hunt wild boar roaming the island to supplement their meager food rations.

During the process of reassembling the Wildcats, Hart was ordered to report to the *Curtiss* for another meeting with McCain. It was the first of a succession of meetings and orders for Hart that would make it impossible to carry out photo reconnaissance missions.

In a makeshift conference room on the *Curtiss*, McCain began to grill Hart with a series of questions. "What is the range of your F4F-3Ps?" asked the vice admiral.

"About 400 miles out and back," replied Hart. With Guadalcanal more than 800 miles from New Caledonia, and about 500 miles from Espiritu Santo, the squadron Wildcats did not have the range necessary to reach the soon to be contested island.

McCain continued the questioning. "Any belly tanks?"

"No sir," said Hart.

"Are your pilots ready for combat?"

"Our pilots have received little more than familiarization in the Wildcats. Some of the pilots have had observation training," answered Hart.

"Are the planes still armed?"

Hart answered in the affirmative.

McCain informed Hart to put all effort in getting his planes in the air at the earliest possible time and initiate an intensive training program in fighter tactics and gunnery. Hart was dismissed and made his way back to the squadron.[12]

A flurry of orders started to come in. Squadron records indicate that on 23 July, Hart and 2Lt. Frank M. Platt, Jr., departed New Caledonia for Espiritu Santo to conduct an inspection of their planned area of operations. So it appeared another move was in the making.

One the same day, Campbell, 2Lt. Roy T. Spurlock, 2Lt. Robert T. Whitten, 2Lt. Carl I. Scheussler and 2Lt. William P. Kirby were assigned to Special Temporary Aviation Duty (STAD) for the impending Guadalcanal operation. Two of these five pilots would not be seen again.

Squadron records indicate that "sometime in late July" Hart informed Captain Claude H. "Windy" Welch that he would be in charge of getting a radar station in operation on Espiritu Santo. Hart, accompanied by Welch, met again with McCain. LtCol. Harold W. Bauer, commanding officer of VMF-212 then operating out of Efate (code name Roses), was also present at the meeting. McCain "promised complete co-operation"[13] from himself and Bauer to get the radar station up and running.

According to Operation Plan Number I-42, Task Group 63-7, the squadron was ordered to Espiritu Santo (code name Ampersand, later Button) "to provide all possible service" to the 11th Bombardment Group based at Bomber One on Espiritu Santo. They would be under the command of Brigadier General William I. Rose, United States Army. Also, in conjunction with Task Group 63.6, they would be responsible for the air defense of Efate and Espiritu Santo, hence the necessity of getting the radar installation operational. As the battle for Guadalcanal heated up, the squadron was also tasked with rotating personnel to supplement the Cactus Air Force.[14]

These demands placed on the squadron effectively prohibited pilots from performing photographic reconnaissance missions with its Wildcats. However, beginning in late July VMO-251 enlisted photographers from the squadron photo section started flying photo missions on U.S. Army B-17s out of Tontouta and later Espiritu Santo. In essence the organization became an ad-hoc fighter squadron while retaining its VMO designation. In addition to its air defense duties and its support for the 11th Bombardment Group, it was also tasked to provide service to other squadrons, groups and area commands.

During a 27 July conference, attended by Vice Admiral Frank Jack Fletcher, commanding officer of Task Force 61, Turner, Major General Alexander Vandegrift, commanding officer of the 1st Marine Division and Rear Admiral Daniel J. Callaghan, Chief of Staff under Vice Admiral Robert L. Ghormley, who was overall commander of the South Pacific Area, Fletcher informed those present that he would pull out his carriers 48 hours after the initial invasion of Guadalcanal. He was hesitant to leave the carriers in an area that did not provide much maneuver room should the fleet be threatened. Vandegrift and Turner would not get the air protection they felt they needed to ensure that their mission was accomplished. It was also on this date that VMO-251 started making preparations for a move to Espiritu Santo in the New Hebrides.

It had been intended that VMO-251 and VMF-212 would make it to Guadalcanal via Espiritu Santo as soon as the field was captured by the 1st Marine Division. Without

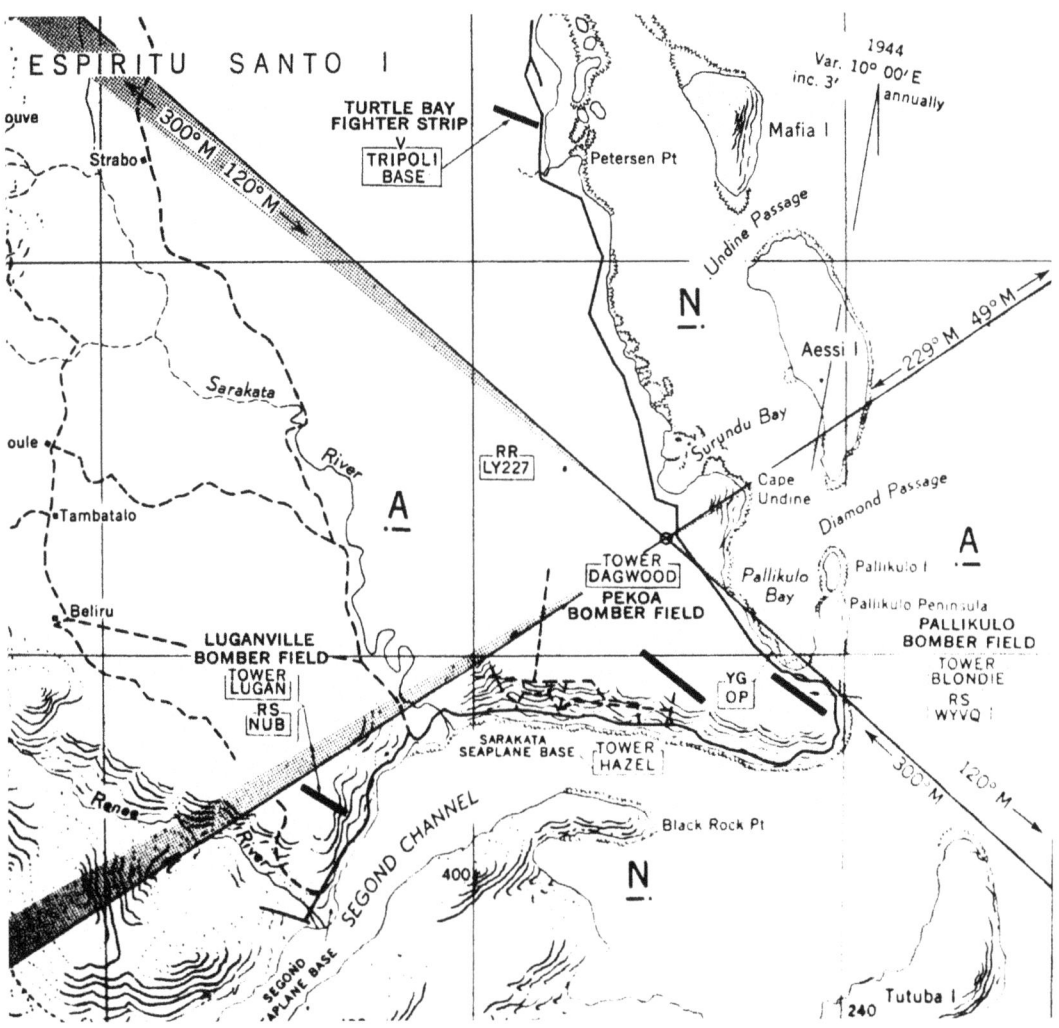

Airfields on Espiritu Santo, dated 1944 (National Archives).

the much needed external fuel tanks, the Wildcats of 251 and 212 did not have the range to make it to Guadalcanal from their respective bases. Nor could the planes make it by carrier, since there were concerns that many of the pilots were not carrier qualified. As a result, VMO-251 and VMF-212 would not be participating in the initial invasion of Guadalcanal. Instead, MAG-23s VMF-223 and VMSB-232 would be the first of many squadrons to fly as part of the Cactus Air Force. These squadrons would depart Pearl Harbor in early August onboard the USS *Long Island*. VMF-224 and VMSB-231 would depart for Guadalcanal later in the month.[15] It would be two weeks after the invasion that the Marines on Guadalcanal would finally get the air support they so vitally needed.

As for the external fuel tanks for the Wildcats, it was suggested by CinCPac that they be transported by ship to Espiritu Santo or Efate. Somewhere along the way this suggestion was changed. The tanks ended up being delivered by B-17 Flying Fortresses.

The Radar Stations[16]

Welch and his crew of seven radar men certainly had their work cut out for them in order to get the radar station built and operating. The station was to be built on Espiritu Santo, but no specific location had been determined. The radar set needed, the SCR-270, was not available on Tontouta. The nearest set available was on the island of Efate, located south of Espiritu in the New Hebrides, so transportation had to be coordinated to get the set to Espiritu Santo. There was no camp equipment available, so all tent supplies, stoves, cots, water cans, water trailers, vehicles, gas and the tools necessary to complete the job also had to be tracked down and transported.

Following Welch's meeting with McCain, Welch flew to Efate and met with Bauer. With Bauer's invaluable help, they obtained the radar set from the 4th Defense Battalion on the island. They also secured the items needed to complete the mission and the gear was loaded onto a barge. Bauer also arranged for the availability of a large unloading barge from the port director. Both barges would be at Welch's disposal as soon as Welch called for them in order to get the supplies to Espiritu Santo. In addition, Bauer supplemented Welch's seven man crew with six radar men.

With the items secured, Bauer assigned Captain F. R. Payne to fly Welch to Cape Cumberland on the northern tip of Espiritu Santo. On 9 August 1942, with Payne at the

Capt. Claude H. "Windy" Welch (courtesy Robert T. Whitten).

controls of a J2F "Duck," Welch made an aerial reconnaissance to get an idea of where to place the radar. After flying across a long, grassy plateau near Cape Cumberland, they decided to land the plane so Welch could scout the terrain on foot. After landing the float plane in the water, Payne and Welch removed a rubber raft from the aircraft and Welch paddled ashore.

Welch was met by natives in the area, and as he was talking with the chief, he noticed the plane was drifting towards the shore and nearby rocks. Payne was able to locate the anchor and tossed it into the water, stopping the plane from drifting into the rocks and avoiding serious damage to the plane. Unfortunately, they couldn't fire the engine back up to move it a better location. The natives, with their outrigger canoes, towed the plane a safe distance away from the rocks. Welch and Payne were stuck for two days until a PBY came by and picked them up.

While waiting for the PBY, Welch scouted the area on foot and determined where the radar would be set up and the path they would take through the jungle to get the equipment to the selected site. Ultimately, Welch found what would be the home of the radar site. The radar site was to be erected atop a small mountain, about 900 feet above sea level and located approximately six miles south of Cape Cumberland.

Welch returned to the squadron on 11 August. As soon as he returned he notified Bauer to send the barge, already preloaded with the gear gathered at Efate, to Espiritu. The unloading barge was also dispatched from Efate. It proceeded to Cape Cumberland to be on hand when Welch and his crew arrived.

While Welch waited for the barge to arrive from Efate, he was able to gather seven more men for the job, including a pharmacist mate. Also acquired was a radio set to remain in communication, a Caterpillar to tow the radar up the mountain, and gasoline.

The preloaded barge from Efate arrived at Pallikulo Bay on 18 August. The equipment rounded up by Welch was loaded aboard. Welch and his crew of twenty men departed later in the evening and arrived at Cape Cumberland at dawn the following day.

Thus began the backbreaking work of unloading and hauling the gear through six miles of jungle and up a mountain to set up the radar. It was impressed upon all the men that the SCR-270 was the only set available in the Pacific and no replacements were forthcoming. Great care had to be taken to unload the three mobile parts of the radar since each section weighed eight to ten tons. The loss of any one piece would effectively end the mission. VMO-251's radar chief, Master Technical Sergeant Howard A. Bailey, and another MTSGT by the name of Merrill, closely supervised the unloading. After six hours of hard physical labor, the radar set and supplies were on the beach.

The barges departed and were soon out of sight of the Marines. A camp was set up near a clear stream just off the beach, and the process of getting the gear moved to the camp began. By nightfall, the beach bore no evidence of the gear. The men settled in for the night, hoping to get some rest in preparation of the next day's work.

Work on cutting the jungle road began early on 20 August. Many of the trees had trunks ranging from 24" to 28" in diameter. Toiling under a hot sun, the work party used hand axes to cut down the trees, since a cross-cut saw could not be located before the mission began. One of the vehicles obtained at Efate, a weapon carrier, broke down on the same day and could not be repaired. It had been intended to use the carrier to haul the barrels of gasoline to the radar site once the site was established. As Welch walked ahead to scout the road path, Bailey and Merrill closely supervised the work. One four man crew led by a member of VMO-251's anti-aircraft crew, Sergeant James A. Cosner, became so adept at cutting down trees they ended up taking down most of the larger ones in the group's path.

After six days of cutting and hacking, the camp set up at the clear creek was moved further inland so the Marines would not have far to walk to the work site every morning.

As the road work continued, three bridges had to be built along the way. Bailey and a Marine named Meing, who had experience building bridges during his civilian days, led the construction of the bridges. They located timber strong enough to support the heavy radar units, and the bridges were in service for as long as the radar station remained in operation.

Just as the Marines broke through the jungle and up the mountain, a hard rain began to fall. The rain turned the newly cut road into a slick mud. With the steep incline of the mountain and the slippery road, the crew was delayed in setting up the radar on the selected site.

On 4 September, after sixteen days of hard, physical labor, the radar set was deployed. They used their Caterpillar to pull the radar units into place since the bulldozer they had planned on using for this purpose broke down several days before. Bailey and Merrill, experienced radar technicians, had no problem setting up the set and putting it in operation. Enough gas was brought in to establish operation and keep the radar's generator running for a few days. The remaining barrels would have to be hauled in from the original camp. There was difficulty in establishing communication with the control center on the southern end of the island. The reception was good, but transmission from the site was poor. The culprit was the low power transmitter. By using a day and night frequency, they were able to maintain reliable contact with the control center.

Once the operation of the radar was established, work crews built an improvised skid to attach to the rear of the Caterpillar. The "Cat" and a loading crew traveled back to the main camp, loaded the barrels of gas onto the skid, and returned to the radar site.

Security procedures were established. The radar installation was rigged with explosives just in case a Japanese raiding party made an attempt to capture the installation. Once Welch was satisfied everyone knew their job, he requested via radio to be sent back to the squadron. Major William "Soupy" Campbell piloted a Grumman F2F and picked up Welch. Welch was back with the squadron on 6 September 1942.

Despite poor food and adverse living conditions, the Marines did not complain. They performed their duty to the best of their ability and accomplished the mission. There was no malaria control (spraying, atabrine, quinine) and despite strict use of mosquito nets, all of them eventually contracted malaria.

If Welch thought he was finished establishing radar stations, he was sadly mistaken. As soon as he rejoined the squadron, he was pegged to lead the installation of a second radar station near a new fighter strip recently built just to the south and west of Turtle Bay. VMO-251 would soon be moving to this new fighter strip.

After an aerial view of several possible sites and a reconnaissance on foot, Welch eventually selected Petersen Plantation for the site. Welch commandeered a construction battalion and ordered them to push down the coconut trees and clear the land. The U.S. government compensated the owner of the coconut plantation by paying $3,700; $10 for each tree knocked down.

Welch recalled Bailey from the northern radar site to help with the establishment of the new site. With the help of a few sailors on loan from COMAIRSOPAC, work began on 18 September. The area was already developed with roads, so getting the SCR-270 radar gear and equipment to the area posed no difficulties. Within a short time, the radar was up and running. As Welch was making plans to move half the crew from the northern radar installation to operate the new radar unit, he became ill and was hospitalized.

Subsequently, all Marines were removed from the northern installation, and the Army took over the operation of the northern radar set. They also took control of the newly established radar station near the fighter field after a short period of time.

Within a span of two months, the Marines of VMO-251 established two fully functional radar stations that provided an early warning of impending Japanese raids (northern radar) at Espiritu as well as close-in fighter direction (southern radar) for the island. Their work in New Caledonia and Espiritu Santo would not go unrecognized.

In June 1946, Brigadier General Laverne G. Saunders, former commander of the 11th Bombardment Group, wrote a letter to the Adjutant General of the United States Army recommending that General Order Number 4—authorizing the Distinguished Unit Citation to the 11th Bombardment Group—be amended to include VMO-251. He wrote:

> 3. For the outstanding manner in which this single Marine Squadron on independent duty, performed its mission in support of our operations and, in addition supplemented the personnel of the 11th Bombardment Group in combat missions and thereby materially and effectively aided in the successful completion of this operation to secure a foothold in the Solomon Islands—our first offensive mission and the turning point in the war in the Pacific, it is recommended that General Orders No. 4 be amended to include Marine Observation Squadron Two Fifty-One and that the personnel attached during the above period be authorized to wear as a permanent part of their uniform, the Distinguished Unit Badge.[17]

Saunders went on to write that "...no reason exists to prevent such an award."[18] It is not known if Saunders' recommendation was acted upon. If not, it certainly should be considered for review by the United States Army. Without the help of VMO-251, the 11th Bombardment Group would have been hard-pressed to accomplish its duties.

Operation Watchtower

The five 251 aviators assigned to STAD on 23 July were told they had an hour to pack their bags. They then boarded an awaiting truck and were transported to the temporary camp of the rear echelon of the 1st Raider Battalion, located south of Tontouta. At a briefing the five pilots learned they would be participating in the invasion of Guadalcanal. Flying as rear seat observers in naval scout planes, their job would be to report any Japanese movement or positions to higher headquarters, and provide target coordinates to the ships participating in the bombardment of Guadalcanal and Tulagi. Along with the Marines of the 1st Raider Battalion, they boarded the USS *Colhoun*—an old WW I destroyer converted into a high speed transport—and sailed off. Within five days the *Colhoun* joined the rest of the Guadalcanal invasion fleet in the Fiji Islands. Scheussler and Kirby were taken by small boat to the USS *Vincennes*, a heavy cruiser of the New Orleans class. Campbell, Spurlock and Whitten were whisked away to the USS *Astoria*, the namesake for the Astoria class of heavy cruisers.

From 28 July to 31 July, while in the Fiji Islands, the invasion fleet conducted a run

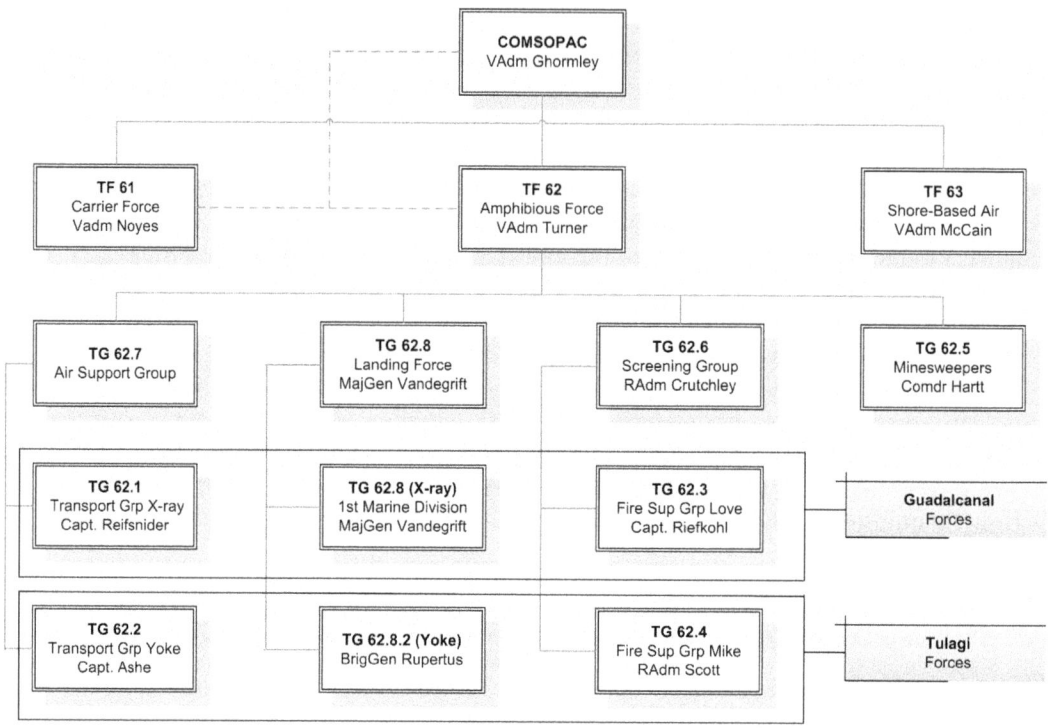

TASK ORGANIZATION AND COMMAND STRUCTURE
Guadalcanal-Tulagi Assaults
August 1942

Chart 1. Task Organization for the Guadalcanal invasion. VMO-251 was under the control of TF 63 (chart adapted from The Guadalcanal Campaign by Major John Zimmerman, USMC Historical Branch, 1949, p. 12).

through of the impending invasion at Koro. Vandegrift and other high ranking officers were not pleased with the results of the practice session. Spurlock, in a scout plane above the fleet, thought "it looked all right"[19] from his advantage point.

The invasion force, comprised of Task Force 61 (carrier-based air) and Task Force 62 (amphibious force) with its attached task groups, departed for Guadalcanal on 1 August, and by daybreak of 7 August, it arrived undetected by the Japanese. Supporting the invasion was Task Force 63 (shore-based air). Ships opened up with their main guns to soften up suspected Japanese positions. Spurlock, on board the *Astoria*, didn't agree with the ship's captain penchant to salvo all his guns simultaneously. For a Marine aviator not used to naval gunfire, the noise and concussion wrought by the *Astoria's* nine 8 in. guns were hard to handle.

During the approach to Guadalcanal, Task Force 62 split into two groups: Task Group Yoke landed Marines at Tulagi on Florida Island while Task Group Xray landed the Marines to the east of Lunga Point on Guadalcanal.

In a report written by Spurlock, he detailed his, Campbell's and Whitten's involvement in the invasion. The report does not give any specifics of Schuessler's and Kirby's involvement during the invasion, but Spurlock notes their actions "no doubt closely paralleled ours (Spurlock and Whitten)."[20]

At 0300 on the morning of August 7th, "General Quarters" was sounded aboard the ASTORIA, and the force entered the harbor between Tulagi and Guadalcanal. No shellfire or aircraft molested us as we swung into position just off Guadalcanal. The attack opened at 0630 with concentrated shelling of the Kukum and Lunga Point areas. Kukum was a small settlement with several docks and shore defense guns of heavy caliber located in an emplacement just back of the beach.

Simultaneously, 12 SBD's and eight TBF-8's began their attacks on the airfield, anti-aircraft batteries, supply and oil dumps, etc. The Japs were completely surprised and were never able to fire a shot at our planes. Grumman F4F-4's also assisted in the attack by dive-bombing and strafing.

Captain Campbell was catapulted at 0600 in a plane piloted by Lt. Tunnel, U.S. Navy, and was over the beach observing at the time fire was opened. He took part in the battle by strafing with his free gun and dropping two 100 lbs. bombs on supply dumps. The ships fired at any target given them by their spotting plane, which was also over the beach at the time.

After all resistance and such AA fire as there was had been beaten down, our transports slung boats over the side and at 0830, after five minutes shelling of the beach west of Lunga Point by the cruisers and destroyers, sent their boats in for a landing which was unopposed. Landings continued in force all day; the ships steaming right into shallow water close to the beach.

Lieutenant Whitten was catapulted at 0930 with Lieutenant (JG) Johnson piloting. Captain Campbell was recovered at 1030. Routine observation continued by Lieutenant Whitten.[21]

Spurlock noted that there was nothing to report "since it was obvious that the Japs had fled to the jungle as soon as the ships appeared."[22] The Marines at Guadalcanal met little resistance and quickly began to consolidate their positions. As supplies were quickly brought ashore the beach became crowded, making an inviting target for the Japanese. At Tulagi it was a different story. Marines of the 1st Raider Battalion and elements of the

2Lt. Roy T. Spurlock (courtesy Robert T. Whitten).

5th Marines met stiff resistance but by the evening of 8 August the small island was deemed secure.

The main Japanese force was quick to respond after receiving word of the invasion from the defenders at Tulagi. Vice Admiral Gunichi Mikawa, commanding officer of the Imperial Japanese Navy's 8th Fleet, quickly assembled a strike force consisting of five heavy cruisers, two light cruisers and a destroyer[23] and made way for Guadalcanal. In the meantime, Japanese aircraft were launched for an immediate counterattack. The planes arrived shortly after 1300 on 7 August. Anti-aircraft fire and carrier pilots beat back the attacks. Only the destroyer *Mugford* received a hit. Another Japanese attack was launched on 8 August and the planes arrived for another attack on the ships.

> At 1230 it was learned that an air raid was impending. At about 1300 I was ordered to make preparations to be catapulted, with Genest piloting. While we were turning up on the catapult just prior to launching, the ship's guns opened up on about 12 or 15 twin-engine Jap bombers directly over-head. The ship was steaming around in a circle and catapulted us when we got into the wind. Lieutenant Whitten was still up at this time.
>
> We took ourselves over Guadalcanal and proceeded with our observation, keeping an eye out for Zeroes, of which only one was in our vicinity that we saw. Our dive bombers and torpedo planes continued attacking land objectives, completely disregarding the air attack. Our fighters attacked the bombers and shot down at least three. Lieutenant Whitten was recovered about 1430, after a second air attack by Jap dive bombers, which I was told was a complete failure, except for one hit on the fan tail of the *Elliott* (transport) and a near miss on the destroyer *Jarvis*, springing some of her plates. Several more dive bombers were shot down here.[24]

Spurlock did not have any documents on which to base his account, but the above description matches closely to what actually happened. The Japanese airstrike contained over three dozen planes. During the attack, the *Jarvis* received a torpedo hit. She tried to make it back to the New Hebrides but sank the following day. As for the *Elliott*, she was damaged when a Japanese plane plowed into her. The *Elliot* beached and was destroyed by U.S. ships.[25]

The night of 8 August and the early morning hours of 9 August would prove to be a disaster for the United States Navy. For Vandegrift's Marines on Guadalcanal, just as Fletcher had promised, they lost their carrier-based air support and the bulk of their supplies still in the holds of the off shore in cargo ships. Citing fuel concerns, loss of aircraft, and the approaching Japanese naval force, Fletcher ordered his carriers to withdraw. Turner was also notified as well as Vandegrift. Without carrier air cover, Turner would be forced to pull back his transports carrying supplies and reinforcements for the Marines on Guadalcanal. Vandegrift would be without any air cover until the airfield on Guadalcanal was brought into operation.

For Scheussler and Kirby, they would lose their lives.

To cover the beaches and to meet the incoming Japanese task force, U.S. Navy screening forces were deployed near Savo Island. The South Patrol Force, comprised of the Australian cruisers HMAS *Canberra* and *Australia*, USS *Chicago* and two destroyers, guarded the southern approach into the Sealark Channel. Further north and to the east of Savo Island, the North Patrol Force comprised of the USS *Vincennes*, USS *Astoria*, USS *Quincy* and two destroyers, attempted to block the northern approach to the channel.

Despite destroyers scouting ahead and radar on some of the U.S. cruisers, Mikawa's 8th Fleet arrived undetected near Savo Island. At 0316, the Japanese commenced firing on the South Patrol Force with guns and torpedoes. They gave the U.S. Navy a harsh lesson in night warfare.

Japanese forces tore into the South Patrol Force, severely damaging the *Chicago* and sinking the HMAS *Canberra*. The strike force turned north, and engaged the North Patrol Force. Immediately sunk were the *Vincennes* and *Quincy*. The *Astoria,* severely damaged from the engagement, sank later in the day.

The *Astoria* took a beating from the Japanese task force. Japanese gunners were accurate as many shells struck the ship, including the ship's aviation section. With its fuel, lubricants, spare parts and ammunition for its scout planes, the section was a powder keg ready to explode and it did. The cruiser quickly was engulfed in flames and became a beacon for more Japanese fire. Spurlock writes:

> My first consciousness that there was something wrong was when I heard muffled explosions from some distance away from the ship, closely followed by terrific bangs outside the entrance to the room I was in. Almost instantly the General Quarters alarm sounded. I sat up in the cot and reached for my clothes. I remember it took forever to get dressed, or so it seemed. By this time there was no doubt in my mind what was happening. There were heavy crashes all over the ship, instantly followed by the sound of sand and gravel being flung against the bulkheads, and the sound of heavy metal barrels bounding down stairways.
>
> I later determined that the sound of steel barrels bounding downstairs was the sound of many shells coming aboard unevenly and exploding on some part of the ship. The 'sand and gravel' I heard was the sound of myriad pieces or fragments of exploding shell casings penetrating the steel bulkheads of the compartments of the ship....[26]

After what seemed like an eternity, the firing ceased. Spurlock picked himself off the steel deck and made his way through the ship. The passageways were filled with smoke; stinking of fuel, burning human flesh and the screams of the wounded. He passed by what remained of the ship's main first aid station. It did not escape the accuracy of the Japanese gunners. A hit to the aid station killed many men, throwing bodies and body parts throughout what remained of the compartment.

Many wounded sailors came to the destroyed first aid station looking for help, so Spurlock grabbed shirts and parachute material from the luggage in his cabin and returned to patch up the wounded sailors.[27]

Capt. Robert T. Whitten in a photo taken late in the war (courtesy Robert T. Whitten).

At some point he met up with Whitten. Neither of them had seen any sign of Campbell. Spurlock and Whitten began to haul wounded sailors from the bridge deck to the main deck. One of the sailors had a shattered leg; his foot hanging on by a few tendons. Whitten told Spurlock that he had seen this type of wound before, having just amputated a foot on another sailor.

Spurlock, who had carried on board the maps and operational codes for the Watchtower operation, had been given a weighted bag in which to keep them. He was instructed to toss the papers overboard if he had to abandon ship. Having seen the devastation topside, he thought the ship wouldn't stay afloat much longer. The documents were kept in the Captain's cabin, so he ran

2Lt. Carl Schuessler on board the USS *Heywood*. Scheussler was later killed while serving on STAD on board the USS *Vincennes* on 9 August 1942 (courtesy Robert T. Whitten).

back to retrieve the bag. Bag in hand, Spurlock walked to the edge of the deck and tossed the bag overboard.

As the *Astoria* was taking a beating, the *Vincennes* began to receive Japanese fire. Initial hits to the ship struck the bridge and she soon received dozens more, including a hit that set off a huge fire in the cruiser's aircraft hangar. Torpedoes quickly struck the ship, grievously wounding her. Power to the guns was lost, as well as communication systems within the ship. A flaming wreck, the *Vincennes* sank at 0250 on 9 August.[28] Over 300 of the ship's crew lost their lives, including VMO-251's Scheussler and Kirby.

At around 0330, the destroyer *Bagley* pulled up along the battered *Astoria* and the wounded were evacuated. About a half hour into the evacuation, the destroyer started firing point blank at another ship. The Captain of the cruiser gave the order to abandon ship and the able-bodied sailors and Marines boarded the *Bagley*. The destroyer then spent the rest of the morning gathering survivors from the *Vincennes* and the *Quincy*, which sank about 15 minutes before the *Vincennes*.

The *Astoria* burned through the morning. An attempt was made to put the ship back in service, but she was too far gone. She rolled over and sank shortly after midnight on 9 August.

Spurlock and Whitten were transferred to the transport ship *President Jackson* and on 11 August, the ship docked at Espiritu Santo. Campbell reported to the USS *Curtiss* (AV-4), anchored in the Segond Channel at Espiritu Santo on 12 August.[29] The next day the three VMO-251 pilots returned to the squadron.[30]

Whitten, as well as Spurlock, were later commended for Meritorious Conduct during the campaign. Whitten's citation reads:

> For meritorious conduct in action as aerial observer in aircraft of a vessel which was damaged during an engagement with Japanese naval forces off Guadalcanal, Solomon Islands, on Aug. 7, 1942. While flying over Japanese positions on Guadalcanal, Lieutenant Whitten descended to dangerously low altitudes to obtain accurate information for the vessel. Later, when the vessel was damaged, he assisted in the emergency treatment and transfer of wounded aboard the ship. His coolness and courage were in keeping with the highest traditions of the United States naval service.[31]

Photographic Missions[32]

In June of 1942, Lieutenant Commander (LCDR) Robert S. Quackenbush, Jr., United States Navy, had been appointed to run the Navy's photographic unit in the South Pacific. Unfortunately, he had no gear and no personnel except on paper. He arrived in New Zealand aboard the Dutch ship *Fontaine* on 16 July 1942. Within minutes after docking, he was ushered away to a meeting with Vice Admiral Ghormley.

Also attending the meeting was Turner. Both informed Quackenbush of the impending Guadalcanal invasion and gave him his first assignment. Quackenbush was to provide up-to-date photographs of Guadalcanal and drop the pictures by air to the invasion fleet. Quackenbush informed Turner of the sad state of his unit: no planes, no equipment, no photographers and no photo interpreters. Turner ignored Quackenbush's dire report and sent him on his way.

The next day, Quackenbush hopped on a PBY Catalina and was flown to New Caledonia where he met McCain on the *Curtiss*. He informed McCain of his mission, and that he was now on McCain's staff. Quackenbush suggested using Catalinas for the mission but McCain—for unknown reasons—shot down that idea.

For the next week, Quackenbush worked on getting the pieces in place to complete his assigned mission. Luckily, elements of the 98th and 42nd Bombardment Squadrons, 11th Bombardment Group, had arrived on 21 July and 22 July respectively.[33] Quackenbush quickly secured the use of two of the group's B-17 Flying Fortesses. It was also around this time that Quackenbush found VMO-251 on the island. Hart, the squadron's commanding officer, and Quackenbush were classmates at the U.S. Navy Photography School at Pensacola, Florida during the early 1930s.

At the time, the squadron photo section consisted of 17 enlisted men and was led by Capt. Carl Longley. Their job was to develop film brought back from pilots for distribution to higher commands and other photographic duties deemed necessary, including recording the squadron activities on the ground. It did have two aerial cameras on hand but these were never used and were soon out of the squadron inventory. Since the squadron was not going to be flying photo missions, that left many of the photographers with a lot of time on their hands.

Quackenbush explained his predicament to Hart. Realizing the importance of Quackenbush's mission, Hart assigned four photographers, TSGT. Marcus N. Harper, Jr., the non-commissioned officer in charge (NCOIC) of the squadron's photographic section,

SSGT. Jay W. Morris, SSGT. Wilbur L. Peak, and SGT. Homer E. Collier, Jr., for the impending photographic mission.

Even though Quackenbush had his planes and photographers, he was still without aerial cameras. He was able to acquire two aerial cameras from the *Curtiss*. The two B-17s were hastily modified to allow the cameras to shoot through a small hole from the belly of the planes.

The two B-17s took off from New Caledonia on 23 July. The nearly 1700 mile flight from New Caledonia to Guadalcanal and back would push the B-17s to the limit of their endurance. Quackenbush flew in the lead plane to direct the mission. Each plane carried a VMO-251 photographer.

As the two Flying Fortresses made their way to Guadalcanal, they ran into severe weather several times. Despite being bounced around, the "Forts" made it through the storms but they consumed precious fuel in doing so. When they finally arrived over Guadalcanal, the weather was perfect for taking pictures.

When the planes were over their target areas, Quackenbush ordered the photographers to start their cameras. The two VMO-251 photographers did as ordered, "taking vertical 60 percent overlap aerial photographs with the Fairchild K3B 12 inch focal length lens. The two B-17 airplanes were flying abreast of each other on a parallel course with a distance between the two B-17s to give approximately 40 percent photo flight line coverage."[34]

It wasn't long before the Japanese jumped on the B-17s. Approximately half way through the mission, five Rufes (the floatplane version of the A6M Zero) attacked the two bombers. Gunners on the B-17s claimed four of the planes. During the attack, Quackenbush was able to complete his mission and turned his planes to head back to New Caledonia.

After flying through storms and loitering over Guadalcanal for the pictures, the planes didn't have enough fuel to return to Noumea, so they put down on an island along the route to their destination: possibly Bellona Island or Rennell Island. Quackenbush contacted the USS *Curtiss*, requesting a Catalina be sent to pick up the film.

The PBY Catalina arrived but ran into a reef while taxing to the beach and sank. A second Catalina was requested. It arrived safely, whisking away Quackenbush and the film for processing and interpretation at New Caledonia. After two days, the pictures were successfully flown to the invasion force where they were distributed to Vandegrift and other commanders.

Another mission was flown on 2 August to snap pictures of Tulagi, the target of the Marine Raiders in the upcoming Guadalcanal invasion. Once these pictures were ready, they too were delivered to the invasion fleet by a PBY Catalina.

For the next several months VMO-251 photographers continued to fly photo missions on B-17s initially out of New Caledonia, then out of Espiritu Santo. They often helped the gunners when the Forts came under attack by Japanese aircraft. From July to October 1942, they participated in 92 flights for a total of 616 hours.[35]

When Quackenbush moved his photo interpretation unit to Guadalcanal, several VMO-251 photographers worked with his unit—unofficially called Quackenbush's Gypsies—and the 1st Marine Division to help with photo analysis.

VMD-154 took over the photographic responsibilities from VMO-251 and the 11th Bombardment Group when it arrived in theater in November 1942.

After a short stay on New Caledonia, the squadron received its orders to head for

Espiritu Santo. On 1 August, all equipment not in use by the squadron was transported to the docks at Noumea. Work details were assigned to load the equipment on board the *Curtiss*. The next day all remaining camp equipment and field facilities were brought to the docks where loading continued until late in the afternoon. When loading was finished, the Marines of VMO-251 boarded the *Curtiss*. The *Curtiss*, along with the USS *Maryland* as escort, departed Noumea. The *Curtiss* reached Espiritu Santo on 4 August.[36]

Due to lack of time and a receding tide, not all equipment made it on board the *Curtiss*. A rear echelon of Marine raiders was enlisted to help move the gear off the docks. The gear was moved to a location near the raiders' camp and an U.S. Army detail was assigned to guard the gear. Twenty-four men, 15 of them pilots, stayed behind to ferry the planes when ordered.

As the VMO-251 Marines waited for word to depart Noumea, a ship carrying the remainder of the squadron's gear from the United States finally arrived. The supplies were the first to leave San Diego before the *Heywood* departed. The USS *Alcyone* (AK-24) dropped anchor at Noumea on 8 August. The *Alcyone* was under orders to load the gear the *Curtiss* left behind and take it to Espiritu Santo. With the help of the raiders the gear was loaded and the *Alcyone* departed on 9 August. The ship arrived at Espiritu Santo the next day. The rear party of VMO-251 Marines departed Noumea on 10 August. The pilots flew the Wildcats to Bomber Field #1 on Espiritu Santo while an Army B-26 Marauder and a Lockheed Hudson flew the nine mechanics to Espiritu Santo by way of Efate.[37]

For Albert Hoffman, a radio operator for the squadron, his days on Espiritu Santo were numbered. Four days after the arrival of the squadron on the island, a PBY-5A with the Commanding General of the 1st Marine Air Wing, General Roy Geiger, landed at Espiritu Santo. Hoffman writes:

> The pilot was Major Jack Cram, and the co-pilot was Lieutenant Walt Giles, a friend I had met when he returned to North Island in 1939, having served as Admiral Byrd's pilot on his last trip to the South Pole. While we were catching up on the latest happenings, he asked me, that as General Vandegrift wanted him for a job on his staff on Guadalcanal, would I be willing to take his place on the PBY. I said I would, and my CO, Col. Hart, had the company clerk type out secret orders transferring me temporarily to General Geiger's staff.
>
> For the next couple months we flew practically non-stop, flying General Geiger to meetings with Admirals Nimitz and Halsey, transporting wounded the 1,000+ mile trip to the Navy Hospital in Noumea, flying replacement pilots in from Australia, and bringing any mail available. When General Geiger was aboard, being a pilot, he usually rode the right seat, which gave me time to read Hemingway's book "The Sun Also Rises," or visit with his aide, Lt. Gray. (Always just along for the ride).
>
> On one flight in November, we retrieved Captain Joe Foss from the island of Malaita. The natives had taken him there in a dugout, after fishing him out of the ocean after he'd been shot down by an enemy float biplane.[38]

Little did Hoffman know his decision would place him in the middle of a Japanese counterattack in October 1942.

Three

Espiritu Santo and Guadalcanal

To the casual observer, Espiritu Santo in the New Hebrides and Guadalcanal in the Solomon Islands look inviting. Covered in a thick, dark green canopy of trees and surrounded by the vibrant blue-green waters of the Pacific, they seem to exude tranquility. They beckon those looking to get away from the grind of everyday life. But looks can be deceiving. For the airmen, sailors, soldiers and Marines who served on these islands, the living conditions were hell. High temperatures, high humidity, constant rain, mud, lousy food,[1] tropical diseases, boredom and the constant stress of combat quickly sapped their strength.

The Marines of VMO-251 served on both islands from August 1942 to May 1943. Many enlisted men and officers served at Guadalcanal on a temporary basis before the squadron transferred there in January 1943. Said Campbell, "We never knew what squadron we were in; we were never carried as an administrative unit."[2]

In 1606, Spanish explorer Pedro Fernandez de Quiros discovered the New Hebrides. However, it was English explorer Captain James Cook who charted the islands in 1774. France claimed the island group in 1853. By 1941, both Britain and France were firmly entrenched on the island. The island group is located north of New Caledonia and southeast of the Solomon Islands, putting it in an ideal position to serve as a transit point for forces heading to the Solomon Islands or south to Australia. Espiritu Santo, shaped like a hand pointing north, is the largest island in the New Hebrides. The island receives plenty of rain and malaria was rampant.[3]

The Solomon Islands were discovered in 1568 by the Spanish explorer Alvaro de Mendaña de Neyra. Guadalcanal, located at the southern end of the Solomon Islands, averages around 200 inches of rain per year. All who served on the island had to contend with many tropical diseases, including malaria and dysentery.[4] In a letter written to his family in late 1942 or early 1943, VMO-251 pilot Kenneth Kirk described the living conditions on the disease-ridden island.

> I guess the rainy season has really begun. It has rained and rained and then rained some more. And when it comes down at its worst you can't see 50 yards. Mud is from three inches to a foot deep and is everywhere. Your clothes get muddy but you get used to that. The mosquitos are bad, but you get used to that, too. Rats run around the tent at night but don't bother us much....[5]

For most of its stay on Espiritu, the squadron was the only unit with a functioning first aid station, staffed by nine sailors. By the end of October 1942, the first aid station had cared for an estimated 1,000 patients.[6] No one was immune from the tropical diseases that infested the island; even the squadron's medical officer, Lieutenant Commander Marion M. Kalez, had to be evacuated due to illness.[7] Many of the sick and wounded returning from Guadalcanal, as well as pilots injured in crashes on Espiritu, received treatment from VMO-251's medical staff. Even survivors from the USS *President Coolidge* were sent to the squadron after the ship struck a mine and sank near the island on 26 October 1942.

By the time the Wildcats arrived from New Caledonia, the ground echelon had set up camp near Bomber Field #1 located south of Pallikulo Bay.[8] Using material found on the island, they constructed rudimentary field facilities made of lumber from felled trees and canvas to protect the planes from the elements as they performed maintenance on the Wildcats. Other ground personnel continued to off load the squadron supplies from the *Curtiss* and the *Alcyone*. Still others were assigned to refueling B-17s of the 11th Bombardment Group, which arrived during the first week of August without their maintenance personnel. The fuel was contained in drums, and the refueling of the bombers was done with the use of hand pumps. The labor intensive work took 16 to 20 hours a day. Ordnance men assisted in loading bombs on the B-17s, as well as Douglas SBD dive bombers. Spurlock recalls:

> At this stage our squadron did not have the luxury of gas refueler trucks, and all refueling had to be done by hand pump alone. This was bad enough when filling our F4F type planes which carried only 144 gallons of gas internally. With the B-17 it was a different matter, since they required as much as 2700 gallons per plane, and there were usually three B-17 planes going out every day to reconnoiter the Solomons and surrounding areas. Our enlisted personnel were frequently up all night just gassing these planes, and as time wore on this chore become more and more onerous.[9]

The fueling of the B-17s was the first in a long line of service jobs the squadron performed during the course of its stay at Espiritu. By reason of its location, the bomber strip became a major staging base for squadrons heading to and from Guadalcanal. Because VMO-251 was the only fully-staffed aviation unit on the island at the time, the squadron took on the responsibility of maintaining the squadrons as they passed through, as well as feeding the men assigned to these squadrons. Naval aircraft also used the field when their carriers were sunk during the course of the seven month long campaign to take Guadalcanal from the Japanese.

Nearly 150 aircraft, as well as the squadron's Wildcats, were serviced by the ground crew of VMO-251 during its stay on Espiritu Santo. Among units serviced were VMF-212, First Marine Air Wing and COMAIRSOPAC PBY-5A Catalinas, VF-71, VF-5, VS-3, VT-8, VB-6, and VMJ-253. Parts and assistance were also provided to the 4th Defense Battalion, 76th Coast Artillery, 182nd Infantry Regiment, CUB-1, and the 7th Construction Battalion.[10] This work would decrease in September after the squadron made another move to the newly constructed fighter strip just south of Turtle Bay, located a few miles north of the bomber strip.

While the squadron performed the work for other squadrons, it also had duties it needed to perform as ordered by COMAIRSOPAC—the air defense of Espiritu Santo. As if that wasn't enough, on 13 August Hart was given command of all interceptor and fighter forces on Espiritu Santo. This included fighters on STAD from VMF-212.

Lacking adequate early warning or fighter direction facilities until the radar stations it was tasked to set up and run were completed, the squadron had to run combat air patrols of four planes each on a daily basis—at dawn, noon and before sunset. Coupled with needed pilot training and the constant assignment of pilots and enlisted personnel on temporary duty to Guadalcanal during the months of the campaign, what few pilots the squadron had available quickly became worn out from the continuous flying.

Top: Bomber Strip No. 1, Espiritu Santo in the New Hebrides as it appeared in November 1942 (National Archives). *Bottom:* A VMO-251 Grumman F4F-3 Wildcat undergoing maintenance in a makeshift hangar on Espiritu Santo, New Hebrides, late 1942 (courtesy Tailhook Association).

VMO-251 Wildcats parked along the fighter strip near Turtle Bay, Espiritu Santo, New Hebrides, late 1942. Note the squadron insignia (courtesy Tailhook Association).

Morale of the ground crew appeared to be good throughout most of its stay on the island despite the long hours of maintenance and guard duty. For the most part, men were kept extremely busy and had little free time. Even if they had some free time, recreational facilities on Espiritu Santo were next to non-existent in late 1942. However, in a few instances military discipline was breached and had to be dealt with. Private Frederick R. Prendergast was court martialed for disobedience of orders and fined $32 over a two month period,[11] the other—Pvt. Dennis Batistich—was put on bread and water rations for 20 days and fined $30 over a two month period.[12] In both cases, the fines were a princely sum for a private making only $52.50 a month.[13]

Batistich, who hailed from Boston, enlisted in the Marine Corps in March 1942. Apparently he had an independent streak and did things his own way. While he may have been a thorn in the side to officers, he was well-liked by his fellow enlisted men. Dan Abrams remembered him as "a comical kid and had lots of fun. Everybody loved him."[14]

The Marines on Guadalcanal were fighting hard to hang on to what precious real estate they held. The captured Japanese airfield, later renamed Henderson Field, needed plenty of work to get into operation. On 12 August Admiral Ghormley ordered McCain to employ "all available transport shipping to take aviation gasoline, lubricants, ammunition,

Henderson Field in the foreground with Fighter Strip 1 in the background, November, 1942 (National Archives).

bombs, and ground crews to Guadalacanal."[15] McCain rounded up four transport destroyers, loaded them with the requested supplies and sent them off to Guadalcanal. VMO-251 Executive Officer Major Charles "Fog" Hayes, 2LT. Oscar P. "Curly" Rutledge, Jr., some of the squadron "ground staff, air controllers, and communicators"[16] sailed with the transport force, as well as over a hundred engineers of CUB-1 and an Australian coast watcher, Lt. Hugh Mackenize, to help with communications.[17] Hayes had the overall responsibility of getting Henderson Field in operation. The CUB-1 engineers were to assist Marine engineers already at work on the field and to serve as ground crew.

The transports arrived on 15 August and the supplies and men were taken ashore. The engineers of CUB-1 began to assist the Marine engineers, who were in the process of extending the field's 2,000 foot runway.

"We had some light bombs, ammunition and hand tools. The men had for their own accommodations just what they could carry on their backs. We ... unloaded on the open beach and tried to get the field ready to accept aircraft. Of course we had no equipment and it was about all we could do to get these sailors shaken down and teach them how to live under those conditions. But we did get the essentials of the shops and communications set up and actually began to operate the aircraft as soon as they arrived," said Hayes.[18] Hayes in effect became the Cactus Air Force's first operations officer and remained at the job for several weeks.

The field was ready to go on 18 August but the engineers didn't have time to celebrate. Japanese bombers arrived over the field the same day, scoring over a dozen hits on the runway. The engineers went back to work and filled in the craters. Within 48 hours the repair work was completed and the first Marine air units—VMF-223 and VMSB-232—arrived, having been launched from the USS *Long Island*. The Marines of the 1st Division were no doubt ecstatic with the arrival of the squadrons, having gone without any air support for nearly two weeks.

It was the performance of the squadron's many activities that inspired 1LT. Eldon H. "Duke" Railsback to design VMO-251's first patch. It was approved by local command authorities in 1942, but not by Naval Aviation. The insignia featured a six-legged octopus against a white cloud with naval aviator gold wings sprouting from each side of its head. The gold wings would change to the bent wings of the F4U Corsair once the squadron began acquiring them in late 1943. The patch would undergo another change in 1945 when it was re-designated as a fighter squadron (VMF). Each arm of the octopus carried an object indicative of the squadron's many responsibilities. Spurlock writes:

2Lt. Eldon H. "Duke" Railsback, the Marine credited with designing the squadron's first insignia—the famed six-legged octopus with gold wings (courtesy Robert T. Whitten).

> The first tentacle grasped a monkey wrench, symbolizing the mechanical aspects of supporting a Marine fighter/photographic squadron which was also fully equipped and served as a radar early warning and control squadron. VMO-251 also maintained an air-sea rescue capability.
> On to the second tentacle, which clasped a machine gun, which along with the bomb in the fifth tentacle, symbolized the ground and air combat functions of the squadron.
> The third tentacle grasped a camera, which was appropriate since part of the assigned mission was photographic. Each fighter plane was equipped to make vertical aerial photographs, and the squadron had substantial photo-processing capability.
> The fourth tentacle gripped a pair of binoculars, symbolizing the reconnaissance aspect of the photographic missions.
> This leaves the sixth and last tentacle. This one grasped a roll of ordinary toilet paper, with which to wipe the Army Air Corps "posterior." It is regrettable that under the trying conditions of war some irritations, aggravations and sometimes outright hostility occurs between services. All of us recognize that such incidents do not really divide us. We were all trying to reach the same objective, which was the defeat of the enemy in front of us.[19]

Amid the multiple duties of the squadron, the daily combat patrols continued. Kobler once again ground looped a Wildcat on 14 August. Fortunately the damage was slight and the plane was quickly brought back into operation by maintenance crews. Kobler was uninjured.

There was a bit of excitement on 18 August when at 1400 air raid sirens gave the alarm. Apparently enemy aircraft were sighted about 200 miles away and heading for the airfield. The squadron launched its planes into the air to meet the incoming threat, but after three hours nothing was sighted of the enemy. By 1700, all planes had been recalled and returned to the field.

Gunnery practice for the pilots was the syllabus for 19 August, and to the relief of VMO-251 maintenance personnel, the Army finally took over responsibility of refueling the 11th Bomb Group B-17s.

More gunnery practice and combat patrols continued for the rest of the month. On 24 August, six VMO-251 photographers flew with B-17s from the 11th Bomb Group for a photographic mission. Tragically one of the B-17s crashed upon return from the mission, killing six of its crew. Fortunately, no 251 photographers were killed. Two of the photographers made it home after the mission while the other four arrived the next day. On the same day, 2Lt. Robert M. "Doc" Livingston damaged his Wildcat upon landing. Livingston suffered minor cuts in the incident. The aircraft was quickly repaired and flying the next day.

On 27 August the squadron was assigned its first F4F-7 Wildcat. The F4F-7 carried no machine guns and was produced strictly for photo reconnaissance missions. With the removal of the guns and non-folding wings extra fuel tanks were added, giving it a range of over 2,000 miles. The increased weight drastically curtailed its performance compared to the F4F-3P.[20] The squadron received at least three F4F-7s during its first combat tour, but squadron records do not indicate if any missions were flown with the planes. Less than two dozen F4F-7s were built by Grumman during the course of the war.

Two days later the squadron received four F4F-4 Wildcats. This version of the Wildcat would eventually replace its F4F-3P Wildcats. The F4F-4 carried six .50 caliber machine guns—three in each wing—and had folding wings. The additional weight of the two extra guns, ammunition and the parts needed for the folding wings increased the aircraft's weight, slightly reducing its performance.

By the end of August, four squadrons stopped at the Bomber Strip on their way to Guadalcanal, among them VMF-224 and VMSB-231. For all the pilots, it was a brief respite to renew old friendships from their training days. During the evening meal at 251's makeshift mess hall, the bantering was loud and for a brief moment the deadly business of war was forgotten.

The three insignia. *Top:* The original insignia designed by Eldon "Duke" Railsback. *Middle:* Insignia after the squadron obtained F4U Corsairs. The gold wings of the original design have been replaced by the bent wings of the Corsair (courtesy John W. Irwin) *Bottom:* Squadron insignia (designed by 2Lt. Danny Johnson) after the squadron was re-designated as VMF-251. They became known as "Lucifer's Messengers" (author's collection).

Seated left to right: Sgt. Glen F. Keithley, Lt. Col. John N. Hart, and Sergeant Major Merle C. Davis. *Standing left to right*: Cpl. Lloyd G. Green, Pfc. Edwin C. Omernick, Cpl. James W. Whitaker, and Pfc. Harold O. Evans (courtesy Robert T. Whitten).

The daily patrols and gunnery practice continued into September. The month also marked the beginning of a series of transfers of planes and rotation of personnel to the Cactus Air Force on Guadalcanal. Usually the rotation assignment for personnel would last anywhere from three to six weeks. For some enlisted men it lasted far longer. Once pilots served their assigned time on Guadalcanal, they were sent back to Espiritu Santo. They then received some R&R, usually a week in Australia, and then back to the grind of combat. The rotations would continue until the squadron was shipped to Bevy in January 1943.

On 2 September, the squadron received orders to ferry six F4F-4s to Cactus. Four of the planes came from 251's inventory, and two aircraft from VMF-224. The aircraft assigned to 224 arrived on 3 September, flown by pilots from VMF-212. VMO-251's 2Lt. Kenneth J. Kirk and 2Lt. Livingston departed Espiritu Santo at noon of the 3rd. On the way to Guadalcanal, Kirk's plane lost its propeller hub, and he had to drop out of formation. Noting Kirk appeared to be in no immediate danger, Livingston continued to Guadalcanal. Kirk was left behind and flew alone. After a 2 1/2 hour flight, Kirk arrived safely with 12 gallons of gas to spare. Kirk and Livingston returned to Espiritu Santo the next day via air transport. Also arriving on 4 September were the long sought after drop tanks for the squadron Wildcats, flown in by B-17s.

The shuttle missions continued on 6 September with Yeaman, 2Lt. Joe H. McGlothlin, Jr., Railsback, and 2Lt. Michael R. Yunck flying the remaining F4F-4s to Cactus. Garton was tasked with flying the squadron's newly acquired F4F-7 (Buno 5265) Wildcat to Cactus. Garton named his -7 "Ferdinand" after Munro Leaf's bull who did not want to fight.[21] Led by Yeaman, and with a B-17 of the 11th Bombardment Group tasked with navigating, the four -4 Wildcats and -7 made their way to Guadalcanal. Orders issued to the Wildcat pilots stipulated that if one of the planes went down, the others would continue to Guadalcanal.

Shortly after the flight cleared the coast, Garton developed a problem with his -7 and was forced to ditch at sea near Cape Quiros, Espiritu Santo. Ignoring their orders, the F4F-4s turned back and circled Garton until a rescue plane showed up. A PBY Catalina was dispatched to retrieve Garton from the drink. Apparently the pilot couldn't land the PBY since the water was too rough. The B-17 continued to Guadalcanal, and the four -4s returned to Espiritu Santo due to low fuel. When 251 headquarters received word of Garton's predicament, it didn't set well with Campbell and Kirk. With Kirk in tow, Campbell commandeered a squadron J2F to rescue Garton.

Campbell landed the "Duck" near Garton's crash site. As the plane approached Garton, Kirk exited the cockpit and walked on the lower wing towards Garton. A blast from the propeller caused Kirk to lose his footing, throwing him into the water with Garton. Campbell now was faced with rescuing two comrades as well as maneuvering the plane in the water.

He taxied the plane as close as possible to the two water-logged Marines, who were staying afloat by clinging to wreckage of the floating F4F-7. Campbell let go of the controls and rushed out onto the wing, and pulled both men out of the water.

With Garton and Kirk strapped in,

Marine Gunner Wendell P. Garton near Guadalcanal ready tent, late 1942 (courtesy Robert T. Whitten).

Campbell took over the controls of the plane to take off. The water was too rough; Campbell had to taxi his plane for at least 10 miles before he was able to find a smooth patch of water in order to lift the plane into the air and head back to Espiritu Santo.

Garton's plane remained afloat after the ditching. A PBY on anti-sub duty decided it was a navigation hazard, as well as being a boon to Japanese intelligence if captured intact, and shot the plane to pieces.[22]

A second attempt to ferry the F4F-4s to Cactus was made on 7 September. Yeaman, McGlothlin, Kobler, and 2Lt. Harry F. Schwethelm took off from Espiritu Santo at 1130. They landed safely at Cactus after a 2 hour, 40 minute flight. The four pilots returned to Espiritu Santo the next day via a RD-1 of VMJ-253.

Schwethelm was back up in the air on 9 September, this time in one of the squadron's SNJ-3s. With him was PFC. William H. Miller, a carpenter. The plane developed some kind of malfunction and was forced to land on the beach at Point Pussei, approximately 35 miles west of the bomber field. The prop was damaged during the landing.

Once again Campbell was called to fly the J2F "Duck" and pick up another VMO-251 pilot. With him were Yeaman and SGT. William C. Holmes, a plane captain. The plane arrived in short order. Yeaman stayed behind with the damaged SNJ while Campbell and Holmes flew back to the bomber strip with Schwethelm and Miller. Back at the base, Campbell, assisted by mechanics PFC. Albert Madden and PFC. John V. Madden, grabbed a spare propeller and tools and loaded it into the "Duck." With both Maddens onboard, Campbell flew the "Duck" back to Point Pussei.

Campbell landed in heavy seas, damaging the wheel mechanism. The spare propeller was off loaded, along with Albert Madden. Campbell and John Madden attempted to return to the bomber strip at dusk, but couldn't land at the strip due to the crippled wheel mechanism. Instead, they tied up to a buoy in the Segond Channel.

Back at Point Pussei, Yeaman and Albert Madden worked to replace the bent prop in a tropical downpour. By the time the sun set, the work wasn't complete. Both spent the night in a nearby village and returned to finish the job the next morning.

With the prop fitted and checked out, Yeaman attempted to fly the plane off the beach. After several aborted attempts at doing so, he was finally able to

John, Albert and Walter Madden in a photo taken prior to being shipped out to the South Pacific in 1942. Compare this photo to the one on page 53 taken later in the year while at Espiritu Santo (courtesy Madden family).

VMO-251 personnel with a squadron SNJ. Photo taken on Espiritu Santo, New Hebrides, late 1942 after move to Turtle Bay (courtesy Madden Family).

get the SNJ into the air. After a short hop, he landed at the bomber strip shortly after 9 a.m. A seaplane was sent to pick up Madden.

While Yeaman was bringing the SNJ back to the strip, Kirk and SSGT Emmett Anderson, another enlisted pilot who recently joined the squadron, were practicing the Thatch Weave when their planes collided. Kirk lost his left wing and Anderson's left wing was smashed inward to the wing spar.[23]

Kirk immediately bailed out. His plane spiraled into the ocean, a total loss. A Navy destroyer was on hand to retrieve him out of the water. Kirk suffered a broken leg and lost a few teeth. He was transported to the USS *Curtiss* for treatment.

Anderson hesitated bailing out of his damaged plane, perhaps thinking he could make it back to the bomber strip. Fortunately, his radio was working. Campbell contacted Anderson, helping him determine just how much control he had of the Wildcat. After the quick tests, Campbell informed Anderson it would be too risky to land his battered Wildcat. He advised Anderson to bail out.

Anderson set a course toward Pallikulo Bay where a picket boat was on standby to pick him up. As he approached the area, no chute was seen. Anderson tried several times to line up his plane before jumping, but failed to do so each time. It was only after his Wildcat ran out of gas that he finally exited the plane. He bailed out without incident and as he floated down, he watched his Wildcat plunge into the bay.[24]

Meanwhile, back at the bomber strip, the squadron received 19 F4F-4s and one F4F-7. The 19 F4F-4s were earmarked for the Cactus Air Force at Guadalcanal. Getting the planes to their destination would turn into a three day operation. To help VMO-251 continue their sea and air patrols during the ferry mission, nine VMF-212 pilots were temporarily assigned to the squadron.

On 12 September, 10 Navy SBD Douglas dive bombers from the carrier USS *Hornet* and six TBF Avengers from the USS *Wasp* arrived at the bomber strip carrying 19 pilots to fly the F4F-4s to the *Wasp* and *Hornet*. The SDBs and TBFs would fly 14 VMO-251 pilots, along with five VMF-212 pilots, to the carriers. These pilots would then fly the Wildcats to Guadalcanal. For most of the pilots of VMO-251, it would be their first flight off a carrier. Hart, who was a qualified carrier pilot, gave the pilots a quick verbal lesson in taking off from a carrier.[25] The pilot assignments were[26]:

USS *Hornet*	USS *Wasp*
Captain Carl M. Longley	Captain Charles P. Weiland
2Lt. Roy T. Spurlock	2Lt. Herbert A. Peters
2Lt. Blaine H. Baesler	2Lt. Robert M. Livingston
2Lt. Robert T. Whitten	2Lt. Oscar P. Rutledge, Jr.
2Lt. Harry F. Schwethelm	+5 VMF-212 pilots
2Lt. Thaddeus Wojcik	
2Lt. Michael Yunck	
2Lt. Joe H. McGlothlin, Jr.	
2Lt. Eldon H. Railsback	
TSGT Wendell P. Garton	

The carrier pilots brought in by the navy planes took the 19 F4F-4 Wildcats to the carriers. The VMO-251 and VMF-212 pilots grabbed what personal gear they could and boarded the SBDs and TBFs to be ferried to the *Wasp* and *Hornet*. During the afternoon, all took off successfully but one. A SBD carrying Railsback crashed into the sea immediately after takeoff; Ensign Philip H. Grant of VB-5 suffered head injuries, and Railsback received head lacerations along with a broken arm. Despite his injuries, Railsback pulled Grant from the floundering SBD and kept him from drowning until they were picked up.[27] The other planes landed safely aboard their respective carriers.

For the Marine pilots assigned to fly the Wildcats to Guadalcanal, the brief respite aboard the carrier was an eye opener. Compared to their less than stellar living conditions at Espiritu Santo, the carrier was a four-star hotel. For the first time in months, they were served a full service meal from a table decked out with linen. And for dessert—ice cream. When each of the pilots retired to their guest quarters, awaiting them was a shower with hot and cold running water.[28]

At 0600 the next day, the engines of the Wildcats roared to life. Both carriers had steered into the wind. With Hart's advice clear in their memory and with flaps down, each pilot rolled his Wildcat down the flight deck and into the air. One of the planes remained behind due to a bent stabilizer and tab.[29]

After a little over an hour, the first of the Wildcats landed at Henderson Field, only to be redirected to the newly cleared Fighter Strip 1, located to the south and east of Henderson Field. The rest of the Wildcats followed suit. The scene that greeted the pilots once they arrived at Guadalcanal was one of devastation. The area bore witness to the repeated Japanese attacks since 7 August. Craters covered the area, and wrecked planes littered the field.

The Cactus Air Force was glad to have these fighters, as well as those that belonged to VF-5, having arrived a few days before. The Wildcats greatly increased the strength of the Cactus Air Force, which had seen its force greatly reduced due to operational losses.[30]

The pilots arrived in the midst of a large Japanese push to retake the airfield. The attacks began on 11 September with Japanese planes attacking Guadalcanal. Japanese bombers arrived the next day in an attempt to bomb the airfield. In conjunction with the 12 September aerial assault, Japanese troops of the 35th Brigade under the command of Major General Kiyotake Kawaguchi launched an attack during the evening about 2,000 yards south of the airfield. The 1st Marine Raider Battalion defending the area successfully repulsed the assault, but gave up ground in doing so.

The pilots and their gear were taken to Henderson Field. The baggage was deposited at a hangar near the pagoda, a Japanese constructed building serving as the headquarters for the 1st Marine Air Wing (1st MAW) and Marine Air Group 23 (MAG-23). Pilots already serving with the Cactus Air Force greeted the new pilots who were hanging around outside the pagoda.

Under the command of Brigadier General Roy Geiger, USMC, the Cactus Air Force was an amalgamation of aircraft from the U.S. Navy, Marines and Army. The planes and pilots flew together; which squadron a pilot belonged to did not matter. "Pilots never knew which plane they would fly until they saw it on the flight schedule just before takeoff. Your wingman might be a member of some other squadron. It was assumed that all pilots were equally skilled in gunnery and tactics," wrote Weiland.[31]

The welcoming committee quickly ended when the first of two Japanese air raids began. Early that morning, eleven planes from the Tainan Air Group, headquartered at Rabaul, departed to harass the Marines at Guadalcanal. Alerted by coast watchers, the pilots scrambled to get back to Fighter Strip 1 only to find all available planes were already manned and taxiing. The Japanese were coming in at over 27,000 feet.[32] With its slow rate of climb, the Wildcats needed as much lead time they could get in order to reach that altitude. It isn't clear how many VMO-251 pilots made it into the air, but at least one, Rutledge, attempted to do so. Unfortunately his plane stalled and crashed while trying to take off. Witnessing the crash, Garton and Weiland made their way to the crash site.[33] When they arrived, they saw an unconscious Rutledge hanging from the cockpit with blood streaming from his head. Weiland and Garton rushed to the plane and attempted to pull Rutledge from the wreck. "The instrument panel and map board were pushed back and had pinned his leg. While I held him in my arms, Garton managed to unbuckle his parachute. Slowly his leg worked free and we laid him on the crumpled wing...," recalled Weiland.[34]

They then carried Rutledge a safe distance away from the still smoking plane. A corpsman arrived to render first aid and an ammunition carrier soon pulled up. Rutledge was carefully loaded onto the ammo carrier and rushed to a field hospital. Weiland tracked down a doctor and was told that while Rutledge was in a coma and had suffered a fractured jaw, he would survive. Rutledge was eventually sent to Efate to recover.

Around the same time Rutledge crashed, Weiland and Garton heard a loud whine and looked up to see a Wildcat in a dive, heading for the ground. The plane slammed into the ground; a large pillar of smoke marking the impact area. The crash killed 2Lt. Richard A. Harring of VMF-212. Apparently Harring may have had an oxygen malfunction, causing him to black out.[35]

The pilots returned from the morning raid and tried to grab a quick lunch of spam and rice. For some of the pilots, it wasn't to be. Another Japanese attack was on the way. Not all the Wildcats had been tanked up and rearmed from the morning raids. Marine pilots, including a few from VMF-212 and VMO-251, hopped into what planes were ready and began another difficult climb for high altitude to meet the Japanese. Weiland's plane was one of those not serviced, so he taxied it to a revetment to protect it from the incoming raid.

Among those VMO-251 pilots flying to meet the Japanese were Garton, Livingston and possibly Whitten. As Garton climbed to meet the incoming Japanese, he noted his Wildcat was performing better than usual and he soon left his fellow pilots behind.[36]

By the time Garton reached the Japanese bombers, they had already dropped their payload onto the airfield and were heading home. Garton lined up one of the bombers in his sight and let loose with his machine guns, but he was too far from the bombers to have any effect. Garton, now alone, was jumped by several Mitsubishi Zeroes escorting the bombers. Recognizing an untenable situation, Garton put his Wildcat into a steep dive and made for Guadalcanal.[37]

Like Harring, VMO-251's 2Lt. Robert T. Whitten may have also been a victim of oxygen starvation during the September 13 raids. Weiland records that Whitten fell victim to the condition during a high altitude climb.[38] Whether it was the morning or afternoon raid is not clear. Several days later after his return to Espiritu Santo, Whitten was sent to Efate to be hospitalized. The incident, coupled with four bouts of malaria, eventually grounded Whitten. By April 1943, he was recovering at the home of his mother. "Well, I did pass out once—just like that. Alone. Snapped out of it just in time," said Whitten to a Wilmington, Delaware Journal reporter.[39]

There was no rest for the pilots after they returned from the afternoon raids. As evening approached, the Japanese once again pressed their attack to retake the airfield. A nuisance raid by Japanese aircraft kept the weary Marines from getting any sleep, destroyers bombarded the field, and Kawaguchi launched another attack. Fighting continued through the night. A scheduled flight to ferry the VMO-251 pilots back to Espiritu Santo at 0300 was cancelled due to the fighting. All they could do was ride the attack out in any available cover. For Garton and Spurlock, it was the side of a water-filled crater.

By the time the sun broke the horizon on the morning of 14 September, Colonel Merritt Edson's raiders had beaten back the Japanese land attack. Kawaguchi's brigade was decimated. The battle became known as "Bloody Ridge" and garnered Edson the Medal of Honor. The Japanese, recognizing the failure of their operation, pulled back to regroup. They would come back in full force in mid–October.

With the fighting all but over, the VMO-251 pilots grabbed their gear and boarded

VMO-251 Line Chief Master Technical Sergeant George P. Bunker looks over a destroyed SBD Dauntless dive bomber on Guadalcanal (courtesy Robert T. Whitten).

a R4D-1 for the ride back to Espiritu Santo. The flight was uneventful. When they arrived back at Espiritu Santo, they found the squadron in a state of flux.

Several officers and mechanics had been assigned to the Cactus Air Force on temporary duty, including radio operator Hoffman, Marine Gunner Richard E. Gilmore, AA crew member Pvt. Paul D. Baer, as well as Captain James P. Adams. Baer was injured on 26 September when he fell from a stand while working on a Wildcat. He suffered multiple contusions and had to be evacuated to a hospital.[40]

A few days after the pilots returned from their Guadalcanal shuttle mission, Garton received secret verbal orders to travel to Tonga to bring back another F4F-7 while Baesler ferried the squadron's only F4F-7 to Guadalcanal. Baesler quickly returned to the squadron while Garton would be absent for several weeks. Longley was then sent to Guadalcanal on temporary duty to pilot the F4F-7 while attached to MAG-23. In cooperation with MAG-23s D-2 (Intelligence) and D-3 (Operations) sections, he would eventually make several photographic runs over Guadalcanal to aid the ground troops.[41]

The Wildcat Garton was ordered to bring back was apparently abandoned by the USS *Saratoga* as she made her way to Pearl Harbor for repairs following a torpedo hit at the end of August. Garton received his verbal orders on 18 September. Assigned no transportation to pick up the -7 Wildcat (BuNo 5263), he basically had to hitchhike from Espiritu Santo to Tonga-Tabu (code name Bleacher), using any mode of transportation available.

On 20 September, Garton secured a ride on a PBY Catalina piloted by Cram, flying to New Caledonia. Five days later, he boarded a cargo version of the B-24 Liberator, a LB-30, and proceeded to Fiji. After a four day stay at Fiji, he hopped on board a RNZAF four-engine DeHavilland and flew to Suva. Finally, on 6 October, a RNZAF Singapore flying boat got him safely to Tonga.

When Garton was taken to the -7, he found it in desperate need of repair. Someone left the canopy open; the tropical rains had filled the cockpit with several inches of water. The ignition harness was missing, cannibalized for use on another Wildcat. With the help of two mechanics from a Navy patrol squadron stationed at Tonga, the -7 Wildcat was brought back into flying condition. After a couple of test flights, the Wildcat was deemed ready to fly back to Espiritu Santo.

On 10 October, Garton got the Wildcat airborne. Flying as escort was a RNZAF Hudson. Unfortunately the Wildcat developed fuel problems and had to put down at Fiji. The fuel problem was repaired and the next day Garton took off, following a B-17 on its way to Efate. The landing at Efate was uneventful. On 12 October, Garton finally arrived at Espiritu. On landing the left brake on the Wildcat failed, causing the plane to swerve to the right. Luckily the plane suffered no damage and Garton was uninjured. Garton soon discovered that the squadron was no longer at the bomber field.[42]

While Garton was away the squadron prepared for another move, this time to the fighter strip near Turtle Bay, located several miles north of the Bomber Strip at Pallikulo Bay. The last two weeks of September were spent getting all the squadron gear to the fighter strip, as well as building facilities at the location in order to perform maintenance on the Wildcats. By the beginning of October, the squadron was operating out of the fighter strip.

Despite the squadron's impending move, the land and sea patrols continued. Kobler cracked up another aircraft while taking off—this time an SNJ—while McGlothlin lost a side panel on his SNJ. Kobler, McGlothlin and his passenger, Private Karl D. James of the squadron's engineering section, suffered no injuries. Both planes were quickly repaired and brought back into operation.[43]

After their failed mid–September attempt to recapture Henderson Field, the Japanese began to regroup their forces for another attempt in October. Air attacks became sporadic. They did manage a strike on Henderson on the 27th, destroying at least one plane and damaging several others. It may have been during this raid, or the day after, that VMO-251 lost one of its enlisted men. During the bombardment, VMO-251's Richard E. Baird went to retrieve his rifle from his bunk, perhaps thinking a land attack was imminent. As he retrieved his rifle the weapon went off, hitting him in the foot. His injuries were severe and he had to be sent to better facilities. He was evacuated on 29 September on board the *SS Matsonia* and eventually returned to the United States. He was still undergoing treatment when the war ended.[44]

After 3 October no air attacks occurred for nearly a week. The Imperial Japanese Army began bringing reinforcements to Rabaul, then shuttling them to Guadalcanal at night onboard destroyers known as the Tokyo Express. By the middle of October the Japanese had approximately 20,000 men, plus supporting artillery on the contested island.

The Marines on Guadalcanal were in bad shape, desperately in need of reinforcements, food, ammo, and fuel for the Cactus Air Force. Vandegrift got the reinforcements and supplies he needed. The newly created Task Force 65 brought in over 4,000 men of the 7th Marines, fuel, equipment, and ammunition a few days after Kawaguchi's failed

VMO-251 enlisted personnel at Espiritu Santo, September 1942. Photo taken by VMO-251 photo section. The strain of operations is evident on their faces (author's collection).

attempt to recapture Henderson Field. And on 13 October, the Army's 164th Infantry Regiment arrived and immediately deployed in defensive positions to the east of the airfield near the Ilu River.

Beginning in late September and continuing into October, the Japanese launched several attacks to the west, east and south of the airfield in another attempt to recapture the airfield and push the Marines off Guadalcanal. These attacks failed, costing the Japanese dearly. In conjunction with the land attacks, the Imperial Japanese Navy set sail for Guadalcanal. During the early morning hours of 14 October, Henderson Field underwent an intense bombardment by Japanese Admiral Kurita Takeo's 3rd Battleship Division (*Kongō* and *Haruna*). For over an hour, 14 inch shells pummeled the air field. When the battleships ceased firing, Japanese artillery took over to continue the bombardment.[45]

Sergeant Vito Murgolo, PFC Louis P. Tuttle and other enlisted men sought shelter in a log-covered foxhole. Crammed like sardines, they couldn't stop shaking. Murgolo felt anger at not being able to do anything against the Japanese and prayed that they would make it through the bombardment. But then duty took over. With the Marines also expecting an air raid by Japanese bombers, he realized that several fighters had not been prepared for flight. With hot shrapnel flying in all directions, he and Tuttle left the shelter of the foxhole and raced for the planes. Both arrived unscathed. They worked feverishly to get the planes ready. As if the artillery wasn't enough, a Japanese sniper harassed them. Murgolo and Tuttle were not hit; Murgolo got two of the planes cranked up and Tuttle cranked up another. Murgolo taxied one of them to a nearby officer. Screaming to be heard, he asked the officer if he was a pilot. The officer replied in the affirmative.

Murgolo then told the pilot to "get in the plane and get that Jap sniper!"[46] For their actions that day, Murgolo and Tuttle were awarded the Silver Star.

The bombardment continued the night of the 14th. By the morning of the 15th, the Cactus Air Force had taken a severe beating. Henderson Field was cratered so heavily that operations from the field were curtailed, but Fighter Strip 1 was still useable. Over half the planes of the Cactus Air Force were either destroyed or damaged, and precious aviation fuel went up in flames. Over 42 men were killed or wounded.[47] Despite this severe blow, the men of the Cactus Air Force retaliated.

Hoffman, a radio operator for the squadron and assigned to Geiger's headquarters on STAD, found himself on Geiger's PBY Catalina—the *Blue Goose*—on 15 October piloted by Cram, Geiger's aide and personal pilot. The day before, Cram had 251 maintenance personnel rig up two torpedo launchers on the Catalina, one on each wing.[48] He then flew the Catalina back to Guadalcanal.

On the 15th, Cram begged Geiger to let him take the Catalina up and participate in an upcoming attack on Japanese ships. The general was hesitant to let Cram fly on the day's mission but gave his approval. Five Japanese transports anchored near Kokumbona were visible from American positions on Guadalcanal. The defenders watched as the Japanese unloaded supplies and troops. In a series of mission throughout the day, Cactus planes pressed their attack, mostly in Douglas SBDs and in one mission, accompanied by Cram's Catalina. Hoffman recalls the attack:

> We took off from Henderson during a lull in the shelling and climbed to around six thousand feet. About one mile from the enemy fleet we started our dive and were indicating 240 knots as we leveled off at 75 feet. We passed over their destroyer screen before they saw us, and suddenly there were the targets. The torpedoes were released a few seconds apart. One of the torpedoes scored a direct hit while I believe the other one missed.
>
> We pulled up into a left turn and headed for Henderson Field. All at once there were Zeros all around us and we were taking a terrific pounding The shells and anti-aircraft flak from the ships firing on us, sounded much like someone was slinging hands full of gravel against the metal hull of the aircraft. We were still traveling at a pretty high speed with a Zero closing on us head on when both engines ceased functioning simultaneously, giving the effect of slamming on the brakes, and the Zero over shot and missed us.
>
> Our aircraft had metal tanks in the starboard wing and self-sealing tanks in the port. We had been using fuel from the starboard tanks, and the Zeros had shot up the metal tanks so when they went dry, we had complete engine failure.
>
> Anderson, our engineer, had immediately switched tanks and cut in the crossfeed fuel pumps; so when both engines re-started with full throttle, mixture and props forward, the aircraft surged forward just as another Zero made his pass and he under-shot, and missed us.
>
> As we approached Henderson Field, Lt. Roger Haberman was returning to land his smoking Wildcat at Fighter One air strip when he saw a Zero chasing our PBY, he saved us by pulling up sharply and shooting down the Zero without even taking time to retract the landing gear on his damaged fighter. It was his first kill and believe me, to me he's a hero![49]

By the end of the day several transports were burning and beached.

The Catalina was badly shot up. Murgolo was present when the plane landed. Hoffman, drenched in sweat, stepped off the plane. "Shot full of holes," Hoffman said to Murgolo. "You can write this plane off."[50] Hoffman recalls that the plane had 175 bullet holes in the wings and fuselage. There were two 20 mm hits in the vertical stabilizer, and other damage by anti-aircraft flak. None of the seven crewmen received a scratch.[51]

Meanwhile, as Cram and the SDBs attacked the transports, Anderson shuttled a Wildcat to Guadalcanal from Espiritu and found himself assigned to VMF-121 for temporary duty. Less than a week later, Anderson was declared missing in action.

Late in the morning of 21 October, a coast watcher informed Cactus of an approaching Japanese air attack, numbering over 30 bombers and fighters. Cactus launched nearly 20 Wildcats, and tangled with the incoming Japanese fighters after the bombers made their run and turned for home. It was during this fight that Anderson was lost. His body was never found and he was initially listed as missing in action. In 1945, he was declared killed in action.[52] VMO-251 was not informed of Anderson's loss and inquiries were sent to Cactus to determine his status. The squadron finally received its answer after a delay of several weeks.

The defenders on Guadalcanal withstood another attempt by the Japanese to retake Henderson Field during the night of 24 October and the next day. And once again they were stopped in their tracks. Just like the previous attempt of 13 October, Japanese air and naval assets added their weight to the attack.

Shortly after this failed attack, four pilots from VMO-251—Yunck, 2Lt. Herbert A. Peters, Campbell, and Livingston—arrived at Henderson Field via ferry in the first of many rotations that would continue until the squadron arrived at Guadalcanal in January 1943.

On 29 October, Hart relinquished his duties as commanding officer of VMO-251, and was assigned as the First Marine Air Wing liaison officer on the staff of Commander Aircraft South Pacific. Hayes took over the duties as commanding officer of the squadron the next day.

At 0445 on 1 November, seven F4F-4 Wildcats took off from Henderson Field for an attack at the Japanese seaplane base located at Rekata Bay on the northwest coast Santa Isabel Island. First Lieutenant Robert F. Stout of VMF-121 led the attack. With him were fellow VMF-121 pilots 1Lt. Watkins and 2Lt. Freeman, and VMO-251 pilots Yunck, Peters, Campbell and Livingston.

The seven Wildcats reached their target in about an hour and began their strafing attack. Despite the heavy anti-aircraft fire put up by the defenders, the Marine pilots claimed five bi-planes destroyed on the beach.

The anti-aircraft fire put up by the Japanese defenders was accurate. All the Wildcats were hit; all but one of the Wildcats made it back to Guadalcanal. Yunck had taken a

VMO-251 enlisted mess. From left to right: Wendell Garton, John Irwin and Emmett Anderson, September 1942 at Bomber Field 1, Espiritu Santo. Garton and Anderson were enlisted pilots. Anderson was lost the next month. His body was never recovered (courtesy John W. Irwin).

hit in his oil line, eventually causing his engine to quit. Yunck was forced to ditch his plane off the southwest side of Santa Isabel in the Austria Sound.

His plane quickly sank. At around a depth of 25 feet, Yunck finally scrambled out of the cockpit and made it to the surface. Gasping for air, he looked around and swam to an islet about 200 yards away. The small island was uninhabited. There, Yunck contemplated his next move and quickly made up his mind.

He swam back to where his plane sank and made several dives to retrieve the life raft. He also cut out the bureau number from the rudder.[53] With the coastline of Santa Isabel visible in the distance, Yunck began to paddle his raft on a southeast course.

After four days of paddling, Yunck made landfall. Before him were several natives cooking a pig on the beach. Using Pidgin English, the creative use of his arms and sound effects, he tried to convey to the natives that he was an American pilot. After about half a minute one of the natives spoke. In a British accent, the native told Yunck he understood and that they would take him to Geoffrey Kuper, the coast watcher on the island.

Using canoes and at times walking inland, the natives delivered Yunck to Kuper on 9 November. Yunck was anxious to get back to the action, even suggesting to Kuper that he head back up to Rekata Bay and steal a Japanese floatplane. After that suggestion, Kuper decided to get Yunck back to the Americans as soon as possible. On 16 November, a large canoe was used to transport Yunck to Tulagi, where he was delivered to American forces after several days. A PT boat then took him back to Guadalcanal. By late November, Yunck was back flying missions against the Japanese.[54]

Following the failed Japanese attacks in October, the commanding officer of the Japanese 17th Army on Guadalcanal, Lt. General Harukoshi Hyakuyake, expected to continue attacks on the Americans, but to do so he needed reinforcements. The 8th Fleet organized a force of 11 destroyers to carry 1300 soldiers and made way for Guadalcanal.[55] On 7 November, search planes spotted the ships northwest of Florida Island and heading in a southeast direction. Cactus immediately ordered an airstrike. Participating in the attack would be three TBF Avengers of VT-8 and 12 Douglas SBD dive bombers—at least seven of them from VMSB-132. Assigned to escort the strike planes were 12 Army P-39 Aircobras and nearly two dozen Wildcats flown by eight pilots from VMF-112, eight pilots from VMF-121, five pilots from VMF-212 and at least three pilots from VMO-251.[56]

The strike force took off from Guadalcanal at 1630. Fifty-five minutes later, the Japanese were spotted. Amid intense anti-aircraft fire, the dive bombers nosed over to line up their drops and several fighters began strafing runs on the ships. As the Marines kept the Japanese busy, the three TBF Avengers of VT-8 lined up for their torpedo runs. It was only after the torpedoes hit the water that the Avengers were detected.

Two ships were hit by the torpedoes, and the dive bombers scored one hit. Three Wildcats—one flown by VMF-112's 1LT. J.L. Secrest and two flown by pilots of VMO-251 claimed to have caused an explosion on a destroyer during a strafing run, sinking it. Each received a partial credit for sinking the ship.[57]

Japanese planes intercepted the attack force. After the aerial melee, all the Avengers suffered hits from the enemy gunfire and one VT-8 crewmember, AOM3c R. L. Shively was critically wounded.[58] One dive bomber from VMSB-141 failed to return,[59] and one VMF-121 Wildcat had to ditch at sea after running out of gas. The pilot was picked up by a PT boat. Five Japanese planes were claimed to have been shot down during the fight.[60]

Unfortunately no Japanese ships were sunk[61] and the damage the ships may have

2Lt. Michael Yunck (courtesy Robert T. Whitten).

suffered did not stop them from reaching Guadalcanal. During the evening of 7/8 November the reinforcements disembarked near Tassafaronga, located north and west of Kokumbona on Guadalcanal's northern shore.

As the Marines and the Navy valiantly defended the Solomon Islands, back in the United States there was talk of merging the Army, Navy and Marines into one fighting force. The idea was to streamline the services and maximize their striking power. All members would wear the same uniform, and be led by one commander. This move, if accepted, would no doubt destroy the identity and esprit de corps of each service. Corporal Albert Madden, one of three brothers serving with 251, wrote a poem that made it known how 251 Marines, and perhaps all Marines, felt about the proposal:

> Aye, Poloticians, send us out
> To light our country's war,
> And while we're raising hell out here
> Disband our gallant Corps.
> Just tear the globe and anchor down,
> Cut out the eagle's heart,
> Clad us all in olive drab
> And split us all apart.
> Take our two-tone suits of blue
> Reclaim our threadbare "greens"

But these traditions still belong
To the United States Marines.
Belleau Wood-Chateau Thierry
St. Mihiel-The Argonne
Wake Island-Midway-The Solomons
Where have those memories gone?

Far better to take our band
And group us all alone
(You'll have to search the far flung fronts
For you won't find us at home)
Then give us all the guns we need
With cartridges to spare
And send us to Japan itself
To make a landing there.
Beneath the canons' thundrous roar
On hot and bloody sand,
While "Wildcats" strafe from up above
Let us Leathernecks make our stand.
While the "Devil-Dog" insignia
Waves o'er the enemy's shore
Let the Gods of war decide
The disbandment of our Corps.[62]

The proposal fell by the wayside. The success or failure of the fight for Guadalcanal was indeed placed in the hands of the gods of war.

As Yunck was making his way back to Guadalcanal, the tide turned in favor of the American forces holding Guadalcanal. The Japanese made one more push to take back the island with air, naval and land forces. Several thousand soldiers of the Japanese 38th Division loaded onto 11 transports and made way for Guadalcanal. Also dispatched was a protective naval force comprised of two battleships, several cruisers and destroyers. During the night of 12 November and the morning of the 13th, American naval forces engaged the Japanese in what became known as the Battle of Santa Cruz. The IJN battleship *Hiei*'s rudder was damaged, severely limiting her maneuverability.

Left to right: Albert Madden, John V. Madden, and Walter F. Madden of VMO-251's engineering section, possibly taken at Espiritu Santo in late 1942. An edited copy of this photo made the cover of the September 17, 1943 issue of *Hat Times* (courtesy John W. Irwin).

On the morning of 13 November, planes from Henderson Field, including those from the USS *Enterprise*, repeatedly attacked the ailing *Hiei*. Numerous hits forced the commanding officer of the ship to eventually scuttle her. At the same time, Japanese forces pounded Henderson Field through 13 and 14 November while they attempted to land reinforcements. It is against this background that VMO-251 pilots scored their first aerial victories.

Shortly after 0900 on 11 November, radar on Guadalcanal picked up an incoming Japanese raid. Nearly two dozen 1st MAW Wildcats scrambled into the air to intercept the incoming attackers. One of the intercepting pilots was VMO-251's Campbell.

VMO-251 officers and others at Espiritu Santo, November 1942. *Standing at rear left to right:* George S. Kobler, Charles P. Weiland, Carl M. Longley, Ralph R. Yeaman, William R. Campbell, Charles H. Hayes, John V. Collins, Claude H. Welch, Raymond D. Little (U.S. Navy, medical officer), Ramon J. Wallenborn (U.S. Navy, dental officer), Robert M. Livingston. *Kneeling left to right:* Lowell M. Witt, Merle C. Davis, Blaine H. Baesler, Frank M. Platt, Jr., Eldon H. Railsback, Kenneth J. Kirk, Jr., Harry F. Schwethelm, Robert G. Straine and Richard E. Gilmore. *Sitting left to right:* Daggett, Seraphin G. Musachia, Thaddeus Wojcik, Joe H. McGlothlin, Jr., Herbert A. Peters, Roy T. Spurlock, Robert T. Whitten, Wendell P. Garton, Walter W. Pardee (courtesy Robert T. Whitten).

Unfortunately cloud cover over the area aided the Japanese, and they snuck in to strike U.S. ships off loading supplies and reinforcements off Lunga. Carrier bombers, covered by Zeros, targeted several ships. The *Zeilin* (AP-9) received several near misses, causing minor flooding when her hull plates were loosened by the exploding bombs.

With the aid of the cloud cover, Japanese Zeros jumped on several Wildcats. During the ensuing dogfight, Campbell was credited with downing one of the two Zeros lost by the Japanese. The Marines lost four pilots, all from VMF-121.[63]

Meanwhile, Japanese bombers escorted by Zeros were on their way from Rabaul to drop their load on Henderson. At around 1130, the bombers let loose their deadly cargo, but missed Henderson Field. Instead, the bombs thinned out a nearby coconut grove and holed Fighter Strip 1. Wildcats intercepted the bombers after their run on Henderson Field. Aggressively pressing their attack, the Wildcats downed four of the Japanese bombers.⁶⁴ Among those credited with downing one of the Japanese bombers was VMO-251's Peters.

Late in the morning on 12 November, the Japanese launched another attack force to hit U.S. ships off Lunga. Forty-six planes, comprised of torpedo bombers and Zeros, made their way to the targets. Coast watchers warned Guadalcanal. With the information provided by the coast watchers, the Navy positioned its ships to greet the attackers. Radar on Guadalcanal picked up the incoming force and constantly gave out approach warnings. Despite this, and with the aid of more clouds moving in, the Japanese attack force surprised the American forces by approaching Lunga from the northeast by way of Florida Island.

Spotting the incoming Japanese planes, 16 Wildcats with army P-39 Aircobras intercepted the Japanese and proceeded to inflict serious damage to the incoming enemy. When the engagement was over, 24 of the enemy planes were claimed to have been shot down by the pilots.⁶⁵ It was during this engagement that Campbell was credited with shooting down his second plane, a Zero.

The action continued on 13 November with planes from Cactus repeatedly flying missions to strike the damaged *Hiei*. Shortly after 0600, six TBF Avengers took off for the Japanese battleship. Two of the torpedo bombers developed problems and had to abort. Following the Avengers were six Wildcats led by Campbell. After little more than an hour, the torpedo bombers made their run on the *Hiei*. The Wildcats jumped on some Zeros broken up by a previous attack. During this engagement, Peters was credited with his second kill.

After the repeated bombardments during the course of the day, the *Hiei* was scuttled early on 14 November. That night, IJN cruisers bombarded Henderson Field and the nearby Fighter Strip 1. At least 15 aircraft were hit by shrapnel, all at the fighter strip. Most were repaired and brought back into operation the next day. A few men were also hit by shrapnel, including VMO-251's Campbell.

On 14 November, the Japanese 11 ship reinforcement convoy arrived near Guadalcanal carrying 10,000 soldiers of the 38th Division, artillery personnel, engineers, and replacements, as well as several thousand tons of supplies.⁶⁶ Seven of the transports were either sunk or became floating hulks after Cactus planes attacked the convoy. Four others retreated and were ordered to beach themselves to deliver the remaining troops and supplies. They did but in the end, it was all for nothing. Around three thousand troops made it to Guadalcanal and less than a week's worth of supplies. Planes from Cactus went out the following day and located several of the floating hulks. Avengers, escorted by Campbell with six Wildcats, ended up sinking two of the transports damaged during the attacks on the 14th. Never again did the Japanese attempt to reinforce Guadalcanal with such a large force. Instead, supplies and forces brought to the island were merely to provide a rear guard for the evacuation of all Japanese forces on the island.

After the disaster incurred by the Japanese during the engagements of 12–14 November, they began to reevaluate their position in the Solomon Islands. The Japanese realized the supplies and reinforcements reaching Guadalcanal weren't enough to sustain any kind of offensive operations on the island. Japanese troops that remained on the island in January 1943 could only rely on meager supplies delivered by submarine. By 1 December, American personnel outnumbered Japanese personnel by nearly a 2 to 1 margin. The 1st Marine Division was relieved by the 25th Infantry Division in December, with Major General Alexander Patch taking over command of ground forces from Vandegrift.

In January 1943, with 50,000 troops under his command, Patch went on the offensive to drive the Japanese off the island.

With U.S. control of the air over Guadalcanal, an increasing U.S. Navy presence, as well as U.S. Army reinforcements and their own inability to keep Guadalcanal adequately supplied, the Japanese eventually decided to evacuate the remnants of the 17th Army from Guadalcanal, dubbed Operation KE-GO. Troops on the island were ordered to move to the northwest corner, near the Cape Esperance area, where they would be picked up and evacuated. The evacuations would begin on 1 February with destroyers from the Tokyo Express tasked with picking up the Japanese troops.

Air operations continued for the pilots of VMO-251. The squadron lost two planes on 17 November, most likely at Espiritu Santo. It cannot be determined with any certainty what led to the accidents. What is known is that the pilots, 2Lt. G. B. Doyle and 2Lt. Kenneth L. Reusser survived. Doyle's plane, an F4F-4 (BuNo 03434), was written off. However the engine was salvageable, and required a major overhaul to be brought back into service. Reusser, flying an F4F-3P (BuNo 1850), lost his plane when it crashed at sea.

The end of November saw the beginning of a series of command changes for the squadron. On 30 November, Hayes relinquished command of the squadron to Yeaman. On 8 December, Yeaman turned it over to Campbell, and on the 11th Major Joseph N. Renner assumed command of VMO-251, with Campbell becoming the executive officer.

On 30 November, 11 VMO-251 pilots received verbal orders to report to Guadalcanal for duty: Hayes, Weiland, Baesler, Kobler, McGlothlin, Railsback, Kirk, Spurlock, Schwethelm, 2Lt. Thaddeus Wojick and Garton. The pilots were at Guadalcanal by 1 December, having arrived by a transport aircraft. Within a span of a week beginning on 11 December, the squadron received an influx of pilots from VMSB-142, VMO-151 and 4thMBDAW.[67] None of the pilots had time in fighter aircraft. Renner was given 25 days to train these men in the Wildcat and teach them the fine art of fighter tactics.[68] Renner designated his executive officer, Campbell, to execute the program. One of the pilots in this crash program was future Marine Corps ace 2Lt. Henry A. "Hank" McCartney. Even enlisted men were not immune from the shuffling of personnel. By the end of December, due to transfers, sickness and casualties, the number of enlisted men in the squadron numbered 167, nearly a 50 percent drop within a span of five months.

Table 1—Pilots Joined from VMSB-142 on 11 December 1942

Name	Rank
Vroome, Ray L.	Major
Booth, Roy L.	2Lt.
Dunn, John T.	2Lt.
Leeds, Philip	2Lt.
McCartney, Henry A.	2Lt.
Rhodes, Richard M.	2Lt.
Harlan, William B.	2Lt.
Hellerrde, Arthur O.	2Lt.

Table 2—Pilots Joined from MAG-13, 4th MBDAW and VMO-151 on 16 December 1942

Name	Rank
Baker, Robert M.	1Lt.

Name	Rank
Baran, Walter A.	1Lt.
Berteling, John B.	1Lt.
Bryson, Robert L.	1Lt.
Christian, Wayne W.	1Lt.
Loban, Glen A.	1Lt.
Klas, Donald L.	1Lt.
Moore, Jack R.	1Lt.
Sabatier, Henry S.	1Lt.
Whitaker, William H.	1Lt.
Erwin, Paul V.B.	2Lt.
Trenchard, Harold R.	2Lt.

Campbell worked up a syllabus which included the following: familiarization in the Wildcat, section and division tactics, gunnery practice at all altitudes, high altitude hops, cross country flights to Efate to teach navigation and the management of fuel consumption, pre-dawn takeoffs, night flying, bombing and strafing on a simulated target, individual combat (plane vs. plane, sector vs. sector and division vs. division). The fledgling fighter pilots were also taught offensive and defensive tactics, gunnery runs on bombers, fighters, dive bombers and float planes. The Thatch Weave was taught "but above everything else the men were taught to stick together and fly in the same air."[69]

The training for the soon-to-be fighter pilots was strenuous and in at least one instance, deadly. On 21 December 2Lt. Roy Booth, who came to the squadron from VMSB-142, was killed when his Wildcat crashed into the water during a practice gunnery run.

Since most of the pilots came from dive bomber squadrons and had not flown at altitudes higher than 15,000 feet, they also had to be trained to use an oxygen mask since the Wildcats flew at altitudes above 20,000 feet.[70]

Meanwhile at Guadalcanal 251 pilots flew daily patrols. Most were escort missions and at times, only AA fire was encountered. However, there were a few missions when the Japanese met the Marine pilots in the air. On 3 December, Yunck, back from his adventure with the coast watcher, led a flight of Wildcats on an escort mission to intercept Japanese destroyers cruising between Georgia Islands and Santa Isabel. Yunck ended up shooting down three Japanese floatplanes. He returned to Espiritu Santo on 11 December for a much needed rest.

Several hours before sunrise on 8 December, dive bombers and Wildcats prepared for an attack on Japanese destroyers said to be heading down the slot and towards Guadalcanal. Weiland would be leading a flight of four Wildcats, with Kobler the tail-end Charlie of his flight. They were to provide cover for the dive bombers.

Fighter Strip 2, located to the west of Henderson Field near Kukum on the north coast of Guadalcanal, was not in the best condition for operations. Overnight rains turned pot holes into water-filled mud pits. Since the field was recently cleared out of a coconut plantation, no one thought to provide navigation aids for the pilots. Beer bottles lit with flares, placed along both sides of the runway, provided the only aid for the airmen.

Weiland was the first to become airborne. He circled the field as the others took to the air. After two of the Wildcats joined up with Weiland, he noticed a white light in his rear view mirror. He thought it was Kobler's plane, thinking a cover fell off one of Kobler's navigation lights.

The Wildcats climbed to 12,000 feet as the dive bombers took off. There was still

Pilots of VMF-121 and VMO-251, late December 1942 or early January 1943, Guadalcanal. Eldon Railsback is standing 2nd from left, Blaine Baesler standing 3rd from left, Harry Schwethelm standing 4th from right, Joe McGlothlin 3rd from right in middle row, Roy Spurlock (with bandage) is 4th from right in middle row, Wendell Garton in baseball cap is 2nd from left in middle row, Pat Weiland is sitting in front row, 5th from right (courtesy Garton family).

no sign of Kobler. Weiland was in contact with Cactus, but radio transmissions from Cactus were non-existent. Finally, after nearly an hour of flying, Weiland received word from Cactus to abort the mission and to return to base.

By the time the Wildcats made their approach, the sun was breaking the horizon. Weiland made his landing and touched down without a problem. As he taxied down the field, he noticed a plume of smoke rising ahead. He finally realized that the white light he had seen was Kobler's plane cracking up. Kobler had somehow lost control of his Wildcat and collided with a plane parked on the left side of the runway. As Weiland rolled by the wreckage, he saw the charred remains of Kobler still in the cockpit.[71]

The missions continued. The next time VMO-251 pilots met up with the Japanese in the air it was 23 December. The Japanese had constructed an airfield near Munda, located on the south side and near the western end of New Georgia, an island in the Solomon chain. At around 1045, approximately 40 Japanese aircraft landed at the field. Major Don Yost, commanding officer of VMF-121, found himself leading a division of Wildcats, and VMO-251's McGlothlin led another. Also flying on the mission was Baesler. Escorting dive bombers, they arrived over Munda Field around noon. Over a dozen Japanese planes were already airborne to greet the Marines. The Wildcats engaged the Japanese while the dive bombers attacked the airfield.

Joe H. "Pete" McGlothlin, Jr. Pete was credited with his first kill in December 1942 while flying with the Cactus Air Force (courtesy Robert T. Whitten).

During the engagement, McGlothlin was credited with his first kill. Yost claimed two fighters, while VMF-121's Irwin Carter and Ben Wisner each claimed one Japanese plane destroyed. Even the dive bombers put in claims for two Japanese fighters destroyed on the ground.

The Marines did not get away unscathed. Baesler's plane was shot full of holes, but he was able to get the Wildcat back to Guadalcanal. VMF-121's Captain David Andre was shot down, ditching his plane in Roviana Lagoon despite being wounded. He hid himself on a small island and after a short time, coast watchers alerted friendly natives to Andre's presence. The natives retrieved Andre and brought him to a friendly village. He finally returned to Guadalcanal via a PBY Catalina on 1 January.[72]

Yost was back in the air the next day leading a division of Wildcats, this time VMO-251's Kirk as his wingman. Along for another strike at Munda were Army P-39 Aircobras and a dozen Dauntless dive bombers. They arrived over the field early in the morning and once again the Japanese were waiting. For some reason the P-39s engaged the Japanese fighters while several Wildcats strafed the airfield, catching Japanese planes as they attempted to get airborne. Yost got four of the planes, Kirk was credited with three, and another VMF-121 pilot claimed one. Along with claims by the dive bombers and the Army P-39's, a total of 18 Japanese planes were claimed to have been shot down. Kirk was awarded the Distinguished Flying Cross for his feat, and the aerial tour de force by the Wildcat pilots made headlines in papers all across the United States.

At least two VMO-251 pilots were back at Munda on 27 December: Weiland and Spurlock. Weiland led one section and Spurlock led a second section. A division of

A wrecked SBD Dauntless dive bomber at Guadalcanal (courtesy Robert T. Whitten).

Captain Kenneth J. Kirk with his Distinguished Flying Cross (courtesy Vermont Historical Society).

Wildcats from VMF-121 were also along for the mission. Their mission was to conduct a fighter sweep before a scheduled bombing mission arrived to pound the airfield.

The Wildcats arrived to find several Japanese fighters in the air ready to meet them. Following a wild engagement with one of the Zeros, Weiland was able to flame it. Along with Weiland, Spurlock and VMF-121 pilot Alex Hearn each bagged a fighter. Once the aerial threat was minimized, the Wildcats began to strafe the field. By this time the dive bombers had arrived. Nearly half a dozen Japanese planes were hit. In addition to the planes, supply dumps and a fuel dump were left ablaze.[73]

Weiland and Spurlock were not finished flying for the day. They were back up in the air in the afternoon for patrol duty. After an uneventful three hours, the sections led by the 251 pilots returned to Cactus. When Spurlock attempted his landing, the Wildcat's wheels dug into the runway and flipped over, ending up on its back. Spurlock scrambled out of the plane with a few bruises and his head badly cut. For a period of time, Spurlock had to wear a bandage covering his head.[74]

On 29 December, it was Railsback's turn to get into the action. Nearly a dozen Marine and Army aircraft ran into intense anti-aircraft fire over Munda airfield. The planes strafed the field destroying one AA gun, flaming a trio of Japanese planes on the ground and possibly destroying a fuel dump. The planes then turned around and headed home.[75]

The next day, Weiland and several VMF-121 pilots flew escort for a quartet of Army P-39s. As the Aircobras dropped their bomb load on barges located in New Georgia's Wickham Bay, the Wildcats flew above them keeping an eye out for any approaching Japanese aircraft. After the army pilots left five barges in flames, they flew on to the Munda airfield. No targets were found but they did encounter AA fire from the Japanese.[76]

December was a successful month for the squadron. Squadron pilots were credited with nine Japanese planes shot down but it came at a cost of two men killed. The success would continue into January 1943. Despite the intense operations on Guadalcanal, and the continual patrols over Espiritu Santo, squadron personnel found time to send holiday greetings to friends and family. They designed a card showing two Wildcats against a partly cloudy sky, with the Marine Corps emblem in the bottom right. Across the top of the card were the words, "Seasons Greetings."

Weiland flew another mission on 2 January with the intent of escorting an approaching U.S. Navy task force reported to be south of Guadalcanal. Unable to locate the task force, Weiland and his fellow pilots returned to Henderson. It wasn't until late in the day when the task force was finally spotted by another patrol.

The 251 pilots who arrived at Henderson on 1 December were sent back to Espiritu on 9 January. When they arrived they found the squadron packing up for a move to Guadalcanal. The USS *Crescent City* anchored in Pallikulo Bay at Espiritu Santo on 7 January with orders to transport several units from Espiritu Santo to Guadalcanal, which included VMO-251 and VMF-122. Three officers and 175 enlisted men were on board by 12 January. Two days later the USS *Crescent City* departed Espiritu Santo.[77]

While the squadron was packing up, those pilots undergoing fighter training were sent to Guadalcanal for temporary duty. They departed on January 10th and the 11th. Campbell led the pilots and planes to Guadalcanal. Renner and a few other pilots were sick and came up a few days later.[78] Up until this time, squadron pilots assigned temporary duty to Guadalcanal were flown to the island via a transport plane. When the USS *Crescent City* carrying the ground echelon of the squadron arrived on 17 January, orders for VMO-251—as well as those of the ground echelon of VMF-122—were to relieve the ground crews of VMF-112[79] (at Guadalcanal since November 1942) and VMF-121 (at Guadalcanal since September 1942). Both squadrons were operating out of Fighter Strip No. 2. The ground echelon set up tents on top of a hill near the fighter strip to begin their work. The squadron's administrative offices appeared to have stayed at Espiritu, as several officers who arrived in January were ordered back to Espiritu for duty with VMO-251.

As the leading line chief, Master Technical Sergeant John Irwin had his hands full keeping track of the location of aircraft sprawled around Henderson Field, as well as ensuring crews were assigned to planes needing repairs. Not only responsible for 251's aircraft, squadron maintenance crews worked on all planes at Cactus. This would eventually include the F4U Corsair, soon to arrive at Guadalcanal. As an aid, Irwin sketched

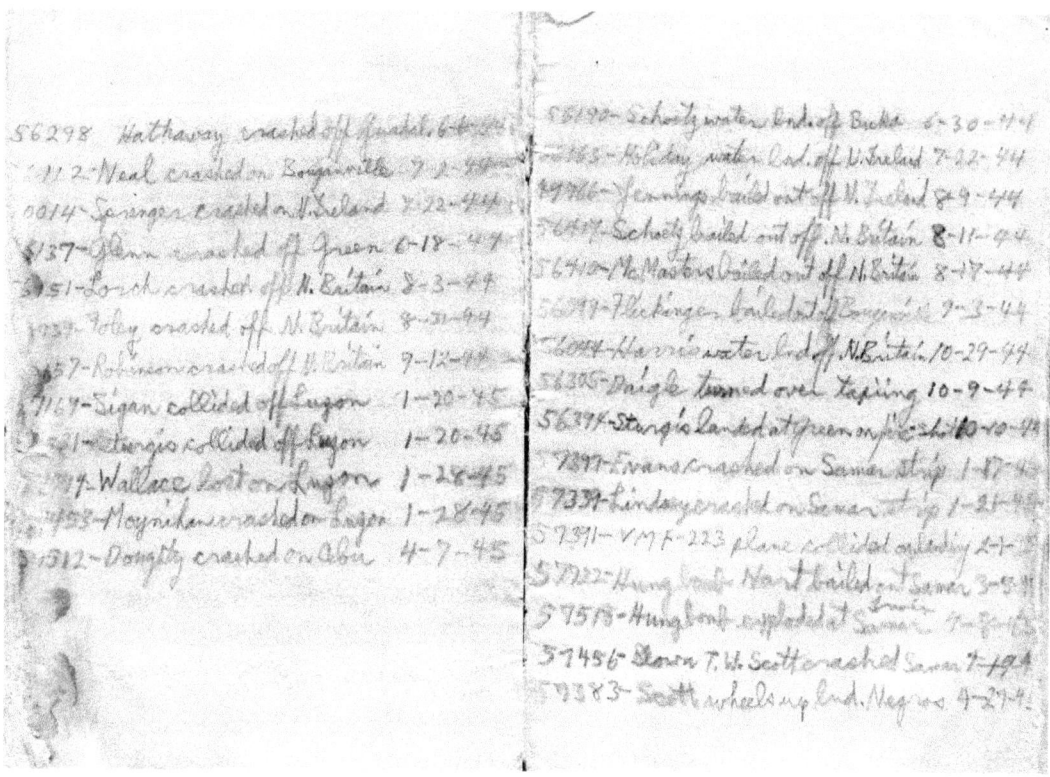

List of Corsair VMO/VMF-251 losses (1944–1945) kept by John W. Irwin. At Guadalcanal Irwin was the NCOIC line chief and by the time they reached Bougainville he was a lieutenant and the squadron engineer officer. His handwritten notes kept up with crew assignments, engine block changes and other items pertaining to maintenance (courtesy John W. Irwin).

out a map of Henderson Field in a notebook no larger than a pocket bible, marking each aircraft's location. Three to four Marines were usually assigned to a plane during maintenance; Irwin kept track of his crews, at times noting which planes they were assigned to repair and aircraft losses. It was a practice he kept up through Bougainville in 1944 and Samar in 1945.

Friday, 15 January proved to be the squadron's best day in the air against the Japanese. Nine destroyers were spotted off the northwest coast of New Georgia, heading home after dropping Japanese troops off on Guadalcanal during the previous night. Shortly after 7:30 in the morning, dive bombers of VMSB-142, escorted by 12 Wildcats and six army P-39s, caught up with the destroyers. Eight of the Wildcat pilots were from VMF-121 and four were from VMO-251: Renner, Baran, Moore and Loban. Of the four 251 pilots, Baran, Moore and Loban were on their first mission after recently completing the crash fighter course ordered by Renner.

The Japanese ships spotted the planes and immediately began to scatter, throwing up anti-aircraft fire in the process. As the dive bombers nosed over to press their attack, the covering Wildcats and Aircobras engaged around two dozen Japanese fighters.[80] During the aerial melee, Renner was credited with downing one Japanese fighter. Baran was also credited with downing a Japanese plane. Moore and Loban were credited with two apiece.[81] Unfortunately, the dive bombers scored no hits.

Moore would have to wait to celebrate his first kills. Japanese fighters latched onto his tail and ended up shooting him down. Moore was able to ditch his plane. After retrieving his life raft, he spent several days drifting in the water before he was met by natives in canoes off Santa Isabel Island. The natives proved to be friendly and coordinated with the area coast watcher to get Moore back to Guadalcanal. By the end of January, Moore was back in American hands.[82]

While the pilots faced the Japanese in the air, the enlisted men continued to endure intermittent Japanese attacks, especially bombardments. Sometime on 22 January at around 0400, Henderson Field was apparently the target of a bombing raid.[83] During the attack, Batistich was killed when a bomb exploded near his position.

"We got there up on the flyer strip and instead of him digging a foxhole, there was a kind of a little arm chair lookin' indent in the volcano rise that was behind the strip there ... him and another guy just got in that, and there's only one way it could've hurt him was the bombs had dropped and come in from, and sure enough, first night that they crawled in there, well a little old bomb went off and killed them both right there in that deal, so it was their time to go I guess," said Abrams.[84]

VMO-251 pilots were back in the air on 23 January. Coast watchers had spotted two Japanese ships sailing in the Slot. Dive bombers from VMSB-233 and torpedo bombers from VMSB-131, escorted by nearly two dozen VMO-251 pilots, took off for an early evening strike. Shortly after 1800 hours the Marines arrived, and were promptly met by Japanese planes. Amid a sky filled with flak, the dive bombers and the torpedo bombers went after the Japanese ships. The Wildcats of VMO-251 engaged the Japanese fighters. Once again the Japanese ships escaped untouched. In the air it was a different story. Renner, 1Lt. Paul V. Erwin and Loban were credited with one Japanese plane each. The Japanese shot down Erwin and 2Lt. Philip Leeds.[85] Erwin was never found and was later declared killed in action. Leeds, who was wounded, returned to Guadalcanal after being missing for 20 days.[86]

While the pilots were wrestling with the Japanese in the air over the past several days, the Japanese were on the move on the ground. Marines and soldiers pursued the retreating Japanese as they slowly made their way towards Cape Esperance to be evacuated. On 25 January, the Japanese geared up for a massive air raid on Henderson Field.

With the Japanese reporting weather to be good all the way to Guadalcanal, 18 Bettys took off from Rabaul to meet up with over 50 Zeros. A coast watcher quickly relayed the Japanese activity to Cactus. As the Japanese formation made its way towards Guadalcanal, they met up with the Japanese fighters in the vicinity of Kahili. Once again, a coast watcher reported the incoming force to Cactus.

The weather deteriorated as the formation followed the Slot towards Guadalcanal. Nearly 20 fighters became lost in the bad weather, and after three hours of fruitless flying, made their way back to Rabaul. The remaining Japanese were quickly picked up on Cactus radar.

Herb Peters, 1Lt. Henry Sabatier, Major Ray Vroome and one other VMO-251 pilot, already in the air on patrol, received orders to intercept the incoming Japanese planes. Shortly after 1 p.m. the Japanese spotted the incoming Wildcats. The Bettys quickly reversed course to head home, leaving the fighters to engage the Wildcats. Attacking from above and aided by overcast skies, the Wildcats pounced on the Japanese. Peters was credited with shooting down two Zeros. Sabatier and Vroome were credited with one Zero apiece.[87]

Squadron pilots would be busy on 27 January. The Japanese struck in full force,

2Lt. Herbert A. Peters. Peters led all 251 pilots with four shot down Japanese planes credited (courtesy Robert T. Whitten).

sending numerous fighters and bombers to Guadalcanal throughout the day. Henderson Field was the target of the first attack during the early morning hours of the day when 14 Bettys dropped over 10 tons of bombs and repeatedly strafed the field. Anti-aircraft gunners put up intense fire, claiming one bomber shot down.

VMO-251 pilots were up in the air at least twice. First was a mid-morning mission. Led by VMF-112's Lt. Joe Lynch, Capt. Jim Anderson and two other 251 pilots took to the air around 1020 and later intercepted Japanese aircraft near Cape Esperance. Anderson and his wingman soon found themselves pouncing on the Japanese from above. Unfortunately, they failed to splash any Japanese. Next up in the late afternoon was an escort mission. Nine Wildcats protected Cactus TBF Avengers and SDB dive bombers as they attacked Japanese ships near Kolobangara. One ship was hit but did not sink. As Japanese planes attacked the Cactus bombers, VMO-251's Sabatier received credit for downing one of the Japanese fighters.[88]

On 29 January, tragedy struck VMO-251 as several planes made their way back from a mission over Munda. The weather had deteriorated, reducing visibility over Cactus as the returning planes made their approach. According to one witness, 1Lt. Glen Loban and 1Lt. Wayne Christian collided when they entered the landing pattern at the same time. Both men were killed in the collision. Their bodies were not recovered.[89]

Three VMO-251 pilots, along with two pilots from VMF-112 joined up with 12 Army aircraft for a fighter sweep over Vila and Munda on 31 January. They encountered AA fire over Vila, but very little could be observed at the airfield. The planes left Vila behind and set a course for Munda. As they approached Munda they ran up against a lone Japanese fighter but failed to shoot it down.[90]

The first day of February would prove to be 251's best outing against the Japanese since 15 January. It would also be the last time they would meet the Japanese in air to air combat for the rest of the war.

During the early morning hours of 1 February, General Patch put ashore a reinforced 2nd Battalion of the 132nd Infantry near Verahue on Guadalcanal's west coast in order to trap the retreating Japanese as they made their way to Cape Esperance.

As Patch's troops were debarking the ships, Dauntless dive bombers from VMSB-233 and 234 took off from Cactus in the early morning light to hit Munda Airfield. Joining the dive bombers were 12 Wildcats piloted by VMO-251 personnel. The Japanese at Munda put up heavy flak as the dive bombers arrived. Several of the planes took hits while attacking the airfield. One of those SBDs was piloted by Capt. Abram Moss[91] of VMSB-234. Flak exploded near Moss's plane, killing him. Sgt. Gil Henze, the rear gunner, grabbed the auxiliary controls and called for help. He was told to turn back and head for Guadalcanal. VMO-251's Major Ray Vroome and his wingman tagged along to protect Henze.

As he made his way back, the engine of Henze's SBD quit working. Unable to contact Henze, Vroome and his wingman could only watch as the SBD made its inevitable rendezvous with the water below. As Henze bailed out, he injured his leg. The two VMO-251 pilots watched in horror as the injured Henze struggled to open his chute. Finally his chute opened and he floated into the water. Vroome and his wingman flew over the sergeant's position as they made their way back to Cactus. What they saw did not look good. It appeared the sergeant was going under.

Henze was rescued by natives and a few days later a PBY picked up the sergeant. He ended up in a hospital in the rear but died a few months after his rescue.[92]

As the morning progressed, Japanese bombers that survived the early morning raid at Munda took off for a mission to bomb Cactus. With them as escort were half a dozen fighters. Several VMO-251 pilots were

Glen Loban (courtesy Mary Janell Timmons).

on strip alert and they took off in Wildcats to meet the incoming Japanese. Soon McCartney, 1Lt. William Whitaker, Baran, Anderson, Berteling and three other pilots found themselves in deadly air to air combat. During the engagement, McCartney finally downed his first Japanese plane, a Lily. McCartney did not come away from the fight unscathed. His Wildcat was shot full of holes. Also credited with shooting down Japanese planes was Baran with one kill, Whitaker with two kills, and Anderson with one kill. As for the Japanese raid, it appears all they did was crater a runway at Henderson Field.[93]

Later in the afternoon, VMO-251 Wildcats along with a variety of U.S. Army aircraft, provided escort for VMSB-234 and the torpedo bombers of VMSB-131 as they made their way to strike a Japanese Navy group—consisting of destroyers and transports—heading for Guadalcanal. The Wildcats provided low cover for the attack planes, while the Army aircraft provided high cover. Nearly two dozen Japanese planes provided air cover to the group. Unknown to the U.S. strike force, it was the first of three missions of the Tokyo Express to evacuate the remnants of the Japanese Army on Guadalcanal.

The Japanese and U.S. forces met just north of Vangunu just before 1830. During the ensuing engagement, the Cactus attack planes appeared to have only hit one ship, while losing several planes from VMSB-131. The Tokyo Express continued to Guadalcanal to successfully evacuate the first contingent of 17th Army off the island.[94]

The Tokyo Express made two more runs to Guadalcanal during the night of February 3/4, and February 7/8. Both runs were successful, and the survivors of the Japanese 17th Army lived to fight another day for the emperor. After seven hard months of fighting, Guadalcanal belonged to the Americans.

There is no record after 1 February of VMO-251 pilots flying combat missions or patrols. By 7 February, over two dozen officers were transferred to VMF-122 or evacuated to Espiritu Santo. Most of the men who left were pilots. By mid–March, only a cadre of officers remained with the squadron. The squadron's commanding officer, Major Joe Renner, was one the officers transferred from the squadron. Windy Welch took over the squadron as it prepared for its eventual return to the states. Yunck—after seeing service with VMF-121—took over just before the squadron departed Guadalcanal in May 1943.

However, the work did not stop for the maintenance men of VMO-251. Strikes continued in the Solomon chain, and at times the work became deadly. On 9 February, VMO-251 lost Pfc. Ralph Abel Lucero. Abrams relates:

Henry "Hank" McCartney joined VMO-251 in December 1942. He scored his first kill while with VMO-251. He became an ace later in the war (courtesy Jack Cook).

We had a kid by the name of Lucero. He was on the fire truck on the airport.... Lucero was talking and he was from Pueblo, Colorado, and we were talkin' about when we got home, and he said that night, he said I'm not goin' home. And oh yeah, you are. And no, no, said I'm not. He said any of you get to be to Pueblo after the war, he said stop and tell my mother. So we all promised we would…. Sure enough, next morning, two planes collided right together. One was taking off one way and the other run head on and one of them hit the fire truck and killed him."[95]

On 12 February, VMO-251 caught a glimpse of their future when Corsairs of VMF-124 landed at Cactus. The squadron would soon be training to maintain and fly the Chance-Vought F4U-1 Corsair once it returned to the states.

VMO-251 suffered yet another casualty when on 23 February Private Clifford Edward Brooks was struck in back by a piece of log shattered by a bomb blast. Whether this was a result of an attack or an accident is not clear. Brooks survived his ordeal.[96]

By early May, the squadron was making preparations for its return back to the United States. Tragically, two days before the squadron's departure, TSGT Robert Lowell Andrews, Jr., was killed in a freak accident. While standing in a puddle of water, he accidently grabbed a live 110 volt line. Andrews ran a short distance and then fell unconscious. His fellow Marines struggled for 90 minutes to revive him but were unable to do so.[97]

John Irwin pays his respects to Robert Andrews, a VMO-251 mechanic who died in an accident at Guadalcanal in May 1943 (courtesy John W. Irwin).

With the death of Andrews fresh on their minds, squadron personnel (9 officers and 205 enlisted men) embarked on the USS *George Clymer* on 12 May and made way for Espiritu Santo. The ship arrived on the 14th, and on the 17th squadron personnel boarded the USS *Kitty Hawk* (AKV-1) for their voyage back to the United States. The squadron's first tour of duty in the Pacific was over.

Four

Home and Transition

The USS *Kitty Hawk's* bow slowly cut through the calm waters of the south Pacific as it made its way to San Diego, California. After nearly a year of service in the south Pacific battling oppressive heat, rain and disease, the Japanese, and coping with the loss of comrades, the officers and men of VMO-251 were ready to set foot in the United States. There they would reunite with loved ones, visit family, and for some, they would get married.

Since the *Kitty Hawk* was not carrying any supplies, there was plenty of space available to quarter the men of the squadron. Enlisted personnel were assigned to a large, open space on the second deck. Each man was given a cot provided by the ship. Ventilation was provided by opening one of the main hatches leading to the main deck. To make it easier for the men to access the main deck from their quarters, makeshift ladders were installed. Officers were housed on the main deck forward and were protected from the weather. To accommodate the Marine passengers, extra toilet facilities were set up on the main deck—one forward and one aft.

The Marines of 251 were not assigned any ship duties and they had very few watches. Boredom could have set in, but the *Kitty Hawk*, with ample deck space due to lack of cargo, set up volleyball courts, badminton courts and shuffleboard courts. The Marines took full advantage of the sports, especially volleyball. They formed 12 teams and over the course of several elimination rounds, the winning team was proclaimed. The winning Marine team took on the winning team of the *Kitty Hawk* in a championship game and defeated them.

Another item the Marines enjoyed on the Kitty Hawk was the chow—especially milk and ice cream. Both items were unavailable to the Marines while they served in the New Hebrides and the Solomon Islands. The demand was so great and the lines so long, it interfered with the cleaning of the mess hall and crew's compartment. Ice cream sales were curtailed, limited to a few hours each day. Despite this, many a Marine skipped his meal to wait for ice cream.

"We have managed to shorten the lines by reducing the sales of ice cream by the scoop and putting it in quart cartons and #10 tins. (A #10 tin holds a little more than three quarts)," wrote the commanding officer of the *Kitty Hawk*, Captain E.E. Duvall, in the ship's war diary. "For one man to eat a quart of ice cream is common; for two men to polish off a #10 tin … is not unusual."[1] According to Duvall, six Marines appeared to have an insatiable appetite for ice cream. The men reserved a five gallon container each day over a four day period during the cruise to the United States.

At 1600 hours on 31 May, the ship received orders to cancel its port of call to San

Diego, and make way for San Francisco. If there was any disappointment it quickly disappeared when shortly after 0900 hours on 2 June, the Golden Gate Bridge was sighted. By noon, the ship was docked at pier 25.² The Marines gathered their gear, and proceeded to Kearny Mesa, near San Diego. Once the men arrived, they were granted 30 days leave.³

As the men returned from leave in early July, the reorganization of the squadron began. Most of the Guadalcanal veterans were transferred out of the squadron to provide needed experience to new squadrons then forming. Retained were four officers and about 30 enlisted men with Major Carl Longley temporarily in command. These Marines would provide the combat experience to the new officers and men that soon flooded the squadron at its new duty station, Marine Base Defense Air Group 44 at MCAS Mojave, located just outside of Mojave, California.

The airfield, established in 1935 by local authorities, was deemed necessary for national defense in 1941. Later in in the year, a modernization program began with the construction of two 4,500 foot long runways, each 150 feet wide. The Marines moved to the airfield in early 1942, adding buildings, a third runway and extending the existing runways. On 1 January 1943 the station was activated, as well as units MBDAG-44, VMF-225, and VMSB-236.⁴

The Marines of VMO-251 knew they would be going back for another tour of combat. It was a matter of when, not if. Training for the pilots would be intensive, and they would be pushed to the limits of their endurance. Accidents piled up at an alarming rate. From September 1943 to January 1944, the squadron lost 11 planes, 27 were damaged and four pilots were killed. In peacetime, heads would have rolled for such a dismal training record. In wartime, it appears to have been a price that had to be paid to defeat the Japanese.

Little has been written on Marine Corps aviation training during World War II. Without a thorough examination it is difficult to determine if the squadron accident rate was an aberration, or the norm. However, two factors may have played a role.

First, Marine Corps aviation saw its greatest expansion during the war years. In the last year of peace (31 December 1940 through 31 December 1941), the number of squadrons grew from 11 to 13. At its peak strength on 30 September 1944, Marine aviation fielded 145 squadrons. Concurrent with the increase in squadrons was an increase in personnel. The Marines had 385 pilots on 31 December 1940. By 30 June 1944, there were 10,416 pilots. Enlisted personnel also grew from 2,630 on 31 December 1940 to a 125,162 by 31 January 1944.⁵ To keep these squadrons operating, and to meet the demands of operations in the Pacific, men were needed and there was never enough. Pilots and enlisted men were rushed through schools; pilots arrived at operational squadrons to complete their training. The Marines had to compete with the manpower requirements of the Army, Navy, Air Corps and the Coast Guard, as well as the industrial needs of the United States.

Second, Marine pilots were classified as Naval Aviators, and as such underwent their training under the control of the Navy. As the war progressed and casualties mounted, the number of student pilots needed every month increased. Flights hours were gradually shortened in order to get pilots to squadrons quickly: new pilots entering their assigned squadron in many cases had little or no time in the type of plane they were assigned to fly. In VMO-251's case during its training: Wildcats and Corsairs. Demand, and a shortage of personnel, may have led to the priority of getting needed men to squadrons quickly at the expense of experience.

The squadron was slated to receive the new Vought F4U Corsair. It is interesting to note that while the squadron would be getting the fighter plane, incapable of photo reconnaissance work, the squadron kept its VMO designation. The training regimen the pilots were about to endure would stress fighter and bombing tactics. The squadron, once it returned to combat, would find itself performing bombing missions on an almost daily basis.

Men were sent on temporary duty to several schools to begin their instruction on the new fighter: F4U School at Bridgeport, Connecticut; Army and Navy Training School at Pratt and Whitney Aircraft, Hartford, Connecticut; Oxygen Equipment School, NAS San Diego; Goodyear Aircraft Corporation, Akron, Ohio; and the Propeller School at Hamilton Standard Propeller Division, East Hartford, Connecticut to name a few. Schooling continued through the months of August, September and October.[6] When not in classes, line maintenance had to be performed as well as pulling duty on firefighting details.

In 1938, the Navy's Bureau of Aeronautics sent out a request for a high speed, single seat fighter armed with at least four machine guns. It also had to have a range of at least 1,000 miles. Vought designer Rex Biesel answered the call with two variations of its Corsair design—each powered by a different engine. The Navy chose the design powered by the supercharged 1800hp Pratt & Whitney XR-2800. A prototype was ordered, designated the XF4U-1.

To accommodate the extremely powerful engine, a large diameter propeller was needed. Hamilton Standard supplied the prop—each blade was slightly over 13 feet in length. To accommodate the large propeller, the undercarriage had to provide enough ground clearance. Biesel used inverted gull wings and put the landing gear at the lowest point of the wing. When the gear was raised, the main strut rotated 90 degrees and brought the gear up into the wheel well parallel with the fuselage rather than in line with the wing. While this solved the prop problem, the increased height would create problems during carrier trials. The prototype also featured leading edge wing fuel tanks as well as machine guns situated in the nose.

It took two years to build the prototype with testing beginning in May 1940. It was evident to the navy during the period of testing that the Corsair—surpassing speeds of 400 mph—far outclassed its two competitors: the Bell XFL-1 Airabonita and the Grumman XF5F-1 Skyrocket. The navy decided to go ahead with production but requested changes to the Corsair: the fuel tanks in the wings were eliminated and replaced by a fuel tank installed in front of the cockpit, necessitating an increase in fuselage length, fuel tanks were also made self-sealing, the nose guns were removed and fire power was upgraded to six machine guns with three in each wing, and armor protection for the pilot was to be installed.

Planes of the first production run—designated F4U-1—began being delivered in June 1942. The increased weight of the modifications made for production was adequately handled by the latest version of the R-2800 engine, now cranking out 2,000 hp. Service trials, including carrier trials, began in September 1942.

The carrier trials did not go well. Degraded pilot vision due to the lengthening of the fuselage to accommodate the fuel tank, high speed upon touchdown and problems with the struts led the navy to declare the Corsair unsuitable for carrier operations until the problems were fixed. This decision allowed the Marines to acquire the Corsair ahead of schedule. If the Corsair had qualified, all squadrons designated for carrier duty were to have received them first, before land operating units. The navy may have been disappointed, but the Marines were overjoyed to have a new plane.[7]

VMO-251 maintenance men work on a Corsair. Piva, Bougainville sometime in 1944 (courtesy John W. Irwin).

Despite this, VMO-251 had to wait until October 1943 before they acquired their first Corsairs. Until then, pilots had to train on F4F-3 and -4 Wildcats, as well as the General Motors built FM-1 Wildcat.

September saw a large number of pilots joining the squadron from VMF-218 and VMF-225. Pilot training also kicked off at a quick pace, and did not let up until the squadron was on its way to the south Pacific for another tour of combat. Each day through January was spent in the classroom and in the air. Ground classes varied—navigation training, recognition classes, gunnery training on a skeet range, Link training, film instruction classes. When pilots were not in class, they were in the air—familiarization flying, formation flying and practice landings were stressed during the month. The month also saw the first of over two dozen accidents the squadron suffered during the period of its refit and training.

The accidents began in the middle of September. On 16 September, 2Lt. Laurence L. Neal ground looped his FM-1 while landing. Shifting winds were to blame. Neal was unhurt but the Wildcat's right wing tip was damaged. Second Lieutenant Robert R. Rosellen ground looped his Wildcat the following day. The aircraft's engine and tail assembly were damaged so severely that each had to be replaced. Luckily, Rosellen walked

Ground officers and pilots of VMO-251 at MCAS Mojave, 25 October, 1943. Irwin made several notations on this photo. Four pilots were killed during training (courtesy John W. Irwin).

away from the crash unscathed. Three days after Rosellen's wreck, 2Lt. John J. McMasters was uninjured when he crashed his Wildcat upon landing, damaging the left wing tip. Eight days after he ground looped his Wildcat, Neal ground looped his second plane, damaging the left wing tip. Neal was unhurt, but his pride may have suffered a blow. To round out the month of accidents, 2Lt. Galen K. Merkel had to make a forced landing 25 miles northeast of MCAS Mojave when an oil line connection burst. Merkel survived the forced landing but his Wildcat (BuNo 12133) was damaged beyond repair.[8]

Despite the number of accidents, the fast pace of the training continued unabated into October. Section tactics was the order of the day for 2 October and 2Lt. Orville F. Lorch was lucky to make it back alive. His engine failed and he had no choice but to make a forced landing. This he did, bringing his Wildcat (BuNo 15373) down in Koehn Dry Lake located in the Fremont Valley 12 miles northeast of California City. Lorch was slightly injured, receiving lacerations on his right cheek. However, his plane was destroyed. It was stricken from the squadron records and the wreck was transferred to Naval Supply at NAS San Diego. Three days later, 2Lt. Richard W. Hildebrand damaged a wing tip when his plane ground-looped. After a successful day of navigation hops and practicing section tactics, on 7 October 2Lt. Russell H. Neilson ground looped his Wildcat after going into a slight skid upon landing. The propeller was damaged but Neilson was unhurt.

The pilots continued to be pushed hard. Coupled with the accelerated pace of operations, it was only a matter of time before someone would be killed. Unfortunately, it happened on 9 October. 2Lt. John Fredrick Osterlund spent his aerial instruction for the day practicing section tactics. All seemed to go well, and when finished he set a course for home. As Osterlund made his final approach he apparently lost control of his aircraft, causing the Wildcat to spin straight into the ground. The impact destroyed the Wildcat (BuNo 32470) and killed Osterlund. McMasters escorted Osterlund's remains to Arlington National Cemetery, where Osterlund was interred on 18 October.[9] McMasters returned to the squadron on 26 October.

During section tactics on 20 October, Hildebrand and 2Lt. William J. Pirages collided in mid-air, approximately 50 miles northeast of MCAS Mojave. The pilots parachuted to safety with Pirages receiving slight bruises in the incident. The planes, both FM-1 Wildcats (BuNo 20123 and BuNo 14260), were destroyed.

Two days after the mid-air collision, four planes were damaged after a day of flying simulating radar problems. Winds were unpredictable on 22 October and severe cross winds may have been a factor in three of the four accidents. 1st Lt. Lee E. O'Harra, struggling to keep his plane from drifting after he landed, damaged the propeller and wing tip of his Wildcat. 2Lt. Joseph A. Condon ran off the runway, damaging his plane's propeller. 2Lt. Howard T. Willey, fighting to control his plane in the wind, partially ground looped his Wildcat damaging the left wing tip. The last plane to go down was piloted by Lorch, but this time his fuel gauge was giving him problems. He was forced to make an emergency landing 2.5 mile southeast of the airfield. The rough landing tore his plane to pieces. Lorch made it through the ordeal, suffering cuts above his right eye.

A bit of good news arrived on 23 October in the form of four FG-1's and 12 F4U-1's. The pilots began training in them the next day. Soon after the squadron began receiving its Corsairs, the squadron patch was modified by replacing the gold wings of a naval aviator with those of the bent wings of the Corsair. As for the Wildcats, they were gradually transferred out of the squadron, the last of them leaving in January 1944.

The flying went well in the Corsairs until 28 October when CPT. Thomas W. Furlow made a wheels-up landing after his engine quit. The plane was seriously damaged: the fuselage buckled underneath the cockpit and the center section inter-beam assembly was fractured. Mechanics traced the cause of the engine failure to a carburetor stoppage. Fortunately Furlow was unharmed.

Longley was sent to MCAS Cherry Point on 30 October and was relieved of command of the squadron on 31 October. Captain Robert W. Teller took over the reins of the squadron until a new commander was named. Taking over on 6 November, having arrived the day before, was veteran combat pilot Major William C. Humberd.[10] Humberd flew with VMF-221 during the battle of Midway, flying the Brewster Buffalo. For his actions there, he earned the Navy Cross. Humberd would go on to command the squadron for over a year, providing solid leadership during the squadron's second tour of combat.

In November, overland navigation, night flying, combat tactics and bomb runs were added to the already crowded training syllabus. As with the last three months, accidents occurred at an alarming rate. The month would turn out to be the deadliest of the squadron's training period.

During the late afternoon of 1 November, Captain Oscar M. Bate, Jr., an experienced fighter pilot with over 200 hours in the Wildcat, led O'Harra, 2Lt. Nick A. Sigan, and 2Lt. Mortimer D. Hathaway in a series of combat exercises about eight miles east of the airfield. Taking each pilot one at a time, Bate taught Sigan and Hathaway the fine art of the scissor maneuver. He took on each pilot twice before releasing them. O'Harra then joined Bate for his turn. Sigan and Hathaway circled to the west about a mile away at around 10,000 feet to observe the maneuvering. Bate and O'Harra went through the maneuver twice, and all seemed to be going well for both pilots.

"When we were about five hundred yards apart I pulled up to show him (O'Harra) that even though he had the altitude advantage I could bring to bear my guns in a head on run as well as he could his," wrote Bate in an accident report describing the accident. "At about two hundred and fifty yards I nosed over intending to pass under him. He nosed over too, to keep his sights trained on my plane. I nosed down some more, still not thinking there was any danger. It was then that he nosed over again, and the only interpretation I can put on this last move of his was that he thought he could pass under me. I was already committed to a downward path at an angle, perhaps about 20 degrees, with him about at about the same angle and twenty-five feet higher than me. Although things happened very fast, I think he finally tried to pull above me. His plane hit the top of mine."[11]

It took a moment for Sigan to realize what had happened. "I noticed one plane go into a spin; I noticed a wing practically off the spinning plane before it occurred to me that there had been an accident."[12]

The spinning plane was O'Harra's. His Wildcat struck Bate's plane—the propeller chewed up his right wing, bent his prop, glanced off his canopy, ripped off control surfaces, the rudder and an elevator. As Bate struggled with his damaged plane, O'Harra's Wildcat (BuNo 15508) spun violently towards the earth.

Hathaway immediately returned to base. Sigan followed both planes down for a short time and reported the accident to Mohave Tower.

Bate's plane entered a lazy spin to the left. Bate tried to recover the Wildcat but his controls did not respond. It was time to bail out. "I opened my hood, cut the main ignition switch and unbuckled my safety belt, crawled out on the right wing, then dropped off." Bate pulled his ripcord at around 1,500 feet.

As he slowly dropped to the earth, Bate saw O'Harra's plane burning in a tract of land about half a mile away. O'Harra was killed when his plane slammed into the deck. Bate landed within 70 feet of where his plane hit the ground, now a crumpled mass of metal. His Wildcat (BuNo 15460) was destroyed. Bate was lucky to receive just minor cuts and bruises.

It was a hell of way to start the month.

The loss of the two planes and one pilot did not put a halt to training. Gunnery practice, bombing practice and night flying instruction took up the next week. The laundry list of accidents grew on 7 November. 2Lt. Francis C. Jennings, after an early morning flight in a Corsair, brought his plane home. As he entered the landing pattern, he lowered his wheels. His landing gear indicator showed wheels down. Coming in at 160 knots to touchdown on Runway 7, the runway duty officer gave the ok sign all the way down through the final approach. Jennings came in at a full stall for a three point landing. 2Lt. J. H. Olmsted, who witnessed the landing and may have been the runway duty officer, saw nothing wrong with the landing.

After Jennings' plane rolled 400 to 500 feet down the runway, the left landing gear inexplicably collapsed, causing the left wing to go down. The plane drastically swerved to the left. Soon after the left landing gear collapsed, the right landing gear collapsed, putting the plane on its belly. After several seconds, the plane came to a halt. Jennings was able to walk away from the crash but his plane would be out indefinitely with the landing gear destroyed, a bent prop and a damaged left wing.[13]

An hour later, Captain Roger A. Haberman, a veteran combat pilot with over 500 hours, took off from Runway 12 in an FM-1 Wildcat at around 10:30 in the morning. Shortly after the wheels left the ground, the prop on the Wildcat failed. Haberman tried to get his plane back on the field but ran off the east edge of the runway. The plane's fuselage buckled under the cockpit, severely damaging the plane. Fortunately for Haberman, he suffered no injuries.[14]

The day following the mishaps involving Jennings and Haberman, 2Lt. John R. Kane was bringing in his Corsair for a landing after a familiarization flight. Shortly after he touched down, his Corsair suddenly swerved to the left. He immediately applied the right brake, hoping to straighten the plane on the runway. It worked, and Kane immediately applied both brakes to slow the plane down. Unfortunately for Kane, the plane flipped over on its back. The plane suffered severe damage and would require a major overhaul to bring back into service. Kane was slightly injured with lacerations on his forehead.[15]

Two days later on 10 November, Lorch brought his Wildcat in for a landing following a hop stressing overland navigation. As he touched down, the right wheel blew out putting the plane into a ground loop to the left. Lorch received no injuries but the right wing of the Wildcat was damaged.[16]

For the next two days, pilots continued to become acquainted with the Corsair with familiarization hops, as well as honing their skills in navigation. On 13 November, section tactics were practiced with the Corsair while several others flew Wildcats for gunnery practice. First Lieutenant George C. Inglehart was one of the Wildcat pilots. At 1630, he began his takeoff roll on Runway 7. While on the roll his plane went off the runway to the left. The tower kept telling Inglehart to take off. He chose to let it roll rather than trying to take off. After rolling 300 yards, the plane struck a truck located between the runways. By the time his plane struck the truck, it had slowed considerably so Inglehart was able to regain control of it prior to impact. The right wing tip hit the top rear of the truck, spinning his plane around in a half-turn ground loop. The right wing crumpled, the left wing tip was damaged, as was the landing gear. Inglehart apparently lost control of his Wildcat, leading to the mishap.[17] Later in the evening, McMasters was making a night landing in a slight crosswind. When his wheels hit the runway, the plane veered to the right causing a ground loop and dragging the left wing. McMasters, after some effort, straightened the plane out. Unfortunately, it immediately went to the left, this time causing a ground loop to the right. McMasters applied the right brake. It grabbed, and with the momentum of the plane, caused the Wildcat to nose over and flip over onto its back. McMasters was unhurt but the plane was severely damaged.[18]

On 14 November, familiarization flights with the Corsair and glide bombing practice were the lessons for the day. 2Lt. Joseph A. Condon, returning from his lessons for the day at 1300, stalled his plane too high upon landing. His plane bounced high, swerved out of control, and after several attempts at braking the plane ran into a ditch off Runway 4. He was unhurt, but the Corsair was hauled off for major repairs. That night, several pilots were practicing night landings when McMasters damaged his second Wildcat in as many days. He brought his plane in too fast and long. Upon touchdown he applied his brakes to slow down to make the turn at the end of the runway. Still too fast to make the turn, he ground looped to the left, dragging the right wing. McMasters was not injured but the plane required its wing to be repaired.[19]

Night flying exercises were on the agenda for 15 and 16 November. It was on 16 November that the squadron lost three of its pilots—two killed—and three of its aircraft in two separate accidents. Shortly before 1900, Captain Thomas R. Furlow, 2Lt. Sidney R. Goldstein, 2Lt. Howard T. Willey, and one other pilot took off for their exercise. Immediately after takeoff, pilots had to go on instruments since poor visibility eliminated any visual of the horizon. As Goldstein was joining up on the flight leader, he may have suffered a case of vertigo or mistook lights on the ground for his flight leader. His plane ploughed into the ground just under two miles northeast of the air station. Willey, either due to vertigo or simply following Goldstein, followed suit. Both Wildcats (BuNo 15225 and 15434) were destroyed. Willey was killed, while Goldstein survived with two broken legs and bruises. Both pilots had less than 100 hours in a Wildcat, and three hours or less night flying in the fighter.[20]

In a separate accident that occurred within minutes of the Goldstein/Willey incident, 2Lt. Galen K. Merkel was killed. At 1900, 2Lt. David J. Schoetz, 2Lt. Max K. Robinson, Merkel, and one other pilot took off for their run at night flying in Wildcats. One plane turned back due to propeller trouble; Schoetz, Robinson and Merkel continued on. The planes were nearly finished with a turn on instruments, and as Robinson joined the formation he noticed "Merkel flip over on his back and go straight into the ground." Merkel was killed when his plane burst into flames upon impact (BuNo 15442). Schoetz, coming out of the turn, looked back and saw Merkel's plane a "mass of flames." Engrossed in the wreckage and not his instruments, Schoetz went into a vertical position. He quickly recovered his plane. Settling down, he called Mojave Tower informing them of the accident. He circled over the wreck until emergency crews arrived. Like Goldstein and Willey, Merkel had slightly over 76 hours in a Wildcat, and only three hours of night flying experience. Vertigo was listed as the probable cause of the mishap.[21]

Over the course of the next several days, flying was halted as the squadron prepared for a move to Camp Pendleton. By 23 November, all pilots and most of the squadron enlisted personnel were in place to resume operations. A small contingent was left behind at MCAS Mohave to guard squadron gear. As the squadron became accustomed to its new, temporary home, pilots took time to take cross country hops and practice division tactics until the end of the month.

Training in December 1943 and January 1944 became much more serious, as word came down that they would be training for combat duty. Pilots engaged with "enemy" aircraft, provided cover for amphibious forces, flew combat air patrols and escort missions. Missions in coordination with ground forces were intensified as pilots honed their skills in the art of close air support. Strafing, dive bombing and observation missions were conducted while in radio contact with participating Marine ground combat units. Division tactics and night flying missions were also conducted as before.[22]

The accidents continued as pilots worked to master the Corsair: seven mishaps in December 1943 and one in January 1944. The first occurred on 6 December when the brakes of 2Lt. Russell H. Neilson's Corsair failed while landing. As he touched down, his Corsair swerved to the right. When he applied the left brake to straighten the plane it locked up. The Corsair nosed over onto its prop, bending the blades. Neilson bruised his nose in the incident and the plane was brought back into service after a week's worth of work by maintenance crews.[23]

Two accidents occurred on 12 December. Second Lieutenant William H. Scoville returned from a successful flight and as he was taxiing his plane to the hardstand, he suddenly had to apply his brakes to keep from running into the aircraft in front of him. The plane nosed over, damaging the prop and a wing tip.[24] The second accident occurred at 1300 when 1Lt. Cecil M. Wilson was taxiing his plane in after a successful hop. As he pulled up near the station tower, the landing gear folded and the Corsair slammed into the ground. The plane required a major overhaul to repair the engine, prop and landing gear.[25]

The next day, Hathaway encountered the same problem with his landing gear. As he was taxiing, the Corsair's landing gear folded. It too required a major overhaul to repair the aircraft.[26] Five days later on 18 December, 1LT. Louis W. Rancourt damaged his Corsair when he ran it off the runaway after landing. The plane nosed over, damaging the prop.[27] The next accident occurred on 21 December. After 2Lt. Robert C. Holiday brought his Corsair in for a landing, it swerved to the right causing the left flap to drag across the runway.[28]

The Desert Room of the Three Oaks Restaurant in Glendale, California, where VMO-251 Guadalcanal veterans held a get together on 10 January, 1944 (courtesy Madden Family).

The last accident for the month of December 1943 occurred on the 23rd. After Kane brought his Corsair in for a landing, his right brake failed and he was unable to control the Corsair. It ran off the end runway and like Rancourt's Corsair, suffered prop damage when it nosed over.[29]

The training continued into January 1944. Despite the rigorous schedule carried over from December, the Guadalcanal veterans of the squadron found time to attend a soiree held in the Desert Room of the Three Oaks Restaurant in Glendale, California on 10 January. Over 60 squadron veterans of the now famous battle attended to recall their wartime experiences and to remember those who did not make it back.

During the course of the month's training the pilots mastered the Corsair, and the number of accidents dropped. Only two were reported, both on the last day of the month. First Lieutenant Francis C. Jennings was taxing his Corsair after returning from night flying exercises when he ran into the tail of the Corsair in front of him, piloted by 2Lt. William A. Erdmann. Jennings' plane suffered minor damage,[30] but Erdmann's plane was out of commission for an extended period of time with a damaged rudder, left elevator, left stabilizer, rear fuselage, left aileron and left wing tip.[31]

Training ceased in February as the squadron prepared to be shipped back to the South Pacific. Planes were turned over, and the squadron was brought up to strength with a flurry of transfers. On 20 February 1944 the Marines of VMO-251 boarded the USS *Tangier* (AV-8) at NAS North Island in San Diego.[32] The next day the USS *Tangier* was on her way—destination Espiritu Santo, New Hebrides.[33]

Squadron Strength, 29 February 1944

Marine

Pilots	40
Ground Officers	8
Enlisted	247

Naval Personnel

Officer (Medical Corps, Flight Surgeon)	1
Enlisted	8

FIVE

Espiritu Santo, Green Island and Bougainville

The USS *Tangier* arrived at Espiritu Santo on 9 March and moored to the pontoon dock in Pallikulo Bay. The Marines of VMO-251 debarked the following day,[1] and proceeded to the Luganville Bomber Field—located off the Segond Channel between the Renee and Serekata Rivers—where they would operate while on the island.

The squadron faced a radically different situation compared to the dire days of 1942. General Douglas MacArthur's forces were marching towards the Philippines through New Guinea and Morotai. Forces under Admiral Chester Nimitz began what would later be called the island hopping strategy with the invasion of Tawara in the Gilbert Islands in November 1943. The next target was the Marshall Islands: Kwajalien in January 1944 and Eniwetok in February 1944. Japanese forces left behind on isolated islands were left to wither, their supply lines cut by advancing Allied forces and their merchant shipping devastated by U.S. Navy submarines. The Japanese, recognizing that their fortunes had changed in the area, evacuated their naval air forces from the strategic base at Rabaul in New Britain to Truk "leaving Rabaul virtually without air protection and depriving the forces throughout eastern New Guinea, New Britain and the Solomons of most of their air support."[2]

Espiritu Santo had become an important island in support of the push towards Japan. It became a staging area for forces entering the theater prior to commitment into combat. Pallikulo Bay and the Segong Channel were good anchorages. Coupled with numerous repair facilities, they provided the U.S. Navy with an excellent rear base. Supply and ammunition depots, fuel dumps, overhaul facilities and other buildings occupied a large swath of the coast along the Segong Channel. Marine aviation made ample use of the island facilities, supporting offensive operations throughout the Solomon Islands and other island chains.[3]

Even though VMO-251 personnel were ready to go, they had no planes to fly. They had to wait nearly a month before Marine Air Group 11 (MAG-11) transferred 20 F4U-1 Corsairs to the squadron. That occurred on 6 April. The next day the squadron began familiarization and training flights. These flights included division tactics, sleeve gunnery and strafing, oxygen hops, instrument flights, radar training and problem solving, and bombing practice. There were at least two mishaps—both occurring on May 3 when 2Lt. Mortimer D. Hathaway and Captain Robert W. Teller (Executive Officer of the squadron) damaged their Corsairs upon landing at Luganville Bomber Field. Both planes suffered a damaged elevator and rudder and were repaired by VMO-251 maintenance crews.[4] The

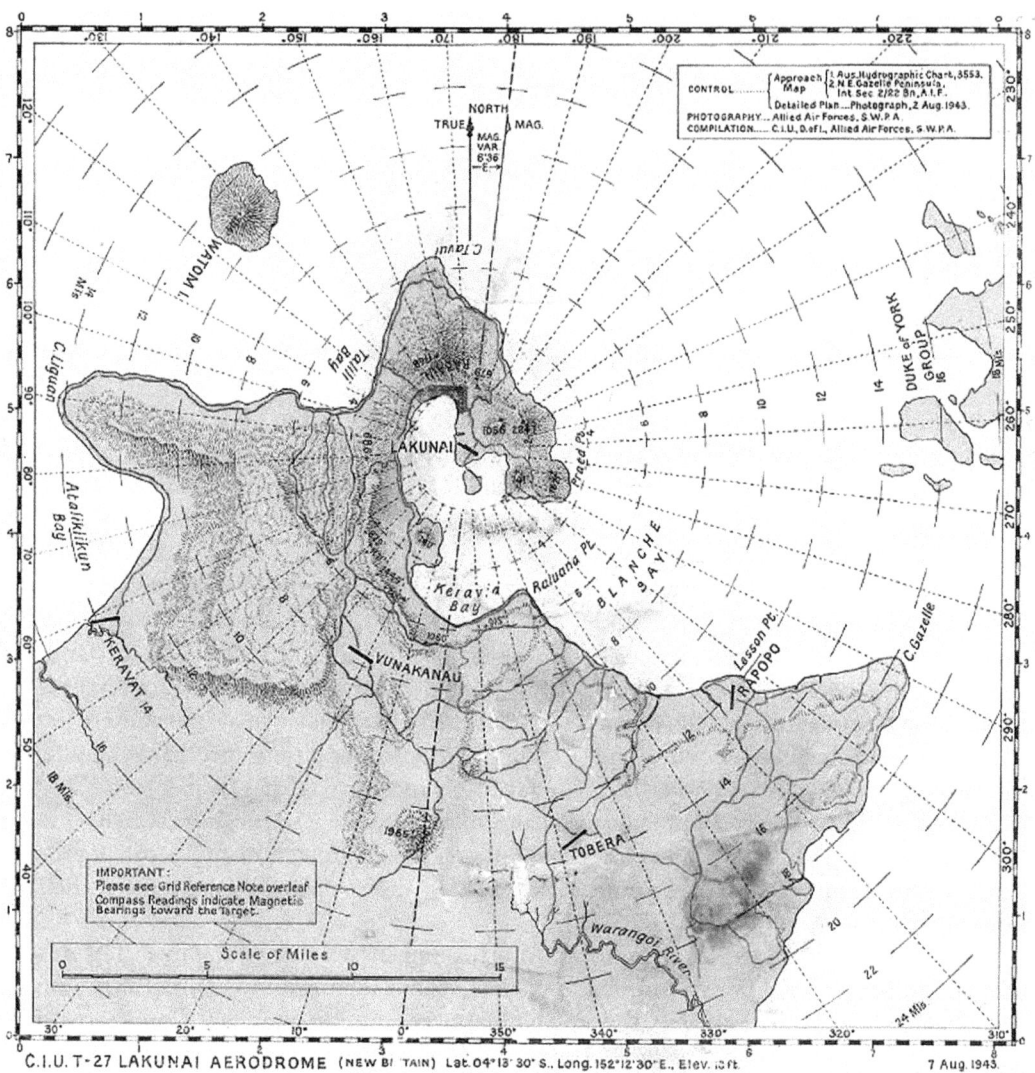

Target map of Rabaul area dated August 1943 (map based on Lakunai target chart [Rabaul] available online at http://ww2db.com, used with permission).

squadron did fly one escort mission, protecting a bomber on a photographic mission on 9 May. The training flights continued for several weeks.

On 6 June, the squadron received orders to transfer four of its Corsairs to the pool of aircraft at Lunga on Guadalcanal. Leading the flight was Teller, with fellow pilots 1Lt. David J. Schoetz, Hathaway, and 2Lt. Michael E. Moynihan accompanying the flight leader.[5] The flight to Guadalcanal was marred by tragedy when at approximately 1345, Hathaway's plane (BuNo 56298) crashed and exploded two to three miles off the southeast tip of the island. Hathaway's body was not recovered.[6] The cause of the crash was never determined. Teller, Schoetz, and Moynihan returned to the squadron via air transport the following day.

Training missions continued until 14 June when the squadron received orders to send all pilots, including the squadron's flight surgeon, intelligence officer and intelligence clerk, to Green Island (also known as Nissan Island)—located between New Ireland and Buka (see map)—where they would be on STAD under MAG-14. Transport aircraft were assigned to take the men to Green Island.

The squadron's ground echelon, as well as its Corsairs, would stay behind. The ground echelon would not rejoin the flight echelon until late July, meeting them at Piva Airfield on Bougainville.

Prior to the squadron's departure on 17 June, an accident injured three officers. A squadron jeep in which CPT. Harold C. Wallace, Lt. John P. Gallagher—the squadron's flight surgeon—and 1Lt. Waldemar D. Maya were riding overturned after striking a soft shoulder on a road leading from the Segond Channel to the Luganville Bomber Field. Wallace, the driver, suffered a broken leg and was hospitalized. Both Gallagher and Maya suffered cuts and bruises but were able to rejoin the squadron. Wallace, due to his injuries, did not travel with the squadron to Green Island.

At around 0600 hours on 17 June, transport aircraft carrying the squadron's flight echelon left Espiritu Santo for Green Island. One aircraft did not make it since it had to be held over at Guadalcanal. Pilots aboard that plane reached Green Island the next day.[7]

The purpose of the squadron's temporary assignment to Green Island was to familiarize the pilots with combat operations—fighter sweeps, escort duty, and combat patrols against isolated Japanese forces with Rabaul as the primary target. These types of missions would occupy the squadron until they left for the Philippines later in the year. Operations commenced on 18 June, the same day the squadron was assigned 13 F4U-1s and three FG-1s courtesy of MAG-14. Pilot assignments for missions were the responsibility of the squadron flight officer. Assignments were posted the night before, followed by a preflight briefing prior to the day's mission and a debriefing after the mission.[8]

While at Green Island, the squadron was divided into two wings, each consisting of five divisions of four aircraft each. Each wing, as well as the divisions, had a designated leader. Combat missions from Green Island and later from Bougainville were flown by these divisions and their designated pilots. As operational losses were incurred, assignments were changed as new pilots joined the squadron but the basic structure remained the same.

Squadron Wings, 18 June 1944

Port Wing
Major Humberd, William C. (Flight Leader)
2Lt. Sigan, Nick A.
1Lt. Inglehart, George G.
2Lt. Sturgis, James B.
CPT. Furlow, Thomas W. (Division Leader)
2Lt. Scoville, William H.
1Lt. Cunningham, Russell F.
2Lt. Webber, William G.
1Lt. Gerety, Edward J. (Division Leader)
2Lt. Rosellen, Robert R.
1Lt. Garrett, James B.
2Lt. Wubben, Hazlett H.
1Lt. Jennings, Francis C. (Division Leader)
2Lt. McMasters, John J.
1Lt. Foley, James A., Jr.

Starboard Wing
CPT. Teller, Robert W. (Flight Leader)
2Lt. Moynihan, Michael E.
2Lt. Sprenger, Robert F.
1Lt. Tanner, Grover K.
CPT. Bate, Oscar W. (Division Leader)
1Lt. Wilson, Cecil M.
1Lt. Schoetz, David J.
2Lt. Hildebrand, Richard W.
1Lt. Henley, Paul B. (Division Leader)
2Lt. Lorch, Orvil P.
1Lt. Maya, Waldemar D.
2Lt. Crutcher, Ernest R.
CPT. Hart, Joseph P. (Division Leader)
2Lt. Holiday, Robert C.
2Lt. Erdmann, William A.

Port Wing
2Lt. Condon, Joseph A.
2Lt. Neal, Lawrence L. (Division Leader)
2Lt. MacLachlan, Archibald W.
1Lt. Robinson, Max K.
1Lt. Glenn, Joseph N.

Starboard Wing
2Lt. Pirages, William J.
1Lt. Smith, Howard F., Jr. (Division Leader)
2Lt. Neilson, Russell H.
1Lt. Kane, John R.
1Lt. Thornton, Powell D.

The Green Island Missions[9]

The Sunday, 18 June mission began as they would until the last mission flown in 1945. Maintenance crews serviced the planes, and loaded ordnance. Pilots received last minute briefings on target assignments, after which they were trucked to the flight line. There, they made their pre-flight walk-around, visually inspecting their planes for any possible issues. Once satisfied, the pilots entered the cockpit and with the help of one of the maintenance men, strapped themselves in. After all men were cleared from the Corsair, the engine was primed and started, belching smoke. Soon the roar of Pratt & Whitney 2,800 horsepower engines was all that could be heard across the small strip. Each plane slowly taxied away, and in assigned order, took off for their mission.

The squadron's first day of their second tour of combat was uneventful. Humberd, along with Bate, Teller and Henley flew a fighter sweep along the coast of New Ireland. No enemy activity was noted and the four pilots returned to Green Island without seeing any Japanese. Hart's division flew the dawn patrol over Green Island while Jennings' division, with Sturgis flying in place of Condon, flew the dusk patrol. In both patrols, no Japanese were sighted. Rounding out the day, Kane and Thornton escorted a transport aircraft (SCAT)[10] to Emirau. The two pilots remained there overnight and returned to Green Island the next day.

The squadron flew its first mission over Rabaul on 19 June. Rabaul, located on the northeast end of the island New Britain, was a major Japanese base in the South Pacific. Simpson Harbor to the south provided a good anchorage for the Japanese fleet. Several airfields were located near Rabaul: Lakunai, Vunakanau, Tobera, Rapopo, and Keravat to name a few, and at least three seaplane bases.[11] With its air support recalled to Truk, and cut off from its supply line by American forces as they advanced toward Japan, Rabaul and its facilities still maintained a strong anti-air (AA) defense—making the area a dangerous target while allied air units attempted to pacify it.

Seven divisions, Humberd's, Teller's, Furlow's (less Cunningham), Jennings,' Bate's, Neal's and Hart's, were assigned to fly combat patrols over Rabaul. Twenty-Seven Corsairs took off during the course of the day. Neal's division was the first to arrive over Rabaul, setting up on their station at 0700. Each division remained over the Japanese stronghold for two hours before returning to Green Island. Apparently none of the squadron Corsairs engaged the enemy.

The only incident occurred in Neal's division as they approached Green Island on their return home. First Lieutenant Joseph N. Glenn ended up in the drink after his Corsair's (BuNo 56137) engine quit at low altitude. A rescue boat was on the scene of the crash within minutes but found no trace of Glenn. Apparently his plane sank quickly, allowing no time for Glenn to scramble out of the cockpit. His body was not recovered.

The squadron did not put up as many planes in the air on 20 June as they did during the previous day's patrols over Rabaul. Cunningham and Webber provided escort for an air transport aircraft (SCAT) making a hop to Emirau, while Hart and Erdmann provided escort for a PBY Catalina rescue plane—commonly referred to as Dumbo—to the same location. Pirages and Lorch also provided escort for a Dumbo on station near Cape Saint George for the day's strikes by other squadrons. The divisions led by Teller and Gerety flew the dawn and dusk patrols. To round out the day's flying, Smith's division flew a combat patrol over Rabaul but found no sign of Japanese activity.

It was also on this date that the 13 Corsairs left behind at Luganville Bomber Field when the flight echelon departed Espiritu Santo were officially transferred over to MAG-11 at Turtle Bay.

It was back to Rabaul on 21 June. Four divisions led by Jennings, Bate, Henley and Smith flew combat patrols over the Japanese held base. Four barges were spotted underway in Simpson Harbor. No action was taken against the barges and the divisions returned to Green Island without trouble. The four pilots who provided escort duty for SCAT and Dumbo on the 20th returned to Green Island.

The squadron returned to Rabaul the next day. Neal's division arrived over the area shortly after 0600 and reported several fires along the coast of Simpson Harbor as well as the small island of Matupi located within the harbor. At around 0620 hours, one of the pilots spotted what appeared to be a medium bomber about 20 miles north of Duke of York Island. The division immediately made a course to intercept the bogey. Excitement was running high. If the plane was indeed a Japanese bomber and they shot it down, it would be the first plane downed by the squadron on its second tour of combat, as well as the first plane downed by the squadron since February 1943. As they closed to within 10 miles, their excitement immediately turned to disappointment when the plane was identified. It was a lone B-25 Mitchell.

Meanwhile, Teller's division spotted what appeared to be Japanese planes on the Keravat airstrip. He ordered Neal's division to go in close and identify the planes. Neal's division flew in at tree-top level, only to find the planes had been abandoned. They were sitting flat on the ground without landing gear, with grass growing all around them.

Furlow's division, patrolling in the vicinity of the Vunakanau—about 10 miles south of Rabaul—spotted several trucks running back and forth across the runway and into revetments. If the Japanese were trying to lure the Corsairs into anti-aircraft range, it didn't work. The Corsairs flew to Tobera Airfield, where they spotted more than a dozen Japanese working on the strip. By the time Furlow's division circled around for a strafing run, the Japanese had disappeared. If Humberd's division was looking for any action during their dusk patrol over Rabaul, they didn't get it. The pilots reported no activity and returned to base empty-handed.

A search for a missing B-25 medium bomber and assisting with a rescue mission occupied squadron pilots on 23 June. At dawn, Neal, MacLachlan and Rosellen searched the St. George Channel as well as New Ireland for the missing plane. They found nothing, returning to base at 0900. Two hours later, Jenning's division took off to search the east coast of New Ireland. They reported a large fire on a hill near Cape Senna and nothing else. They returned to Green Island at 1340.

Taking off at 0845, Robinson and Sigan flew as escort for a Dumbo while the plane looked for a downed New Zealand Corsair pilot in the waters off the coast of New Britain. After hours of searching, the pilot was spotted and rescued. While Robinson and Sigan remained on station while the Dumbo rescued the pilot, they spotted a large fire at Bulbuk on New Ireland. Occupied with their current mission, they could not fly to the fire to investigate further. The two VMO-251 pilots finally returned home at 1340. Humberd's division was called to assist in the rescue, but were ordered to return to base when it was determined they were not needed.

Divisions led by Furlow and Smith flew the dawn and dusk patrols over Green Island, while Bate and Wilson escorted a Dumbo to Emirau for an overnight stay.

Over the last few days, maintenance crews worked around the clock to equip MAG-14 Corsairs with bomb racks. By 24 June, several of VMO-251's Corsairs were outfitted with the bomb racks and would fly their first bombing mission to New Ireland.

The day started early. At 0530, Hart's division flew the dawn patrol. They returned two hours later with nothing to report. Bate escorted a Dumbo from Emirau, landing at 0930 hours. Along the way he spotted a few friendly vessels, but no Japanese. While Bate was escorting the Dumbo, Schoetz and Hildebrand provided escort for a Dumbo for the morning strikes by other squadrons. They returned at 1210. Robinson and MacLachlan escorted a Dumbo to Emirau, while Smith's division continued the search for the missing B-25. The search turned up nothing.

Henley's division had the honor of flying the squadron's first bombing mission. Two barges were spotted tied up along the shore at Cape Roloss, New Ireland. Armed with 500 pound bombs, the four Corsairs took off to sink the barges. Quickly spotting the barges, they nosed over for their bomb run. Unfortunately, no direct hits were obtained, but one bomb was reported to hit right between the two barges, and all hit within one hundred feet of the target. Informed of the results, Humberd's team went out for a second try but when they arrived they found the barges burning. Someone else had plastered the barges for them. Undaunted, Humberd took his division up the west coast of New Ireland until they found another target, two small barges 20 to 30 feet long tied up to a pier. They too missed their target; the bombs overshot the barges by 150 to 200 feet.

To round out the day, Foley led his division on dusk patrol over Green Island. After an uneventful two hours, the four Corsairs returned home with nothing to report.

After several raids over Rabaul without once pulling the trigger on the Japanese, the squadron struck the Japanese bastion with a vengeance on 25 June. During the entire day, the squadron attacked the area every two hours, dropping several tons of ordnance during the course of the day.

At 0520, Neal's division took off with each Corsair carrying a 500 pound bomb. With no specific target assigned to them, they ended up attacking the revetment area at Rapopo Airfield. They nosed over and entered their dive for the target, releasing their 500 pounders at 5000 feet. Unfortunately, the pilots did not lead the target enough since the bombs exploded 1500 feet short of the revetment area. Recovering from their bomb run, the four Corsairs turned for home. They landed at 0840. On their tail were Robinson and MacLachlan, returning to Green Island after providing escort for SCAT.

Humberd's division took off at 0720 but the four Corsairs carried no bombs. After reaching the Rabaul area, they noted that Rapopo Airfield was cratered and a fire one mile northeast of Vunakanau was putting up a column of smoke extending 1500 feet. Apparently not spotting any Japanese, they returned to Green Island at 1110 hours.

Furlow's division was up next, taking off at 0945 with three of the planes carrying a 500 pounder. On the way to Rabaul, Scoville's plane developed a hydraulic leak causing the main landing gear to come down. Scoville jettisoned his bomb and returned to base, escorted by Webber. Furlow and Cunningham pushed on. Reaching Rabaul, they dropped their bombs on the town—one was a dud, the other exploded but caused no observable damage. As they passed Rabaul and after they had climbed to an altitude of 5,000 feet, Japanese anti-air guns opened up on the Corsairs from nearby Hospital Ridge. Neither Furlow nor Cunningham received hits. Their patrol over, the pilots spotted two trucks moving southwest of the Vunapope supply area, located approximately 20 miles south and east of Rabaul. They strafed the trucks, forcing them to stop. After the run, they headed home, arriving at 1300.

Next up for their chance at Rabaul was Teller's division, taking off at 1115. Two of the four Corsairs carried 500 pound bombs. Arriving over their target after about an hour's flight, the Corsairs carrying the bombs went into their bombing run. One bomb fell 150 feet short of the revetments at Vunakanau Airfield. The other would not release, and later fell off the plane into a wooded area. After turning around the Corsairs started a strafing run on the town of Rabaul. Japanese AA fire was intense, forcing the Corsairs to break away for home rather than risk flying through the wall of lead.

Bate's division took off at 1315, and were on station over the Rabaul area from 1400 to 1600. Each plane carried a bomb with a 1/10 second delay fuse for a run at buildings southwest of Vunakanau. Two were duds, one was unobserved, and one bomb exploded among the buildings. After dropping their bombs, the planes gained altitude as they made their way back to Green Island, touching down at 1650.

Smith's division was the last to hit Rabaul, taking off at 1515. Thornton developed mechanical problems during his take-off run and had to stay behind. The remaining three planes each carried a 500 pounder. As the Corsairs arrived over the Rabaul area, each plane attacked a different target. One plane dropped a bomb aimed at buildings north northeast of Keravat, falling 100 yards short. Another, aimed at buildings 200 yards southeast of the Vunakanau revetments, scored a near miss. The third Corsair almost

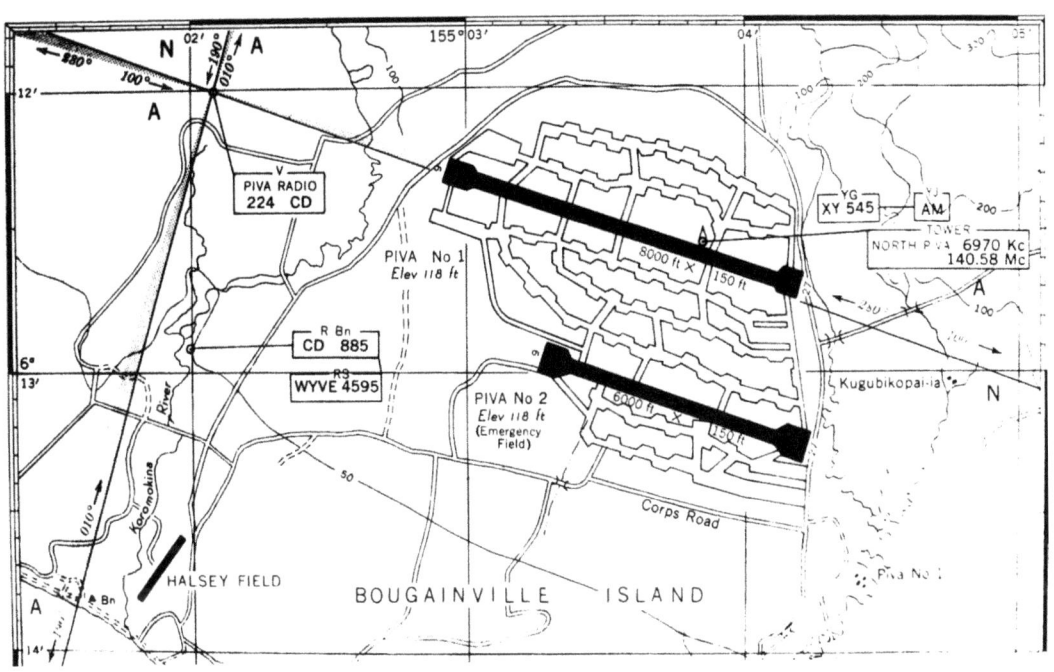

Piva Airfield, Bougainville (National Archives).

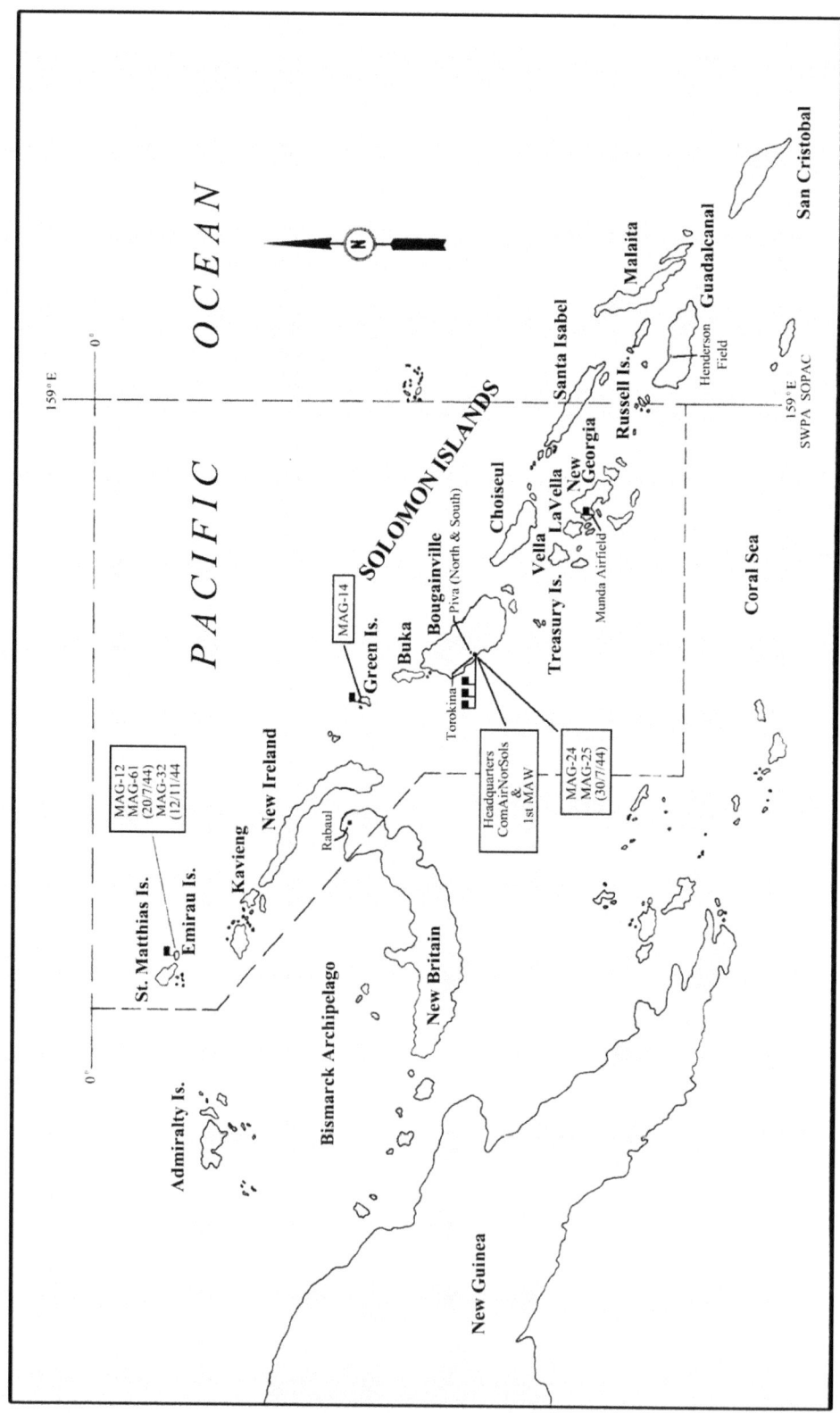

sank an Emily[12] parked in Simpson Harbor. On the way home, the three Corsairs strafed a dock and a group of buildings at the Neinduk Plantation—located to the west of Rabaul—with no observable damage. The three planes made it back to Green Island unharmed.

Bad weather scrubbed the early missions to Rabaul on 26 June. Late in the morning the weather cleared enough to allow Hart, MacLachlan Garrett and Wubben to take-off at 1130 for a strike on Rabaul. Each plane was armed with a 500 pounder. Weather over their target was overcast and at times totally socked in with lousy weather. Their target near Vunakanau consisted of a line of trees to the southwest suspected of hiding Japanese planes. With a break in the clouds the four Corsairs released their ordnance between 4,000 and 6,000 feet. One bomb failed to explode; the other three fell short of the tree line. Their patrol over, the four Corsairs made for Rapopo airfield. They let loose their .50 caliber machine guns at around 2,000 feet. If they hit anything they couldn't see it. After the strafing run they laid in a course for Green Island, landing at 1445.

While Hart led his team back to base, Jennings' division took off shortly after 1400. The four Corsairs each carried a 500 pounder and made their way to the Rapopo and Vanukanau airfields, and the supply dump at Ralum, located near the town of Kokopo about 20 miles southeast of the town of Rabaul. Apparently Hart's team awakened the Japanese defenders at the two airfields as anti-aircraft fire greeted Jennings' team at both locations. The fire was inaccurate and no Corsair was hit. Leaving the two airfields behind, the planes attacked the Ralum supply dump. Three of the four bombs fell squarely on the target but the damage could not be assessed since they retired at over 300 knots. The four Corsairs made it back to base at 1710.

The last raid of the day, as well as the last raid on Rabaul from Green Island, turned out to be less than stellar. Furlow's division, without Cunningham, took off in midafternoon with only one bomb and it failed to explode when dropped. The patrol spotted nothing else; no Japanese activity was seen. The three Corsairs were back at Green Island at 1800.

Compared to the last several days, June 27 was quiet. Furlow's division had dawn patrol duty over the base. Nothing was spotted and they returned to base in a few hours. After they returned, Furlow and Scoville were back in the air to escort a Dumbo over the St. George Channel. Humberd flew alone to Bougainville where he picked up orders for the squadron and returned to Green Island. To round out the day, Robinson led Sigan, Erdmann and Tanner for the dusk patrol over the base. Once again nothing was spotted and the four returned safely to the base.

The squadron had orders to move to the Piva Airstrip, located north of Torokina on Bougainville's south central coast. The flight echelon, except for the divisions led by Humberd, Furlow, Hart, Smith, and Robinson, were transported via SCAT on the 27th. On the following day, the five divisions flew their 20 Corsairs to Piva. A rear party consisting of Gallagher, 2Lt. Henry B. Welch (intelligence officer) and Jones (intelligence clerk) were flown to Bougainville via SCAT, arriving at 1400. The squadron would be flying their missions from Piva's North Field until the end of the year.

Opposite: Area of Operations in Northern Solomons, 1944 (map adapted from Marine Monograph–Marine Aviation in the Philippines, p. 9 http://www.ibiblio.org/hyperwar/USMC/USMC-M-AvPhil/USMC-M-AvPhil-1.html).

The Bougainville Missions[13]

The jungle-covered island of Bougainville—the northernmost and largest island in the Solomon chain—was the target of an Allied invasion on 1 November 1943. Elements of the 3rd Marine Division of the I Marine Amphibious Corps staged an amphibious assault at Cape Torokina on the island's south side, and quickly moved ashore. The Japanese made several attempts to push the Marines off the island but failed. It was not the allied intent to capture the whole island, but to secure the area for the establishment of airfields to support the allied advance. Within a week, the rest of the 3rd Marine Division came ashore, as well as the Army's 37th Infantry Division. Construction of the Torokina airfield began the day of the invasion and went into operation of 10 December. On 15 December I Marine Amphibious Corps was relieved by the Army's XIV Corps and on 28 December, the 3rd Marine Division was relieved by the Americal Division. Work on Piva Airfield was completed on 30 December, and operations from the field began on 9 January 1944. Both Torokina and Piva were approximately 200 miles southeast of Rabaul.

Piva airfield had two runways: an 8,000 foot strip known at various times as Piva No. 1, Piva North, Piva Uncle or Piva Bomber Strip, and to the south a 6,000 ft. long runway running parallel to Piva North known as Piva South, Piva No. 2, Piva Yoke, or Piva Fighter Strip. This runway also served as an emergency airstrip.

Piva Airfield, Bougainville, looking towards the south. Piva North strip in foreground with Piva South in background (National Archives).

By the time VMO-251 began operations, facilities were established but spartan in function. While MAG-24 tried to provide services to keep the Marines entertained, many found there wasn't much to do so each man in the squadron found his own way to fight the boredom. For the pilots, poker was the game of choice during their off time.

Second Lieutenant Hugh "Yogi" Irwin, who would join the squadron in November 1944, wrote that "conditions at Bougainville and Samar might be described as "primitive" so far as running water and toilet facilities but no more so than boy scout camps of my youth, except that at Piva there would be no hiking since the island was primarily populated by disbanded Japanese troops. I had no personal experience with such but was told of occasional harassment enemy fire into our encampment from the surrounding jungle."[14]

Flying the squadron's first mission out of Piva on 29 June were divisions led by Humberd, Furlow, Jennings and Gerety. Their 16 Corsairs were loaded out with 1,000 pound bombs. Taking off at 0850, their orders were to hit two AA gun emplacements protecting the Ralum supply dump. The four divisions approached the target area from the east at an altitude of 10,000 feet. Each peeled over and entered a 50 to 70 degree dive angle, with speeds reaching 380 knots. Bombs were released between 3,000 to 5,000 feet. Of the 16 bombs dropped, 12 hit in the target area, two other bombs dropped were not observed, and two were misses. The Marines encountered accurate AA fire on their departure south of target. Condon, a pilot in Jennings' division, felt his plane jolted by a burst of AA fire but was otherwise unharmed. All 16 Corsairs made it back safely to Piva North, arriving around noon. Impressed with the results of the day's missions, the squadron was commended by higher authorities.

Not a bad start for the squadron flying from their new home.

Unfortunately, the next day's mission wasn't as stellar. Divisions led by Teller, Hart, Bate and Henley took off at 0845 to attack AA emplacements east of the Tobera Airfield. Moynihan, flying in Teller's division was late taking off due to a flat tail wheel. By the time he was able to take-off his fellow pilots were well ahead of him. Unable to catch up with the attack force, he jettisoned his bomb and returned to Piva.

Approximately 30 minutes into the flight, Schoetz began to have engine trouble. His oil pressure was dropping, and oil was leaking from his plane. He turned around for home with his wingman, Hildebrand, at his side. Both planes jettisoned their bombs.

Ten minutes later, his engine quit at an altitude of 6,000 feet. As his plane lost altitude, Schoetz tried to restart his engine without success. There was only one option left—ditch the plane.

The sea was running in swells. With no white-caps, it made the spacing between the swells difficult to judge. Schoetz ditched his plane into the wind, hitting one of the swells. The impact caused him to slam his head into the forward cockpit frame, causing severe cuts and bruises. Unaware of his injuries, he quickly escaped his sinking plane, inflated his life raft and pulled himself into it. His plane (BuNo 56190) slid beneath the waves. He released a dye marker into the water. Staying close to the dye marker would make Schoetz easier to spot from the air. He pulled out his signaling mirror and noticed his bloody face in the reflection on the back of the mirror.

Hildebrand circled the downed pilot. Noticing that Schoetz was drifting away from his dye marker, he flew low over the raft and dropped his own dye marker. Schoetz paddled over to it and fought to stay with the drifting marker. Hildebrand continued to circle Schoetz until Dumbo arrived. The first Dumbo to reach the scene refused to land because of the large swells, but the second one did land and pulled Schoetz out of the water. Schoetz, battered and wet, was taken to Green Island where he was hospitalized. He quickly recovered, returning to Bougainville two days later via SCAT.

While Schoetz tried to save his plane, the remaining 13 Corsairs reached Rabaul but found both primary and secondary targets completely socked in with weather. Bate and Henley's division turned around for home, jettisoning their bombs along the way. Teller and Hart brought their divisions back by way of Buka Airdrome on Buka Island, located just off the coast of northwest Bougainville, where they unloaded seven bombs near the southwest end of the strip. As they continued on to Piva, they noticed a column of smoke rising about 200 feet from where the bombs struck. The seven Corsairs touched down at Piva North 15 minutes before noon.

By now the pilots of VMO-251 knew what they would be facing each day. So it came as no surprise when they learned they would be returning to the Rabaul area on 1 July 1944.

Humberd led a flight of sixteen Corsairs, taking off from Piva at 0825. Each plane carried a 1,000 pound bomb to be delivered on AA emplacements to the east of Tobera Airfield. McMasters soon developed engine problems shortly after departing Piva. He aborted his flight, jettisoned his bomb and turned for home, accompanied by Kane.

The remaining 14 Corsairs continued on. After about an hour's flight they arrived at their target. Apparently no AA fire greeted the Corsairs as they made their run on the target. Thirteen of the Corsairs hit the target. Humberd ended up dropping his bomb on a hut at Kulon Plantation, located on the east coast of New Britain, due east of the airfield. The planes returned home at 1040.

Teller led the afternoon flight of 16 Corsairs, taking off at 1350. Their target was the Ralum supply dump located near Kokopo. Like Humberd's earlier flight, each Corsair carried a 1,000 pounder. First Lieutenant William J. Pirages soon developed engine trouble and had to return to base. Not long after Pirages returned home, Hildebrand's Corsair developed engine trouble. He let loose his bomb, and with Kane at his wing, returned to Piva. The remaining Corsairs pushed on to Ralum, dropping their bombs with unobserved results. They returned home 1545.

The next day Teller was picked to lead a flight of 16 Corsairs back to Rabaul to hit AA emplacements near Tobera Airfield. All but one took off at 0840. Crutcher had a scare when his 1000 pound bomb fell off his plane and rolled onto the taxiway. Fortunately it did not explode and Crutcher was able to slow his plane to a stop.

Shortly after 1000 hours, Teller's remaining 15 Corsairs plastered the target with 7.5 tons of ordnance, scoring nine hits on the AA guns and wiping out what appeared to be an ammo dump. Neilson saw two bomb bursts northeast of the airfield, followed by a series of small explosions which produced many fires and several columns of black smoke. Teller's flight returned home unscathed at 1100.

The afternoon flight to the Ralum supply dump near Kokopo was marred by the loss of a popular pilot. At around 1340 Humberd and 12 other Corsairs, each loaded with a 1,000 pound bomb, lined up to take-off. Twelve Corsairs made it into the air. One did not. First Lieutenant Lawrence L. Neal's Corsair crashed and burned as it took off, destroying the aircraft (BuNo 56112). With fires whipping around in the cockpit, Neal somehow pulled himself out of the flaming wreckage but suffered severe burns. He was immediately transported to the 52nd Army Hospital. Luckily for all in the area, the bomb his plane was carrying did not go off.

Five. Espiritu Santo, Green Island and Bougainville 91

VMO-251 Corsairs at Piva, Bougainville, late 1944 (courtesy John W. Irwin).

Humberd and his remaining Corsairs reached Ralum at 1430. AA fire was light, but for 1Lt. Nick A. Sigan it was accurate. Several rounds pierced his Corsair, destroying his radio in the process. Results of the attack were good, with five tons of bombs dropped right in the target area. Satisfied, Humberd led his flight home.

On 3 July, VMO-251 and VMSB-235 would be hitting the same target—AA emplacements northwest of Tobera Airfield. VMSB-235's Dauntless dive bombers—flying out of Green Island—took off first at 0810, followed by Humberd and his 12 Corsairs fifteen minutes later from Piva.

About 50 minutes after takeoff, the dive bombers arrived over the target and were greeted by intense AA fire. Four of the dive bombers were damaged and one plane, piloted by 2Lt. Edward J. Becker with Sgt. Robert F. Van Derhaeghan as his gunner, took several 20mm hits, forcing the plane down five miles off the east coast into Blanche Bay. Both men were listed as missing in action. Despite the hot reception, the planes dropped their bombs in the target zone.[15]

Humberd's Corsairs arrived as the dive bombers were finishing up their run. The AA fire continued but was not as accurate. None of the Corsairs were hit. Despite the havoc caused by the dive bombers, nine of the 12 pilots hit their assigned targets. The planes of both squadrons were on the ground at their respective airfields by 1045.

There were no afternoon flights for the squadron but the men did receive bad news. At 1400, Neal, who was severely burned in his accident on the previous day, died of his wounds at the 52nd Army Hospital. Neal had joined the squadron when it was rebuilt upon its return from its first combat tour in 1943. The squadron stood down on 4 July so that all pilots could attend Neal's funeral. In a solemn ceremony, Neal was laid to rest at Bougainville Cemetery.

Combat missions resumed on 5 July. VMSB-235 and VMO-251 were ordered to strike the same target they hit on 3 July. Thirty-three SBD dive bombers, armed with one 1,000 bomb and two 100 pound bombs each, took off at 0830, with 16 Corsairs of 251 following 10 minutes later. Each of the Corsairs carried a 1,000 pound bomb. Second Lieutenant Robert C. Holiday had mechanical problems soon after take-off and returned to base. The two squadrons were supposed to rendezvous at Cape St. George but according to VMSB-235's mission report, the 251 Corsairs did not show up. This may have been due to two factors: the weather was overcast, reducing sighting capabilities, and the fact that the dive bombers arrived early at the rendezvous point over Cape St. George. VMSB-235 did not wait long at the rendezvous point, and proceeded to the target area. The dive bombers, at 13,500 feet, approached the AA emplacements near Tobera Airfield from the south ahead of schedule. They pushed over at 9,500 feet, releasing their bombs at 2,200 feet. Several hits were noted, but the ordnance they dropped obscured the target area for the Corsairs.[16]

As the Corsairs approached the target, Neilson's Corsair developed engine trouble. He immediately turned around and made a bee line toward the sea. He had lost 3,000 feet of altitude before he was able to get his engine restarted. With his engine running smoothly, he turned back to strike the target area.

Meanwhile, the remaining 15 Corsairs arrived over the target area at 0950 only to find it covered in smoke. They pushed over, reaching dive angles of nearly 60 degrees and speeds of 350 knots. Strafing targets as they dived, the Corsairs released their 1,000 pounders at approximately 2,000 feet. Several hits were scored despite the smoke covered target area. As the Corsairs turned for home, they strafed buildings and piers along the coast with no observable damage.

The planes of VMSB-235 landed at Green Island 1110, while the VMO-251 Corsairs touched down at Piva at 1135.

The squadron stood down on 6 July and resumed operations the following day. The morning strike on AA emplacements near Rapopo Airfield was supposed to have been led by Humberd but his radio failed prior to take-off. Furlow took over, leading 14 other Corsairs armed with 1,000 pounders to the target. Joining them on the strike would be 35 SBD Dauntless dive bombers of VMSB-341, flying out of Green Island, led by Major W. D. Persons. The dive bombers departed Green Island at 0855. Furlow's Corsairs left Piva at 0900.

Again there was confusion at the target area. The two squadrons arrived over the target area at the same time at approximately 1030. Planes of both squadrons apparently got in the way of each other, affecting the accuracy of their drops and creating some dangerous moments between individual aircraft. Inglehart had to abort his bomb run when one of the SBDs cut in front of him, and went straight for the target Inglehart had lined up in his sights. Despite the confusion several bombs struck the target area, damaging several of the AA guns. No planes were lost by either squadron and all planes were on the ground shortly before noon.

Each squadron pointed fingers at the other for the problems over the target area. Persons blamed 251 for the confusion, saying the Corsairs—who were to strike first—arrived late and at the same time as the SBDs "making the SBD attack and dives difficult." Furlow, while not directly blaming VMSB-341, wrote that the SBDs interfered with the Corsairs during their bomb runs.

Kneeling: Albert Madden, Walter F. Madden, Robert E. Conroy. *Standing:* William C. Ordway, John V. Madden, Joseph N. Meyers, John W. Irwin, and Robert Greenwood at Piva Airfield, Bougainville, 1944 (courtesy John W. Irwin).

It was a new target for Bate and his 15 Corsairs for the afternoon mission. They were ordered to strike buildings in the Liguan Bay area, located a few miles west of Rabaul. Armed with 1,000 pounders the planes took off at 1330. The 16 Corsairs reached the target area a little over an hour later and made life miserable for the Japanese. Erdmann and Kane scored direct hits, blowing up several buildings and creating plenty of fire and smoke. Second Lieutenant Robert C. Holiday's bomb release mechanism failed so he had to carry his bomb home. Once the Corsairs let loose their half-ton payloads, the pilots strafed the remaining buildings and beaches. As they escaped to the east, light inaccurate AA fire from Kabagada Point—located west of Rabaul—attempted to down the Corsairs to no avail. Once over water, the Corsairs turned southeast and made for home, arriving at Piva at 1550.

Sixteen VMO-251 Corsairs, carrying their standard load of one 1,000 bomb on each plane, were assigned to strike targets near Liguan Bay once again on the morning of 8 July. Fifteen of the Corsairs made it to the target area; Webber had to abort and returned to base. Several fires south of Liguan Bay were spotted as the squadron Corsairs arrived over New Ireland. Light AA fire greeted the Corsairs as they approached the area from the west at 12,000 feet shortly before 0900. They descended to 10,000 feet before pushing over, releasing their bombs between 2,000 and 3,000 feet. Cunningham's bomb released late, and Condon's bomb carried its bomb rack. While several damaging hits were scored, most of the bombs fell in the target area with unobserved results or missed all together. As the Corsairs retired to the east, they strafed huts and roads with unknown results. The 15 Corsairs were on the ground at Piva by 1000.

Before the squadron's afternoon mission to the same target, 36 SBDs from VMSB-235 struck the Liguan Bay area leaving behind plenty of smoke and fire after several direct hits were scored on targeted buildings.

Fifteen Corsairs led by Teller arrived to strike their targets from the northwest at approximately 1420. Sixteen had taken off, but 1Lt. Cecil M. Wilson had to turn back. The Japanese greeted the pilots with intense but inaccurate AA fire. Most of the Corsairs plastered the target area; for reasons unknown Maya and Bate had to jettison their bombs before the strike. Lorch was the only pilot to score a direct hit; his 1,000 pound bomb blowing up a building to pieces at Kabagada Point. As they made their way home the Corsairs strafed targets of opportunity. They made it home just before 1600.

Back they went the next day. Teller led 16 Corsairs to bomb and strafe buildings surrounding Liguan Bay. Sprenger developed problems with his Corsair and turned for home. The remaining 15 Corsairs arrived over the target area with clouds all but obscuring the target. Overcast skies hampered visibility and storms were beginning to form over the target area. Luckily the AA fire was ineffective. One damaging hit was scored on a building when a bomb dropped by Lorch sent flames and smoke through the structure. Once all the bombs were dropped the Corsairs strafed the area. Neilson may have struck a truck along the coast road since he saw a large part fly off the vehicle as he hit it. After the strafing runs the Corsairs retired to Piva, touching down at 1230.

An afternoon strike on Rabaul was quickly ordered with all available aircraft to take part in the mission. Only seven planes were made ready, taking off armed with 1,000 pound bombs at 1430 with Humberd as the leader. Rabaul was socked in with bad weather so they set in a course for their secondary target: gun emplacements on Sohana Island, situated between the northwest tip of Bougainville and Buka Island.

The guns were obscured by mostly cloudy skies. Despite this, the Corsairs dropped their payload but scored no hits. The planes circled around and returned to Piva, landing at 1635.

On 10 July, the assigned targets for Humberd's flight of 16 Corsairs were AA gun positions on Raluana Point, marking the eastern entrance to Keravia Bay, where they were to hit barges spotted in the bay. Only 15 of Humberd's Corsairs took off at 0800. Webber developed problems with his plane and did not get off the ground. As with previous missions, each Corsair carried a 1,000 pound bomb. They were over the target area in 60 minutes. The Corsairs spilt up, with some attacking the gun positions and others attacking the barges. The Japanese opened up on the Corsairs with intense AA fire. Gerety's Corsair was hit, losing part of its ring cowl, nearly all of the right aileron, and the plane's radio antenna was destroyed. Fortunately Gerety was not hurt.

Not much damage was done by the 15 1,000 pound bombs and the strafing conducted during and after the bomb drops. Sturgis scored a direct hit on an ammunition dump which caused a huge explosion which could be seen for miles. McMasters silenced an AA gun firing at him from a high cliff along the shore of Keravia Bay, and observed what appeared to be steel doors leading into the base of the cliff.

As for the barges tied up off shore in Keravia Bay, Condon scored a damaging hit when his bomb exploded between two barges that were tied together. The pilots found the barges hard to destroy with the standard .50 caliber ammunition for their machine guns, preferring incendiary ammunition. With most of their ammunition expended the Corsairs turned for home, arriving at Piva at 1030 hours.

Teller's wing had the honor of striking a new target for the afternoon mission. They were ordered to hit AA guns at Vulcan Crater, located on a spit of land along Keravia Bay and northwest of Raluana Point. Carrying the standard ordnance, sixteen Corsairs took off at 1250. Thunderstorms were spotted on the way to the target, but the weather cooperated with the Marines over the target. Visibility was unlimited. Unfortunately it worked both ways. Japanese AA fire was heavy as the Corsairs approached and let loose their bomb loads. Neilson noted the AA fire was "pretty accurate"[17] as his Corsair was tossed around by several near misses. First Lieutenant Powell D. Thornton scored a direct hit on a trench system along the northwest shore of the bay. According to Thornton's division leader, 1Lt. Howard F. Smith, Jr., the hit "caused fire to race down the entire length of the trenches."[18] Hildebrand, while missing the AA guns, appeared to have damaged a couple of barges with his bomb. Teller rounded up his Corsairs, and set a course for Piva. They made it home by 1530.

Teller's wing was back up in the air on 11 July. Sixteen Corsairs took off for Rabaul at 0820. The planes ran into a solid front of nasty weather about 100 miles from Piva. The decision was made to turn back and strike the secondary target—gun positions at Bonis Airfield located on the northwest tip of Bougainville along the Buka Passage. They arrived over the target area at 0920. Hart got the only direct hit, scoring a strike on a fuel or ammunition dump. The planes were back at Piva 20 minutes after arriving over the target.

Humberd was the wing leader for the first mission on 12 July. Sixteen Corsairs took off at 0800 to bomb and strafe AA guns about 2,000 yards due north of Tobera Airfield. Soon after takeoff Condon had to turn around since his landing gear would not retract. Weather as they approached the target from the southeast was good, with broken clouds between 2,000 and 8,000 feet. After over an hour in the air, they arrived over the target area. No clouds obscured their vision. As they began their bomb runs, the Japanese opened up with AA fire. Webber received a hit in his left wing, but was otherwise ok. The Corsairs entered their bomb runs at 10,000 feet, releasing their 1,000 pound payloads at 3,500 feet. Gerety scored the only direct hit, knocking out three AA guns. The other 14 bombs scored two damaging hits, five hit in the target area, and the others were either misses or duds. Once the bombs were dropped, the Corsairs began strafing runs. Rossellen and MacLachlan paired up to silence one machine gun on the west end of the airfield.

On the way home, they strafed roads and huts and smoked a barge along the shores of Kabanga Bay. Another mission was in the books as the Corsairs touched down at Piva shortly before 1100.

The afternoon mission singled out one structure as the main target. It was a concrete block house located northeast of Rapopo Airfield. This building was apparently spotted by Jennings during a previous mission so he was tapped to lead the mission.[19] Four Corsairs, armed with 1,000 pounders fused for an eight second delay, were wheels up at 1230. They arrived over the target after a 50 minute flight. The four pilots spent nearly an hour looking for the building to no avail. As they searched, the pilots saw several cultivated gardens underneath cocoanut trees on Ulaveo Plantation east of Rapopo Airfield. Most likely it was a sign the Japanese were trying to supplement their dwindling food supply. Most importantly they saw that heavy gun emplacements running from Rapopo to Tobera to Cape Gazelle were empty. It may explain why they encountered no AA fire while searching for the concrete block house. Frustrated, they dropped their bombs from 50 feet onto a group of thatched huts, as well as what appeared to be a concrete underground shelter whose roof was flush with the ground. No hits were scored. The four Corsairs turned for home and arrived at Piva shortly after 1500.

There was no flying on 13 July. Missions resumed on 14 July when Bate led 16 Corsairs armed with 1,000 pound bombs to strike gun positions north of Tobera Airfield. When they arrived over the target area at 0925, they found their primary target obscured by cloud cover. Bate made the decision to strike secondary targets, attacking buildings in several areas including Vunapope (a small beach town along Blanche Bay), Timbur (a village located near Kokopo), Tulaen Plantation, and Bitagalip (located south of Kokopo). Neilson was the only one to score a hit when his bomb obliterated a building west of Vunapope. Most of the pilots strafed targets as they finished their bomb runs but no results were observed. All planes made back safely, landing at Piva at 1035.

Meanwhile back at Espiritu Santo, the ground echelon—having waited nearly a month for transportation to join its flight echelon—boarded the USS *Alnitah* (AK-127), moored at Berth 37 in lower Pallikulo Pay. By 1500 hours, all men were aboard. Three hours later the *Alnitah* was underway, setting a course for Bougainville.[20]

Seventeen Corsairs were put into the air for the 15 July mission—sixteen from the squadron and an extra Corsair piloted by Colonel Jim Neefus, assistant operations officer with the staff of the Commander Air Solomon Islands (ComAirSol). Neefus was flying as an observer for the mission and was assigned to fly in Humberd's division. Each plane, as in previous missions, carried a 1,000 pound bomb. Taking off from Piva at 0900, their mission was to strike two supply dumps near Vunapope, located just to the east of Kokopo.

Divisions for Vunapope Mission, 15 July 1944

Division 1	Division 3
Humberd	Furlow
Sigan	Scoville
Inglehart	Cunningham
Sturgis	Garrett
Neefus	

Division 2	Division 4
Gerety	Robinson
MacLachlan	Wubben

Division 2	Division 4
Rosellen	Kane
Webber	Thornton

As the planes made their way to the target, Robinson was forced to turn back due to engine trouble. Accompanying him on his return to Piva was his wingman Wubben. The remaining 15 Corsairs were greeted with clear weather as they approached the target area at around 1000. Anti-aircraft fire was light and inaccurate. One at a time the Corsairs went into their dives, releasing their payloads between 1,600 and 2,500 feet, and pulling out of their dives anywhere from 900 to 1,500 feet. Three direct hits were scored. Gerety wiped out a fuel storage dump, sending a huge column of orange-colored fire and smoke bellowing into the air. Humberd and Sigan each wiped out a building, sending columns of smoke 600 feet into the air.

On the way back to Piva, MacLachlan reported observing four guns situated on the Credner Islands, a small group located between New Britain and Duke of York Islands. He lowered his plane and lined up for a strafing run. Letting loose with his .50 caliber machine guns, he ended up destroying three of the four gun emplacements.

The rest of the return trip was uneventful. The Corsairs were back at Piva by 1100. After the pilots were debriefed, some went for chow while others returned to their living quarters only to find some of their fellow pilots missing. A lucky few had packed a few belongings for a well-earned trip. Bate, Hildebrand, Schoetz, McMasters, Condon, Foley— who joined the squadron shortly after it had arrived on Espiritu Santo—Wilson, and Jennings quickly boarded a SCAT plane for Sydney, Australia on a week's leave for rest and recreation.

VMO-251 was back in action the next day. Teller led 16 Corsairs to strike gun emplacements near Vulcan Crater. The planes took off shortly after 0800. Hart developed engine trouble, and accompanied by his wingman, Erdmann, returned to Piva.

The remaining 14 Corsairs approached the Vulcan Crater area at an altitude of about 14,000 feet and immediately received intense but inaccurate AA fire. The Corsairs descended about 2,000 feet, lowered their main landing gear to use them as dive brakes,[21] and pushed over into 70 degree dives to release their 1,000 pounders. No direct hits were observed, but 11 of the bombs struck within the target area.

During the rendezvous after the attack, Holiday saw a thin column of gray smoke from the target area going up to 5,000 ft. As the planes reached the Duke of York Islands on their way back to Piva, they descended to strafe huts and buildings, smoking two of them.

As the 14 Corsairs entered the traffic pattern at Piva, Holiday reported tracer ammunition being fired at the squadron Corsairs, missing the plane in front of him. The fire appeared to be coming from a bivouac area atop a butte located about three miles east of Piva North Field. No one was hit, and the 14 Corsairs landed safely at Piva by 1050.

For the afternoon mission, Furlow ended up leading 16 Corsairs to bomb and strafe a supply area about 3,000 yards northeast of Tobera Airfield. Take off was at 1250, but three planes did not get off the ground. Humberd, who was to lead the mission, Sigan and Hart all had mechanical problems and could not start their Corsairs. As the remaining Corsairs made their way to the target, Garrett's engine cut out. He was able to get it restarted but it was running rough. He turned back for Piva, escorted by Scoville.

The remaining 11 Corsairs reached the target area at around 1355, ranging in altitude from 8,000 to 10,000 feet. The Japanese opened up with light AA fire; no Corsairs were hit. The Corsairs nosed over releasing their 1,000 pounders between 1,500 and 2,000 feet. Ten of the bombs hit inside the target area, with Webber's bomb scoring a direct hit inside a grove of rubber trees. What he struck is not known but it caused a huge explosion, throwing a large mushroom cloud of smoke and fire into the air.

The Corsairs formed up and turned for home. Several of the planes, skimming the surface at 50 feet, strafed a square concrete block house located 2.5 miles east of Tobera Airfield. Gerety's aim was on the mark as he knocked out a 20mm gun emplacement. The rest of the trip back to Piva was uneventful. All Corsairs were on the ground by 1500.

The mission conducted on the morning of 17 July was a rather unusual one. Humberd and Hart would lead their divisions (each consisting of four Corsairs) on a low level attack against an underground storage dump near Keravia Bay. The target was several large doors leading into the base of a 100 foot cliff. In order to ensure the destruction of the dump, the fuses of the 1,000 pound bombs the Corsairs would carry were set with an 8 to 11 second delay. Prior to VMO-251 hitting the target, VMSB-235 SBDs at Green Island were assigned to neutralize AA guns in the area.

Each of the 36 SBD dive bombers was armed with one 1,000 pound bomb and two 100 pound bombs. Led by Captain Edward C. Willard, all planes were in the air shortly after 0800. About 90 minutes later, the SBDs arrived over the target area, coming in from the west at 13,000 feet. They were promptly greeted with intense, accurate AA fire from a variety of weapons, possibly including 5" guns. Several planes were damaged; two severely.

Despite the AA fire, the planes pushed over at around 9,000 feet and released their bombs at 3,200 feet. They pulled out of their dives at 2,000 feet and retired to the east. Several of the gun emplacements received damage and an ammunition dump or an oil dump was blown to bits. The massive explosion of the dump created a huge column of orange flame that rose nearly 2,000 feet into the air.[22]

While the dive bombers of VMSB-235 were softening the target area, the eight Corsairs of VMO-251 circled over St. George Channel awaiting a call to proceed to their target. It soon came. At around 0935, flying at speeds in excess of 300 knots, they approached their target at 100 feet. AA fire was still being directed at the retiring dive bombers; the Corsairs went in untouched. Seven of the eight bombs were believed to strike the target area, with one reported to be a direct hit—credited to Robinson—on the doors. Hart had a problem with his release mechanism and could not drop his payload. He ended up shaking it loose in the vicinity of Duke of York Islands. Within a span of 10 minutes, over 20 tons of ordnance was dropped by the two squadrons.

Explosions were not witnessed by the 251 pilots for two reasons: the planes retired at a high rate of speed to the west to clear a 1,000 foot cliff, and the delay fusing of the bombs. The results were apparently witnessed by VMSB-235. The Corsairs circled back around for another look at the target area via Talili Bay, over Rabaul, then down St. George Channel. A thin haze of smoke and fire greeted the pilots. They also saw the huge column of smoke from the dump destroyed by VMSB-235.

All the SBDs from VMSB-235 made it back to Green Island, as well as the eight Corsairs to Piva. Despite the AA fire that greeted the planes, there were no casualties. VMO-251's mission report called the coordination of the attack with the dive bombers "perfect."[23]

The mission for 18 July saw the squadron getting a respite from Rabaul. Two divisions, led by Teller and Henley, were assigned to bomb and strafe targets along the coast of New Ireland. Teller's division of four Corsairs was assigned the east coast, while Henley's four Corsairs drew the west coast. The Corsairs, armed once again with 1,000 pound bombs, took off from Piva at 0800, and arrived over their target areas after 0900. Teller's division found the east coast socked in with overcast skies and rain squalls, so they ended up attacking gun positions on Sohana Island. No hits were scored.

Henley's division had better luck with the weather on the west coast. Attacking targets located near the Kamdaru River, Henley scored a direct hit on a camouflaged hut, throwing up plenty of smoke and dust, while Crutcher scored a damaging hit on a group of huts. Lorch's bomb was a dud and Maya missed with his bomb.

The Corsairs regrouped and turned home, arriving at Piva by 1040.

Humberd led the strike to New Ireland on the morning of 19 July. His 16 Corsairs, armed with their usual payload of destruction, were to strike a series of bridges and gun positions on New Ireland. The Corsairs took off at 0930, arriving over the target area an hour later and stayed to pound their targets until 1300 hours. Sigan and Gerety scored direct hits on bridges spanning the Sae River, rendering both unusable. Scoville's 1,000 pound bomb scored a direct hit on a bridge on the Selik River, completely destroying it. Inglehart and Sturgis encountered AA fire from several gun emplacements near Cape Namaroda. Unscathed, they proceeded to bomb and strafe the guns, destroying two of them.

Once the attacks on the bridges and gun emplacements were complete, the Corsairs set fire to a few huts after a strafing run. Flying low along a road servicing the west coast, they spotted several small bridges as well as a mine washed up on a beach about 40 miles up the beach from Cape St. George. Several barges were also spotted in a river near Kanam Plantation and were strafed. No damage to the barges was recorded.

All Corsairs made it back to Piva by 1400.

The 20 July mission found the squadron striking targets closer to home. The morning strike to Rabaul was washed out due to weather so in the afternoon, 12 squadron Corsairs, to be armed with 1,000 pound bombs, were ordered to strike bridges along the east coast of Bougainville and attack a Japanese bivouac along the Bovo River in the Rumba Mission village located near Kieta on the northeast coast of the island. Four of the squadron Corsairs, led by Hart, would precede TBF Avengers of Royal New Zealand Air Force (RNZAF) Squadron 31 to attack the bivouac area, while Teller led the remaining eight Corsairs to attack the bridges.

The Corsairs of VMO-251 took off first, getting into the air at 1420. The New Zealand Avengers followed 25 minutes later. Within 10 minutes of taking to the air, Hart's division struck first, destroying one hut and starting a large fire in the bivouac area.

Next to attack were the remaining eight Corsairs, attempting to knock out two bridges located on the Toberei Plantation at the base of the Kieta Peninsula. Unfortunately no hits were scored but they did strafe huts located in the area.

Last up were the RNZAF Avengers. After releasing 53 500 pound bombs and numerous strafing runs, they destroyed one large house, several huts and damaged at least a dozen more—leaving behind many fires to mark the damage.[24]

No planes were damaged during the assault. All were on the ground at Piva by 1600.

It was back to New Ireland for the 21 July mission. Armed with 1,000 pound bombs 16 Corsairs led by Humberd were to strike bridges and targets of opportunity in the same area they pounded on 19 July. The 16 Corsairs were in the air by 0845. With partly cloudy skies, they set a course for the target area. After about an hour's flight they were ready to strike.

Divisions for the 21 July Strike on New Ireland

Major Humberd, William C.
(Flight Leader)
2Lt. Sigan, Nick A.
1Lt. Inglehart, George G.
2Lt. Sturgis, James B.

CPT. Furlow, Thomas W.
(Division Leader)
2Lt. Scoville, William H.
1Lt. Cunningham, Russell F.
1Lt. Garrett, James B.

1Lt. Smith, Howard F., Jr.
(Division Leader)
2Lt. Neilson, Russell H.
1Lt. Kane, John R.
1Lt. Thornton, Powell D.

1Lt. Gerety, Edward J.
(Division Leader)
2Lt. Rosellen, Robert R.
2Lt. Webber, William G.
2Lt. MacLachlan, Archibald W.

A bridge was spotted to the south of Borpop, as well as buildings near Namatanai. The planes approached the bridge along the long axis of the structure and dropped their payloads. Neilson scored a direct hit, completely demolishing the bridge. Thornton may have also hit the bridge but no one observed the result. Kane scored a direct hit on a large building in the vicinity of Namatanai. The rest of the bombs were either misses or duds.

After their bomb runs, the Corsairs hit the deck and let loose with their .50 caliber machine guns. Over two dozen cattle and horses—valuable livestock to the starving Japanese—were killed. Many huts were left smoking and several were set on fire. Maclachlan strafed what he thought was camouflage netting covering several barges along a river near Kamiraba Plantation.

The pilots also shot up gun emplacements at Namatanai Airfield and Cape Namaroda. Light but inaccurate AA fire met the Corsairs in the Cape Namaroda area but no hits were scored by the Japanese. Rosellen flew low enough to spot twin guns believed to be 20mm. No guns were destroyed by the pilots.

After spending over two hours pummeling the Japanese, the 16 Corsairs of VMO-251 regrouped and set a course for Piva. All wheels were down on the ground by 1300.

It was back to New Ireland for a late morning raid on 22 July. Sixteen Corsairs, led by Teller, were to bomb a bridge near Lagogon Bay, and strafe targets all along the east coast of the island. Fifteen planes got off the ground at 0855. Crutcher's plane developed mechanical problems and remained on the ground.

The weather on the run to the target was clear, and it remained that way as the squadron Corsairs approached New Ireland. Sighting their target, the 15 Corsairs dropped their bombs at 600 feet. They immediately gained altitude upon release since the 1,000 pound bombs had instantaneous fuses and exploded upon impact. Erdmann scored the only direct hit on the bridge, while seven of the bombs crated a nearby road. The rest were either misses or duds.

With their payloads expended the pilots searched to strafe targets of opportunity. Hart's division—consisting of Holiday, Pirages, and Erdmann—spotted barges in a river near Putumbu Bay. They appeared to be the same barges spotted during the 19 July mission. The four pilots pummeled the barges with six strafing runs, expending thousands of rounds of .50 caliber ammunition. The barges were not set on fire but the four pilots believed that the barges were unserviceable after being shot full of holes.

While Hart's division was busy shooting up the barges, the remaining eight pilots were attacking gun positions to the east of Namatanai Airfield on Cape Namaroda. The Japanese filled the sky with lead, and this time their aim was on the mark.

Teller's division was the hardest hit. As the planes made their strafing runs, Sprenger's plane (BuNo. 50014) was severely hit by the AA fire. Whether Sprenger was killed by the Japanese fire or his plane rendered uncontrollable, the result was the same. It plowed into the jungle, exploding in flames. He was missed immediately after the run; either his wingman (1Lt. Grover K. Tanner) or division leader Teller turned back to find him.[25] All that could be seen was a column of black smoke rising from the jungle about 400 yards inland from Cape Namaroda. It may have been at this time that Teller's plane was hit in the left wing. The ammunition pans exploded, blowing a large hole in the wing. Teller was able to maintain control of his Corsair, and flew it back to Piva.

Holiday's plane was also hit by AA guns as he started to make a run on them. His oil pressure began to drop, but was able to keep his plane aloft until he reached a point north of Feni Island when his engine quit. He ditched his plane (BuNo. 56163), escaped from the cockpit and retrieved his rubber raft. Luckily Holiday was uninjured, and was rescued by a Dumbo out of Green Island in less than an hour.

To date, it was the squadron's roughest mission of their second combat tour: two planes destroyed and one pilot lost, presumed dead. If there was any consolation, the squadron was beginning to earn a reputation that would later garner it a recommendation for a Navy Unit Commendation award: it flew every mission assigned to it, and did so with nearly all its planes available for each mission.

No one had time to grieve for Sprenger. The pilots were back at it on 23 July. Twelve Corsairs, led by Humberd, were assigned to bomb and strafe targets from Cape Gazelle to Ralum. Smith and Neilson were assigned an Able-Charlie search. This assignment entailed searching the entire coastline of Bougainville and Buka to observe Japanese activity and strafe targets of opportunity.

Humberd's Corsairs took off at 0630, reaching the Ralum supply dump in about an hour. The usual dive bombing tactics were employed. The planes approached the target at 10,000 feet, pushed over into 60 to 70 degree dives and released their bombs at 2,000 to 3,000 feet. Eleven of the bombs struck in the supply area and one bomb was a dud. No damage was seen. As the planes high-tailed it out of the area, they shot at a group of buildings one to two miles west of Rapopo Airfield, which put up a 100 foot column of smoke. After the strafing run the planes made for Piva, landing at 0900.

Smith and Neilson took off at 0830 and remained in the air until 10:45. During the course of their search, no enemy activity was spotted. They ended up strafing a few huts to the west of Tabago, smoking a few of them. Both pilots returned safely to Piva.

To the southwest of Piva, the USS *Alnitah* anchored off Puruata Island to the west of Cape Torokina, and began discharging cargo and passengers, among them the ground echelon of VMO-251. By late afternoon, the men were settled in at Piva.[26] The flight echelon was relieved from STAD and began operations as a complete squadron, now attached to MAG-24.

On 24 July, the squadron flew its first mission under MAG-24. Three squadron divisions were assigned to attack targets from Cape Gazelle to Raluana Point. Smith and Nelson once again drew the Able-Charlie search. Pilots assigned to fly were:

Teller (Division Leader)	Hart (Division Leader)	Henley (Division Leader)
Moynihan	Erdmann	Lorch
Kane	Holiday	Maya
Tanner	Pirages	Crutcher

With Teller leading the mission, the 12 Corsairs took off at 0635 hours, each carrying one 500 pound bomb. The weather cooperated with scattered clouds on the way to the target and with clear skies when they arrived over the target area 55 minutes later. Unlike the previous day, no AA fire was encountered. Without the AA fire to disrupt their bomb runs, the Corsairs scored three hits on the main coastal road west of Rapopo, three area hits on the Vunapope Supply Dump, three hits on a supply area two miles west of Rapopo Airfield, one damaging hit on buildings near the coast, and one hit inland of a large derelict ship near Vunapope. For an unknown reason, Holiday was unable to drop his bomb. During the attacks in the Rapopo area, Kane flew at tree-top level over Rapopo Airfield, spotting many craters in the runway.

The trip back home was uneventful, and all landed safely on Piva by 0855.

Humberd led the first strike on the morning of 25 July to attack a supply dump near Vunaknaua along Keravia Bay. Only six of the twelve Corsairs carried one 500 pound bomb to deliver to the supply dump.

Moderate AA fire welcomed the Corsairs as they approached the target from the west at 12,000 feet. Braving the defensive fire, they nosed over into 60 degree dives, releasing their payload at 2,500 feet and strafing on the way out as they pulled out of their dives. All bombs hit in the target area, but results of their attack went unobserved. The Corsairs were back at Piva at 1020, the mission lasting 2 hours, 10 minutes.

Divisions led by Teller, Smith, and Hart took off 1315 on 25 July with only six of the twelve planes carrying one 500 pound magnesium cluster each, to bomb and strafe buildings from Tayui Point to Rataval, an area northwest of the town of Rabaul. William Bacheler, who would join the squadron on 28 July, described the clusters as "cylindrical slatted baskets containing as many small incendiaries as they could pack in and slung from the bomb pylon underneath."[27] The purpose of these bombs was to start as many fires as possible.

Of the six planes carrying bombs, all were reported as having gotten hits in the area. At least 12 fires were started, two of which smoked up to 500 feet. It was the squadron's first experience with dropping magnesium clusters, and found they had a tendency to drop short of the target.

Once the planes dropped their bombs, the strafing runs started. A parked truck carrying lumber, covered with branches, was shot up just south of Cape Tawii and a boat, approximately 20 feet long, was shot up near Tawii Point. During the course of their attacks, squadron pilots observed what appeared to be a large, new building with a cover on its roof on the tip of Cape St. George.

Throughout the attacks, the Corsairs received intense AA fire. Near Talili, Thornton's plane was especially hard hit—a portion of his left outboard flap was shot away, the fuselage aft of the cockpit received several holes, and his vertical stabilizer was shot up.

All planes returned to Piva at 1540. Other missions flown during the day had Robinson and Wubben on the Able-Charlie search duty, while Lorch and Maya flew test hops.

For the 26 July mission 12 Corsairs, consisting of divisions led by Teller, Smith and Henley, were once again assigned to attack the Ralum Supply area. All but one Corsair got into the air at 0800. Tanner's plane developed a problem, and remained on the ground. Following a 1 hour, 10 minute flight the planes entered their dives from 10,000, pushing over into 70 degree angle of attack. By the time the planes began their pullouts between 2500 and 3500 feet, they were flying at speeds in excess of 400 mph. Eight of the bombs struck the target area but no damage was observed. The Corsairs returned to Piva by 1030.

Five. Espiritu Santo, Green Island and Bougainville

While their squadron mates were attacking Ralum, Holiday and Pirages drew the Able-Charlie duty, while MacLachlan and Erdmann flew test hops.

For the afternoon strike, Humberd led 12 Corsairs for another strike on Ralum. Armed with 500 pound general purpose bombs, they took off at 1350. After slightly over an hour in the air, they were greeted by inaccurate AA fire as they arrived over the target area. They Corsairs pushed over at 9,000 feet and released the 500 pounders between 2,500 and 3,500 feet. Eleven of the bombs hit in the target area but the damage was negligible. The planes regrouped and set a course for Piva, touching down shortly after 1600 hours.

The mission for 27 July was a bit unusual. Sixteen Corsairs, once again led by Humberd, were ordered to strike a supply area northeast of Tobera Airfield. Each Corsair was to carry one 500 pound magnesium cluster. However, since none were available to the squadron at Piva, they had to fly to Green Island where MAG-14 ground personnel would arm the squadron Corsairs with the clusters.

All went according to plan. Fourteen of the 16 Corsairs took off from Piva at 0655 and made way to Green Island. Once the Corsairs arrived, ground crews hustled to load the clusters on the squadron planes. The work took about an hour. One by one the Corsairs took off and arrived over the target area by 1015.

The Corsairs approached New Britain at around 12,000 feet. No AA fire was encountered. As they neared the target area, the Corsairs were at 10,000 feet when they pushed over, entering dive angles ranging from 60 to 70 degrees.

Having learned the clusters had a tendency to fall short of their target, the pilots led their targets and released the clusters at 2,800 feet. The lesson was learned well—all the clusters hit the target area. Retirement from the target area was made before results of the strike could be determined. As the Corsairs passed to the east of Tobera Airfield, Gerety strafed a concrete block house with undetermined results. All the Corsairs made it back to Piva by 1115. A photographic mission conducted the next day revealed that 16 of 32 buildings were destroyed.[28]

For the mission on 28 July, 16 planes (Divisions led by Henley, Smith, Teller and Hart) were assigned to bomb and strafe buildings and supply areas located near the same target they struck the day before. They took off at 0805 and reached the assigned target area about an hour later. Unfortunately, a solid overcast prevented a good dive bombing run. Each division searched for a break in the clouds in order to attack targets of opportunity. Their search was successful, striking targets near Tobera, Nordup, and Rapopo Airfield. Despite sometimes intense AA fire from the Japanese, all but one of the 1,000 pounders the Corsairs were carrying struck within the target areas, causing several fires to buildings. Aerial photos taken immediately after the strike near Tobera showed that three of 20 buildings were destroyed.

While their fellow pilots were pounding the Japanese on New Britain, Sturgis and Inglehart flew the Able-Charlie search around Buka and Bougainville. As they flew around Buka, they spotted a trio of Japanese in the water off the northeast coast. Both planes pushed over and lined up for a strafing run. The Japanese struggled to get out of the water and head for cover on the shore. Sturgis and Inglehart pulled the trigger on their .50 calibers, killing at least one of the soldiers.

The squadron also saw a change of personnel to its flight echelon. Gerety, Maya, Kane, Thornton, Webber, Holiday and Wubben were transferred out of the squadron. Coming in to replace them were Major William L. Bacheler from VMF-115, 1Lt. Glenn

L. Bowers, 1Lt. Ned J. Corman, 1Lt. Alfred L. Johnson, 1Lt. Harry C. Johnson, 1Lt. Earl W. McCabe, 1Lt. Robert A. Enders, 1Lt. Millard F. Fowler, 1Lt. Albert Jolink, 1Lt. Orville. R. Swick and 1Lt. Thornton F. Spindler. Bacheler replaced Teller as the squadron's executive officer.

On 29 July, divisions led by Humberd, Hart, Furlow, and Smith took off at 0815 to hit guns positions on Praed Point on the approach to Blanche Bay. Each Corsair carried the usual 1,000 pound payload. As they cleared Bougainville, Humberd received instructions via radio to hit their assigned secondary target—two missions near an area designated Point Dog. A solid front of bad weather covered most of New Britain, precluding any attack on Praed Point. With the pilots not being familiar with the Point Dog area, Humberd made the decision to strike gun positions on the northeast tip of Sohana Island. They set a course for the gun positions, arriving to attack at 0910. Japanese AA fire was light and did nothing to distract the Corsairs from their bomb runs. All bombs hit in the target area, but results were unobservable as the 16 Corsairs retired to Piva.

Divisions led by Humberd and Hart, as well as Furlow and Henley, were in the air for the afternoon mission to bomb and strafe huts on Motupena Point in southwest Bougainville. When the 16 Corsairs arrived over their target, the ceiling was down to 2,000 feet with numerous rain squalls. It became necessary to perform a level bomb run at 1,800 feet instead of their normal dive bombing runs. Thirteen 1,000 pound bombs hit the target area, and two damaging hits were also scored. No Japanese activity was observed as the Corsairs retired to return to Piva. They were back on the ground by 1450.

While Motupena Point was under attack, MacLachlan and Rosellen drew the Able-Charlie search. No Japanese were observed, but they did strafe a few huts before returning to Piva.

Rataval was the intended target for the 30 July mission. Fourteen Corsairs led by Furlow, carrying 1,000 pounders, took off at 0815 only to run headlong into a solid front of bad weather extending from Buka Island to Wide Bay, New Britain. Furlow gave the order to turn back and attack gun positions on Sohana Island. Thirteen bombs hit the target area. Spindler's bomb hung up and he later jettisoned the bomb in the sea. The extent of the damage went unobserved as the planes made way for Piva, all planes returning by 1045.

The squadron stood down on 31 July. However it was not a day off for the flight echelon. All pilots attended a three hour survival lecture, "The Birds and Bees; the Flowers and Trees," given by two Australian army officers.

August 1944

If the pilots were looking for a change of scenery when it came to target selection, they were sadly mistaken. It was back to the Rabaul area for an early morning mission on 1 August to strike Japanese gun positions north of Tobera Airfield. Divisions led by Humberd, Bacheler, Furlow and Jennings drew the assignment. Fifteen out of the 16 Corsairs got into the air shortly after 0800.

About an hour later, the Japanese greeted the Corsairs with light and inaccurate AA fire. Unshaken by the paltry Japanese reception, the Corsairs dropped all their bombs in the target area, but results could not be seen as they retired.

All planes were back at Piva by 1030. More personnel changes occurred with four officers being transferred out of the squadron: Bate, Condon, Hildebrand and Wilson. Eleven others drew a week's leave to Sydney, Australia.

Missions continued on 3 August. Two divisions, led by Bacheler and Henley were to bomb and strafe separate targets. Each Corsair was loaded with a 500 pound bomb with four to five second delay fuses. Bacheler's division drew the Duke of York-Cape Lambert sweep while Henley's division drew the Put-Put, Malabunga, Keravat sweep. Flying in Bacheler's division were Pirages, Swick and Spindler. Flying with Henley were Lorch, 1Lt. Judson, Flickenger and Crutcher.

The eight Corsairs lifted off at 0835 and arrived over their respective target areas a little over an hour later. Bacheler's division encountered little AA fire and ended up getting an area hit near plantation buildings on Watom Island.

Henley's division struck Malabunga first, getting an area hit near some huts. They flew to Tobera Airfield where they received a hot reception from the Japanese. Crutcher scored a direct hit on some huts just southeast of the airstrip, while Flickenger cratered a nearby road. Soon after Lorch dropped his bomb, he leveled out at a 1,000 feet to line up for a strafing run on gun positions about two miles southeast of the airfield when he was hit by Japanese AA fire.

Lorch set course for St. George's Channel, gained 3,000 feet in altitude when his engine froze somewhere between the mouth of the Warangoi River and Cape St. George. With the other three planes of his division following him to the water, he glided down, jettisoned his canopy and appeared to be in good shape for a water landing. There were many whitecaps and swells on the water. The plane's tail struck the water first, and made one low bounce before it settled on the water. The Corsair (BuNo 56151) sank in less than 10 seconds, taking Lorch with it.

The other three pilots sent out a distress signal to Dumbo at Green Island, and circled the area barely 50 feet off the surface for 30 minutes looking for any sign of Lorch. Unfortunately no trace of him was found. During debriefing, held after the remaining pilots returned to Piva, those in the same division as Lorch stated they could not tell why their comrade was unable to escape from the cockpit.

The same area was the target for the afternoon mission. Fowler's division had the Put Put-Keravat sweep while Jolink's division had the Duke of York-Cape Lambert sweep. Seven Corsairs, each armed with one 500 pound bomb with a 4 to 5 second delay fuse, took off at 1230. McCabe's plane had mechanical difficulties and did not take off. Corman, flying plane number 724, had to turn back due to a hydraulic leak, leaving six Corsairs to

1Lt. Orville F.S. Lorch. He was listed as MIA on 3 August 1944 following a strike on Tobera Airfield near Rabaul (courtesy Brenda Lorch Puttoff).

complete the missions. Fowler and 1Lt. Harry Johnson scored direct hits on buildings along the Keravat River, about three to four miles from Keravat Airfield. During their sweep, pilots in Fowler's division noticed the Japanese had cleared out underbrush near a farm as if they were making a new supply or garden area. They also spotted several log structures to the southeast of Keravat.

Jolink's division on the Duke of York sweep and flying at tree top level, dropped bombs on buildings located at Gavit Plantation, which appeared to be a bivouac area. They also observed fires near Vunakanau, and strafed huts along the shore of Ataliklikun Bay with unobserved results.

Neither division met any AA fire. The Corsairs retired to Piva, landing at 1550. With the Japanese activity seen on the ground, the squadron was sure to return for another strike in the area.

Two divisions were up in the air on the morning of 4 August. Humberd led a four plane fighter sweep covering the area from Duke of York to Cape Lambert. Jolink led his division for the Put Put–Keravat sweep. Both divisions took off at 0835, and arrived over their respective target areas within 90 minutes.

Humberd's planes dropped their 500 pounders on rows of huts on Makada Island, Duke of York, which appeared to be a camp or bivouac area, scoring one hit in the area, one miss, and two unobserved.

One plane from Jolink's division dropped its 500 pounder from 100 feet altitude for an area hit among shacks at Malabunga. The three other planes dropped their bombs near Put Put Harbor, with Enders getting a direct hit on a small structure.

Reconnaissance from 1000 feet along the whole sweep area was unproductive—no Japanese were seen. Both divisions did not meet any Japanese AA fire, and returned safely to Piva just before noon.

Two divisions, led by Furlow and Jennings, took off at 1205 to pound the same target areas assigned to Humberd and Jolink in the morning. Furlow got the Duke of York—Cape Lambert sweep while Jennings got the Put Put—Keravat sweep. Seven of the eight planes made it into the air; Scoville remained behind due to a mechanical problem. In both sweeps, several buildings and huts were targeted but results were less than stellar—several misses, duds and three area hits. The main excitement for the afternoon sweep occurred when Jennings strafed a truck heading south on a road between Vunakanau and Malabunga. His tracers slammed into the cab of the truck, forcing it to veer off the road and crash into a ditch.

On 5 August, Henley's division took off at 0820—with each Corsair armed with one 500 pound bomb with a delay action fuse—to attack targets of opportunity while flying the Put Put—Keravat sweep. Upon reaching the Keravat area, they scored three area hits among buildings about three miles southeast of Keravat.

During their sweep no enemy activity was seen but they did observe a couple of columns of smoke coming from trees about two miles south of Vunakanau road. The pilots also noticed many new huts in vicinity of the Malabunga-Vunakanau road. The road from Keravat to Vunakanau to Tobera appeared to be in excellent condition, but no traffic was seen on it. While flying over and along the Warangoi River the Japanese appeared to be absent but they did spot many logs and sandbars clogging the river. During debriefing, the pilots made it known that they thought the river would be difficult for the Japanese to navigate due to the obstructions spotted, unless they were in an extremely small boat.

For the afternoon, Bacheler's division flew the Put Put—Keravat sweep while Fowler led the Duke of York—Cape Lambert sweep. Both divisions took off from Piva at 1200. A solid front of nasty weather, running north to south near Cape Gazelle, forced the Corsairs to turn around. They ended up striking their secondary target, Sohana Island in the Buka Passage, scoring four area hits with their 500 pounders with no observed damage or enemy activity noted.

The weather had an impact on the missions flown on 6 August. Heavy cloud cover and rain forced Humberd's division to abort the Put Put—Keravat sweep and head for Bohana. The weather was slightly better over Bohana, but visibility was still reduced. Despite the foul weather, the division dropped all four of their bombs in the target area but the results could not be ascertained. The Japanese offered no resistance and the four pilots made it back safely to Piva.

While Humberd's division was pounding Bohana, Flickenger and Jolink took off at 0930 for the Jaba River—Kieta sweep (Bougainville). Within 10 minutes of taking off, visibility quickly deteriorated. Heavy rains soon began, quickly reducing visibility to zero. The two pilots aborted their mission and were back at Piva by 0950.

By the early afternoon, the weather cleared enough to launch Fowler's division for the Ebery Plantation—Toburai sweep. They were to attack huts and gardens located in a three mile long stretch of land a few miles north of Ebery Plantation, located on the south end of Bougainville. They carried no bombs: strafing was the order of the day.

Fowler's division lifted off at 1530. Within 40 minutes they were over the target area. Despite heavy but inaccurate AA fire, and solid clouds with haze and mist at around 3,000 feet, the four Corsairs came in at tree top level to strafe the target area. Evidence of Japanese activity abounded—huts, small fires, cultivated gardens and well-traveled roads. They pasted the area with thousands of rounds of .50 caliber ammunition but smoked only one hut. The Corsairs suffered no damage, returning safely to Piva by 1700.

Humberd and Furlow led their divisions for the morning sweep on 7 August, with Humberd leading the Put Put—Keravat sweep and Furlow leading the Duke of York—Cape Lambert sweep. The eight Corsairs took off at 0755, each armed with one 500 pound bomb with 4 to 5 second delay fuse. Weather in route to the target areas was cloudy but as the Corsairs approached their targets they found clear skies.

Humberd's division dropped to treetop level to make their attack on a road just south of Tobera. Humberd spotted a truck with 6 to 8 people running away from it. He lined up his Corsair and let loose with his guns. Flying too low, his right wing hit a tree, causing extensive damage. The truck was riddled with bullets but did not burst into flames.

Sigan, Humberd's wingman, sighted another truck going west on the same road. It appeared to have a machine gun mounted on a rear platform with two men manning the weapon. He turned around to line up his strafing run but by the time he was ready to fire his guns, the truck had disappeared. On his way out, Sigan dropped his 500 pounder on some huts near a cocoanut plantation on the north side of the Warangoi River.

As Humberd's division continued their sweep, Sturgis bombed and strafed a civilian-type automobile at Toma, southeast of Vunakanau with unknown results.

With their sweep complete, Humberd's division flew home to Piva, landing at 1100. Humberd's plane required a wing change to be brought back to operational status.

Furlow's Duke of York sweep was uneventful. His four Corsairs dropped their bombs on some huts on Rokunda Plantation. None exploded—all four were duds. The planes did not strafe. They turned back and set a course for Piva.

It was back to the same areas for the afternoon sweeps. Jennings, with fellow pilots McMasters, Foley and 2Lt. Lewis C. Frank following him, took off at 1200 for the Duke of York—Cape Lambert sweep. Following an uneventful 1 hour, 15 minute flight, the four Corsairs dropped their 500 pounders near a group of buildings approximately 100 yards south of a wharf on Garreer Bay east of Cape Lambert. A strafing run followed the release of the bombs. Unfortunately no damage was observed. The four pilots turned for home and arrived at Piva at 1530.

Bacheler led Pirages, Spindler and Swick on the Put Put—Duke of York sweep. Armed with 500 lb. bombs, they took off at 1230. They arrived over their target area an hour later. The four Corsairs went into a low level bombing run, releasing their payloads at 50 feet on buildings at Neinduk Plantation. Bacheler, Spindler and Swick missed with their bombs but Pirages scored a direct hit on one building, sending debris hundreds of feet into the air. Strafing began after the bomb runs, resulting in several smoking huts and one Japanese soldier killed.

The four Corsairs made it back to Piva at 1550. Once Pirages landed and exited his plane, he walked around to inspect it. He found a large hole—possibly from either a .30 or .50 caliber bullet—in the fuselage near the horizontal stabilizer No AA fire was encountered so who fired the weapon was a complete mystery.

The eighth of August would be a busy day for the squadron. Henley led his division for the Duke of York—Cape Lambert morning sweep. Armed with 500 lb. bombs, the Corsairs took off at 0730. They ended up dropping their bombs on a group of buildings at St. Paul near Cape Lambert to the west of Rabaul City. All four bombs hit well within the target, and two were believed to be damaging hits. Strafing afterwards proved to be ineffective. All planes were back at Piva by 1030.

Furlow's division drew the Ebery Lease—Takasago Farms sweep. Without a bomb load, they took off at 1050. Theirs was strictly a strafing mission. They ended up putting over 6,000 rounds of .50 caliber in the target area but saw no sign of Japanese or enemy activity. Over Kahili Airfield, they drew heavy, but inaccurate AA fire. They did spot one truck which pulled onto the runway. Thinking the truck was bait to draw the Corsairs closer to the field, the four Marines opted not to strafe. The Corsairs retired and landed at Piva at 1330.

Fowler's division took off nearly an hour after Furlow's division. They flew the Duke of York sweep with one 500 pounder slung underneath each plane. All four Corsairs dropped their explosives on a group of buildings and huts at Vunalama Plantation. Two of the pilots, Fowler and Flickenger, scored direct hits, demolishing two buildings. McCabe and A. Johnson overshot. No one saw any trucks or signs of Japanese, but they did spot a column of smoke inland from Raluana Point. The Japanese offered no resistance and the four Corsairs returned undamaged to Piva at 1515.

Bacheler's division was next to fly. The division, armed with the standard 500 pounders, took off at 1215 for the Put Put—Malabunga—Keravat sweep. They reached their target area about an hour later and remained over the area for 50 minutes. During that time, they damaged one hut near Malabunga by bombing, but did no damage while strafing near Toma. They did observe nearly a dozen camp fires in several clearings about three to six miles south of Vunakanau. Swick and Spindler photographed roads between Malabunga, Keravat and Vunakanau. Squadron records do not indicate how this was accomplished. The Corsairs did have gun cameras, so it may be the photos were taken with them. Following their sweep, the Corsairs returned to Piva by 1450.

At 1300, Jolink led his division for a strafing mission on the Ebery's Lease—Takasago Farms area. Arriving over their target area at 1320, they strafed for the next 50 minutes with no results. They saw plenty of gardens and huts, but no vehicles. Near Kahili, they saw a Japanese soldier run from a hut and jump into a ditch but were unable to shoot at him. Jolink, Enders, Bowers and Corman returned to Piva by 1520.

On 9 August, Major Humberd's and Jennings's divisions had the assignment to bomb and strafe targets of opportunity from East Cape to Namatanai, New Ireland. Reaching the target area about an hour after they took off at 0830, they smoked five or six huts during their strafing runs, started a grass fire, and bombed a bridge across the first river south of Kandau, north of Cape Senna, scoring one area hit with no visible damage. Three of the pilots bombed buildings just south of Cape Senna, with McMasters's 500 pounder destroying one building with a direct hit and damaging two others.

On the way home, Jennings' Corsair (BuNo 49766) was lost about 30 miles west of Buka Passage. Jennings had no choice but to abandon his plane. Apparently, small arms fire during their bombing and strafing runs near Cape Senna struck the Marine's Corsair. While heading back to base, he noticed his RPMs fluctuate between 500 and 800. Jennings struggled to keep his Corsair in the air. It was a losing battle: he was losing altitude at a rate of 300 feet per minute.

Jennings realized he wasn't going to make it back to Piva. With his Corsair at 1,800 feet, he bailed out, injuring his foot when it struck the vertical stabilizer as the Corsair went past him. He waited two hours in the water until Dumbo rescued him. Crowded radio traffic made it difficult to report Jennings' predicament to Piva in order to facilitate his rescue. His injury kept him off flight status for several days. Later, when he returned to Piva, Jennings reported that his engine was running fine and that prop failure was to blame for the aircraft's loss. The remaining seven Corsairs made it home safely.

All but four pilots had the day off on 10 August. Fowler's division got the only assignment for the day: the Put Put—Keravat sweep. Armed with 500 pounders, the four Corsairs took off at 1240. An hour later they were over the target area and commenced their attacks. Buildings were bombed two miles northwest of Malabunga but no direct hits were scored. The Corsairs then strafed many huts and buildings in the town, setting one ablaze. As for enemy activity, they did observe truck activity in the vicinity of the Experimental Farms. One truck was parked on a road approximately halfway between Malabunga and Vunakanau but was not strafed. Once again there was no Japanese resistance and the Corsairs landed at Piva at 1515.

As they had done for the last few months, pilots of VMO-251 grabbed their flight gear for another early morning flight to New Britain. The first mission for 11 August went to Jolink's and Henley's divisions. Jolink would handle the Put Put—Keravat sweep, and Henley the Duke of York—Cape Lambert sweep.

Jolink's Corsairs, armed with 500 pound bombs with instantaneous fuses, took off at 0800. An hour later they were over the target area. Each Corsair attempted to bomb and strafe warehouses between Keravat and the Experimental Farms. The bombs missed but the pilots were surprised to find their .50 caliber ammo bouncing off the warehouse. Huts were also strafed, but none were set on fire. During their sweep, no enemy activity was spotted. Jolink, Enders, Bowers and Corman were back at Piva by 1030.

Henley's division took off at the same time as Jolink. Following a 75 minute flight, the four Corsairs entered the target area. At a point approximately two miles north of Vunagalip, east of Cape Lambert, Schoetz's Corsair (BuNo 56417) was hit by AA fire. No one saw where the Japanese fire came from but suspected a red-painted building in the vicinity.

The sweep was immediately abandoned. The pilots jettisoned their bombs, and stayed with the crippled plane. Henley immediately contacted Dumbo and requested assistance, keeping them apprised of their location.

Schoetz headed north, smoke pouring from his engine. At a point about 50 miles from Rabaul and at a course of 290 degrees, Schoetz attempted to bail out of his Corsair. As he scrambled out of the cockpit, his arm became stuck. In wrenching it free, he pulled several ligaments, bruised his arm and broke two fingers. When he was clear of his Corsair, he pulled his ripcord and floated into the waters of the Bismarck Sea. Shortly after he hit the water, a Dumbo out of Emirau rescued him. Upon arrival at Emirau he was taken to a hospital. Once Schoetz was picked up, the three remaining Corsairs turned for home, arriving at Piva at 1145.

The strikes to New Britain continued on 12 August. At 0800, Humberd's division, with no bombs, took off for the Put Put—Keravat Sweep. Very little strafing was done due to a lack of targets. However, Sturgis did spot a lone Japanese soldier running along a road on Livuan Plantation. He fired his guns, but did not hit the soldier who scampered into some cover. The flight did strafe huts west of Varzin Plantation, as well as huts southeast of Mt. Varzin. Inglehart's Corsair was hit by AA fire near Malabunga resulting in a severe oil leak. Inglehart diverted his plane to Green Island, landing with his oil pressure near zero. Ground crew at Green Island examined the plane. Finding three cylinders pierced by the fire, it required an engine change. Humberd, Sigan and Sturgis returned to Piva unscathed, landing at 1100.

At 1215, Bacheler's division took over the Duke of York—Cape Lambert sweep, minus one plane. Pirages was unable to take off because of a flat tail wheel. No enemy activity was sighted. Bacheler's three Corsairs dropped bombs along the north shore of Cape Lambert and may have slightly damaged several huts. They returned to Piva without a scratch at 1530.

Furlow's division departed for low level strafing runs on the Put Put—Keravat sweep, taking off at 1230. However, one plane was left behind. At start up, Garrett's cockpit filled with smoke which forced an immediate shutdown of his engine. Furlow, Cunnningham, and Scoville strafed many huts, but saw no signs of enemy activity. The three Corsairs landed at 1500.

The mission for 13 August was a coordinated strike with VMF-223. Each squadron put sixteen Corsairs in the air, each carrying one 500 pound bomb to strike a Japanese bivouac and supply area along the Bovo River near Arawa Bay on the north coast of Bougainville.

VMO-251 put four divisions in the air: those led by Bachelor, Jolink, Furlow and Fowler. The squadron's divisions took off while it was still dark, getting into the air at 0555. Twenty minutes later they were over the target area. The Corsairs loitered over the area until there was enough light to enter their bomb runs. If there were any Japanese below, they would be in for a rude awakening.

Of the squadron's 16 planes, 12 put their bombs on the target. All but one of the planes strafed all the way down the area and to the sea. No enemy activity or actual damage was seen in the target area because of the dense jungle growth, but thin wisps of smoke were seen rising from an area about 10 miles up the coast. All of the squadron's Corsairs were back at Piva by 0715.

Five. Espiritu Santo, Green Island and Bougainville 111

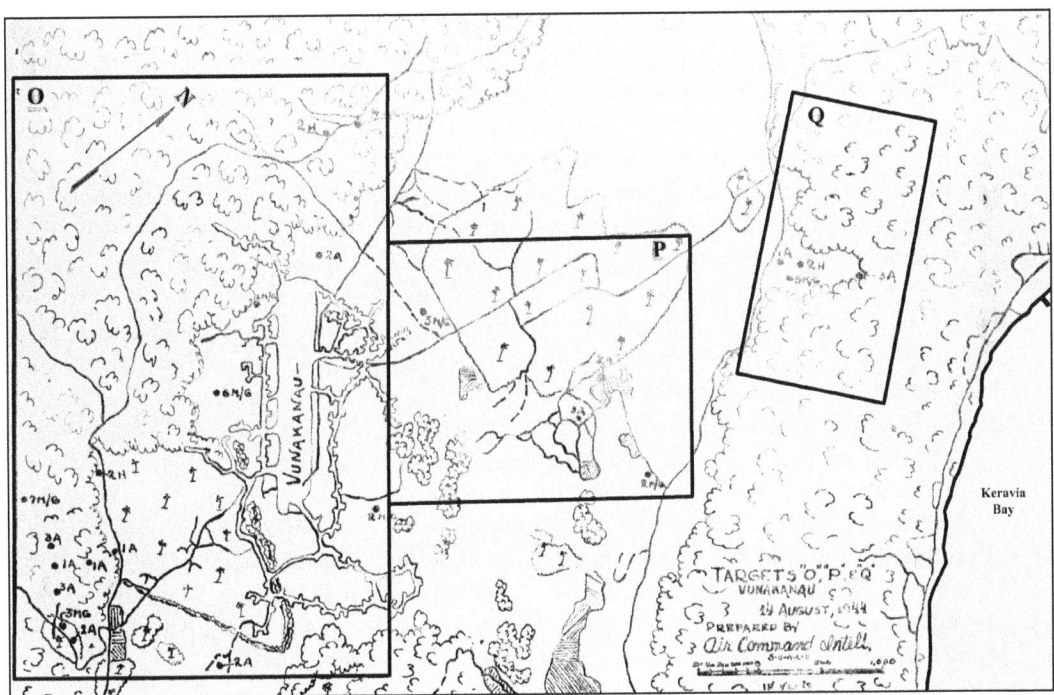

Vunakanau target areas. Adapted from VMSB-243 Mission Report dated 15 August 1944 (National Archives).

As for VMF-223, their results could not be determined. Records covering the 13 August mission, as well as the war diary for the month could not be located.

Taking off at 0720, Henley's division set a course for the Put Put—Keravat sweep. They would not accomplish this mission. As they approached Cape St. George from the south, they ran into a solid wall of nasty weather extending from sea level to 30,000 feet. Henley got on the radio and requested instructions. They were diverted to Arawa Bay and the Manatai Mission—located on the east coast of Bougainville—where they strafed and took photographs with their gun cameras. No damage was observed from the attack. The Japanese offered no resistance and four Corsairs returned to Piva without damage.

At 1400, Fowler's division was assigned the afternoon Put Put—Keravat sweep, but it was stopped by the same front that had diverted Henley's division. Fowler took his division up the east New Ireland coast in an effort to get through the weather. He found the conditions so bad that he opted to abort the mission and returned to Piva.

The bad weather continued to have an impact on the squadron's missions on 14 August. Taking off at 0745, Humberd led his division for the Put—Keravat sweep. Shortly after takeoff, Humberd was forced to return to Piva due to a hydraulic leak. Inglehart took over as division leader but found his way blocked by the same front that stopped two flights on 13 August. With the front extending from seal level to 15,000 feet, Inglehart found no way to get around the wall. The mission was aborted and Inglehart led the Corsairs home, returning two hours after they took off.

At 0905, Furlow led McMasters, Foley and Frank on the Duke of York—Cape Lambert Sweep. The weather appeared to be breaking up, allowing the four Corsairs to fly through scattered rain squalls on their way to the target area. They ended up dropping their 500 pounders on a group of buildings at Mandres Sawmill, gaining several area hits on an already devastated target. As they continued their sweep, buildings located on the northwest side of Watom Island as well as buildings on Duke of York Islands were strafed. Upon return to Piva, Foley and Frank filed a report indicating a breach of radio discipline by two other squadrons in the area. If any Japanese activity was spotted, or if a downed crewman's position needed to be reported, the crowded airwaves made it difficult to contact Piva, as happened on 9 August when Jennings went down.

Jolink's division flew the afternoon Put Put—Keravat sweep with no bomb load, taking off at 1300. Flickinger returned to base immediately after takeoff when his Corsair developed a hydraulic leak. The three Corsairs ended up strafing huts and buildings from the shores of Kabanga Bay to Keravat. No enemy activity was seen by the pilots, but numerous fires were spotted running from Malabunga to Vunakanau to Mt. Varzin. Jolink, Enders, and 2Lt. Wilson G. Barton returned to Piva without a scratch, landing at 1530.

On the heels of Jolink's division, Bacheler led his division for the Duke of York—Cape Lambert sweep, taking off at 1345. Each Corsair carried a 500 pound bomb set with an instantaneous fuse. It's not clear where the pilots dropped their bombs but all were misses. As they sought targets of opportunity for strafing, Bacheler smoked a hut east of Cape Lambert. While in the same area, the flight also strafed several tin-roofed huts in plantations along the coast. The pilots were surprised when the huts did not burn, despite their tracers going through the flimsy structures. After their strafing run, Bacheler's Corsairs returned home, landing at 1645.

Several pilots flew the Motupena Point—Kieta sweep over Bougainville during the course of the day: Flickinger and Barton, Henley and Crutcher, Alfred and Harry Johnson, and Fowler and McCabe. No enemy activity was seen by any of the sections flying the sweep.

The morning mission for 15 August was a large scale strike on AA targets and revetments at Vunakanau Airfield. Squadrons from Torokina, Piva and Emirau participated in the attack. Flying out of Piva: VMO-251, led by Humberd, supplied eight Corsairs, and Major Dave Drucker led seven VMF-223 Corsairs: From Torokina, RNZAF Squadrons 19 and 21 combined to put up 20 Corsairs. From Emirau: VMSB-243 supplied 17 Dauntless dive bombers, VMF-115 supplied 10 Corsairs, VMF-211 put in the air eight Corsairs and VMF-215 provided 12 Corsairs. Eighty-two aircraft ended up striking the Japanese airfield with each aircraft carrying one 1,000 pound bomb with an instantaneous fuse.

The two New Zealand squadrons were the first to get into the air, taking off at 0725. After flying for 30 minutes, RNZAF squadrons 19 and 21 rendezvoused, less two aircraft due to mechanical problems, with VMO-251 and VMF-223. The four squadrons then made their way for Vunakanau Airfield.

At Emirau, The Dauntless dive bombers took off first, with wheels up at approximately 0730. Corsairs with VMF-215, VMF-211, and VMF-115 took off next, at 0735, 0750, and 0800 respectively.

Arriving over the target area at 0840, first to strike were the New Zealanders. The Japanese were ready for the approaching planes and they threw up all they had in the way of AA fire. They kept up the fire throughout the attack by all squadrons. From 11,000 feet, the Corsairs of RNZAF Squadron 19 nosed over for the bomb run. At an altitude of 2,000 feet they released their payloads, registering a possible hit on an automatic weapons position, and several near misses on other gun positions. The New Zealanders returned to Torokina by 1020.[29]

At 0847, VMO-251 Corsairs led by Humberd and Fowler were next to strike Vunakanau. The eight Corsairs planes attacked automatic AA positions to the east of the plantation and three machine guns at the west end of the runway. The Corsairs nosed over at 10,000 feet and entered a 60 degree dive angle. At an approximate altitude of 2,000 feet they released their bombs without using dive brakes, scoring five area hits. Two bomb drops went unobserved and Alfred Johnson had to jettison his bomb when it did not release during his run at the target. The attack appeared to go according to plan, but because of the high-speed dive and pullout of the Corsairs at speeds exceeding 380 knots, it was impossible to get a view of any damage that may have been caused. Despite the hot reception the Japanese gave the pilots, all planes returned safely to Piva at 1015.

About 15 minutes later, VMF-223 commenced their attack. Drucker's Corsairs entered their dive bombing runs at 10,000 feet, diving at speeds in excess of 380 knots. Between 3,000 and 4,000 feet the planes released their bombs, claiming two direct hits on revetments located near the south side of the runway. The Corsairs retired to the east and set a course back to Piva.[30]

Right on the heels of VMF-223's attack, the four squadrons from Emirau arrived at 0920 to drop their 1,000 pound bombs on the Japanese. The Japanese continued their heavy AA fire for the incoming squadrons. VMF-115's Corsairs claimed a direct hit on machine gun positions, as well as several near misses.[31] Corsairs from VMF-211 scored a possible direct hit on an AA position, as well as scoring a few near misses.[32] The 12 Corsairs of VMF-215 hit their target area but no direct hits were observed. One plane from the squadron was hit by the intense AA fire, gaining a hole in one of its flaps as a 25mm shell passed through it.[33] Lastly, dive bombers of VMSB-243—less one that had to turn back due to engine trouble—got their shot at Vunakanau. Three damaging hits were reported on AA positions northwest of the airfield by their pilots before the squadron retired for the return trip to Emirau.

Despite the large scale effort, the Japanese got away relatively unscathed after having 41 tons of bombs dropped on them. Despite the claims made by the squadrons, a photo reconnaissance mission after the strike revealed new craters around two gun positions with no apparent damage to the guns.[34] There would be another mission to Vunakanau.

While the divisions led by Humberd and Fowler were on their way back from Vunakanau, Jolink led his division on the Put Put—Keravat sweep. The Corsairs carried no bombs. They ended up strafing many huts and buildings along the route, but observed no damage. During their sweep, they saw no smoke or other evidence of damage at Vunakanau as result of the eight squadron strike. They did spot a cloud of dust on the northeast end of Tobera Airfield but couldn't determine what caused it. The division encountered no Japanese resistance, and was back at Piva at 1210.

Soon after Humberd's and Fowler's divisions landed, Furlow led his division back into the air for the Duke of York—Cape Lambert sweep, dropping 500 pounders on a group of buildings located on Kakada Point on Duke of York Island. Cunningham and Garrett also strafed Utuan and Micko Islands adjacent to Duke of York. No results of bombing or strafing were seen, and no Japanese activity during the Cape Lambert sweep was observed. The four Corsairs were back at Piva at 1230.

Henley's division flew the afternoon Put Put—Keravat sweep, taking off at 1330 without bombs. The pilots strafed and took pictures of several locations with their gun cameras during the sweep. No Japanese were spotted. They observed a few brush fires a couple of miles north of Malabunga. Flying over the Warangoi River they observed no traffic.

Between Malabunga and Keravat, more than two dozen thatched huts were spotted. They received no Japanese fire and returned home at 1545.

McMasters, Frank, and Scoville flew the Motupena Point—Kieta sweep over Bougainville, while Fowler and McCabe flew to Sterling[35] to stand local security alert. Fowler and McCabe returned the next day to find the squadron standing down. Lousy weather in the area scrubbed all flying for 16 August.

Major Humberd's division was the first in the air on the morning of 17 August. Taking off at 0820, and armed only with .50 caliber ammunition, they drew the Put Put—Keravat sweep. Arriving over the target area an hour later, they ended up strafing a wharf, buildings and huts at Vunapaldig Bay. The buildings began to smoke as they were hit, but none of them caught on fire. After spending 15 minutes shooting up the area they continued on their sweep, observing a brush fire inland from Vunapaldig, as well as a small fire at the Experimental Gardens. They received no Japanese fire and returned safely to Piva at 10:50.

Taking off 20 minutes after Humberd's division were divisions led by Bacheler, Furlow and Foley. The 12 Corsairs, armed with one 500 pound bomb each, were scheduled to strike Vunakanau. However due to bad weather, the target was changed to a ration dump located along the Hongarai River on Bougainville. Arriving at the target area at 0900, they nosed over for their attack runs, releasing their bombs at 2,000 feet. All 12 bombs appeared to hit the target area, but due to the thick jungle coverage results could not be seen. Several of the planes ended up strafing the dump during their dives. The 12 Corsairs turned for Piva and landed by 0930.

Fowler's division flew the Put Put—Keravat sweep in the afternoon, taking off at 1315. They carried no bombs, and very little strafing was done as there was a lack of targets. They did spot two small fires burning to the north of Mt. Varzin. The four Corsairs returned from their uneventful flight at 1530.

After the less than stellar results of the attack on 15 August, COMAIRNORSOL (Commander Aircraft Northern Solomons) decided to launch another large scale attack on Vunakanau Airfield, targeting AA guns around the strip. The target areas were designated "O" and "P" on the north end of the strip (see map) and designated "A," "B," and "C" on the south end.

Once again, squadrons from Torokina, Piva and Emirau were ordered to prepare for the attack: from Torokina, RNZAF 21 Squadron; Piva, VMF-223 and VMO-251; from Emirau, VMF-115, VMF-211, VMF-215 and VMSB-243. The bomb load for each plane participating in the mission consisted of one 1,000 pound bomb.

First into the air were squadrons from Piva and Emirau, followed by squadrons from Torokina and the remainder of the squadrons from Emirau. In overall command of the squadrons flying out of Piva was VMF-223's commanding officer, Major Dave Drucker. Bacheler, VMO-251's executive officer, had command of the squadron's divisions for the strike. Bacheler called the briefing for the strike "extensive and boring, since we all knew by now the location of just about every gun in and around Rabaul."[36] The pilots suited up and took to the air. Belly tanks were carried by the squadron Corsairs since the first plane to take off had to wait for the last in order for the squadron to form up and head to Vunakanu. The process took 30 minutes.[37] VMF-223, putting up 17 Corsairs, took off at 0715. Ten Minutes later, 18 Corsairs consisting of divisions led by Bacheler, Fowler, Jennings and Jolink, plus pilots Rosellen and MacLachlan, took off. At Emirau, 12 Corsairs of VMF-215 took off, followed by 15 Dauntless dive bombers of VMSB-243 at 0730. Five minutes later at Torokina, 12 Corsairs of RNZAF 21 Squadron took to the air. Back at Emirau, the remainder of the squadrons participating in the attack—VMF-211 and VMF-115—took off at 0750 and 0800 respectively.

VMO-251 Pilots Participating in the Vunakanau Airfield Strike of 18 August 1944

Name	Division	Call Sign
Bacheler (leader)	1	Garnet 1
Pirages	1	
Spindler	1	
Swick	1	
Fowler (leader)	2	Garnet 2
McCabe	2	
Johnson, A.	2	
Johnson, H.	2	
McMasters (leader)	3	Garnet 3
Jennings	3	
Foley	3	
Frank	3	
Jolink (leader)	4	Garnet 4
Enders	4	
Bowers	4	
Corman	4	
Rosellen (leader)	5	Garnet 5
Maclachlan	5	

If the pilots of VMO-251 were expecting a combat formation on the way to the target, they received a surprise from Drucker. Bacheler recalls:

Finally setting out for Rabaul, Dave ordered us into parade formation. Okay, we reasoned, this is for practice, since we haven't had an entire Group together before, and all four squadrons tightened up wingtip-to-wingtip. As I looked across the massed formation, I was very proud of the job all our guys were doing, which would have done credit to an air show. But it wasn't an air show and as we neared New Britain I began to wonder when Dave was going to loosen us up into battle formation. Still we droned on in parade formation, each pilot concentrating so hard on staying in tight that he was unable to see anything except the guy he was keying on, a very unsafe way to fly in enemy territory, where a constantly swiveling neck is mandatory. We were also heading straight for Tobera Airdrome, an enemy hotspot that was not our target for today. The target was supposed to be Vunakanau which was miles ahead yet, and it was not our habit to expose ourselves to fire from areas we did not intend to hit. Yet here we were, passing straight over Tobera Airdrome in parade formation, unable because of the mass of aircraft to jink up or down, right or left, to avoid flak. Grumbling began on the radio....

... Nothing happened. There was no flak and we passed over and beyond Tobera serenely. Either the japs were so surprised that they refused to credit their senses at the sight of 96 airplanes passing right over their guns in such tight formation that a single 40-millimeter shell could knock an entire division out of the air, or they figured that if they kept quiet we wouldn't notice them and would go away, which we did. I lean toward the latter guess, since we packed a lot of fire power.

On we went, like The Charge of the Light Brigade, droning toward Lakunai Airdrome, another enemy hotspot but it was still not our primary target. Sure as hell, we flew right over Lakunai, only this time we weren't so lucky, as ground batteries began to open up on us. The flak was either above or below our altitude, and we went through unscathed. With Vunakanau in sight now, Dave ordered all squadrons to the right and each squadron echeloned, finally in battle formation. When in position, Dave dropped his belly tank and "peeled off" into his dive. We bombed "around the clock" that is, each airplane dived from a slightly different direction from that of the guy ahead of him, all the way around 360 degrees of a circle, with Vunakanau Airdrome in the center. Each pilot had been assigned a specific target from intelligence photos, but we found that it was not always possible in a "Group Grope" to be that choosey once we began our diving runs.[38]

Weather forced VMF-223 and VMO-251 to swing north over Borpop, New Ireland, then approach Vunakanau from west to east. A cloud layer over the target between 5,000 and 8,000 feet made it difficult to get a good visual on designated targets in areas "O" and "P." The two squadrons were the first to attack, arriving over the target area by 0845. Drucker took his planes, as well as those of VMO-251 through a hole in the clouds and the Japanese filled that hole with plenty of lead. They threw up intense AA fire throughout the entire attack, and by the end of the day the Marines would pay a price for their assault.

The 17 Corsairs of VMF-223 pushed over at 12,000 ft. with a 60 degree dive angle. All but one of the bombs was released in the target area, but any hits went unobserved. As the planes escaped at tree top level, four of the Corsairs strafed a truck, pouring .50 caliber rounds into its front. As the squadron made its way back to Piva, a bomb was dropped on buildings and huts at Kara Plantation on Bougainville.[39]

The Corsairs of VMO-251 fared a bit better than VMF-223 when it came to hitting their designated target. All of the bombs appeared to hit in the target area except one, which had to be jettisoned. McMasters' Corsair (BuNo 56410) was hit by intense AA fire. Unable to keep his plane in the air, McMasters had to abandon it about 15 miles northeast of Praed Point. He attempted to roll the plane over on its back, but the nose dropped off and the plane side-slipped out of the roll just as he bailed out. McMasters struck the horizontal stabilizer, suffering a broken leg near the hip. Jennings and Foley circled overhead, noticing an object fall from McMasters' chute. At first they thought it was the pilot falling out of his chute, but it turned out to be his rubber boat with oxygen bottle attached, which fell out of the boat pack and was lost on the way down.

With his broken leg, hitting the water must have been painful for McMasters. Despite the injury, he struggled free of his parachute harness and kept his head above water with the aid of his Mae West. Dumbo rescued him within thirty minutes after he hit the water.

Jennings' plane was also hit by AA fire. His plane was hit beneath the right wing just outboard of the gull angle, making a six inch hole and peppering the topside of the wing with nearly a dozen shrapnel holes. His plane was also hit by a .50 caliber bullet which traveled the entire length of the fuselage and exited on the port side just forward of the vertical stabilizer. Jennings was able to get his plane back to Piva with the remaining Corsairs of his squadron, but it did require a wing change upon return.

Right on the heels of VMO-251's attack, the 12 Corsairs of VMF-215 began their run on the target. Diving in from 13,500 feet they released their 1,000 pound payloads. All the bombs appeared to hit the target area, with one damaging hit claimed. Two of the Corsairs were damaged during the attack; one was hit in the engine cowling, and another plane was hit in the air intake by shrapnel. None of the pilots were injured, and all of VMF-215's Corsairs returned to Emirau safely by 1045.[40]

Next up were the 12 Corsairs of RNZAF 21 Squadron at 0915. Unfortunately they reported no hits on the gun positions, but claimed two hits on revetments near the southeast end of the airstrip.[41]

Five minutes later, VMF-115 and VMF-211 attacked. The six Corsairs of VMF-115 came in from the south to attack the gun emplacements, and started their dives at 13,000 feet. They released their 1,000 pound bombs between 5,000 and 6,000 feet. The Corsairs strafed during their dives, and on retirement out to the shore. One division attacked gun emplacements south of the airfield, while the other division could not attack its primary target on the south end and ended up dropping on a secondary target. Unfortunately no fires or explosions resulted from the attack. One plane could not release his bomb over the target, but dropped it over huts just south of Mission Point as the planes retired. The Corsairs made it back to Emirau undamaged by 1055.[42]

Coming in from the southeast, the 12 Corsairs of VMF-211 were assigned to attack areas "A," "B," and "C." Japanese AA fire assaulted the Corsairs before they made their attacks and during their bomb runs. All bombs were believed to have been dropped in their designated target areas, but no direct hits were observed on any AA gun. Disappointed, they turned for Emirau and arrived at 1030.[43]

Last to make their attack were the Dauntless dive bombers of VMSB-243 at 0925. They claimed one direct hit and four damaging hits on AA gun positions, as well as a damaging hit on an underground storage dump in target areas "S" and "T." Their success came at a price: one plane lost and three possibly damaged. First Lieutenant Herbert L. Chaitin was last seen to pull out of his dive with his engine on fire—an apparent victim of AA fire—flying at tree top level. His gunner, PFC Jospeh Letronico, was firing his gun at anything worth targeting. His fellow squadron mates did not see Chaitin's plane crash. The wreckage was found approximately one mile north of Keravat, about 100 yards from the beach. Apparently, Chaitin tried to make a forced landing on a nearby road. The plane's left wing was torn off, and the plane was burning. Both Chaitin and Letronico were listed as MIA—presumed dead. The remaining planes of the squadron landed at Emirau at 1055.[44]

The results of the 18 August strike were not any better than the 15 August strike and it came at a higher cost: two planes lost and five damaged. Despite months of pounding, the Japanese let the Marines know they still packed a punch.

Bad weather grounded all missions on 19 August. Seven of the squadron officers earned a ticket to Sydney, Australia for a well-earned rest: Humberd, Sigan, Inglehart, Sturgis, Furlow, Scoville and Cunningham. With Humberd gone, Bacheler assumed temporary command of the squadron until Humberd's return.

Weather was still a concern on 20 August for the planned attack on AA positions and a supply area at Tonolei Harbor facilities on southern Bougainville. Teller and Corman took off early in the morning for a weather hop in preparation of the strike. As they made their way towards the planned target, the weather front appeared to be breaking, allowing the mission to go ahead. Teller and Corman returned to the base.

Participating in the attack were VMO-251—providing divisions led by Teller, Smith and Jolink—VMF-223 providing another dozen Corsairs, and 12 Corsairs from RNZAF 21 Squadron out of Torokina. One of VMO-251's Corsairs was unable to take off due to a flat tail wheel. The attacking planes arrived over the target area at around 1125. Unfortunately, no direct hits were observed by the 1,000 pounders dropped by the Corsairs. However, pilots of VMF-223 reported seeing two fires burning on Kleiner Island hit by Teller's division. Japanese fire was light and inaccurate and no planes were hit. However, Foley's plane had the skin ripped off its port wing tip, bottom and topside. It's unclear what caused the damage but it was not attributed to the AA fire. The planes returned to their respective bases by 12:25.

Pilots got a break from the stress of combat on 21 August when flying was secured for the day. Bacheler would need the rest for the next day's mission. It would put his flying skills, as well as his leadership skills, to the test.

On 22 August, 12 Corsairs consisting of Bacheler's, Hart's, and Fowler's division, along with 12 Corsairs led by Drucker of VMF-223 were to strike Rataval—a Japanese bivouac and supply area southwest of Rabaul on Talili Bay. They were to carry 500 pound magnesium clusters but to get them the two squadrons had to fly to Green Island. This they did but the weather was so bad between Green Island and Rabaul that the strike to Rataval was scrubbed. Bacheler and Drucker got together and decided to strike a Japanese bivouac near the Bovo River in the Arawa Bay area, about 30 miles across Bougainville from Piva. Ten of the 12 squadron planes took off from Green Island at 1125—two Corsairs developed starter problems—with Bacheler in overall command of the strike.

The Corsairs hit bad weather to the north of Bougainville. VMF-223 turned back to Green Island, but Bacheler's Corsairs continued to the agreed target. Bacheler writes:

> The weather was clear and sunny as we took off at Green Island, but fifteen minutes after takeoff we came to a massive squall line extending from the surface to some astronomical altitude far above our capability and blacker than coal. It seemed to stretch as far as we could see in either direction. After paralleling it for awhile in an easterly direction Dave announced that he was taking his four-plane division[45] back to Green and that I could do as I liked, but he was satisfied that he had done his best. I decided to try to find a soft spot in the front by dropping down to sea level and going under it, to which Dave replied that he thought I was crazy and he would "join me in hell some day, only not now!"
>
> As the division swung around and headed back, I told my guys that anybody who wanted to join the other group was under no obligation to stick with me. Nobody defected, which I considered a nice tribute and down we went to about 100 feet above the water, still paralleling the squall line. After about ten minutes I spotted a light area to my right, indicating sunshine beyond a curtain of light rain, turned my division around to head southwest and went on instruments, hoping like hell that I wasn't leading them into the "eye" of a typhoon. This time I didn't have to worry about ice, although the rain was quite heavy for about five minutes. My guys all hung in tight, and suddenly we burst out into sunlight again, with nothing but blue sky ahead. Five more minutes and Bougainville Island appeared on the horizon. We pasted our target at Arawe Bay as planned and landed back at Piva North for lunch as though we had been out for a Sunday sight-seeing jaunt. I have always been proud of that mission, a sense of having done a good job. I received an Air Medal and accompanying citation for it. I was happy with the fact that I had done the RIGHT THING, in pressing home the attack under adverse conditions.[46]

The weather that had hampered strikes to New Britain and New Ireland over the last few days finally broke on 23 August, allowing COMAIRNORSOL to continue pounding the Japanese on the two islands. VMO-251's target, along with Corsairs from VMF-223 and RNZAF 19 Squadron, was Rataval.

Flying for VMO-251 were divisions led by Teller (flight leader), Smith and Jennings for a total of 12 Corsairs. VMF-223 consisted of 12 Corsairs for the strike, as well as RNZAF 19 Squadron out of Torokina. The mission was staged out of Green Island where the Corsairs of the two Marine squadrons were loaded with 500 pound magnesium clusters, while the New Zealanders were armed with 500 pound incendiaries. RNZAF 19 Squadron took off from Green Island at 0830, while the two Marine squadrons took off at approximately 0930. One of VMO-251's Corsairs, piloted by Robinson, was unable to take off on time due to starter trouble. Maintenance crews were able to correct the problem, allowing Robinson to try and catch up with his squadron.

The New Zealanders arrived over Rataval at approximately 0930 and dropped all of their incendiaries in the target area, starting several fires and sending columns of black smoke 1,500 feet into the air. Japanese AA fire from the east side of the target was inaccurate, causing no damage to the New Zealand Corsairs.

Next to attack was VMF-223. As they approached the target, one of the planes developed engine problems, causing the pilot to abort his attack on the target. Accompanied by his wingman, the two Corsairs returned to Piva, jettisoning their clusters along the way. Despite no AA fire from the Japanese, the remaining 10 Corsairs dropped only five of their bombs in the target area. No fires or explosions were observed by the retiring planes.[47]

The VMO-251 Corsairs were the last to attack—coming in from the sea—dropping all 11 of their clusters in the target area, starting several small fires and creating plenty of smoke over the area. As they gathered at the rendezvous point for the return trip home, they saw three columns of smoke, perhaps started by the New Zealanders an hour before. The 11 Corsairs arrived home at 1040.

Robinson, taking off late from Green Island, could not catch up with the squadron. He returned to Piva via Hapan, Buka Island, where he dropped his 500 pound cluster on a group of thatched huts, setting fire to three of them. He then turned for Piva, arriving there before the squadron.

The last few months of constant operations put a severe strain on the aircraft. Maintenance crews did a superlative job to keep the planes serviceable: the squadron always had the assigned number of planes ready for any mission it was ordered to fly. Despite this, many of the planes required extensive maintenance so on 24 August the squadron stood down, giving the maintenance crews a full, uninterrupted day to work on the Corsairs.

The next day was a busy one for the aircraft under COMAIRNORSOL. The main effort on 25 August was directed at Rabaul's Simpson Harbor. Targets on New Ireland as well as targets in Bougainville were also hit.

Three squadrons participated in the strike on Simpson Harbor: VMSB-236 providing 17 Dauntless dive bombers, VMF-223 providing 18 Corsairs, and VMO-251 providing 18 Corsairs that included divisions led by Bacheler, Jolink, Hart, Fowler as well as a section of two aircraft piloted by Rosellen and MacLachlan. Eight Corsairs from 223 and ten Corsairs from 251 carried a 1,000 bomb, while the dive bombers of 236 carried one 500 pounder and two 250 pounders apiece. Eight planes led by 251's Hart were assigned to strafe, as were eight planes from 223. These planes did not carry any bombs.

The attack plan called for VMSB-236 to strike AA gun positions near Hospital Ridge and Matupi Island guns to the east and south of Simpson Harbor while the two Corsair squadrons were given to the assignment of knocking out gun emplacements along the southwest shore of the harbor. The planes designated to strafe were given the mission of knocking out barges along the west shore of the harbor.

Unfortunately a solid bank of white clouds over the target, with a base at about 4,000 feet and stretching to 11,000 feet, interfered with the attacks of all the squadrons. First to encounter problems was VMSB-236, arriving over the target area at 0940.

The seventeen dive bombers of VMSB-236 could not attack their primary targets due to the cloud cover. They turned around and ended up striking guns to the west of the harbor. They scored two direct hits on buildings and three damaging hits on gun emplacements.

The attack came at a cost. AA fire struck Captain Ralph L. Pasley's plane, damaging a leading edge flap near the wing root and hitting Pasley in the foot. He struggled to keep his plane in the air, making it to Green Island where he crash landed the plane. Both he and his gunner survived. The plane was written off.[48]

As VMSB-236 began their attack, the Corsairs of VMF-223 entered the fray. The eight Corsairs carrying bombs could not attack their primary target due to the clouds so they attacked 20mm gun positions north of Vulcan crater, reporting a damaging hit on a gun director. As for the planes assigned to strafe, they ended up peppering four to six unserviceable barges south of Walaur since the weather obscured the barges on the west side. Upon retirement, one of the planes strafed the west end of Lakunai, and three or four barges north of Matupi Island with unknown results.[49]

Last to put their mark on the attack were the Corsairs of VMO-251. The dive bombing attack began at 10,500 feet when the 10 Corsairs nosed over into 60 degree dive angles. At 3,000 feet the bombs were released. Four of the planes released their bombs, with Rosellen scoring a direct hit on the AA position. Three of the planes had trouble finding their assigned targets, so they turned around and dropped their bombs at 1,800 feet while in a very shallow glide. Three other planes did not drop on their assigned targets: one pilot's windshield became covered with oil, obscuring his vision; another pilot forgot to turn to turn on his master gun switch, preventing the bomb from releasing; and Enders' cockpit was showered with urine which had collected in a clogged up relief tube just as he pushed over to make his run. The three pilots ended up striking targets of opportunity on New Ireland and Duke of York.

The two divisions assigned to strafe did not do so due to reduced visibility over the target, which hindered their ability to determine if all the bombers were clear of the target. As they retired from the area, two of the planes strafed a barge north of Vulcan Crater.[50]

All of the squadron's planes returned safely, landing at Piva by 1115.

At 1330, Jennings led his division consisting of Barton, Maclachlan and Neilson to strafe and bomb a coastal defense gun position at Moila Point on the southeast tip of Bougainville. Carrying 500 pounders, they dropped their bombs at 25 feet scoring three damaging hits and destroyed three huts which were set on fire while they strafed during their attack run. On the return trip to Piva by way of Buka Island, the division spotted a barge—apparently in working order—just off the west coast of the island, at Karsorilao.

The four planes landed at Piva around 1600. Ordnance crews loaded up each plane with one 1,000 pound bomb, setting the fuses for a 4 to 5 second delay. Forty-five minutes later they were back in the air to attack the barge they had located earlier. Find it they did and dropped their bombs in level flight at 25 feet. Unfortunately, all four bombs fell short, skipped over the barge, and exploded on the beach. The four planes turned around to strafe the barge, pumping over 3,000 rounds of .50 caliber ammunition at the barge, turning it into a sieve. During the strafing run one of the planes struck a tree, damaging a wing. The planes returned safely, landing at 1800. Maintenance crews immediately went to work to replace the wing on the damaged Corsair.

AA guns and barges in and around Simpson Harbor were once again the target of the attack on 26 August. Fifteen Dauntless dive bombers from VMSB-236, each armed with one 500 pounder and two 250 pounders, as well as Corsairs from VMF-223 and VMO-251 (consisting of divisions led by Teller, Hart, Smith and Jennings) participated in the attack. Eight Corsairs in 223 and 251 were armed with 1,000 pound bombs with the remainder of the Corsairs in each squadron assigned to strafe. Also getting into the action was a dive bomber squadron out of Green Island.

The dive bombing squadron out of Green Island was the first to strike, with the attack commencing at approximately 0930. They hit AA positions near Hospital Ridge and Matupi Island. The squadron reported direct hits on machine gun positions and damaging hits on several automatic weapons. The Japanese put up a stout defense, damaging two of the dive bombers.[51]

Five minutes later, the remainder of the squadrons began their attacks. Confusion reigned, with at least one squadron disrupting the attack of another. VMO-251's attack plan called for its Corsairs carrying the 1,000 pounders to attack gun positions south and west of the harbor. The first two fighters hit two auto AA gun positions on the southeast side of Vulcan Crater with no results seen. The next four planes struck suspected AA positions north of a facility called the Vulcan Barge Hide. The first two planes had one dud and one hung bomb, which later fell off as the plane retired. As the next two Corsairs were about to release their bombs, dive bombers of VMSB-236 slid in underneath them for their attack run. The Corsairs broke off their attack to prevent any mishap, and flew on to strike gun positions near Vulcan Crater. The last two Corsairs ended up bombing an auto AA position north of Vulcan Crater.

As for the bomb carrying Corsairs of VMF-223, they struck targets south and west of the harbor but apparently scored no hits.[52]

The dive bombers of VMSB-236 attacked gun positions northwest and west of the harbor. A gun position was blown to bits, witnessed by a Corsair that saw its gun flying into the air.[53]

The Corsairs assigned to strafe barges fared better than the dive bombers. VMO-251's Jennings and Barton set two barges on fire at Toboi Wharf while Hart's division holed three other barges. Jennings also started a fire among some buildings on Kabakon Island, Duke of York as the planes retired from the target area. Damage caused by the strafing Corsairs of VMF-223 is unknown.

Squadron Corsairs retired to Piva by way of Matupi Island and Raluana Point. One Corsair was slightly damaged upon landing when its tail wheel failed to extend.

VMF-223 (15 Corsairs) and VMO-251 (16 Corsairs) paired up once again to bomb and strafe the Rataval supply area inland of Talili Bay and west of Rabaul on 27 August. Both squadrons first flew to Green Island where each plane was loaded up with one 500 pound magnesium cluster. The squadrons took off from Green Island, less three VMO-251 planes, at 0930. One plane damaged an elevator while taxiing, another had starter problems and one aircraft returned to Green Island after developing engine problems.

Following a 50 minute flight, both squadrons commenced their attack. All the Corsairs covered the target area, starting numerous fires. One fire was large enough to create a column of smoke extending nearly 1,500 feet into the air. The Japanese offered little resistance, and all planes made it back to Piva by 1050.

Both squadrons were back up in the air on 28 August. Carrying 1,000 pounders, 16 Corsairs of VMO-251 and 15 Corsairs of VMF-223[54] struck the Wunawatung truck park and a gun position on Cape Liguan, several miles west of the town of Rabaul.

Teller had overall command of the 251 Corsairs consisting of his division and those led by Hart, Smith and Jennings. Arriving over the target, both squadrons commenced their attack. Both the truck park and the AA gun position were apparently destroyed. VMF-223 reported that the 12 251 pilots attacking the truck park covered it thoroughly, obliterating the target. Four 251 Corsairs dropped three bombs on the AA position, apparently scoring a direct hit. The planes of both squadrons landed back at Piva by noon.[55]

Neilson, MacLachlan. Jennings, Foley, Frank and McCabe flew fighter sweeps around Bougainville and Buka during the course of the day. No Japanese activity was spotted and all planes returned safely.

COMAIRNORSOL put up nearly its entire strength of aircraft on 30 August to hit suspected Japanese personnel areas in the Pondo—Toriu district on the west coast of the

Gazelle Peninsula on New Britain. Beginning at 0725, squadrons from Green Island, Emirau and Piva pounded the Japanese continuously for five hours, dropping over 66 tons of ordnance.[56]

VMO-251's turn in the attack came shortly after 1000. Bacheler led 15 Corsairs consisting of his division and divisions led by Jolink, Jennings and Fowler. One plane remained behind due to engine failure on takeoff. Barton kept control of his aircraft, landing it with only damage to the tires.

Each of the Corsairs carried a 500 pound bomb, and all were dropped in the target area. The thick jungle prevented the pilots from observing any damage their bombs may have caused. Several huts were set on fire during a strafing run as the Corsairs flew over the Toriu River as they retired.

One plane was damaged during the attack. Gaining a 4 inch hole in the top of his cockpit hood was 1Lt. Orville R. Swick. He suffered lacerations to the face around his right eye due to the damage. What caused the hole could not be determined. Despite his injury, Swick was able to bring his Corsair safely to Piva. All the Corsairs were back in time for noon chow.

The mission for 30 August was another trip back to the Japanese supply area inland from the eastern shore of Talili Bay—Rataval. Bacheler led the mission, which consisted of his division and Hart's division.

The planes staged through Green Island in order to load up with 500 pound magnesium clusters. Arriving over the target area at 1010, they dropped all the clusters in the target area igniting a dozen fires and sending plenty of smoke into the air. As the last planes made their attack runs, some of the smoke columns extended to 1,000 feet.

The Japanese remained silent; no AA fire was encountered. All eight Corsairs landed at Piva by 1130.

While Bacheler led the attack on Rataval, 12 other pilots flew fighter sweeps to several locations. Jennings' division took off at 0710, armed with 500 pounders. They ended up bombing huts along a road about two miles south Keravat Airfield. The second division, led by Smith, took off at 0800 to strafe huts along the Cape Lambert shore. They ended up smoking two of them before returning at 1100. Armed with 500 pound bombs, Fowler's division took off at 1245 and struck buildings on the west end of the Buka Airstrip on Buka Island. They returned at 1400 without knowing if there bombs caused any damage.

The squadron was back to bomb and strafe Rataval on 31 August. Hart led the 16 plane strike, consisting of his division, and that of Smith, Jolink and Jennings. The Corsairs, each armed with one 500 pound general purpose bomb, took off at 1010. They reached Rataval an hour later, finding it obscured by clouds. Only two of the 16 Corsairs attacked Rataval, the rest selected other targets, among them buildings further south along Talili Bay. Several hits were made, and a few huts started to smoke. Hart had engine problems, so he and his wingman jettisoned their bombs and returned to Piva.

Foley, thinking he had made a direct hit on his target, turned around to try and get a confirmation. Flying at 1,200 feet and accompanied by his wingman Barton, they encountered AA fire between near Tawui Point. Foley's plane (BuNo 56261)[57] took a 20mm hit in the engine. His plane continued in a northerly direction, did a half roll, went into a vertical dive and plunged into the water about 1.5 miles northwest of Tawui Point. Foley's body was not recovered and he was declared Killed in Action. The rest of the Corsairs returned to Piva, landing at 1250.

September 1944

The first day of September saw the squadron hit a Japanese bivouac area near Malabeta Hill in southern Bougainville. Bacheler led the 12 plane strike, taking off at 1035. Within 35 minutes they were over the target area. Clouds hampered the attack but the pilots dropped all their 500 pounders in the target area, strafing as they went into their dives. Unfortunately, the dense jungle hid any results of the attack. No AA fire was encountered and the Corsairs returned to Piva by 1135.

On the morning of 2 September, Hart led his division on the Put Put—Keravat sweep. The four Corsairs took off at 0700 and reached the target area a little over an hour later. Huts at Keravat were strafed with no results to show for the expenditure of 3,000 rounds of .50 caliber ammunition. They were back at Piva by 0925.

Jennings' division followed Hart for the Duke of York—Cape Lambert sweep. The four Corsairs were in the air by 0755, each with a 500 pounder slung underneath it. They ended up scoring direct hits on huts one mile southeast of Keravat. As they continued their sweep, Jennings used his gun camera to photograph the truck park east of Cape Liguan. No Japanese activity was reported and the Corsairs returned to Piva by 1055.

Jolink's division took off at 1230 on the Put Put—Keravat sweep. Arriving over the target at 1330, they too had no luck strafing at Keravat. They were back home by 1500.

Smith's division was the last to fly for the day. Armed with 500 pounders, three of the Corsairs were wheels up by 1330. Rosellen had a flat tail wheel, delaying his takeoff while ground crews did a quick repair. He tried to catch up with the squadron once back in the air, but failed to do so. Rosellen ended up dropping his bomb on a large building on Buka Island and returned to Piva. Meanwhile, the other three Corsairs in his division hit Takis Plantation near Cape Lambert, smoking six huts. On their way back to Piva, they ended up strafing targets of opportunity on Duke of York. By 1615, the landed back at Piva.

It was back to Rataval on the morning of 3 September, with Teller leading 14 Corsairs to strike the Japanese supply area on the east coast of Talili Bay on New Britain. The attack was staged out of Green Island where each Corsair was armed with one 500 pound magnesium cluster.

The fighters took off from Green Island at 1000. When they arrived 50 minutes later, they saw numerous fires burning—started by planes from other squadrons that had already hit the target. The planes nosed over, strafing in their dives and released their clusters at 2,500 feet, placing all 14 clusters in the target area. AA fire was moderate with Flickinger's plane taking a possible hit. As the planes retired north, they strafed a group of buildings on the northeast shore of Watom Island, setting fire to them.

As the Corsairs made their way home, Flickinger began having problems with his hydraulic system. As he approached the base, he extended his landing gear. But there was a problem; one wheel remained partially retracted. Flickinger tried every trick in the book to get his stuck wheel in the down and locked position: using his CO2 bottle, manual pumping, and putting "G's" on the plane. None worked, and Flickinger decided to give up his plane (BuNo 56099). At 6,000 feet and four miles west of Puruata Island in Empress Augusta Bay, he bailed out.

Flickinger was not injured and he was pulled from the bay within minutes by a Navy launch cruising in the vicinity. Flickinger made it back to Piva North to meet his comrades for noon chow, who had landed at 1210.

Weather pretty much scrubbed out the missions set for 4 September. Three divisions took off at various times during the course of the day but all had to turn back due to the lousy weather. One division, carrying 500 pound bombs, detoured to Buka Island on the way back to Piva. They dropped their bombs in level flight at 2,500 feet on huts and buildings on the west coast of the island, but results were not seen. The last division landed at Piva at 1440, No other missions were flown for the remainder of the day.

Sixteen Corsairs, each armed with a 1,000 pound bomb, took off at 0735 on 5 September to attack a Japanese supply area located to the north of Praed Point, east of Rabaul. Led by Teller, 14 of the 16 Corsairs dropped their bombs in the target area. No results were seen, and no smoke was spotted as the Corsairs retired from their strike. They were back at Piva by 1015.

Weather washed out the missions for 6 and 7 September. Bacheler was to lead a 16 plane strike on Kahili on 6 September, but 15 minutes after takeoff they were forced to turn around due to bad weather. Flying was cancelled for the rest of the day. Fowler's division was able to fly the dawn patrol on 7 September, but Jolink's division, assigned the Put Put—Keravat sweep was unable to complete his mission as weather forced them to return to Piva. The day also saw the return of Humberd and Furlow from their stay in Sydney, Australia.

The squadron flew two missions on 8 September. The first, with Humberd leading his division and divisions led by Teller, Furlow and Hart, was to strike the suspected location of the Japanese Naval Headquarters at Kahili. The 16 Corsairs, each loaded with a 1,000 pound bomb, took off at 0710 and arrived over the target at 0745. Fifteen of the Corsairs put their bombs in the target area but jungle growth prevented any visual confirmation of damage. As Captain Hart retired over water, he received intense AA fire from a large hulk lying just off shore from Kahili. Hart returned the favor by blasting the hulk with his .50 caliber machine guns. Luckily, Hart's plane was not hit, and all the planes returned to Piva by 0815.

The second mission for the day involved the division led by Jennings. The four planes were assigned the Cape Gazelle—Lemingi fighter sweep. Each plane carried a 500 pound bomb for the sweep, and took off at 1330. Weather prevented the Corsairs from hitting their primary target so they were diverted to a secondary target. They ended up strafing and dropping their bombs on huts at the northern tip of Bougainville. Because of weather over Piva, the planes were diverted to Green Island where they landed at 1645. They returned to Piva the following morning.

The following morning the squadron once again struck two different targets. Divisions led by Hart, Teller and Furlow took off at 1110 to hit a Japanese supply area near Kiano, Bougainville. Following a 20 minute flight, the twelve Corsairs pounded the target area with 500 pounders and over 3,500 rounds of .50 caliber ammunition. Cloud cover over the target prevented the pilots from confirming any damage. They were back at Piva 10 minutes after striking the target.

Jolink led his division for another afternoon mission to hit Buka Island. They took off at 1320 and arrived over their selected target—a group of huts on the north coast of the island—at 1415. Haze and clouds obscured the target and no hits could be seen. Enders couldn't release his bomb during the attack; he ended up jettisoning it over water as they retired back to Piva. The four Corsairs touched down at 1525.

Flying patrols was the order of the day for 10 September. Six two plane patrols, taking off at 0615 and continuing until 1800, searched the entire southern coast of Bougainville extending all the way to Buka.

Japanese were spotted on the beaches of Buka and at Metong Point in south Bougainville. The planes strafed the enemy, killing at least 12. In doing so they expended 14,000 rounds of .50 caliber ammunition throughout the day.

The severe tropical weather rolled in again on 11 September, making flying impossible for the day. The next day, weather played a role in the loss of one of the squadron pilots.

September 12 started out well enough. Henley led his division on an early morning strike to Keravat, taking off at 0730. A half hour later, Furlow led his division on an attack at Vunabal Plantation. The planes dropped their bombs in their respective target areas, but jungle growth prevented the pilots from determining the results of their attack. All planes returned to Piva by 1045.

Taking off at 0730, Teller led his division on the Duke of York—Cape Lambert sweep. At 0915, the planes struck huts at Barnard Plantation on Duke of York Island, scoring four area hits with unknown results.

As the four aircraft returned to Piva, they ran into a solid front 20 miles east of Cape Gazelle. The Corsairs entered the front through a small opening in the clouds, but quickly lost sight of each other. Tanner did catch a quick glimpse of Teller, Robinson and Moynihan turning back. Tanner stuck to his course and flew through the front. Moments later Teller and Moynihan appeared, and Tanner quickly joined up with them. Robinson's plane (BuNo 50157) did not make it through. He was last seen flying on a course of 120 degrees at 1,000 feet, about 20 miles east of Cape Gazelle. He was originally listed as MIA, but was later declared KIA. Teller, Tanner and Moynihan returned safely to Piva.

The pace of operations for the squadron slowed down for the next two days. Weather scrubbed all missions on 13 September, while the squadron flew several patrols over south Bougainville on 14 September with no results to show for their efforts. On the 13th, eight officers joined the squadron: 1Lt. Roy C. Gray, Jr., 1Lt. Thomas B. Heisel, 1Lt. William E. Mussman, Jr., 1Lt. Arthur W. Poehlman, 1Lt. Arthur J. Warren, Jr., 2Lt. Bernadine J. Daigle, and 2Lt. Preston L. Kammeyer.

Major Humberd led a 16 plane strike on 15 September. Carrying 1,000 pounders, their mission was to bomb and strafe a Japanese supply dump at Chabai in northwest Bougainville. Over the target by 0840, the pilots found it difficult to locate the target due to the dense jungle growth. Despite this, the planes dropped all their bombs in the designated target area. The last division to attack reported the target area was well covered. However, results were difficult to observe and no smoke was seen as the planes retired to Piva. The Japanese offered no resistance; none of planes were damaged in the attack. They were back at Piva by 1000.

The squadron put up another 16 Corsairs on 16 September, attacking the same target as the previous day. Humberd once again led the strike. The results were the same; the target area was thoroughly covered but results could not be determined.

Also on 16 September, three new officers joined the squadron: 1Lt. John A. Kennicott, 2Lt. James M. Gorman and 2Lt. Archibald A. Harris. With the previous addition of new officers on the 13th, a large change in squadron personnel appeared to be around the corner.

The 17 September mission was a bust. Smith, Neilson, MacLachlan and Henley took off at 1300 for the Duke of York—Cape Lambert sweep. No attacks were made since the four pilots saw no sign of Japanese activity, and no targets of any value were spotted.

Detail of Cape Gazelle, New Britain, targets. Map adapted from ComAirNorSols Intelligence Summary, 23 September 1944 (National Archives).

Sixteen Corsairs were assigned to attack the supply and bivouac area at Raluana Point, New Britain on 18 September. Each plane was armed with a 500 pounder and loaded with 4,600 rounds of .50 caliber ammunition to accomplish their mission. With Furlow in the lead, the Corsairs took off at 0850. Arriving over the target an hour later, the pilots strafed and bombed the target area, but once again results could not be ascertained. Japanese resistance was non-existent, and all planes returned to Piva unscathed.

In addition to the officers joining the squadron over the last few day, two more found themselves assigned to the squadron: 1Lt. Joseph A. Conroy and 1Lt. Ollie O. Jones.

On 19 September, sixteen planes each armed with a 1,000 pound bomb and led by Humberd, took off 0630 to attack a Japanese bivouac position on Porton Plantation in northwest Bougainville. After a 30 minute flight, 13 of the 16 Corsairs unloaded their bombs on the plantation getting good coverage of the target area. Three planes had hung bombs, two of which were jettisoned and one carried back to Piva. In what was becoming a frustrating problem, results of the attack could not be determined. All planes made it back to Piva shortly after 1000.

The following day, Teller led 16 Corsairs to hit an enemy bivouac area at Makurapau Plantation located to the east of Tobera Airfield on New Britain. Taking off at 0915, weather forced the strike force to turn back and hit the secondary target—Porton Plantation. The target area was plastered, but once again the results of the strike could not be determined. The Corsairs were back at Piva by 1010.

On 21 September, 16 Corsairs led by Humberd were scheduled to attack suspected Japanese troop concentrations near Raluana Point in the Rabaul area. At Green Island, the flight stopped to load up with 500 pound magnesium clusters. Ordnance crews had the planes loaded in about an hour. As the squadron Corsairs took off to resume their mission, four of the planes developed starter or tire problems and stayed behind as the remaining planes pushed on to hit their assigned target.

The 12 Corsairs that pressed on to the target commenced their attack at 1040. The target area was covered well by the magnesium clusters, but no specific results were observed as the planes retired. As for the four Corsairs that were late in taking off, they ended up attacking the Japanese bivouac area at Baniu Plantation in northwest Bougainville. They too covered their target area with all their clusters, and once again results could not be determined. Planes from both missions made it back to Piva without damage.

The mission for 22 September involved four squadrons, all from Piva: VMF-223, VMO-251, VMSB-236 and VMSB-133. COMAIRNORSOL assigned these four squadrons to attack a suspected Japanese bivouac and supply area in the region of Makurapau and Kulon Plantations near the northeast tip of the Gazelle Peninsula on New Britain. This was the main effort by COMAIRNORSOL, which also ordered strikes near Rabaul and Bougainville.[58]

The Dauntless dive bombers of VMSB-133 and -236 were the first to attack. They combined to destroy or damage nearly a dozen huts.[59] VMO-251, with 16 Corsairs led by Bacheler, scored two direct hits on a group of buildings—probably pulverizing a few of them—while placing their 1,000 pounders in the target area. VMF-223 Corsairs were the last to attack, knocking out a MG position as well as destroying three houses.[60]

It was a good day for COMAIRNORSOL; 184 sorties were flown, with 65 tons of ordnance dropped on Japanese targets. The tally: over 15 huts destroyed, seven buildings destroyed, three huts set on fire and probably destroyed, four huts and four buildings damaged, and four bridges destroyed. All this was accomplished without a single loss from the participating squadrons.[61]

Major Humberd led sixteen Corsairs for an early morning strike on 23 September. Fifteen of them took off at 0640; Jolink stayed behind due to a flat tail wheel. Armed with 1,000 pound bombs, the remaining Corsairs struck a Japanese bivouac area on Baniu Plantation in northeast Bougainville 30 minutes after takeoff. It was difficult to see the target because of dense jungle growth in the area, hence only one bomb was observed to hit the target area. Two of the planes had hung bombs which were eventually shaken off. Once again the Japanese were quite, offering no resistance. The Corsairs returned to Piva without a scratch, landing at 0740.

On 24 September COMAIRNORSOL ordered another big strike, this time on the Ralum supply dump. Once again the squadrons called on to fly the main strike on 22 September flew this mission: VMF-223, VMO-251, VMSB-133 and VMSB-236. Unfortunately the weather did not cooperate. The ever present tropical storms forced planners to have the squadrons strike secondary targets on Bougainville.

Within 10 minutes starting at 1015, several targets were hit. The Corsairs of VMF-223 were the first to strike, hitting several locations including Koromira, Kieta, Anusagaro Island, and Arakawaun. Clouds interfered with their strike on Koromira with four misses, and the rest of their bombs falling out of the target area. Results of strafing attacks on the remaining three locations went unobserved.

At 1020, SDBs of VMSB-133 bombed and strafed huts near Kieta Airfield and Chivorante. Pilots reported obliterating 11 huts, damaging six others and destroying a bridge.[62]

Furlow led his 16 Corsairs for a strike on suspected Japanese occupied buildings in Auda located 15 miles south of Kieta on the east coast of Bougainville. Even there, clouds prevented the Corsairs from performing their customary high angle dives to strike the target. Instead, they went in at a 45 degree angle, releasing their bombs at 2,500 feet. Five direct hits were seen, destroying at least 10 huts.

The squadron from Piva to hit their target was VMSB-236, bombing huts at Mabiri Plantation down the coast to the Kieta airstrip. Three huts were destroyed at Makiki, and six others were damaged on the beach at Puk Puk Island.

With other squadrons participating in strikes throughout the Northern Solomon Islands and the Bismarck Archipelago, the day's tally was a good one. With 158 sorties flown, 60 tons of bombs were dropped on Japanese positions. Forty-two huts and one bridge were destroyed. Eighteen huts and one bridge were damaged. At least three Japanese were killed. In all instances Japanese resistance was non-existent to meager. The squadrons lost no planes, and all returned safely to Piva.

Weather washed out flying on 25 September, and would linger to affect flying for the next several days.

On 26 September, Humberd was to lead 16 Corsairs on a strike on the Ralum supply area. One plane did not get off the ground due a flat tail wheel, and one other developed engine trouble on the way to the target. Bowers, accompanied by his wingman, turned back to Piva. Humberd and his remaining Corsairs pushed on to Ralum, but found their way to the target blocked by a huge storm front. Finding no way through the front, they turned around to hit their secondary target: the Koromira Mission located about 15 miles south of Kieta on Bougainville. Four direct hits were scored, destroying at least seven buildings or huts, and damaging several more. Three planes bombed a bridge on the Meton River near Koromira but did not destroy it. The Corsairs returned to Piva by 1000.

No missions were flown for the rest of the month, bad weather scrubbing all flying. The only flying that occurred was on 29 September when 16 pilots received practice in night flying division tactics.

October 1944

Since it started flying missions in June, targets in New Britain and New Ireland received the brunt of the squadron's attacks. That changed in October when locations on

Five. Espiritu Santo, Green Island and Bougainville

the island of Bougainville became the primary focus of the squadron. Such was the case on 1 October when the squadron was tasked to strike the town of Numa Numa on the east coast of Bougainville. The mission was scrubbed due to weather, as was the dawn patrol. The only flying accomplished was the dusk patrol with Bacheler leading Crutcher, Pirages and Kennicott. Nothing was spotted during the patrol.

It was also on this day that the squadron was relieved of duty with MAG-24 and attached to MAG-14. The squadron would remain with MAG-14 for the remainder of its time in the war.

To round out the day, Schoetz and McMasters received Purple Hearts for their injuries received while in combat.

Strikes on Bougainville resumed on 2 October, with the squadron putting up 14 Corsairs for the day. Furlow led his and Hart's division on a mission to bomb and strafe Numa Numa Plantation. Seven of the eight Corsairs got off the ground; Garrett did not take off because of a flat tail wheel. The planes carried a mixed load of ordnance: four planes carried a 1,000 pounder and three planes carried a 500 pounder. All seven bombs landed on the target, creating two columns of black smoke 700 feet high. At least one structure was destroyed in the attack.

Jennings' division had the Put Put—Keravat sweep, but bad weather put an end to their mission. Unable to get through the storm front, the Corsairs were instructed to land at Green Island. This they did but only after they dropped their payload of 500 pounders on a village located in the center of Buka Island, and strafed huts throughout the island.

Daigle, Tanner and Kammeyer flew the south Bougainville patrol, strafing a bridge on the Tautaua River as well huts north of Kahili, setting two of them on fire.

The first of several transfers of officers out of the squadron began. Bowers, Corman, Enders, Fowler, Alfred and Harry Johnson, Jolink, McCabe, Spindler, and Swick were detached from the squadron for eventual transfer to the United States.

There were three missions flown on 3 October, all hitting targets on New Britain. Bacheler's division took off at 0800 on the Put Put—Keravat sweep. They dropped their 500 pounders on the Experimental Gardens at Keravat, cratering the gardens. Jones' division was wheels up at 0820—except for Harris whose plane was grounded at the last minute—for the Cape Gazelle—Lemingi sweep. The three Corsairs dropped 500 pounders on a road intersection, cratering it, and huts on Wat Wat Plantation on the east coast of the Gazelle Peninsula. Humberd's and Henley's divisions—less Henley, whose plane had a flat tail wheel—took off at 0920 to strike the Japanese Medical Depot at Waitavalo. They arrived over the target at 1025, and dropped seven 1,000 pounders. Luckily for the Japanese, none hit the depot. No Corsairs were damaged or destroyed the entire day.

Despite being busy with the fighter sweeps, the squadron's day wasn't finished. As the sun began to set, divisions led by Humberd, Hart, Jennings, Smith, Bacheler and Henley practiced night flying for a couple of hours and also worked on squadron tactics.

The squadron put up several divisions, as well as three two plane patrols, to strike various targets on Bougainville and New Britain on 4 October. Bacheler and his wingman, Pirages, smoked two huts—one at Luluai Point and the other north of Kieta. They also spotted Japanese expanding their gardens in order to supplement their food supply. Crutcher and Frank strafed a bridge at the mouth of the Tauraua River. They also spotted two Japanese soldiers near Kaukaui, but could not get their .50 caliber machine guns to bear on the fleeing soldiers. Henley and Harris strafed huts from Kieta to Koromira Mission. They too discovered the Japanese cultivating gardens near the Kiriwina Plantation.

Hart's division flew the Put Put—Keravat sweep. Carrying 500 pounders, they bombed buildings on the northeast end of the Experimental Gardens at Keravat. After they retired, the Corsairs strafed huts and villages at tree top level from Keravat to Tobera to Kabanga Bay.

Divisions led by Smith and Humberd handled the Cape Gazelle—Lemingi and the Duke of York—Cape Lambert sweeps respectively. Smith's four Corsairs bombed Tamalili Plantation and smoked 12 huts while strafing. Humberd's division bombed a village on Duke of York, damaging several huts while their strafing set two of the huts on fire.

Furlow led a 12 plane strike on a Japanese supply area near Talili Bay on 5 October. They attacked the target at 0835 following a one hour, 10 minute flight. Most of the bombs fell in the target area but no damage could be seen except for a small fire. As in the previous missions during the last few days, no Japanese AA fire was encountered.

Friday 6 October was a busy day for the squadron, sending three two plane patrols over the southern portion of Bougainville and several division strikes over New Britain. The first mission of the day began at 0735, when three divisions led by Furlow, Scoville, and Garrett took off for the Put Put-Keravat sweep. One pilot, Frank, did not take off because of a flat tire. He ended up flying with the next mission which took off ten minutes later. The remaining 11 Corsairs, carrying 500 pounders, ended up bombing huts at Balu Plantation and gardens at the Experimental Farms. No huts were damaged at Balu, while one of the gardens was cratered.

Smith, Neilson, Rosellen and MacLachlan, with Frank tagging along, were also assigned the Put Put-Keravat sweep and took off at 0745. Reaching the target at 1030, they remained to bomb and strafe various Japanese locations for 30 minutes. Smith smoked two huts at Kurrajong Plantation and a building at Wat Wat Plantation. Neilson drew fire from a lone Japanese soldier—apparently shouldering an automatic weapon—standing in a road on the plantation. Neilson lined up for strafing run on the soldier and let loose with his six .50 caliber machine guns. The strafing run was effective in silencing the machine gun. Next, during two strafing passes, Neilson smoked a hut at Malabunga. While flying over Vunabal Plantation, he spotted what appeared to be gasoline drums on a dirt road, with spurs from the road leading into several copse of trees. Rosellen, looking for a bridge on the Keravat River near the Experimental Farms, found none. After strafing huts at Malabunga, he followed a road from the village to the Warangoi River without spotting any Japanese activity. Maclachlan, after strafing huts at several of the locations mentioned, found truck activity in several open, grassy fields north of the Warangoi River. While flying near the Kabanga Plantation at 1,500 feet, MacLachlan's Corsair received a two inch hole in the starboard wing from a burst of enemy AA fire. The five planes expended over 4,000 rounds of ammunition during the sweep. The five pilots made it back to Piva by 1200.

Taking off at 1000, Henley, Harris, Heisel, and Poehlman for the Duke of York—Cape Lambert sweep. Reaching Duke of York at 1115, they strafed several villages on the island. They then moved on to Watom Island to the west. Following strafing runs on the small island, they ended up dropping their 500 pounders on a group of houses west of the Nambung River, east of Cape Lambert. Heisel scored the only hit, destroying two buildings.

Bacheler, Pirages, Schoetz and Crutcher, their Corsairs loaded with 500 pound bombs, took off at 1030 for the Cape Gazelle-Lemingi sweep. They strafed a barge at Kabanga Point and huts and buildings at Wat Wat and Put Put Plantations, with unknown results. Three of the planes dropped their bombs on huts at Makurapau Plantation with Bacheler scoring a damaging hit with his bomb. It was then on to strafe Ralabang Plantation. Bacheler, flying at tree top level at 200 knots, took several hits of 25mm AA fire in his port wing. His plane, as well as the others returned safely to Piva at 1245.

The first two plane patrol began when Teller and Moynihan took off at 0800. Following a short flight, the two pilots spotted a lone Japanese soldier tending a garden north of Kahili. He made a break for the jungle upon spotting the Corsairs as they began strafing the area. It's not known if the soldier escaped with his life. As the two pilots continued their patrol, they spotted an observation tower, and more Japanese working several gardens north of Kahili Airfield. Fifteen minutes later, Inglehart and Sturgis took off for their patrol but found a rain squall blanketing the southern part of the island. Sturgis spotted and strafed a Japanese soldier on Puk Puk Island while patrolling the northern coast near Kieta but did not get him. Cunningham and Daigle took off at 1000 for the last south Bougainville patrol for the day. They spotted an enemy soldier washing his clothes on rocks near the sea east of Moila Point. Spotting the Corsairs, the soldier made a run for the nearby jungle with Cunningham and Daigle soon strafing right behind him. When the two pilots returned an hour later as they made their way back to Piva, the soldier's clothes were still on the rock where he had left them.

The sweeps continued the next day. At 0745, Humberd, Sigan, Inglehart and Sturgis took off for the Duke of York—Cape Lambert sweep. The four planes attacked Urukukur village and Waterhouse Cove with 500 pound bombs. Humberd scored the only hit when he demolished several buildings in the village. The four Corsairs continued on to Cape Lambert, strafing huts and villages along the way. Upon return to Piva at 1105, the pilots reported that huts they observed during their sweep all appeared to be bombed out.

Taking off at 0800, Teller, Moynihan, Jones and Gorman flew the Cape Gazelle—Lemingi sweep. During their sweep, they dropped two bombs on a bridge at Put Put Harbor and a trench system north of the Warangoi River. The bridge was missed, but the pilots did crater the road leading to the bridge. They too observed that the huts and buildings all appeared to be shot up.

The afternoon sweep to Put Put, flown by Hart, Warren, Mussman and Gray was hampered by weather. Two parallel tropical fronts, running north to south, blocked their flight path. Hart called off the sweep and directed his flight back to Bougainville, where they dropped their payloads on a group of buildings at Butchkombo on the northeast coast of the island. Gray's bomb was seen to explode within the buildings but no one was able to confirm any damage.

Jennings, Erdmann, Conroy and Barton took off for the last sweep of the day. The two sections became separated due to the weather which turned back Hart's division. The sections did not join up again. Both sections, however, pushed on to their intended destination—Duke of York Island—and attacked separate targets on the island. Jennings and Erdmann damaged a few buildings on the northeast coast, while Conroy and Barton attacked huts on the south side of the island with Barton damaging one of them. All four planes strafed as they flew around the island after their bombing attacks before they flew home. Jennings and Erdman landed at Piva, but by the time Conroy and Barton reached Piva, weather had forced the closure of the field. They were directed to fly to Torokina to land. Conroy was able to land but by the time Barton was able to make his approach,

Photo taken in front of the squadron engineering office, location is not known. *Left to right:* **Al Madden, John Irwin, unknown and John Madden (courtesy Madden Family).**

weather socked in Torokina. After several attempts to land, he finally brought his plane down safely at 1610 after nearly four hours in the air.

The results of the first week of October after dropping 21 tons of bombs and expending over 70,000 rounds of .50 caliber ammunition stood at seven buildings destroyed, 13 smoked and four set on fire with an undetermined number possibly damaged. Two gardens were cratered as were two roads, and three Japanese may have been killed.

No combat missions were flown on 8 October since the squadron spent the day honing their gunnery skills. However, the day was marred when Daigle's plane (BuNo 56305) ran off the taxiway after landing during a rainstorm and flipped over on to its back. Upside down in a water-filled ditch, the uninjured Daigle scrambled out of the cockpit to safety.[63]

Several patrols flying over south Bougainville the next day would get a chance to put their strafing skills to the test. Five two plane patrols were scheduled, each lasting on average two hours. Heisel and Poehlman had the first patrol, taking off at 0615. Their patrol was uneventful except for some small activity between Kieta Airfield and Mt. Senfft, and Kaino-Kupai. They strafed both areas but any damage could not be determined. Having received reports from a friendly native of a Japanese observation post on a hill west of Koromira Mission, Henley and Harris took off at 0800 to investigate. They did find the post, basically a lean-to with a thatched roof. They also spotted well-maintained buildings at the base of a cliff four to eight miles south of Buka Passage. Both the observation post and the buildings were strafed by the pilots. Taking off at 0950 were Maclachlan and Sigan. Both observed many native huts and gardens within the area of Mt. Lawernz and along the shore two to three miles west of Kahili. They ended up strafing three derelict cargo vessels lying off shore from the village, huts at Kapui and a long catwalk bridge at Moro. Unlike the previous patrols, MacLachlan and Sigan received moderate AA fire from Kangu Hill but were not hit. Weather hampered Inglehart's and Sturgis' ability to observe any activity during the noon patrol. Clouds hung at 2,000 feet among the mountains which rose in some cases to 5,000 feet. They set a hut on fire at Bomamu during their strafing run there. After they retired from Bomamu, both pilots spent the next hour machine gunning huts and villages from Kupai to Kieta. The last patrol, flown by Cunningham and Daigle, took off at 1400. As they flew in the vicinity of Totavi, they observed six khaki-dressed soldiers carrying rifles. They were walking on the beach in the direction of Kahili. Both pilots decided not to strafe the soldiers who were near an area off-limits to any attacking allied aircraft. A dozen more soldiers were spotted on the beach closer to Kahili but for some reason Cunningham and Daigle could not get a shot at them.

The missions on 10 October had five divisions attacking targets in the New Britain area. Humberd's division, consisting of fellow pilots Sigan, Inglehart and Sturgis took off at 0750 for the Put Put—Keravat sweep. In addition to the sweep, Humbard and Sigan were given the additional assignment of making a low-level strafing run on revetments at the southwest end of Vunakanua Airfield. Intelligence suspected a serviceable twin-engine bomber at the field. The four Corsairs put their 500 pound bombs in the personnel area of the Experimental Farms at Keravat. The pilots were unable to observe the results. They then flew to Vunakanau Airfield where Humberd and Sigan began their strafing run. Flying at tree-top level from north to south, they strafed the field and the revetments. They didn't see the suspected bomber, only wrecks that had been at the

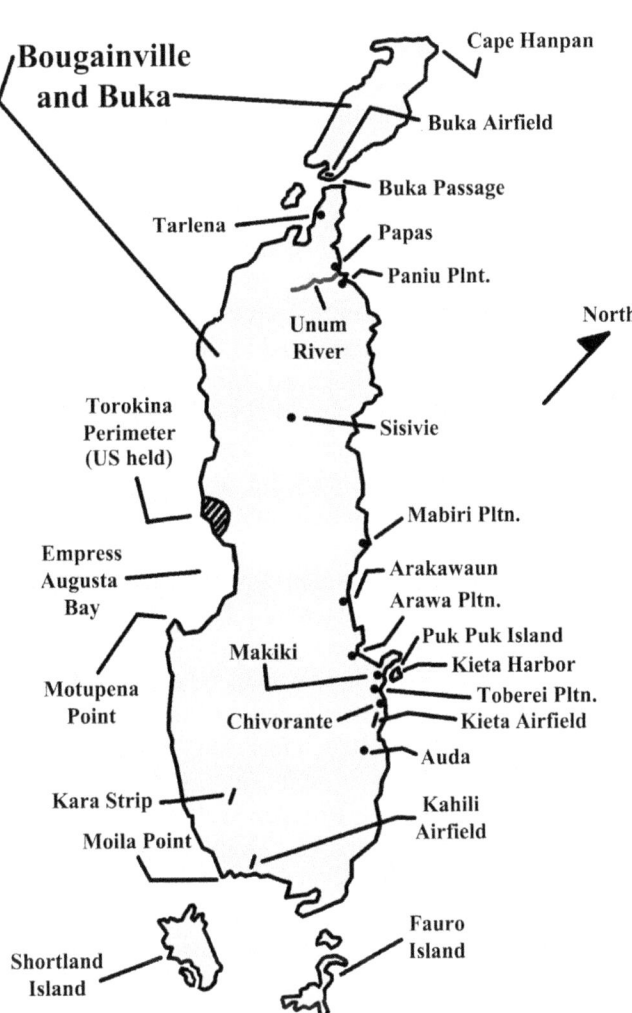

Detail of Bougainville targets. Map adapted from Com AirNorSols Intelligence Summary, 25 September 1944 (National Archives).

field for months. As they continued at low level to Malabunga Junction, then to Toma, they spotted and strafed seven trucks along the road joining the two locations. None of the trucks burned but the pilots felt certain they damaged several of them.

While Humberd and Sigan attacked the trucks, Inglehart and Sturgis strafed the village of Malabunga. They were greeted with accurate machine gun fire. Several rounds struck Sturgis' Corsair, damaging his fuel pump. He began losing fuel, and accompanied by Inglehart, barely made it back to Green Island. As he landed he was notified by the tower that his Corsair was belching flames. Sturgis quickly got out of the Corsair while it was still rolling at a speed of 30 knots, spraining his right ankle and cutting his right hand in doing so. Crash crews quickly responded and had the fire out in minutes before the plane had stopped rolling. However, unlike Sturgis who made it, his Corsair (BuNo 56394) did not. The Corsair was burned beyond repair and was written off.

Five minutes after Humberd's division took off Teller, Moynihan, Jones and Gorman were wheels up for the Duke of York—Cape Lambert sweep. Carrying 500 pound bombs, they were given a specific target to attack. Intelligence had information that a 400 foot fishing sloop was spotted entering the Toriu River on the west coast of New Britain. Teller's division was to sink the boat.

They had difficulty finding the boat. It was only after Jones and Gorman dropped their bombs on a plantation house on the north side of the river that the boat was found. It was spotted in a cove about 100 yards from the house. Teller and Moynihan nosed over at 50 degree angles and released their bombs: one dropped within 100 feet while the other overshot the boat by 300 feet. After the bomb drop, the Corsairs circled around and made several strafing passes at the boat and the house. No specific damage was observed. The flight returned to Piva at 1110.

At 0810 Hart, Flickinger, Mussman and Gray, armed with 500 pounders, took off for the Cape Gazelle—Lemingi sweep. Reports had been received that Japanese infantry were staying in Lemingi, so that's where the four pilots were to drop their ordnance. They did, as well as strafed, but any damage that may have been caused by the attack was obscured from view of the pilots. As they retired they also strafed gardens along the coast near Put Put Plantation. Upon returning to Piva, Hart's plane was found to have several holes on the underside of his fuselage. Where the damage came from could not be determined but Hart suspected he received the fire from the vicinity of the Warangoi River as they flew their sweep.

Shortly after noon, Bacheler's division took off for the Put Put-Keravat sweep. Weather hampered their sweep; any hope of getting some good hits was nullified by cloud cover from 2,000 to 10,000 feet. They had to enter shallower dives as they dropped their bombs on the Experimental Gardens, cratering several of them.

Henley, Neilson, Rosellen and MacLachlan took off at 1220 to finish the job that Teller's division failed to do: sink the boat anchored in the Toriu River. Their four 500 pounders all fell within 30 feet of the boat. The boat was wrecked from the near misses but still afloat. The Corsairs swung around, strafing the boat until it sank. As they departed the area, they pumped a few rounds into the nearby plantation house. Flying towards Cape Lambert, the four planes strafed a tin-roofed building at Pondo Plantation, setting it on fire.

For the last mission of the day, Furlow, Scoville, Garrett, and Frank were wheels up at 1255 for the Cape Gazelle—Lemingi sweep. They deposited their bombs on the 7th Day Mission building south of Put Put Harbor with unknown results. Their .50 caliber guns were kept busy strafing huts as they flew from the Narangoi River to Cape Gazelle before they returned to Piva at 1555.

No combat missions were flown on 11 October since 25 pilots participated in gunnery practice throughout the day.

Patrols resumed on 12 October. Furlow, Scoville, Garrett and Frank were assigned the dawn patrol. After a couple of hours in the air no Japanese activity was spotted. Upon return to Piva, they stood scramble alert until noon. The four pilots were relieved by Teller, Moynihan, Jones and Gorman who stood on scramble alert the rest of the afternoon. The rest of the squadron performed continuous patrols over south Bougainville throughout the day strafing Japanese soldiers, gardens and huts near Kukugai, Kara Airfield, Tugiu, and inland from Kokomira.

Pouring rain and storms cancelled flying for 13 October, and more aerial gunnery practice occupied the pilots on 14 October. Despite the limited activity for the week, it was estimated that the squadron probably wrecked three trucks, sank one boat, cratered four gardens, smoked one hut and set another on fire, and probably killed two Japanese soldiers.

The squadron continued the dawn patrol, scramble alert, and south Bougainville patrols on 15 October. Bacheler, Pirages, Crutcher and Kennicott flew the dawn patrol, then were assigned to be on standby should they be needed to be scrambled to intercept any incoming Japanese aircraft. At noon, Heisel, Flickenger, Mussman and Gray relieved the four pilots and stood on alert for the rest of the day.

As for the south Bougainville patrols, the first patrol of the day brought the most excitement. Conroy and Erdmann took off at 0610 and made for Tonolei Harbor. There Conroy spotted a canoe with three Japanese struggling to make shore. Conroy strafed the canoe, sinking it. He came back around three more times to finish off the Japanese in the water. He then made six strafing runs on supplies stacked up under camouflage netting on the west side of the harbor. Further up the north shore of the harbor he spotted a boat pulled up underneath camouflage and strafed it. His wingman, Erdmann, had to be content with strafing huts and gardens near Kara Airfield.

The rest of the daily patrols saw strafing runs on huts north of Kieta Airfield, Numa Numa Plantation, Kieta, a barge hideout near Lake Lahala, gardens and bridges north of Kahili, and a Japanese soldier on the east shore of Buka Island. The last patrol of the day, which was to be flown by Inglehart and Barton, was cancelled by Piva Operations.

Most of the pilots participated in aerial gunnery practice on 16 October. Smith, Neilson, Rosellen and Maclachlan flew the Put Put Keravat sweep but were turned back by bad weather soon after takeoff. Two other sweeps, the Duke of York and Cape Gazelle, were also cancelled due to weather.

The next day saw a sixteen plane strike on New Britain. Divisions led by Humberd, Smith, Henley and Gray took off at 0810. Carrying 1,000 pound bombs, the sixteen Corsairs were assigned hit a Japanese bivouac positions at Kanakdraw, located near Wide Bay. Arriving over the target at 0910 they released their deadly payload, scoring two direct hits and nine area hits. As the planes rendezvoused for their trip home, they saw two columns of black smoke rising from the target area. A photographic mission flown after the strike showed the bivouac was completely destroyed with only a few trees left standing.

The squadron returned to the Wide Bay on 18 October, this time to strike a bivouac area, headquarters area and a medical post at Waitavalo Plantation. Carrying 1,000 pounders, divisions led by Furlow, Major Quinton R. Johns, Cunningham, and Jones took off at 0825 and arrived over the target area at 0917. Furlow's division struck the bivouac area, scoring two area hits; Johns' division scored three area hits on the headquarters area; divisions led by Cunningham and Jones pummeled the medical post, reporting all bombs in the target area. For their effort, the pilots could not see any damage from their strike as they retired back to Piva.

Combat operations resumed on 20 October with a twelve plane strike near Ruri Bay located on the northeast coast of Bougainville. Divisions led by Bacheler, Cunningham and Gray were off the ground at 0800. The pilots had difficulty spotting the target due to the thick jungle and hills, spending 45 minutes in the air before dropping their 1,000 pound bombs. Most of them exploded 200 to 400 yards north of the target; only four hit the target area. Following the release of the bombs, the Corsairs made several strafing runs. Results could not be observed since the terrain hid from view any damage caused by the attack. The twelve Corsairs landed at 0930.

No combat operations took place for the next three days. Flying was halted on 21 October for aircraft maintenance; weather prevented any combat missions on 22 October, while 23 October was occupied with aerial gunnery practice.

Combat missions resumed on 24 October when Humberd led 12 Corsairs on a strike on the Rumba bivouac area situated close to the Bovo River. The area was suspected to be the home to two companies of Japanese solders: the 3rd and 12th. The divisions led by Humberd, Gray and Jones took off at 0710 with each Corsair carrying a 1,000 pound bombs. Humberd's and Gray's divisions dropped their bombs in the 3rd Company area but seven of the eight bombs fell 500 yards short of the intended target. Jones' division missed the 12th Company target area; their bombs falling within the river fork to the west of their assigned target. All divisions strafed their target areas before returning to Piva. As in many previous missions, no damage was observed.

Aerial gunnery practice was also on the agenda for the day with six pilots giving their trigger fingers some exercise, while divisions led by Humberd, Furlow, Henley and Cunningham practiced squadron tactics during a 2 ½ hour night flight.

More gunnery practice occurred on 25 October with six pilots participating. The squadron also received a new officer, 2Lt. Alexander D. Beattie.

On 26 October, 16 Corsairs led by Bacheler were assigned to hit a Japanese regimental storage area at Rumba, located near Arawa Bay on the east coast of Bougainville. The planes loaded with 1,000 pound bombs, were in the air shortly after 1000. Within 25 minutes the attack began, but finding the target was difficult. Fourteen of the 16 bombs were believed to have hit in the target area. Results were obscured by dense foliage and deep ravines. Two pilots, Garrett and Flickenger, had hung bombs and could not shake them loose. Both returned to base. Before departing the remaining Corsairs strafed the area. During the strafing runs, one of the Corsairs was hit by expended .50 caliber shells from the plane in front of it, damaging the front and right glass of the canopy, severed a spark plug lead, and broke off several cooling fins of one cylinder. Despite the damage, the plane and the others made it back to Piva by 1100.

The squadron received two more pilots on 27 October: Captain Frank A. Robinson and 2Lt. Arthur C. Evans, Jr. While the two new men were processed, twenty squadron pilots were in the air throughout the day for aerial gunnery practice.

The following day, divisions led by Furlow, Henley, Cunningham and Jones took off at 0645 to bomb and strafe a Japanese ammo dump at Rumba. At 0715, nine of the 1,000 pound bombs the Corsairs were carrying fell in the target area, with three of the bombs striking a storage dump located near the ammo dump. The terrain prevented any visual confirmation of damage. The pilots then made a strafing run and were rewarded with smoke rising from the target area. Unfortunately, it was a false alarm; the smoke dissipated as the planes departed the area for home.

Sunday, 29 October was a busy day for the squadron. Five sweeps were flown, putting 20 different pilots into the air. On all sweeps, the Corsairs carried one 500 pound bomb each, some set with a delayed fuse.

Bacheler, Harris, Barton and 2Lt. Ray G. Ward took off at 0825 for the Duke of York—Pondo Plantation sweep. Just northwest of Stockholm Plantation, Bacheler, flying straight and at treetop level, dropped his bomb on a thatched hut built on stilts. Harris, his wingman, was a short distance behind his leader, did not see Bacheler drop his bomb. He commenced a strafing run on the same building that Bacheler targeted with his bomb. Just as he passed over the hut at an altitude of 50 feet Bacheler's bomb exploded, setting fire to a nearby building and sending bomb fragments tearing into Harris' Corsair (BuNo 56044).

Harris was able to control his Corsair but he realized he wasn't going to make it back to Piva. Showing great piloting skills, he was able to ditch his plane five miles offshore in Palangumar Bay on the northwest coast of New Britain. Harris scrambled out his Corsair, still wearing his parachute harness. It helped him stay afloat, along with his Mae West.

A Dumbo was in the area, and witnessed Harris ditching his plane. The PBY soon landed to rescue Harris. A seaman aboard the plane noticed the Marine pilot was having difficulty getting to the Dumbo. He stripped off his clothes down to his trunks and with no life vest jumped into the water. The sailor swam about a hundred yards to Harris and helped him to the plane. Harris was not injured but exhausted from the ordeal.

Barton's bomb missed his target at Stockholm Plantation while Ward overshot his target, a dock at Lassul Bay. The three Corsairs regrouped and returned to Piva at 1145.

Forty minutes after Bacheler's division took off, Humberd, Sigan, Inglehart and Sturgis were in the air for the Put Put—Keravat sweep. The division unloaded their bombs on huts at the southeast end of the Experimental Gardens, gaining only one area hit. The planes did little strafing was done. The pilots noted that gardens and roads near Keravat Airfield appeared to be in good condition. No enemy activity was witnessed and the planes were back at Piva at 1130.

Jones, Gorman, Heisel, and Poehlman were up in the air at 0920, assigned the Cape Gazelle—Lemingi sweep. The four Corsairs bombed a road junction at Ralabang Plantation and shot up gardens and huts between Tobera and Kabanga Bay. All Corsairs returned safely to Piva.

The last sweep of the day was flown by Furlow, Scoville, Garrett and Frank. Assigned the Duke of York—Pondo sweep, they were wheels up at 1255. Their sweep was successful. They scored a damaging hit in the village of Urukukur and Uri, both on Duke of York Island. They also strafed huts and buildings in Seragi, Watom Island and Lilinakala Plantation. Unlike most of the previous missions, they did observe the damage they had wrought: three huts burning and three destroyed. All the Corsairs returned to Piva by 1635 but Scoville's landing could have been catastrophic. His bomb had hung up during the attack and as he touched down at Piva, his 500 pounder fell from his plane and skidded off to the side without exploding.

On 30 October, all flying was cancelled for the day as the squadron prepared its planes for a ferrying mission to Guadalcanal the following day. On Halloween day, all 20 Corsairs of the squadron were flown to Guadalcanal to exchange them for 22 brand new F4U-1Ds. That same afternoon, 19 of the new Corsairs took off to head back to Piva but only five of them arrived. Twelve of the planes landed at the Russell Islands and two landed at Munda due to bad weather blocking the route to Piva. These planes, plus the three left behind at Guadalcanal all arrived at Piva on 1 November.

Due to losses and transfers in and out of the squadron, the divisions underwent restructuring. For the remainder of its time at Piva, most of the missions were flown by the assigned pilots:

Division Leader	Wingman	Section Leader	Wingman
Humberd	Sigan	Inglehart	Sturgis
Henley	Flickinger	Frank	Harris
Jennings	Erdmann	Moynihan	Tanner
Furlow	Scoville	Cunningham	Garrett
Smith	Neilson	Rosellen	MacLachlan
Bacheler	Pirages	Crutcher	Kennicott
Hanson	Daigle	Holderer	Kammeyer
Johns	Wolf	Schoetz	Ward
Jones	Gorman	Heisel	Poehlman
Schroeder	Beattie	Barton	Evans
Gray	Warren	Mussman	Conroy
Wallace[64]	Flickinger	Barton	Harris
Tanner	Beattie	Crutcher	Lingenfelter
Erdmann	Daigle	Frank	Jernigan
Moynihan	Wolf	Barton	Ward

Events north of Bougainville, unknown to the personnel of the squadron, dictated where they would soon be flying. The two-pronged assault by MacArthur's forces to the west towards the Philippines and Nimitz's forces through the Gilbert, Marshall and Caroline Islands had effectively cut off the Solomon Islands and New Guinea from the Japanese. Coupled with the daily aerial assault by U.S. and Allied planes to keep Japanese forces pinned down in the isolated islands, the forces left behind by Imperial Japan were rendered ineffective.

While Nimitz's forces prepared for the coming assault on Iwo Jima, MacArthur's forces landed on Leyte on 20 October and began the long campaign to liberate the Philippine Islands from Japanese forces. As the year drew to a close, the Marines of VMO-251 would soon find themselves helping MacArthur's forces.

November 1944

On 1 November, the squadron underwent a re-organization by enacting a Ground Defense emergency bill. Every officer and enlisted man was given an assignment for the defense of the squadron in case of a ground attack by the Japanese.

Each department—Engineering, Line and Ordnance—was reduced to the absolute minimum to keep their 22 Corsairs flying. Should a situation arise that prevented aircraft from being launched, the men were to serve as demolition squads for their respective departments. They were to be utilized as combat troops after the demolition took place.

Training for the men continued through the month, on top of the daily pace of operations. Organized into three rifle platoons, four .30 caliber machine gun crews and for .50 caliber machine gun crews, the men received training on their weapons. Weapons were obtained from the Americal Division and the 164th Infantry Regiment, with qualified instructors provided by the 164th. After two weeks several of the men qualified on the .30 caliber machine gun according to Army regulations. By the end of the month, the crews receiving instruction on the .50 caliber machine gun had yet to qualify.[65]

On top of their new defensive responsibilities, the squadron spent the first six days of November working on the new F4U-1Ds, allowing maintenance crews to check all systems and prep them for combat. The -1D was not substantially different from the F4U-1. The plane now came with a one piece bubble canopy which replaced the birdcage of the -1 model, and the outboard internal wing tanks were removed. The plane now had factory installed hard points to carry a combination of up to three 500 or 1,000 pound bombs, a centerline external fuel tank and eight 5 inch rockets.

The pilots got their chance to try out their new Corsairs on 6 November. Furlow's division flew the dawn patrol. Seeing no evidence of enemy activity after a couple of hours in the air, they returned to Piva. At 0800, Henley and Barton took off to patrol south Bougainville. At Motupena Point, heavy rain forced them to turn back. They retraced their route up the west coast only to hit a storm front running north to south over Buka Island. Both pilots crossed over to the east coast of Bougainville. As they approached Arawa Bay, they spotted three small fires—apparently the Japanese were getting ready to cook a meal—at a nearby coconut plantation. The pilots lined up for a strafing run and fired their .50 caliber machine guns. As they retired back to Piva the fires were still burning.

The squadron again flew patrols over Bougainville on 7 November. Divisions led by Cpt. Frank A. Schroeder and Cunningham flew the dawn and dusk patrol and then stood scramble alert for a half-day each.

At 0630 Inglehart and Sturgis flew the south Bougainville patrol but the weather hampered visibility. Nothing was spotted of the enemy. The next patrol was flown by Furlow and Scoville, taking off at 0845. They ended up strafing huts north of Kara Airfield. Their patrol was cut short when Scoville's plane developed a hydraulic leak near Kieta. Both planes made it safely back to Piva shortly after 1000. They too saw no signs of the enemy. Humberd and Sigan drew the next patrol. Their 1 hour, 45 minute patrol was hampered by bad weather and like the previous two patrols, saw no signs of the enemy. The last patrol of the day was flown by Gray and Warren. Shortly after takeoff, Gray noticed his oil temperature gauge registering an abnormal high temperature. Gray turned back for home while Warren was instructed to return to Piva by operations a few minutes later.

Afternoon missions were the order of the day for 8 November. Three divisions took off within an hour of each other starting at 1305 to strike separate targets on New Britain and Duke of York Island. Johns' division struck both locations bombing huts and buildings on the Wunataishi and Towannmaronga Rivers, Pondo Point, and Naliwan Plantation on Duke of York Island. Heisel scored the only damaging hit at Naliwan. After the pilots dropped their 500 pounders, the pilots strafed villages along the coast from Pondo Point to Cape Lambert to Keravat, setting a few fires during the strafing runs.

Bacheler, Ward, Kennicott and Harris flew the Gazelle—Lemingi sweep. The target area was covered solid with clouds so Bacheler led his pilots to Duke of York Island, firing a few huts during a strafing run. He then led them to Cape Lalahan near Buka Island to bombs huts. Two bombs hit near the huts but any damage caused by the strike could not be observed. Two of the bombs hung up during the attack; one was jettisoned and the other was brought back to Piva.

Cunningham led 1Lt. George M. Holderer, Daigle and Kammeyer on the Put Put—Keravat sweep, armed with 500 pounders with delay fuses. Kammeyer developed engine trouble soon after takeoff and returned to Piva escorted by his wingman, Holderer. Cunningham and Daigle pushed on. Cunningham's bomb damaged several huts in a village on Duke of York Island while Daigle's bomb cratered a garden at Keravat Farms.

Operations slowed down on 9 November with only one morning strike scheduled for the day. Bacheler led a 16 plane force, consisting of his division and those led by Smith, Gray and Jones to strike an enemy bivouac and supply area—designated as Ratsoa #2—in northwest Bougainville. Carrying a payload of one 500 pounder each, they took off from Piva at 0750. Thirty minutes later they commenced their attack on Ratsoa. Fourteen of the 16 bombs hit the target area; bombs carried by Harris and Warren hung up and were brought back to base. If any damaged was scored by the pilots it could not be determined; jungle growth obscured any observations. By the time the Corsairs retired from Ratsoa to return to Piva, smoke caused by the attack had dissipated.

The missions for 10 November found the squadron flying the obligatory dawn patrol, and sweeps over south Bougainville. Jennings' division flew the dawn patrol, and then stood on scramble alert until noon. For the first south Bougainville patrol, 1Lt. Howard L. Hanson and Frank were wheels up at 0615. They observed two fires at Koromira Mission and two more south of the Puriatia River about 75 yards inland from the river. The pilots strafed the fires, plus huts at Rumba and Kieta. Holderer and Kammeyer left Piva at 0800. Near Cape Friendship, they machine gunned three Japanese in a garden just south of the cape. They also spotted a lone man standing on the beach east of Lake Lahala but did not attack. At 0940 Schoetz and Tanner took off for their patrol. They ended up strafing Rubi Bay and the east coast of Buka. Between Lonahan and Cape Tosahui they drew machine gun fire from caves dug in the side of a cliff in the area. Both planes plastered the caves with their .50 calibers, silencing the Japanese weapon. They also set a hut on fire in the village of Trihup, north of Numa Numa, and returned to base, touching down at 1045. The squadron stood down for the afternoon, due to the cancellation of the afternoon sweeps and the dusk patrol because of weather.[66]

It was back to the New Britain—Duke of York area with six missions on 11 November: three in the morning and three in the afternoon. All planes in every mission carried one 500 pound bomb each. First off the ground was Smith's division, taking off at 0730 for the Duke of York—Pondo Plantation sweep. During a low level bombing run over Rangarere and Vunipa Plantations, Smith and Neilson destroyed at least one building each. Rosellen's bomb was a dud and MacLachlan's was a miss. The division continued its sweep by strafing every plantation from Pondo to Cape Lambert to Ataliklikun Bay and hust on Duke of York Island. During one of the strafing runs, MacLachlan hit a tree, tearing a seven-inch gash in the leading edge of the port wing.

Twenty minutes after Smith's division took to the air, Bacheler led his division on the Cape Gazelle—Lemingi sweep. Entering a 30 degree dive, they dropped four 500 pounders on Lemingi village, damaging an unknown number of huts. Much dust and smoke was hanging over the village when they came back around for a strafing run. No resistance was met by the enemy and the four planes returned to Piva at 1030.

At 0820, Johns' division consisting of 2Lt. John C. Wolf, Schoetz and Ward, took off for the Put Put–Keravat sweep. They bombed the Japanese Experimental Gardens near Keravat Airfield, scoring three area hits. One bomb hung on release and was later dropped on two dump trucks on the road between Wat Wat Plantation and Arara village. The division made several strafing runs on the trucks, setting both on fire. The Japanese retaliated with small arms fire, hitting the planes piloted by Schoetz and Wolf near the tail section.[67] Johns let loose with his machine guns at a driver of one of the trucks who was running into the woods. About one mile north of the burning trucks Ward strafed a tree-covered road setting fire to an unseen target. Whatever was burning, it put up two columns of smoke over 100 feet high. All planes made it back to Piva by 1120.

From left to right: Irwin, Crutcher, Schroeder and Beattie during a debriefing after a mission over Rabaul (courtesy Hugh E. "Yogi" Irwin).

The first of the afternoon strikes was led by Hanson, with Daigle, Holderer and Kammeyer making up the rest of the division. The four Corsairs, armed with 500 pounders, took off at 1300 for the Duke of York—Pondo sweep. The four planes attempted to bomb a large house situated at the Seragi Plantation, but missed with three bombs. The fourth pilot failed to arm his bomb before dropping it so it failed to explode upon impact. The division then made a strafing run on the house. By the time the aircraft retired, the house was smoking. On the way back to Piva, the four Corsairs strafed huts at Cape Pomas, Raganga Plantation and the Vulanlama Coffee Plantation, all located on New Britain. The planes were back at Piva by 1555.

A half hour after Hanson's division took off, Jennings' division was wheels up for the Lemingi—Gazelle sweep. Due to clouds and an error in navigation by Jennings, the four Corsairs dropped their 500 pounders on huts and a crossroad three miles northwest of Namatanai, New Ireland instead of bombing targets on New Britain. One of the bombs missed the target while the other three went unobserved. As the planes returned to Piva, the Corsairs strafed the west coast of Buka and the northwest coast of Bougainville to Soraken Plantation. The results of the strafing went unobserved. Once the strafing runs were complete, the planes returned to Piva, landing at 1630.

The last strike of the day took off at 1400. Smith led his division on the Put Put sweep. Fifteen minutes after takeoff, Rosellen began to have trouble controlling his Corsair and returned to base. Smith, MacLachlan and Neilson pushed on to complete the sweep. Smith and MacLachlan dropped their 500 pounders on revetments on the north side of Vunkanau Airfield while Neilson delivered his 500 pound bomb on a supply area at Wat Wat Plantation. Results of the bombing went unobserved. On the way back to

Piva, the three Corsairs strafed huts at nearly a dozen locations between Keravat and Put Put. They met no resistance during the strike and arrived back at Piva by 1615.

Prior to the strike launched on 12 November, friendly natives had reported the discovery of a Japanese stockade. Called the Kapauinavi Stockade, it was protected by several machine guns and said to be situated about 12 miles inland from the Koromira Mission in southeast Bougainville. Three squadrons were assigned to hit the stockade: RNZAF squadrons 15 and 23, and VMO-251.

The plan called for the two RNZAF squadrons to strike first, followed by VMO-251. Unfortunately, all the squadrons involved in the attack had difficulty locating the target due to dense jungle growth covering the stockade. RNZAF 23 Squadron Corsairs dropped their 500 pounders on huts south of the stockade, destroying six of them. Next came the 12 Corsairs of 15 Squadron, also dropping their bombs on huts to the south but results could not be determined.[68] Because of the problem of locating the target, the RNZAF squadrons were late exiting the target area—set for 0830. The 16 Corsairs led by Bacheler circled for 20 minutes waiting for the allied squadrons to retire.

At 0850, Bacheler, Jennings, Schroeder and Jones led their divisions in the attack. Of the 16 bombs carried by the squadron, four were damaging hits and five were area hits. After the bomb run, the Corsairs circled around for a series of strafing runs, expending 4,000 rounds. Despite the three squadrons dropping nearly 10 tons of ordnance, it could not be determined if the stockade was destroyed. The Japanese offered no resistance and all VMO-251 planes returned safely to Piva.

The squadron was back to flying the dawn and dusk patrols, scramble standbys, and the south Bougainville patrols on 13 November. For the south Bougainville patrols there were five flights of two planes each; the first takeoff was at 0605 and the last patrol came back at 1720. Not much was seen by the pilots during the day. During the patrols, 12 Japanese soldiers were spotted walking along a beach within a no fire zone so the pilots had to let them go free. Smith sighted and strafed a barge with a cabin amidships in Tonolei Harbor. Neilson spotted six of the enemy swimming at Tabut, south of Buka Passage, and gave them a burst of machine gun fire at 1,000 yards. The six soldiers were last seen running into the jungle. More soldiers were spotted during the afternoon but they too were in a no fire zone.

It was back to New Britain for six missions on 14 November. Their orders were very generic: bomb and strafe any target sighted. Three missions were flown in the morning, the rest in the afternoon. Each plane participating in the missions carried a 500 pound bomb set with a delay fuse.

First off the ground was Bacheler's division, taking off at 0730 for the Duke of York—Pondo Point sweep. The four Corsairs flew straight to Pondo Point on the west coast of New Britain. Arriving at 0900, they entered a 35 degree dive and bombed several buildings, scoring one damaging hit, one dud, and two misses. As they retired to patrol the Cape Lambert area, the Japanese opened up with AA fire but missed the fleeing Corsairs. Upon arriving at Cape Lambert, rain squalls covered the area so the Corsairs did not search for Japanese. Returning across the peninsula as they made their way back to Piva, the four pilots strafed the village of Reit, about 15 miles south of Ataliklikun Bay. No enemy activity was seen throughout the entire mission. All planes landed safely at 1035.

Thirty-five minutes after Bacheler's division took to the air; Jones led his division—less Poehlman—for the Cape Gazelle—Lemingi sweep. Jones tried to sink an abandoned barge at the mouth of the Warangoi River, but missed with his bomb. Gorman dropped his 500 pounder on a group of huts at Wat Wat Plantation to no apparent effect while Heisel dropped his bomb on a road intersection at Put Put Harbor but missed. As they regrouped to return to Piva, they strafed huts from Put Put to Cape Gazelle but any results went unobserved. As with Bacheler's division, no sign of the enemy was seen by the three pilots and all were back at Piva by 1145.

Smith's four plane division departed Piva ten minutes after Jones' division for the Put Put—Keravat sweep. One bomb missed a truck parked on a road near Napapar by about 75 feet, and bombs were dropped on a footbridge and huts at the Experimental Farms but confirmation of any damage was not possible. Neilson scored the only hit on four huts about a half mile south of Rapopo Airfield. As the division retired to Piva, they shot up divers huts at Ralabang, Wat Wat Plantation and Raviola, as well as a Japanese soldier in a garden in the village of Raviola. As they flew between Livuan and Kamar on the east coast of the Gazelle Peninsula, they observed five abandoned ground defense gun emplacements along the beach. No enemy AA fire was encountered, allowing the planes to return to Piva unscathed at 1045.

The afternoon sweeps eventually fared much better than the morning sweeps. Johns' division took to the air at 1245 and 55 minutes later dropped their 500-pounders on buildings at Wirawir Point, Pondo Plantation with no damage seen. As they regrouped to head back to Piva, they strafed huts and the mouth of a cave on Stockholm Plantation. They also deposited thousands of rounds of .50 caliber ammunition into every village from Cape Lambert to Vunapaldig, and shot up two iron water tanks at the village of Kulkil near Mandres Plantation. As they left the swath of destruction behind them, they observed at least four huts in flames. Johns' division was back home at Piva at 1540.

Taking off at 1330, Schroeder, Beattie, Barton and Evans handled the Cape Gazelle—Lemingi sweep. Schroeder and Beattie scored a direct hit and a damaging hit on huts at Put Put Plantation, while Barton and Evans scored direct hits on huts at Lemingi. Their 500-pounders left five huts obliterated, and damaged at least six. They were back at Piva by 1610.

Jennings, back to flying following a bout with appendicitis, led four Corsairs on the Put Put–Keravat sweep for the last mission of the day. They left Piva at 1400 and following a roughly 40 minute flight, began their bomb runs. Two of planes scored damaging hits on huts northwest of Wurawunurur while the other two planes scored area hits on huts at the Experimental Farms. They made a strafing run on the village of Ulagun as they made their way back to Piva, landing at 1645.

The squadron stood down on 15 November, allowing maintenance crews to give their Corsairs some much needed attention. The squadron also received three new pilots: 2Lt. Hugh E. Irwin, 2Lt. Curtis D. Jernigan, and 2Lt. Robert E. Lindsey.

Australian troops on the west coast of New Britain were having a difficult time pushing Japanese troops out of the Pandi River area south of Open Bay. They put in an urgent call for an air strike. MAG-14 headquarters responded by launching an early morning 42 plane strike on 16 November. VMO-251 would lead the attack with 16 Corsairs, to be followed by 14 Corsairs of VMF-212[69] and 12 Corsairs from 223.[70] Each Corsair in all squadrons carried one 500 pound bomb—10.5 tons of ordnance to be delivered to the Japanese. The mission marked the first time the squadron would fly in direct support of ground operations.

At 0645, squadron divisions led by Bacheler (who was also the mission lead), Smith, Erdmann and Johns took off and commenced their attack 0800. They approached the target area—a small rectangular island formed by the split mouth of the Pandi River—from south to north and at 10,000 feet with wheels down, entered their dives. At 2,000 feet they released their bombs, with 15 of the 16 Corsairs placing their bombs in the target area. As with many previous missions, any specific damage could not be determined. The planes regrouped to strafe the target area, making the run from the same south to north direction. Once the strafing runs were complete, Bacheler's Corsairs returned to Piva, landing at 0930.

Soon after VMO-251 retired from the area, 12 of the 14 Corsairs of VMF-212 made their attack. Two remained behind at Piva due to mechanical problems. They made their bomb run from the southwest to northeast, releasing their 500-pounders at around 2,000 feet. All the bombs struck the target area and like VMO-251, direct damage could not be ascertained. The planes circled to the left and made a strafing run from east to west before retiring back to Piva.

Hugh "Yogi" Irwin (courtesy Hugh E. "Yogi" Irwin).

Last to deliver their payload on the Japanese were the 12 Corsairs of VMF-223. At 0830, approaching the target area from the north, the Corsairs entered their dive runs after a making a 180 degree left turn. Like the two previous squadrons, VMF-223 Corsairs released their bombs at 2,000 feet, placing all of them in the target area. The planes regrouped over water, and again approaching the target area from the north, made a strafing run before returning to Piva.

Despite the well-coordinated strike and the apparent success of putting the 500-pounders on target, its effect on the Japanese appears to have been negligible. They would be back for another strike to the same area in four days.

It was back to the standard routine for the squadron on 17 November: dawn and dusk patrols and south Bougainville patrols. Erdmann's and Jones' divisions flew the dawn and dusk patrols, spotting nothing of the enemy. Six two plane sections flew the south Bougainville patrols; the first section taking off at 0600 and the last at 1520. Gray and Warren, flying the first patrol, caught two Japanese soldiers in a rowboat off the west coast of Poporang Island in the Shortland group. The two pilots made five strafing runs, each time drawing machine gun fire from a hilltop on the southern tip of Faisi Island. The Corsairs were not hit and in return, Gray and Warren claimed they sank the rowboat and damaged a barge tied up at a pier about 100 yards from the rowboat's location.

Five. Espiritu Santo, Green Island and Bougainville

Johns and Wolf took off at 0825 and flew around the island of Bougainville. Johns spotted a lone enemy soldier in a field near Iula. The soldier fell in a fusillade of .50 caliber machine guns following a strafing run by Johns.

Taking to the air at 1035 were Bacheler and Wallace. They had specific orders to search for a reported mine seen in the Bougainville Straight. They did spot what appeared to be a mine: a floating gasoline drum. Confirming that it was indeed a gasoline drum, they continued on with their patrol and ended up spotting a Japanese soldier on a beach west of Koromira Mission. The soldier fell to the ground following a strafing run by both pilots.

Barton and Evans took off at 1250 for the first of two afternoon sweeps. Looking for vessels that had been reported in Matchin Bay, they found none. They then flew on to Buka island, strafing huts along the coast of the island. Weather prevented them from flying over south Bougainville.

The last sweep was flown by Schoetz and Ward. They too searched for surface vessels in Matchin Bay and the west coast of Buka Island but found none plying the waters, nor any anchored. Like Barton and Evans before them, they too strafed huts along the east and west coast of Buka. Clouds hampered any search over southern Bougainville so they returned to Piva, landing at 1725.

Allied intelligence had received reports from friendly sources of a possible hideout for Japanese seaplanes at Kurakakul, located off Talili Bay, that had been harassing U.S. Navy PT boats patrolling the area during the evening hours. The hideout consisted of three heavily protected storage areas and occupied a small area. VMO-251 drew the mission to destroy the target.

For an unknown reason, a high angle dive bombing attack was planned for the assault, rather than a low level bomb run. Also, the 1,000 pound bombs the Corsairs were to carry were set with instantaneous fuses, rather than delay fuses to allow for a more destructive hit on the storage facilities.

At 0805, divisions led by Bacheler, Schroeder, Hanson, and Gray took off from Piva. As in previous missions, Bacheler had overall command of the flight. Holderer's Corsair remained on the ground due to a flat tail wheel. Soon after takeoff, Kennicott was forced to drop out of formation due to a severe vibration. His wingman, Conroy, stuck with his leader. While the remaining 13 Corsairs continued on to Kurakakul, Kennicott and Conroy flew on to Buka and unloaded their bombs on Soraken Plantation, south of Buka Passage. They then returned to base.

Bacheler's 13 Corsairs approached the target from south to north, so that retirement could be made towards water to avoid AA fire. At 10,000 feet, the Corsairs nosed over one at a time to commence their dive bombing runs. With wheels lowered to act as dive brakes, the planes exceeded 300 knots before releasing their bombs at 2,500 feet. The 1,000-pounders hit in the vicinity of the target but actual damage could not be assessed. The Corsairs returned to Piva by 1100. A photographic interpretation unit reported the following day that only three bombs exploded close enough to do any possible damage.

No combat operations were flown on 19 November. Instead, 12 pilots flew training hops to hone their gunnery skills.

Four days after their first strike to help Australian ground troops on New Britain, the squadron was called upon again on 20 November to help them out in the Pandi River sector. The Japanese were reported to be dug in along the wooded right bank of the west mouth of the river. Assisting the Corsairs would be dive bombing squadrons VMSB-236 and -133, also operating out of Piva North Airfield.

The 15 dive bombers of VMSB-236[71] and the 14 dive bombers of VMSB-133[72] were each armed with one 500 pound general purpose bomb and two 250 pound bombs. The dive bombers were the first to leave Piva, taking off at 0715. Bacheler's 16 Corsairs, armed with one 500 pound bomb each, took off at 0740. The Japanese put up meager AA fire when the squadrons arrived over the target area at 0900.

It is not clear who went in for the attack first, and who went in last. But the results were the same for each squadron: most of the bombs hit the assigned target area but any specific damage went unobserved due to the thick jungle growth. The dive bombers retired back to Piva but the Corsairs of VMO-251 remained to make one strafing run against the Japanese defenders, expending over 7,000 rounds of .50 caliber ammunition. As with the bomb run, the dense foliage obscured any evidence of damage. The Corsairs were back at Piva by 1030. As for the Japanese, they remained in place.

Bacheler led another 16 plane strike on 21 November, consisting of his division and divisions led by Schroeder, Moynihan and Gray, to hit a suspected Japanese bivouac at Soraken Plantation, located along the northwest shore of Bougainville and south of Buka Passage. Armed with one 500-pounder each, the Corsairs took off at 0720. Twenty-five minutes later they deposited 14 of the bombs on the plantation. Any specific damage went unobserved. Following the bomb run, each of the Corsairs circled around for a single strafing run. All planes were back at Piva by 0825.

Sometime after the pilots returned from their strike, they and the rest of the squadron pilots were trucked to the shores of Empress Augusta Bay. There, squadron intelligence officer 2Lt. Henry B. Welch gave the officers a demonstration on the use of a new emergency drinking water kit, which converted salt water into drinking water—definitely a useful tool to have should one find himself in a raft in the vast expanse of the Pacific. The new kits were now standard issue in pilot back packs.

Due to the daily onslaught of aerial bombing during the year, isolated Japanese troops and installations had been pounded into virtual non-existence. There just wasn't much left standing in the way of viable targets—especially in and around the Rabaul area. In reaction to this, sweeps to Rabaul were reduced by higher command. Instead of the normal four to five sweeps in a day, the sweeps were reduced to two: designated Watom Island—Cape Lambert—Pondo Plantation and Watom Island—Duke of York—Cape Archway.[73] On 22 November, VMO-251 handled the two sweeps, plus three other missions.

Erdmann's division, carrying the standard 500 pound bombs, took off at 0800 on the Duke of York to Cape Archway sweep. They deposited their bombs on a group of huts on the southeast coast of Duke of York Island for three area hits, but no damage was seen. On the way back to Piva, the four Corsairs strafed many villages and isolated huts on the island. As with the results of the bombing, no damage was observed.

Fifteen minutes after Erdmann's division took off, Smith's division departed for the Watom Island to Pondo Plantation sweep. Seeing some huts between Cape Lambert and Pondo Plantation, the four pilots decided to drop their 500-pounders on them. The result: three misses and one dud. As Smith's division continued their sweep, they strafed every village and hut they could see from Cape Liguan to Cape Lambert to Pondo Plantation, setting fire to two huts and left 12 others smoldering. The Corsairs returned to Piva, landing at 1040.

The first mission for the afternoon was flown by Jones' division, taking off at 1220. They too had the Watom Island—Pondo Plantation sweep. Heisel spotted a 40-foot

Japanese landing craft on the beach at Pokoloma Point; its flag flying from the stern. The four Corsairs immediately attacked the barge, but missed with their 500 pound bombs. The explosions were close. The concussions shook the landing craft from the beach and it began to drift into the water. Undaunted, the pilots circled around to strafe the barge. After several runs, the barge was finally sent to the bottom. As they returned to Piva, huts and cooking fires were strafed along the coast to the east from Cape Lambert. By 1530, the four Corsairs were back at Piva.

Tanner's division took off at 1315 for the Duke of York—Cape Archway sweep. With weather preventing a sweep of the cape area, the division attacked targets on Duke of York Island. No hits were scored following bombing and strafing runs on huts in numerous villages on the island. The planes were back at Piva by 1410.

During the early afternoon, COMAIRPIVA received an urgent call to once again help the Australians. Since the last time the squadron flew to support the Aussies, they withdrew about 10 miles west of the Pandi River area. They reported by radio that the Japanese held the village of Ulamona on the west coast of New Britain, and were holding up Australian patrols in the area.

Piva rounded up 11 Corsairs of VMO-251, 16 Corsairs from VMF-223, 12 Corsairs from VMF-212, and six Corsairs from RNZAF 15 Squadron to hit Ulamona. All of the Corsairs carried one 1,000 pound bomb for the strike except for the planes of VMF-212; they carried 500 pounders.[74]

VMO-251's executive officer, Bacheler, was in overall command of the squadron's eleven Corsairs, consisting of his division and Schroeder's divisions, plus pilots Moynihan, Wolf and MacLachlan. They were wheels up at 1440 and arrived over the target at 1610. They dropped all eleven bombs right in the village, with Barton and Lindsey scoring direct hits. As the pilots circled the area to line up for a strafing run, they saw to their amazement that the entire village appeared to be leveled.

Next to strike was VMF-223 at 1621,[75] and VMF-212 at 1640.[76] Like VMO-251, both squadrons put their bombs on the village. By the time they and RNZAF 15 Squadron finished their attack runs, the village of Ulamona appeared to be no more. With the Japanese putting up no AA fire, all Corsairs from all squadrons returned safely to Piva.

Patrols flown on 23 November were a bust from dawn to dusk. Gray's division flew the dawn patrol while Smith's division flew the dusk patrol. Nothing was spotted during these patrols. In addition to their patrol duties, both divisions were instructed by COMAIRNORSOL to search the Matchin Bay area for a possible enemy submarine which was reported to be making monthly calls to the bay. The patrols saw no sign of the Japanese submarine.

The squadron also flew the south Bougainville patrols, with Tanner and Beattie leading off at 0622. Then came Crutcher and Lingenfelter, followed by Heisel and Poehlman, then Erdmann and Daigle, and last Frank and Jernigan, who landed at 1730. None of the patrols, flown throughout the day, saw any signs of the Japanese.

VMO-251 was part of a two squadron strike on Ebery's Lease, a plantation located north of Japanese held Kahili Airfield in southern Bougainville, during the morning of 24 November. VMF-223 took the lead in the mission, providing 16 Corsairs carrying one 500 pound bomb each. They took off at 0800,[77] with VMO-251's Corsairs taking off 15 minutes later with Bacheler leading the squadron's 16 Corsairs.

Following a 27 minute flight, VMF-223 Corsairs commenced their attack. They scored near misses on two AA emplacements and a bridge at the northwest end of the target area. The rest of the bombs fell in a cluster of buildings on the north end of the lease.[78]

Twenty-three minutes after 223's arrival over Ebery's Lease, VMO-251 Corsairs arrived over the target area to commence their attack. Bacheler's division, with two planes from Smith's division, hit gun positions on the plantation. No direct hits were scored. The Japanese responded with 40 MM AA fire, but scored no hits on the Corsairs. The remaining Corsairs placed their bombs in a bivouac area north of the lease's garden area.

On the way out, the Corsairs drew Japanese machine gun fire from a hill west of Kahili Airfield and from a derelict vessel offshore to the east of Kahili. At least six of the Corsairs strafed the machine gun on the derelict vessel, causing it to put up a cloud of yellowish smoke. As the planes rendezvoused to head back to Piva, the vessel was still smoking. Neither squadron suffered any losses due to the AA fire.

It was another coordinated strike for the squadron on 25 November, this time with VMF-212. The target this time was a Japanese bivouac and supply area at Hahela Mission on Buka Island. The target had been sighted by pilots of VMF-212 a few weeks earlier.[79] Corsairs from VMF-212 were responsible for hitting the supply area while VMO-251 was tasked with suppressing the AA guns in the area before hitting the supply area. All Corsairs involved in the attack carried one 500-pounder each.

Shortly before 0800, the attack commenced. Of the 16 Corsairs from VMF-212 assigned to attack the target, 14 were able to do so. Two were left behind at Piva. Making a standard diving run from 10,500 at nearly 70 degree dive angles, 11 of the bombs hit the target area but specific damage was not observed.[80]

Ten minutes later, Bacheler's 16 Corsairs began their attack. Bacheler's division attempted to take out the AA guns but their bombs missed the emplacements set on top of a cliff nearby the mission. Apparently the misses were good enough; the Japanese could only put up meager, inaccurate machine gun fire.

With the AA guns somewhat quieted, divisions led by Erdmann, Moynihan and Tanner hit the bivouac area. The attack caused a huge explosion, sending a plume of black and yellow smoke over 600 feet into the air. As the pilots regrouped for the trip home, fire and smoke continued to billow into the sky.

No Corsairs from either squadron suffered damage, and all returned safely to Piva by 0900.

VMO-251 and VMF-212 paired up again on 26 November to strike a radar installation on New Britain. The Tomavatur Radar Station consisted of two large radar screens with two control buildings, one for each screen and was situated along a road on top of a steep ridge about two miles southeast of Vunakanau Airfield.

Both squadrons decided to make a southwest to northeast approach to attack the installation. It put their exit over water and away from any possible inland AA fire. VMO-251 would be the first in, followed by VMF-212. As in the previous day's mission, each Corsair carried one 500 pounder each.

The 16 Corsairs led by Bacheler took off from Piva at 0940. The flight was comprised of four divisions led by Bacheler, Schroeder, Smith and Gray. At 1055, they were over the target. Bachler's division attacked surrounding gun positions, located from 200 to 600 yards from the radar screens, and no AA fire was offered by the enemy. The remaining 12 Corsairs dropped their 500 pounders on the primary target but due to the high rate of speed as they retired, no actual damage was observed. As they retired, the Corsairs strafed a seven mile long area along "Nine Mile Road," which ran from the radar stations to the shores of Blanche Bay.

Within minutes of VMO-251's attack, VMF-212's 15 Corsairs began their attack run. Four of the Corsairs went for the AA guns, while the rest hit the radar stations. Two of the 4 bombs dropped on the AA guns were seen to explode near the guns, while two of them missed. Of the bombs dropped on the primary target, 8 of the 11 bombs were observed to have exploded in the vicinity of the radar installation, with two of those bombs possibly hitting the control buildings.[81]

None of the Corsairs involved in the attack received any damage and all returned to Piva by 1230.

Flying was secured on 27 November to allow needed maintenance to be performed. Combat operations resumed the following day with several sweeps to the New Britain area.

First off was Smith's division, taking off at 0800 to perform the Watom Island—Pondo Plantation sweep. About 45 minutes out of Piva, Rosellen's plane dropped out of formation with a severe oil leak. He immediately made for Green Island where he landed without further incident. The rest of the planes continued their sweep, attacking several targets of opportunity in the area.

Smith and Neilson attacked huts at Banpfragwerk Plantation along the Toriu River south of Open Bay. Smith scored a direct hit on one of the huts, destroying it while Neilson damaged another. MacLachlan attempted to bomb a barge pulled up on shore on Pondo Point, but missed. As the flight continued its sweep, they set fire to a dozen huts at Sergai, Vunalama, New Mobisberg, and Maitairuitap plantations, as well as other locations between Cape Lambert and Ataliklikun Bay. All were back at Piva by 1135.

Erdmann's division was next, taking off at 0830. Flying the Duke of York—Cape Archway sweep, they concentrated their attention on Duke of York Island. Two 500-pounders each were dropped at Ulu and Pal Pal plantations. Only one bomb was seen to cause any damage; Erdmann knocked over one hut. During strafing runs, Frank set fire to one hut on Pal Pal Plantation. The four Corsairs were back at Piva at 1055.

Moynihan's division led the first afternoon mission, taking off at 1230 for the Watom Island—Pondo Plantation sweep. The fighters plastered several huts on Pondo Plantation—which appeared to be uninhabited and severely damaged—scoring three direct hits with their 500-pounders. Strafing runs after the bomb run burned three more huts at Pondo Plantation, started a fire a couple of miles inland from Cape Lambert, and burned several huts at St. Johns. The Japanese offered no resistance and all planes returned to Piva unscathed at 1535.

Jones' division flew the last mission of the day, taking off from Piva at 1305 for the Duke of York—Cape Archway sweep. The four Corsairs ended up putting bombs on huts between Vunakanau and Tobera, Matala Plantation and buildings at Tobera Airfield. No damage was observed. The flight then strafed a 16 foot boat pulled onto the beach near Talili Plantation, and smoked a few huts and gardens between Vunakanau and Tobera Airfield. Before returning to Piva at 1550, the Corsairs searched for trucks spotted by New Zealand pilots the previous day near Utavalo Plantation but saw none.

Ten Corsairs of VMO-251 flew five two plane patrols over south Bougainville on 29 November with Schroeder's division flying the dawn patrol and Moynihan's division flying the dusk patrol. Both patrols reported no Japanese activity.

Jennings and Beattie flew the first south Bougainville patrol, taking off at 0615. Near

Mosiga, Jennings shot and killed a Japanese soldier during a strafing run, and he and Beattie killed another at the same location as they returned to Piva. In between the two strafing runs, they flew at tree top level over the Shortland Islands without spotting any huts or other targets. Near Kara Airfield and at Tonolei Harbor, they spotted many cooking fires and strafed them, as well as buildings at Kahili Airfield. Any damage caused by the strafing runs went unobserved.

The next patrol was flown by Crutcher and Lingenfelter. With wheels up at 0750, they quickly found themselves over Kahili, where they spotted two Japanese soldiers tending a garden and two others who bolted into some bushes upon spotting the Corsairs. Crutcher and Lingenfelter couldn't bring their Corsairs around fast enough to strafe the soldiers. By the time they arrived to strafe, the soldiers were no longer visible. They continued their sweep to Kieta and the north shore of Shortland Island where they strafed several huts.

At 1025, Gray and Warren took off at 1025 for the next patrol. As they flew over Moisuru near Kahili Airfield, they spotted two boat slides made of logs, leading from the water into a line of trees past the beach. As they closed in, they saw a large boat or barge under the trees on one of the slides. They let loose with their .50 caliber machine guns and set the craft on fire. As they continued their patrol, they drew AA fire from several locations: Ballale Island, Faisi Island, Kangu Hill and Ebery's Lease. The gunfire ranged from light to moderate but as in previous missions where AA fire was encountered, it was extremely inaccurate. The Corsairs were not hit. While it may not have been accurate fire, it did force the Corsairs to cut short their patrol and return to Piva.

Rosellen and MacLachlan were up next and after taking off at 1300, strafed a large thatched building at Koliai on Shortland Island. It burst into flames, sending a column of smoke 75 feet high into the air. The building was still burning 30 minutes later when the Corsairs left to continue their sweep. They drew AA fire from Faisi and Ballale Islands; MacLachlan's windshield was shattered as he flew over Ballale. Both pilots observed many villages on the eastern shore of Shortland Island and other islands in the area, as well as a coastal defense gun at Moila Point. They were back at Piva by 1510.

Bacheler and Pirages flew the last two plane patrol of the day, taking off at 1500. They made a complete circle of Bougainville and Buka Island, seeing very little of Japanese activity. Before returning to Piva at 1745, they set fire to three huts north of Mt. Bai on Buka.

Flying was scrubbed on 30 November due to lousy weather, putting an end to operations for the month of November 1944. The squadron's strength at the end of the month stood at 23 F4U-1D Corsairs, 55 officers and 255 enlisted men.

December 1944

The squadron stood down on 1 December for maintenance reasons. Combat operations resumed on 2 December when the squadron was ordered to hit AA gun positions at Raluana Point. Assigned to the mission were divisions led by Bacheler, Henley, Smith, and Jones. Bacheler had overall command of the flight. Armed with 500-pounders, all but one of the planes took off at 0900. Jones was not able to get off the ground due to mechanical problems with his Corsair.

When the Corsairs arrived at the target, a solid layer of clouds at 4,000 feet obscured the target from the pilots. Despite this, Bacheler decided to press the attack which commenced at 1020. Surprisingly, the Japanese put up no AA fire. His division was the first to drop their bombs, but all fell far south of the gun positions. The other divisions were able to place their bombs in the assigned target area scoring no hits. No visible damage was caused and the 15 Corsairs returned home at 1155.

Patrols at dawn and dusk, scramble alerts and south Bougainville patrols occupied the squadron on 3 December. Gray's division, with Warren, Mussman, and Poehlman, flew the dawn patrol. While Gray's division flew the early morning patrol, Erdmann's division, with Daigle, Moynihan and Wolf, stood on scramble alert. The roles were reversed for the dusk patrol. Both patrols saw no signs of enemy activity.

Scoville and Jernigan flew the first south Bougainville patrol, taking off at 0615. Their patrol was mostly uneventful except for the strafing of cooking fires at Monuito Mission and Kara Airfield. They were back at Piva two hours after they took off.

Frank and Ward were next in line for the south Bougainville patrol. As soon as Scoville and Jernigan pancaked at 0815, Frank and Ward took off to complete their mission for the day, which included a complete circuit around Bougainville and Buka islands. At Hanpan, they set fire to three huts after a strafing run. They continued their patrol to Rigu Mission, where they spotted a small camouflaged building on top of a hill rising from the water's edge. Next to the building was a 70-foot pole. The pilots could not figure what the installation may have been, and inexplicably, they did not strafe it. They continued on to Teop Island where they spotted a Japanese soldier on the beach but were over him before they could strafe. They also strafed locations along the Purita River in southwest Bougainville, suspected of housing Japanese soldiers. Frank and Ward were back at Piva at 1020.

The third south Bougainville patrol was flown by Cunningham and Barton. The two took off at 1000 and ended up strafing locations along the beach from Motupena Point to Kahili Airfield, then up to Kieta Harbor on the east coast. During a strafing run at Koromira Mission, they started a brush fire. Any damage caused by the two pilots went unobserved. Both were back at Piva at 1155.

Inglehart and Sturgis took off for the next south Bougainville patrol, leaving Piva at 1245. They found the weather had deteriorated so badly they turned around to return to Piva, landing at 1345.

Weather delayed the take off the last patrol for the day, flown by Schroeder and Evans. The two were able to get off the ground at 1430. They found south Bougainville covered solid with heavy rain and low hanging clouds. Getting around the weather front, they spotted a U.S. gunboat northwest of Choiseul Island and strafed huts between Luluai River and Koromira. Both were back at Piva by 1625.

The village of Hari in southwest Bougainville was the target of two strikes flown by the squadron on 4 December. The village was suspected of being the home of a large concentration of Japanese soldiers.

The first of the two strikes took off at 0715, comprised of divisions led by Bacheler, Henley, Smith and Jones (see table below). Each of the Corsairs carried one 1,000 pound bomb each. When Bacheler's flight arrived over the target area, they found the target covered with a thick layer of clouds stretching from 1,500 feet to 4,000 feet. Bacheler made the decision to abort the attack and the flight returned to Piva with their bombs, landing at 0800.

0715 Strike	1015 Strike
Bacheler (Division Leader and Flight Leader)	Wallace (Division Leader and Flight Leader)
Pirages	Pirages
Kennicott	Jernigan
Irwin	Irwin
Henley (Division Leader)	Henley (Division Leader)
Beattie	Beattie
Schoetz	Schoetz
Ward	Ward
Smith (Division Leader)	Smith (Division Leader)
Neilson	Neilson
Rosellen	Rosellen
MacLachlan	MacLachlan
Jones (Division Leader)	Jones (Division Leader)
Gorman	Gorman
Heisel	Heisel
Poehlman	Poehlman

At 1015, the second attempt to strike the target took off. Wallace had overall command of the flight, and with the exception of himself and Jernigan, consisted of the same pilots as the attempted morning strike (see above table). They arrived over Hari at 1040 and proceeded to strike the village. All bombs hit the target area, and following two strafing runs by the 16 Corsairs at tree-top level, left the village in ruins. As the planes departed the area, two 100 foot columns of smoke were seen to rise from the village. The Japanese offered no resistance, and all Corsairs were back at Piva at 1115.

The Rabaul area sweeps were the order of the day for 5 December. Armed with 500-pounders, Schroeder's division, consisting of himself, Evans, Frank and Lindsey, took off at 0900 for the Cape Archway—Duke of York sweep. Schroeder and Frank scored direct hits on villages on Duke of York Island, destroying at least four buildings. Evans dropped his bomb on a village on Malapoa Plantation while Lindsey dropped his on a village near Tobera Airfield, both with unobserved results.

The Japanese put up meager machine gun fire, striking Evans from a location near the coast and north of Warangoi River. The damage was minimal; puncturing his starboard wing about four feet from the fuselage. No one else was hit and the four Corsairs pancaked at Piva at 1210.

Five minutes after Schroeder's division was in the air, Gray led Warren, Mussman and Kammeyer on the Watom Island–Pondo Plantation sweep. They dropped three of the 500-pounders one mile southeast of Keravat Airfield with unknown results. They continued the sweep, spotting a truck parked under trees near a road juncture. After Mussman dropped his 500-pounder on the truck, all four repeatedly strafed it. They left the truck burning fiercely as they retired to Piva, landing at 1225.

Cunningham, Sigan, Scoville and Jernigan took off at 1300 for the Cape Archway—Duke of York sweep. They found the east coast of the Gazelle Peninsula covered in clouds, so diverted to attack a village on the northeast coast of Duke of York Island. Cunningham and Sigan scored direct hits, destroying many buildings. As they continued their sweep no signs of the enemy were observed. They returned to Piva ta 1530.

Thirty minutes after Cunningham's division left Piva, Jennings, Erdmann, Moynihan and Wolf flew the Cape Lambert sweep. Jennings, Erdman and Wolf dropped their bombs on buildings at Langinda Plantation, scoring three misses. Moynihan scored a direct hit on a building in the village of Kamanakam, located south of Cape Lambert on the west coast of the Gazelle Peninsula. The Japanese offered no resistance and all Corsairs were back at Piva by 1645.

It was back to dawn and dusk patrols, and south Bougainville patrols for the squadron on 6 December. The south Bougainville patrols would provide plenty of action for the pilots who flew them.

Jones' division was assigned the dawn patrol while Wallace, Lingenfelter, Garrett and Harris stood the morning's scramble alert. The roles were reversed for the dusk patrol. As usual, no sign of the enemy was observed by both patrols.

The first of the south Bougainville patrols was flown by Smith and Neilson, who were wheels up at 0715. They found a thick ground fog obscuring the area near Kahili airstrip east to Tonolei Harbor. Strafing runs at Morone, Kakurai and Moro smoked five huts. South of Kara Airfield they saw at least six AA guns either enclosed in dugouts or situated in craters. The guns were not strafed. However, they did strafe and kill a Japanese soldier who was lying flat in a road near the guns.

As they continued their patrol, they strafed a barge on the shore in a small inlet west of East Point in Tonolei Harbor. As they pulled out of the strafing run, they spotted what appeared to be a 20 MM AA gun covered with a camouflaged poncho. Smith and Neilson made three strafing runs on the gun, possibly damaging it.

Jennings and Crutcher departed at 0800 for the second south Bougainville patrol. Flying at tree-top level over the derelict vessel east of Kahili Airfield, they spotted one 20 MM and two 12.7 MM guns aboard the rusting wreck. The barrels appeared to be in good working order but the mounts were crumbling with rust. Oddly the Japanese did not open up on the Corsairs, nor did Jennings and Crutcher strafe the guns.

They did smoke three huts near Kahili but saw no signs of Japanese activity. Crutcher ended up striking a tree with his port wing during the strafing runs on the huts. The damage appeared to be slight and he continued with the patrol. As they flew north of Kahili, they spotted two enemy soldiers walking along a road but were past them before they could open up on the soldiers. When they returned to Piva at 1030, maintenance crews looked over the damage on Crutcher's wing and determined it had to be replaced.

Next up were Moynihan and Pirages, departing Piva at 1025. They spotted a camp fire at Tinputd Mission and a Japanese soldier with a backpack two miles south of Tsimba Mission. Neither was strafed as they both were within a restricted zone, forbidding any attack by allied forces. Deteriorating weather cut short their patrol and on their way back, they smoked some huts on the central west coast of Buka.

At 1255, Kennicott and Irwin took off for the fourth patrol of the day. They spotted, strafed and no doubt killed a Japanese soldier at Mugai Mission, and three other soldiers near Moisuru. They spotted another soldier on a beach at Aitapa and saw smoke rising from the jungle in the center of Popatala Island but neither target was strafed. Rain squalls along the coastline cut short their patrol; they were back at Piva at 1455.

Departing Piva at 1510, Henley and Barton flew the last patrol of the day. They were accompanied by Hart, who once flew with the squadron and now with the 1st Marine Air Wing. Unlike the other patrols of the day, they carried 500-pounders. They had a specific target they were going after: the AA gun at Tonolei Harbor spotted by Smith and Neilson earlier in the morning. Each dropped their bomb within 50 feet of the gun but it escaped damage. They circled around for two strafing runs on the 20 MM gun but did not damage the gun. Leaving the gun behind, the three pilots strafed huts in the Kara Airfield—Plano Mission–Mt. Senfft area, setting three of them on fire. Strafing runs along the Monuito Mission—Kahili road yielded no results. Following this strafing run, the three pilots returned home.

On the three year anniversary of the attack on Pearl Harbor, Bacheler led 16 Corsairs for another strike on the village of Hari. With Bacheler's division were divisions led by Schroeder, Gray and Cunningham. The sixteen Corsairs were in the air at 0730 and an hour later, four tons of bombs were dropped in the target area but the target escaped damage. Disappointed, Bacheler led his Corsairs back to Piva, landing at 0900.

Only two missions were flown on 8 December. First in the air at 0600 were Henley, Barton, Schoetz, and Ward for the Cape Archway—Duke of York sweep. With a weather front that extended from Gazelle Peninsula to New Ireland to Green Island, Henley led his division through the front after finding a break in the clouds and dropped their bombs

VMO-251 Corsair, BuNo 56691. Pilot is Russell Cunningham. Location is Piva Airfield, Bougainville, late 1944 (courtesy John W. Irwin).

near Tobera Airfield. The pilots did not stick around to see if any damage was inflicted by their attack; instead they returned to Piva and landed at 0830.

Jones, Gorman, Poehlman and Daigle, who were assigned the Pondo Plantation—Watom Island sweep, were up in the air at 0820. They ended up dropping their bombs on huts at Pondo Plantation that were barely standing. Three hit in the vicinity of the huts and one was a dud. The flight continued with their sweep, hitting the front seen by Henley's division lying across the Gazelle Peninsula south of Cape Lambert. It forced them to turn around to return to Piva and they landed at 1105.

Any remaining combat operations for MAG-14 ceased the same day. By order of the 1st Marine Air Wing, MAG-14 was placed on 48 hour alert in anticipation of movement of all units of the group to the Philippine Islands.[82] Leave was canceled for all personnel and those on leave were recalled back to their assigned squadrons. The squadron continued to fly, practicing squadron and division tactics.

On 14 December, the squadron was alerted for the move to the Philippines. Three days later Humberd flew to Green Island to meet with MAG-14 commander Colonel Zebulon Hopkins to discuss the move. The squadron was ordered to move on 18 December. When Humberd told Hopkins of his orders from 1st MAW, Hopkins was surprised; he was not aware of any such orders. In fact the field in which MAG-14 squadrons would eventually end up—Guiuan—was still under construction and not ready to receive any aircraft. According to Hopkins, it wasn't until the end of the month that he received permission to send one of his squadrons to Guiuan; he chose to send VMO-251.[83] On 28 December, the squadron finally received its orders to depart for Samar, Philippine Islands. Twenty-five Corsairs were to fly the distance to Samar via Emirau, Hollandia, Owi Island, and Peleliu. Take off time was set for 0600, 30 December.

The use of R4D transport aircraft was arranged to provide transportation for extra pilots, mechanics with their toolkits and personal gear. Most of the squadron's organic gear would stay at Bougainville. To make up for the loss of gear, the Seabees at Samar would help out.[84]

Pilots received lectures from the squadron's intelligence officer as well as a representative from 1st MAW's intelligence section. The briefings covered a variety of topics: the latest methods to authenticate messages, survival methods; the state of the current guerrilla situation in the Philippines, and recognition of Japanese aircraft.

With the briefings complete, all that remained was to make the nearly 3,000 mile flight to the Philippines.

Six

Guiuan Field, Samar, Philippine Islands, and Deactivation

The big day arrived. At 0620 on 30 December, despite bad weather, the R4Ds carrying the ground echelon took to the air from Piva for Samar. At 0730, the squadron's 25 Corsairs, plus their PBJ escorts to guide them all the way to Samar, followed the transport aircraft. Following a 3.5 hour flight, the Corsairs landed at Emirau.

The next day, 22 of the squadron's Corsairs took off at 0730 for the next leg of the trip. Two of the Corsairs remained behind to be transferred to another squadron and another developed starter and engine problems. About 75 miles out, the flight of Corsairs ran into a storm front forcing them to return to Emirau where they waited for a break in the weather. That came early in the afternoon when at 1400, the Corsairs returned to the air. The weather again deteriorated but the squadron pushed on, landing at Hollandia at 1830.

On New Year's Day 1945, the Corsairs departed Hollandia for Owi Island. Following its arrival there, the squadron remained overnight and continued its flight the following day.

Early on the morning of 2 January, the flight departed Owi and after a 3 hour, 15 minute flight the the planes of VMO-251 arrived at Peleliu at 1030. The planes were refueled, pilots grabbed a quick bite to eat, and following a quick briefing, took off at 1400. After nearly three hours in the air, their new home appeared on the horizon—Guiuan Airfield, Samar, Philippine Islands. "There were no taxiways and no buildings, only a coral strip 7,000 feet long, running east to west on a tiny narrow peninsula, from water's edge to water's edge," wrote Bacheler.[1] Bacheler was the first in the squadron to land, Irwin was second.[2] By 1745, all 22 Corsairs were on the ground, as well as two R4Ds.[3]

The base was crowded with other planes and construction gear; the pilots found it difficult to find a space to park their planes. VMO-251 was the first Marine squadron under MAG-14 to arrive at the airfield and would be the group's first squadron to commence combat operations. The rest of MAG-14 would follow later in the month.

Unfortunately, a mishap upon landing marred what was otherwise an accident-free island hopping deployment. While taxiing, Lindsey's plane struck another Corsair. Damage was slight to the plane struck, but Lindsey's Corsair was grounded until a replacement wing could be found for the aircraft.

By the time VMO-251 moved to Samar, General Douglas MacArthur's campaign to

Six. Guiuan Field, Samar, Philippine Islands, and Deactivation

Guiuan Airfield, Samar, Philippine Islands, March 1945 (National Archives).

take back the Philippines was well under way. Leyte was assaulted on 20 October 1944. At the end of the month, some of the U.S. troops moved from Leyte to Samar and with the help of guerrillas, quickly gained control of the lightly defended island. In order to establish advanced bases for the upcoming invasion of Luzon, U.S. troops went ashore at Mindoro in December.

Once Samar was secured, work began in early December 1944 to construct the airfield at Guiuan, located on the east coast of the island near its southern tip. The 61st and 93rd Construction Battalions (Seabees), using crushed coral to cover the runway, worked diligently to get the 1.5 mile long strip ready for operations. By 1 January 1945, the airfield was deemed ready for business for Army, Navy and Marine aircraft. It may have been ready to receive aircraft but it was far from complete; the field lacked taxi ways, there wasn't enough room to properly stage aircraft, tents provided temporary shelter, supplies had yet to be stockpiled to sustain operations and daily heavy rains created potholes in the runway requiring engineers to resurface the field on a continuing basis. The poor conditions led to numerous operational losses due to accidents, and made maintaining the aircraft difficult.

In the coming months, the harsh conditions and the number of missions demanded by the 5th Air Force forced maintenance personnel to work long into the night, and with the help of civilian factory representatives, found solutions to maintenance problems not in the books. Most of the squadron Corsairs in the coming months would spend anywhere up to nine hours in the air during the course of a day, forcing ground personnel to maintain strict schedules to keep the planes in opertion. If a required inspection came due for a plane, the work started as soon as the pilot shut his engine down.

As an example, coral dust on the runway made life miserable for hydraulic specialists in the squadron. The dust would accumulate on the landing gear struts and eventually ruin the hydraulic seals. Master Technical Sergeant Robert E. Conroy built metal scrapers and mounted them at the base of the struts. As the gear was raised and lowered, the scrapers would prevent the dust from clogging the rings, keeping the plane operational for a longer amount of time.[4]

There were no facilities to house the squadron upon arrival, so initially the squadron was quartered with the Seabees. It was an eye-opener for Irwin. "The Navy mess seemed to have access to supplies far more palatable than what we had become accustomed to," wrote Irwin. "The Seabees had constructed their own chapel and after 251 relocated to the east side of the island, I would often journey back for a Sunday evening service and supper."[5] Squadron personnel remained with the Seabees for two weeks before moving to their own area on the east side.

Like Piva, there wasn't much the men could do to keep themselves busy when not flying combat missions. Playing poker remained popular but until MAG-14 settled in and provided the men with entertainment in the form of sports and movies, the men improvised.

"During some leisure hours and with a native lad as guide, Beattie and I found ourselves in the native jewelry business," recalls Irwin. "At low tide we collected hundreds of cowrie shells from the coral reef off shore from camp. When rid of their occupants, these would be stuffed with cotton (from sickbay) and linked together with fine wire (from flight line) for a necklace/bracelet combination to send home loved ones and sell to compatriots for such purpose.

"With the shell business having run its course, Alex (Beattie) and I ventured into a Japanese flag enterprise, obtaining a "surveyed" chute from the parachute loft, cutting it to size and applying red "meat balls" and appropriate Japanese characters with paint (once again) from flight line. I had taken a semester of Japanese language before leaving college to enlist in the Navy Flight Program. Although we explained to potential buyers that the flags were "fake," they found a ready market since genuine ones available from ground forces were scarce.

Six. Guiuan Field, Samar, Philippine Islands, and Deactivation

Living conditions on Samar, Philippine Islands. *Left to right:* James "Tiny" Robinson, Curtis D. "Red Dog" Jernigan, John W. "Honest John" Wyatt, and Hugh "Yogi" Irwin (courtesy Hugh E. "Yogi" Irwin).

"I obtained two genuine flags from ground troops in exchange for medicinal alcohol. Although beer was occasionally available to all hands, pilots were supposedly the only personnel with access to stronger spirits as allotted by the ounce following each mission; however, a friendly flight surgeon might allow accumulation until a full bottle's worth was available for consumption on special occasions."[6]

In addition to poor facilities, the squadron lacked the ordnance to fly anything but escort duty and patrols. Until supplies could be built up, the squadron's Corsairs were armed with .50 caliber ammunition only. It would be nearly a month before the squadron resumed carrying bombs on their missions.

By noon of 3 January, squadron maintenance personnel repaired one of the two Corsairs damaged upon arrival at Guiuan, bringing the number of operational planes of the squadron to 21. MAG-14 and all its squadrons were placed under the operational control of the 5th Air Force, and later the 85th Fighter Wing.[7] The squadron commander, Humberd, located an Army signal station and with a bit of pride "notified the Commanding General, Fifth Fighter Command that the Marines had landed and the situation was well in hand."[8] Combat operations began with several divisions flying combat patrols over Samar and Leyte Gulf throughout the day. None of the divisions saw any signs of the enemy.

The patrols continued the next two days, with the addition of escorting C-47 transport aircraft to Panay on 5 January and to Mindoro on 6 January. Four officers joined the squadron on 5 January: 2Lt. Frank J. Rhodes, 2Lt. James W. Robinson, 2Lt. Harold G. Sandbach, and 2Lt. Charles Scott. During both days, nothing was seen of the enemy during the patrols.

On 7 January, Wallace's division flew cover for part of MacArthur's invasion force

The muddy field at Guiuan Airfield, Samar, P.I. in a photo dated 5 January 1945. Corsairs in background are those of VMO-251 (National Archives).

on its way to Lingayen Gulf off the northwest coast of Luzon, where it was scheduled to arrive on 9 January. Divisions led by Inglehart, Jones, Gray, and Henley, plus pilots Scoville, Jernigan, Cunningham and Beattie provided escort for many C-47s flying from Leyte to Mindoro and back. On one of the hops, Gray's division, with the addition of Scoville and Jernigan, were airborne for nearly seven hours.

The squadron continued to fly cover for several convoys on their way to Lingayen Gulf on 8 January. Humberd's division, augmented with pilots Jennings and Erdmann, flew until relieved by Wallace's division which was reinforced with Moynihan and Wolf. Unfortunately Wallace was forced to turn back after 30 minutes due to a mechanical problem with his Corsair. The Japanese offered no resistance leaving the pilots disappointed that they would not have the opportunity to meet any Japanese aircraft in the air. During the course of the day, divisions led by Henley, Gray and Schroeder flew patrols over Leyte Gulf from dawn to dusk.

At 0700 on 9 January, ships in MacArthur's invasion force opened up with a pre-assault bombardment, and an hour later the landings at Lingayen Gulf began. Over 170,000 men of General Walter Krueger's Sixth Army were ashore within several days.[9] While Krueger's men began the first steps in the liberation of Luzon, Corsairs of VMO-251 were busy with several sweeps to the south and west of Samar.

Cunningham, Frank, Scoville, and Jernigan left Guiuan Airfield at 0822 to sweep Panay, Negros and Cebu. At Panay, the four pilots made several strafing runs at San Jose

Airfield. The Japanese put intense AA fire and as Jernigan was making his strafing run, his plane was raked with 7.7 MM fire causing his engine to spew smoke. He broke off his run and turned for home, followed by the other pilots. He was able to nurse his plane back to Guiuan, landing safely with the others at 1140.

It was the same sweep for Gray, Warren, Mussman and Daigle; taking off at 1105. Unlike the first four pilots, they received AA fire from every location they strafed. As they flew over Japanese held Cebu Airfield, they saw no serviceable aircraft. It was on to Negros Island. At San Erique, the pilots spotted four trucks and an unarmored vehicle on a road next to the airfield. Circling around they lined up for a strafing run and within minutes, all five vehicles were a mass of flames. They also fired at several aircraft—most appeared unserviceable—at the south end of the runway. During his strafing run at 200 feet, Gray was hit by 20 MM fire. The fire was accurate. The rounds impacted around the cockpit, destroying Gray's aerial and shattering the top of his canopy. Gray suffered many cuts on his face but was able to maintain control of his aircraft. It was then on to Bacolod Airfield where they set another truck on fire following several strafing runs. On a road southeast of Bago, Gray and Warren set fire to four vehicles: two trucks and two cars. The flight also strafed a supply area containing 50-gallon drums, but the drums did not explode. Near San Jose, the four pilots combined to sink two 60-foot motor launches near a pier. It was a productive day, and the pilots were all smiles when they finally touched down at Guiuan.

Weather moved in for the 1415 sweep to Panay, Cebu and Negros, making things difficult for Humberd, Inglehart and Sturgis. Thick clouds stretching from 1,500 feet to 10,000 feet prevented thorough observations from being made. They only got one strafing run in at San Jose Airfield, firing at what appeared to be wrecked planes at the south end of the runway. As they flew over San Erique Airfield on Negros, Sturgis spotted what may have been two serviceable twin-engine bombers. For unknown reasons, the bombers were not strafed. The Japanese did not retaliate; the three Corsairs drew no AA fire the entire mission. The planes were back at Guiuan by 1730.

In addition to the patrols, Smith's division, with the addition Crutcher and Irwin, and another flight composed Jones, Harris, Poehlman, 2Lt. John W. Wyatt, Kammeyer and Beattie, flew escort for C-47s to Mindoro Island and back to Leyte. Moynihan and Wolf flew the Leyte Gulf patrol but bad weather forced them to be recalled back to base.

The rain that curtailed the patrol flown by Moynihan and Wolf the previous day continued to plague the missions assigned to the squadron on 10 January. Divisions led by Gray and Schroeder were able to successfully fly the Leyte Gulf patrol but spotted nothing of the enemy. Humberd's division, however, cursed the weather. Taking off at 0915, they had been assigned to escort C-47s destined for Mindoro. They reached the rendezvous point but found no C-47s. Humberd decided to stay and wait for the transport planes. After two hours, Humberd received a call to return to base due to deteriorating weather—apparently the C-47s never got off the ground or were themselves recalled. After nearly three hours in the air, Humberd's Corsairs were back at Guiuan by 1215.

Earlier in the morning, Jennings, Erdmann, Moynihan and Wolf departed for a sweep over the Visayan Islands (consisting of the larger Islands of Panay, Negros, Cebu, Bohol, Leyte, and Samar) in the Philippines. During the course of their sweep they spotted what appeared to be an abandoned cargo vessel dead in the water at Liloan Point, north of Cebu City, strafed points from Binalbagan to Bacolod and Jennings destroyed a truck at San Erique. They had to abandon their run over Negros due to bad weather and returned to base. The rest of the missions scheduled for the day were scrubbed; the tropical rains had settled in.

The rain continued through the night, finally dissipating enough to go ahead with the one mission scheduled for 11 January. Two flights of four planes each—consisting of Smith, Sigan, Rosellen, MacLachlan, Schroeder, Crutcher, Pirages and Kammeyer—were wheels up at 0720 to strafe Del Monte (consisting of seven strips, numbered 1–7) and Butuan Airfields located in northwest Mindanao. Smith, Sigan, Rosellen and MacLachlan came in at tree-top level to make their strafing runs. Sigan scored big by destroying four trucks west of Del Monte #1. The Japanese opened up with AA fire, peppering MacLachlan's Corsair in the port wing with 20 MM fire, ripping a hole about 1x3 feet in size in the top portion of the wing. MacLachlan broke off his attack, and accompanied by Sigan, headed back to Guiuan.

The remaining planes continued their attacks. Schroeder, Crutcher, Pirages, and Kammeyer gunned houses and revetments at Del Monte and Butuan but no results were observed. The planes regrouped and turned for Guiuan, landing after nearly four hours in the air.

During the strafing runs at Del Monte, the pilots saw a crashed Corsair on its belly about 10 miles west of Del Monte #3. Upon arrival back at Guiuan, reports were sent to Fifth Fighter Command concerning the downed plane. Fighter command remained silent; headquarters at 251 could only assume that the higher-ups were aware of the matter.

The squadron drew the Leyte Gulf patrols from dawn to dusk on 12 January. Tapped for the patrols were divisions led by Jennings and Gray, along with fellow pilots Inglehart, Rhodes, Sturgis and Scott. The two divisions drew additional duty; they were ordered to find a reported radar station near Jugban on northwest Mindanao as well as fly a reconnaissance patrol over Surigao. The radar station was never seen, and the recon mission was unproductive.

At 0730 Wallace's division was ordered to fly to a point west of the Calamian Island Group, located to the north and east off the coast of Palawan, and await further instructions. Before they hit the rendezvous area, the flight hit a solid front of bad weather. Wallace attempted to contact headquarters for further instructions but could not raise anyone. With no answer forthcoming, Wallace turned his flight around and returned to Guiuan, landing at 0945. His division took off on two other missions during the day and each time they were turned back by weather. It was certainly a frustrating day for Wallace.

Lousy weather hampered one of the missions flown in the afternoon by the squadron on 13 January. Bacheler, Robinson, Pirages, and Sandbach, along with Cunningham, Beattie, Scoville and Jernigan flew combat air patrols over Mindoro, encountering no Japanese. Jones's division escorted a Dumbo to Luzon, while Jennings' division flew the Leyte Gulf patrol. Gray's division, with Inglehart and Scott tagging along, took off at 1340 to cover a convoy. The pilots could not locate the convoy; thick clouds and rain covered the area. They turned around for home, landing at 1650.

Convoy duty was the order of the day for 14 and 15 January. Divisions led by Humberd, Wallace, Henley and Gray flew cover for a convoy bound for Luzon. The day proved uneventful for the pilots; the Japanese did not attempt to attack. On 15 January, divisions led by Bacheler (flying twice), Schroeder, Smith, Cunningham and Jones protected another Luzon bound convoy from dawn to dusk. While Smith's division was flying cover, Rosellen and MacLachlan assisted one of the destroyers in an attack on a suspected submarine lurking in the area. The results of the attack went unobserved.

The following day would prove to be a long one with some of the squadron pilots spending six hours in the air. Divisions led by Humberd, Henley, Wallace—with Kammeyer as a section leader—and Jennings flew cover for convoys making way between Leyte Gulf and Lingayen Gulf. When they weren't flying cover for the convoys, they were flying sweeps over southern Luzon.

At 1015, Gray, Warren, Mussman and Daigle took to the air to attack Japanese rolling stock and other targets of opportunity on southern Luzon. They quickly found three camouflaged trucks near Naga and set fire to two of them after a strafing run. Still over Naga, they found a locomotive with five cars; it appeared to be in disuse but they strafed it anyway. It was on to Igira where they left another three trucks smoking. Stormy weather quickly moved in cutting short the patrol at Basiad Bay. They turned around to head back to Guiuan. As they made for home, they flew over Legaspi Airfield but saw no enemy activity or aircraft at the field. They were back at Guiuan by 1420. Later in the day Gray's division flew a patrol over Leyte Gulf.

Humberd's division flew their patrol to southern Luzon at noon, looking for a railroad roundhouse at Pamplopa. They located the building and had a successful strafing run: incendiaries and tracers smoked 15 railroad cars and turned a water tower into a sieve. An approaching storm front cut the patrol short; they changed course and made way for Guiuan, landing at 1540.

Henley's division departed at 1240 to pick up where Humberd's division left off. They flew over the southern Luzon target area from 1330 to 1630 but found very little to shoot. When they arrived back at Guiuan at 1700 they reported that all railway and highway bridges were unusable to the Japanese, and six trains seen from above by the pilots were burning.

Jennings' and Wallace's divisions took off at 1450, rendezvoused with four P-47 Thunderbolts over Leyte Gulf and made for Ioilo, Panay Island. The 12 fighters had orders to strafe fuel tanks had been reported on the west coast of Guimaras Island. Arriving at the target area, the fighters commenced their strafing runs. However, they found the fuel tanks heavily protected with concrete making them look like pillboxes. Their efforts to destroy the fuel tanks were ineffective. They left the area and continued with the patrol. They spotted several derelict barges, and shot up roads along the west coast of Negros Island near Bacolod. No Japanese AA fire was encountered, and the Corsairs were home by 1700.

Missions over southern Luzon occupied the squadron on 17 January. From 0800 to 1645, the squadron maintained a four-plane fighter sweep over southern Luzon. Each division was relieved on station by the next. Bacheler's division had the first sweep but saw very little to report except for a burning locomotive near the town of Oas.

Relieving them at 0915 and remaining on station until 1115 were Schroeder, Robinson, Evans and Lindsey. Their sweep over the target area was much more productive. Schroeder smoked a car and a truck northwest of Naga, while Lindsey exploded a truck northeast of the same town. As they patrolled over San Jose Airfield, Schroeder's plane took six hits of .50 caliber ammunition in the aft section of the fuselage. The damage was superficial. Their sweep completed, the four planes set a course of Guiuan and landed at 1215. During Evans' approach he was caught in the slipstream of the plane in front of him, dragged his port wing and spun off the runway into a ditch. Evans was able to walk away from the crash with cuts and bruises to his head but his plane (BuNo 57297) was a total loss.

Squadron maintenance area at Guiuan Airfield, Samar, Philippine Islands, 1945 (courtesy Madden Family).

Jones' division arrived over southern Luzon at 1045, taking over for Schroeder, Robinson, Evans and Lindsey. They ended up smoking a barge secured to a pier near Samiepan. Cloud cover up to 13,000 feet in the vicinity of Lucena and the surrounding area hindered the rest of the patrol, making sighting any Japanese activity impossible. They retired back to Guiuan at 1300 after being relieved by Cunningham's division, which arrived at 1215.

Cunningham's four Corsairs set several box cars on fire and smoked a car at Libmanan and Catabangan. While in the vicinity of Binahalan they strafed a boat and as they flew over San Jose Airfield they spotted a couple of vehicles that appeared to be unusable. They retired at 1400 when Bacheler's division returned for another sweep.

Bacheler's Corsairs encountered rain covering southern Luzon. Heading west they went around the rain and looked over the town of Lucena. There, a runway that appeared serviceable was noted. Flying on to Castillo, they strafed a locomotive but were unable to determine if they did any damage. Schroeder's division, relieving Bacheler's division at 1500, finished the southern Luzon patrols by strafing a Japanese radio station at Legaspi Airfield. Despite the radio towers being plainly visible to the pilots, the station apparently received no damage from the .50 caliber machine guns.

On 18 January, troops with Krueger's Sixth Army were meeting stiff resistance from the Japanese in the vicinity of Rosario and requested help. MAG-14 responded by ordering

VMO-251 to execute the close air support mission; their first against the Japanese in the Philippines.

With Humberd in the lead, 16 Corsairs took to the air at 0835. Wallace had to turn back soon after taking off due to a hydraulic leak. The rest of the flight continued with the mission. About 100 miles south of Manila, the Corsairs ran into a solid front of clouds extending thousands of feet into the air. Humberd took his Corsairs up to 23,000 feet in order to get over the front, but it was impossible. The clouds appeared to go on, far past the safe operating altitude for a Corsair. Humberd had no choice but to turn his Corsairs around and head back to Guiuan. The disappointed pilots landed at 1200.

Operations were secured on 19 January due to bad weather and resumed on 20 January. Flying over Luzon the entire day, five divisions hit several locations on the island and combined to destroy 21 trucks, three cars, and one 35-foot motor launch.

But the squadron paid a high cost for their success. At 1405 Humberd's division was strafing targets north of the town of Muntinglupa. Flying below 1,000 feet, Sigan (BuNo 57169) and Sturgis (BuNo 57531) sighted a truck and lined up for a strafing run. Apparently neither one was aware of the other's position. They approached the target from opposite directions, letting loose with their .50 calibers when they collided head-on and crashed in flames. To Humberd and Inglehart, it appeared the two Corsairs exploded when they hit the ground. They saw no chutes, nor did they find any sign of life when they circled the wrecks. Sigan and Sturgis were listed as Missing in Action and later changed to Killed in Action. Sigan's remains were eventually recovered[10] and buried at the Manila American Cemetery (Plot N, Row 17, Grave 167).[11] Sturgis' body was never located. Both men were well-liked in the squadron, and their loss was keenly felt.

The aircraft action report was blunt in its assessment in what caused the collision, stating "the accident was obviously caused by the fact the two pilots who crashed head-on, did not know the whereabouts of the other three planes in the flight. This rule must be instilled into all pilots engaged in this type of operation that no pilot will make a strafing run until he is positive of the whereabouts of every other plane in the flight."[12] This may be true, however the pace of operations the squadron was maintaining taxed the pilots—fatigue may have been a factor. By the time January 1945 was relegated to history, MAG-14 squadrons—consisting of VMO-251, VMF-212, VMF-222, and VMF-223—flew over 5,000 combat hours, with VMO-251 flying nearly half of those hours.[13]

The men of the squadron had to quickly shake off the loss of the two pilots. There was a war to be fought and operations did not stop because of casualties. It rained through the evening and into the morning of 21 January, turning the airfield into a pool of oozing mud. As pilots manned their planes for the day's mission, the heavy rains had given way to a fine mist and overcast skies.

The missions started just before sunrise. At 0615, Jones, Sandbach and Poehlman took off to patrol the west coast of Leyte near the village of Palompan. Their job was to intercept a Japanese plane reported to have visited the area in the past to perform strafing runs. Their patrol was uneventful; apparently the Japanese plane made no appearance. The three pilots were back at Guiuan in two hours, pancaking at 0815.

At the west end of the runway, B-24s of the 22nd Bombardment Group waited for the green flare that would signal them that the scheduled mission to strike Heito, Formosa was to proceed as planned. Takeoff time was set for 0655. Commanding the mission and in the lead plane *Our Honey* was group commander Col. Richard W. Robinson. In the cockpit's left seat was veteran group pilot Cpt. James C. Hume. Also on board was an extra passenger, combat photographer SSGT George E. Sharp. The B-24 was fully loaded with aviation fuel, 11 men, and five 1,000 pound bombs.

At the opposite end of the airfield, Bacheler, Beattie, Irwin, and one other pilot—possibly Pirages—were ready to take off for their early morning mission. On the field early, a rain squall delayed their initial departure time. Their takeoff was further delayed when they received word from the tower that they would have to wait until the B-24s were on their way to Formosa. They were also directed to take off from east to west when it was their turn to go. Bacheler led his Corsairs as they taxied—straddling the runway to do so—towards the other end of the strip. They pulled off the strip on the north end with engines running to await their turn.

After an isolated storm passed over the field, the tower fired its green flair. Despite the hanging mist and occasional rain that reduced visibility, the B-24s spotted the flare. They also received word via radio that the mission was a go. Hume pushed the throttles forward, and the fully loaded *Our Honey* began its takeoff roll down the slick runway. Irwin, monitoring the radio frequency, heard Hume relay to the tower, "Tell them to get out of the way, we have a date in Formosa."[14]

"As we sat in the abutment we had parked in, we could only watch aghast as the four-motored Liberator thundered out of the storm's mist—obviously well left of runway center and dangerously close to our aircraft," recalled Irwin. "There was nothing we could do. As somewhat mesmerized, I watched the behemoth pass the first three of us safely but as it went by Alex (Beattie) in plane four a tip of the wing flew into the air as it sliced through the Corsair's 13 foot propeller. For a moment all was silent as Beattie and I stared at one another from our cockpits."[15]

It was more than the tip of the wing; the Hamilton prop had cut off a six foot section of the left wing and part of the aileron. Hume struggled to control the bomber, and got it airborne for a few seconds before it crashed and burst into flames, taking with it a nearby construction vehicle. Within minutes, some of the 1,000 pound bombs exploded, sending concussion waves and debris across the field. Red flares were fired from the tower, aborting further takeoffs.

With shrapnel and debris falling around them, the four Marine pilots scrambled out of their cockpits and sought refuge underneath the wings of their Corsairs until the rain of metal subsided. Their mission aborted, they made their way back to the flight line. When they arrived, bomb fragments were found throughout the ready room and surrounding camp areas. No VMO-251 Marines were injured as a result of the incident.

It was a different story for the bomber. All 11 crewmen were killed, as was a Seabee manning the construction truck.[16]

At 0845, Smith, Robinson, Rosellen, CPT. Joseph P. Hart—back to the squadron after a stint as Assistant Operations Officer with the First Marine Air Wing—and MacLachlan took to the air to escort a flight of C-47s to Mindoro. While the transport planes landed and unloaded their supplies, the Corsairs circled the island. Once the C-47s were back up in the air, the Corsairs escorted the transports back to Leyte. They then flew back to Guiuan. From takeoff to landing, the pilots spent 6.5 hours in the air.

Schroeder, Harris, Frank, Lindsey, Scoville and Jernigan also pulled escort duty, protecting another group of C-47s on their way to Mindoro and back to Leyte. All but Lindsey landed safely at 1710. Lindsey lost control of his plane as he touched down, flipping it over on its back, shearing off the engine and both wings as it slid into mud off the side of the runway near where the squadron Corsairs were parked. Squadron ground crew personnel rushed to the scene of the crash and pulled Lindsey out of the cockpit. Lindsey suffered many cuts and bruises to the head and had to be hospitalized. His plane (BuNo 57399) was a total loss.

The squadron pulled continuous air patrols over Leyte Gulf, putting 20 planes in the air on 22 January. In addition, Jennings, Erdmann, Moynihan and Wolf took off at 0710 to fly a reconnaissance patrol over southern Luzon. Drawing light AA fire, the flight made several strafing runs on a radar station and power plant at Caluauag with no apparent results. During their patrol, they also spotted a grass-covered runway east of Negritos Camp. All made it back to Guiuan, landing at 1145.

Wallace's division escorted a flight of C-47s to Mindoro, taking off at 1015. As the four Corsairs covered the transport planes, they ran into bad weather. Wallace and his wingman lost sight of the C-47s and could not relocate them. Both turned around and returned to Guiuan. Garrett and 2Lt. Ernest E. Poor stuck with the C-47s to complete the escort mission. They were back at Guiuan by 1500.

The last mission for the day was flown by Humberd, 2Lt. Virgil A. Lingenfelter, Inglehart and Scott; taking off at 1400 to sweep southern Luzon for reported Japanese seaplanes seen in the area. Lingenfelter returned early to Guiuan when his Corsair developed hydraulic problems. The remaining pilots continued with the sweep, smoking three trucks east of Soragon Bay. No seaplanes were spotted. Humberd and his two fellow pilots returned to Guiuan, landing at 1800.

Six divisions were assigned to fly combat air patrols over Leyte Gulf from sunrise to sunset on 23 January with orders to cover convoys moving through the gulf. Three divisions flying during the afternoon were called back to base early because of declining weather. Another four aircraft flew an early dawn patrol of the Camotes Sea and the western shore of Leyte. None of the divisions saw any sign of the Japanese.

The squadron flew a variety of missions the next day. Divisions led Wallace and Henley flew the dawn and dusk patrols over the Camotes Sea; Humberd and Jennings led their divisions as they flew fighter cover for a convoy southwest of Negros Island; Gray and Lingenfelter flew two Leyte Gulf patrols; and Garrett and Poor escorted C-47s to Bohol and back.

Perhaps the most interesting mission for the day was flown by Wallace and Rhodes. They had specific orders to hunt barges along Cebu Island. To help them, they were to coordinate with PT boats assigned to the area. Unfortunately, radio contact with the PT boats could not be established, forcing Wallace and Rhodes to return to base.

Bacheler wasn't flying this particular day and witnessed another operational accident caused, in part, by the poor field conditions. "Under the pounding of countless landings and heavy rains, the runway began to deteriorate dangerously, with chuck holes evident in many places. We began to put up pilot notices such as, "When landing to the east, touch down on the right side. After passing VMF-251 (sic) ordnance tents, veer left in your rollout." Take offs were equally "hazardous," wrote Bacheler.[17]

It was fatal for one VMF-222 pilot. At 0940 2Lt. Karl Oerth was taking off when he hit a rough spot in the runway, and according to Bacheler, blew a tire. Oerth lost control of his Corsair, struck a coral rock and careened into VMF-222's revetment area, striking Pvt. D.M. Budy, Pfc. P. F. Irish and a Filipino,[18] and wiping out tents housing the intelligence, parachute, material, and oxygen departments. Also destroyed were tents housing VMF-212's intelligence and parachute departments, and the pilots' ready tent.

Personnel for VMF-222 and nearby VMF-212 rushed to Oerth's burning plane to rescue the pilot. As several of the men were pulling Oerth from the wrecked plane, flames ignited the fuel tanks causing a tremendous explosion and setting off the .50 caliber ammunition. Instantly killed were Oerth, and two men who were attempting to rescue Oerth: Sgt. W. H. Rowan and Pfc. C. Hero. About 50 more VMF-212 personnel were hospitalized with burns—six of which died several days after the horrible accident. Several of the men suffered burns so serious they had to be evacuated to the hospital ship USS *Refuge*. Additionally, three pilots and 16 enlisted men from VMF-212 were injured, suffering burns in their attempt to help rescue Oerth.[19]

And so the operations continued. At 0645 on 25 January, the squadron sent out 12 Corsairs to patrol Mindanao and sweep the islands of Cebu, Panay and Negros. Bacheler's division patrolled the east side of Mindanao but bad weather forced a change in plans. Unable to reach Davao—their destination—they cut across the island and ended up flying over Butuan and Del Monte airfields and Surigao. If any Japanese were present, they did not make their presence known, perhaps staying under cover after being hit previously by Hart's Corsairs.

While Bacheler's division was fighting the bad weather, Hart, Wyatt, Jones and Frank strafed Butuan Airfield in northwest Mindanao. Concentrating their fire on buildings and 50-gallon drums stacked along the northwest side of the runway, the four Corsairs burned two of the buildings. Hart pumped hundreds of .50 caliber rounds at a radio station north of Butuan, as well as two trucks on a nearby road. They flew on to Del Monte, then Suragaio where Jones set two trucks smoking. As the Corsairs headed home, Hart set a motor boat smoking after a strafing run near Tagoloan.

Smith, Neilson, Rosellen and Crutcher had an eventful day over Cebu, Panay and Negros. At various locations on Negros, they strafed and burned five vehicles. One of the vehicles exploded so violently that debris blown into the air damaged Neilson's engine cowl. They also flew over all known Japanese airfields on the three islands, finding no Japanese but spotted an abandoned Dauntless SBD at Tanjay Airfield on Negros. The Japanese put up spotty AA fire at several locations with Smith having his port aileron obliterated by 20mm guns.

Cunningham's division flew the last morning mission—a sweep over Cebu Island—taking off at 1020. After flying for a few hours over the island, they finally spotted three trucks hidden underneath some trees near Lahug Airfield located just outside of Cebu City on the east coast of the island. They strafed the trucks but the thick foliage prevented any confirmation of damage. On the way home they drew AA from Japanese guns on Mactan Island but no planes were hit. Cunningham's division returned safely to Guiuan, as did the other planes flying during the morning.

The destruction of vehicles continued with the afternoon sweeps. Four Corsairs took off at 1345; Hart, Wyatt, Jones, and Frank—following a quick meal and a debriefing after their morning mission—flew to Negros. Fifteen minutes later Schroeder, Harris, Evans, and Robinson took off for Mindanao. Smith's division was right behind them, also heading to Mindanao.

Upon arriving over Negros, Hart's division strafed every known Japanese airfield on the island with the exception of Dumaguete, which was socked in with bad weather. During their strafing runs Jones destroyed a truck at Alicante, Hart and Wyatt thoroughly holed a truck near La Carlota and Wyatt strafed another near Camang with results unobserved.

As Schroeder's division approached Mindanao, they headed for the northwest coast

Six. Guiuan Field, Samar, Philippine Islands, and Deactivation

of the island where they began their strafing runs. Robinson spotted two trucks along the coast and shot them up but whether he destroyed them could not be determined. Next up was Butuan Airfield. Flying in below 1,000 feet, they strafed the airfield but no results were seen by the pilots. It was on to Del Monte where Harris and Robinson holed three trucks. The flight proceeded to Davao on the southeast coast where they spotted numerous trucks. With their fuel running low, they were unable to make a pass at the trucks. They turned for home, battling lousy weather along the way. After four hours in the air, they finally made it home.

The bad weather that plagued Schroeder's division moved in over Mindanao, forcing Smith's division to backtrack. They made their way to Davao and as they approached the town at 8,000 feet, Neilson radioed that his oil pressure dropped to 40 PSI, well below the desired 60 to 90 PSI range. Smith immediately called off the mission, and turned around for the 150 mile flight home. The flight was tracked by three radar stations—two land-based and one ship based. They also picked up escorts along the way; one escort flew at 10,000 feet to remain in communication with Guiuan and one flew just above the water to mark Neilson's position in case he had to ditch his plane or bail out. It is a testament to Neilson's skill as a pilot that he was able to nurse his plane back home; by the time he landed at 1645 his oil pressure was down to 8 PSI—far below the minimum of 50 PSI.

The relentless pace of operations continued for the squadron on 26 January. From 0620 to 1830, four divisions flew continuous cover over Leyte Gulf. Henley and Barton provided cover for a convoy from 1145 to 1450, when they were relieved on station by Schoetz and Warren who then flew until 1800. Poor teamed up with a VMF-223 Corsair[20] for a barge hunt along the coast of Cebu. Over Cebu for an hour they found nothing to shoot, but were themselves shot at by Japanese AA fire near the town of Cebu. They weren't hit and made it back safely to Guiuan.

Flying cover for convoys continued on 27 January. Four divisions—led by Bacheler, Smith, Schroeder and Cunningham—provided continuous cover for a convoy from Negros to Samar.

Meanwhile, Hart and Wyatt flew over Cebu from 1500 to 1630 looking for barges. They discovered two hidden near a bridge across an inlet north of Cebu City and left them belching smoke after a strafing run. At Carmen, Hart spotted a metal barge that appeared to be dry-docked. It looked to be set up on wooden horses off the beach and under some trees. Hart and Wyatt plastered the boat with their .50 calibers. It did not burn but both pilots felt the barge would cease to be of any use to the Japanese.

Sunday, 28 January would prove to be another deadly day for the squadron. It started out well enough with Inglehart, Kammeyer, Warren and Scott flying the dawn patrols over the Camotes Sea and the west shore of Leyte. Nothing was spotted and the planes returned at 0840.

While Kammeyer and crew were on patrol, Wallace led his division for a fighter sweep over southern Luzon, taking off from Guiuan at 0730. The sweep area extended from southern Manila (heavily manned by Japanese AA guns) to Legaspi Airfield. They made two strafing runs, firing at a barge near Mabio Point and a car on a road along the northwest shore of Laguna De Bay near Taytay. No AA fire was encountered during the strafing runs. At approximately 1000, south of Taytay, the other pilots noticed that Wallace's plane was nowhere to be seen. The pilots saw no evidence of a crash and were in radio contact with Wallace up to a minute before he disappeared. Repeated attempts to raise him by radio were unsuccessful.

Why Wallace went down remains a mystery to this day. He was originally listed as MIA and later upgraded to KIA. His body was recovered about a month later and buried at the USAF Cemetery Manila #1 in March 1945. His remains were eventually interred at the Manila American Cemetery, Plot N, Row 10, Grave 200.[21]

Jennings, Erdmann, Moynihan and Wolf left Guiuan at 0915 to patrol the same area as Wallace's division. Arriving over the target area 75 minutes later, they struck several locations. One truck was smoked at Alitagtag and two barges were shot up at Laguna De Bay. At Nielson Auxiliary Field, Jennings spotted a biplane and lined up his plane for a strafing run. As he began to fire, Japanese AA guns opened up on him from a position on the south side of the runway. Erdmann, flying Jennings' wing, immediately turned into the AA positions and opened up with his .50s, silencing the guns.

Moynihan, leading the second section, started his strafing run on the field. After he passed it, he got on the radio to see if everyone was OK. Within seconds of the call the other pilots looked back and witnessed an explosion near or on the ground. They circled around and saw Moynihan's plane on its belly a quarter mile from the field. Its engine was smoking; the ailerons and tail surfaces were on fire. Despite the damage, the plane appeared to be intact. Moynihan could not be seen, nor whether the canopy had been jettisoned in an attempt to escape. What caused Moynihan's plane to go down was never determined but AA fire was suspected. Like Sturgis, Moynihan was listed as MIA and is memorialized at the Manila American Cemetery.

As soon as word was received back at Guiuan that Wallace was missing, Henley's division took off at 1340 to search for him. Staying aloft for five hours, they searched the Laguna De Bay area finding no trace of the plane and Wallace. While conducting the search for Wallace, the flight spotted a truck at the east end of Nichols Field and strafed it. Ward was credited with destroying the truck; the tremendous explosion indicated it was carrying a load of ammunition.

Gray's division, with Daigle flying as second section leader, also flew the Luzon sweep. Daigle wasn't in the air long; he developed hydraulic trouble. Accompanied by his wingman Lingenfelter, he returned to Guiuan. Gray and his wingman continued the Luzon sweep but found nothing.

Rounding out the day's slate of missions Inglehart, Kammeyer, Warren and Scott flew the dusk patrol over the Camotes Sea. Like the dawn patrol, nothing was spotted and the flight returned home.

The squadron went back to covering convoys all day on 29 January. Five divisions were involved with Bacheler's division flying twice. Cunningham's division, once its mission was complete, landed back at Guiuan just minutes before a rainstorm closed the field. Bacheler's division, flying the last patrol had to be diverted to Tanauan on Leyte because of the persistent rainstorm inundating Guiuan.

The storm kept all planes on the ground until around 1300 on 30 January. With a break in the weather, Gray's division was quickly sent out to patrol Leyte Gulf. They found the gulf covered solid with clouds and rain and were ordered back to base, landing at 1515. Flights scheduled for the rest of the afternoon were canceled.

On 31 January, VMO-251 received special instructions from MAG-14's Colonel Smith, Executive and Operations Officer, to search Naga for 14,000 Japanese troops reported to be in the vicinity. Smith's division was the first to take off with wheels up at 0645. Upon arrival, they found Naga covered in rainstorms. Despite this, they went low to the deck and were able to make several passes over the area. They saw a few people running for cover; whether they were Japanese troops or Filipinos could not be determined. An area a mile south of Naga was discovered to be a large open farm land with no cover, and this was where the 14,000 troops were said to be. Needless to say the Japanese were nowhere to be seen.

The flight continued on to Lucena Airfield, approximately 100 miles south of Manila. As they were flying over the field, Neilson spotted a message on the runway that appeared to be written in cloth strips: "45th Inf. Reg. 44th (Hunters) Div. Aid Badly Needed. Ref. to Maj. Vanderpool, LO. SWPA. Hunters Here."[22] Neilson copied the message on his target map and tucked it away.

There were two Philippine guerrilla units active in the region: the Hunters ROTC group and President Quezon's Own Guerillas (PQOG).[23] "Hunters" in the message may have referred to the Hunters ROTC group. Vanderpool may have been a reference to Maj. Jay D. Vanderpool, who volunteered to lead a group of men on a liaison mission to the area in November 1944. They were to be dropped off by submarine in northern Luzon but heavy Japanese resistance forced a change of plans, hence they were dropped off in the Lucena area. Vanderpool eluded numerous Japanese patrols before finally meeting with the Hunters ROTC group. Seeing himself as a coordinator, he was able to arrange for supplies for the guerrillas as well as getting the numerous bickering guerrilla groups to fight together against the Japanese. Vanderpool was so effective with the guerrillas "that Japanese intelligence soon concluded that he was a major general."[24]

With the message copied down, the Corsairs turned for Guiuan. Upon arrival, the message was telephoned to Group Operations by the squadron intelligence officer for action by higher command.

Cunningham's division, with Beattie, Wolf and Jernigan, left Guiuan at 1000 to patrol the southern Luzon area. Bad weather hampered their patrol; they were able to check out Legaspi Airfield before turning back for Guiuan. As they approached Bulan Airfield they were met by inaccurate 40MM AA fire; no one was hit. At the field, they shot a garage housing cars and trucks and about a half mile west of the airfield, they strafed and riddled a truck, rendering it useless. The planes were back at Guiuan by 1300.

Pirages, Irwin, Frank and Harris also flew a sweep over southern Luzon, departing Guiuan at 1300. They had to contend with bad weather the entire sweep while they completed the non-productive mission. They were back at Guiuan by 1815.

In a long overdue move, the squadron finally shed its observation designation and became Marine Fighting Squadron 251—VMF-251— by authority of COMINCH dispatch 262132, effective 31 January. Two months later, the gull-winged octopus patch was retired and a new one was created. According to Hugh "Yogi" Irwin, the "Lucifer's Messengers"

Close up of the "Lucifer's Messengers" insignia designed by 2Lt. Danny Johnson (courtesy Hugh E. "Yogi" Irwin).

patch was designed by VMF-251 pilot 2Lt. Danny W. Johnson (joined the squadron on 16 March), a man with some artistic talent. The patch depicts a caped red devil riding a gull-winged general purpose bomb with "Lucifer's Messengers VMF-251" written in the background.[25] It was an apt description for the squadron which had been raining death and destruction on the Japanese since it returned to the Pacific theater in March 1944.

February 1945

Flying cover for a convoy was the order of the day on 1 February, The squadron put up 22 Corsairs to protect an eastbound convoy south of Negros Island. Divisions handling the patrols were Smith's, Inglehart's, Erdmann's, Garrett's and Henley's. Henley and Barton failed to take off when a violent storm prevented ground crews from fueling the two planes. For those who ended up flying cover, the convoy sailed unmolested by the Japanese; the enemy offered no resistance.

The squadron did lose one Corsair in an accident. VMF-223 pilot 2Lt. Eugene F. Proulx, while coming in for a landing following a mission near Liloan, was caught in the slipstream of the plane in front of him. He skidded as he hit the runway, ripping off his left wheel. The out-of-control plane veered to the left and slammed into a parked Corsair in VMF-251's revetment area. Proulx was unhurt, but his Corsair (BuNo 14505)[26] as well as 251's Corsair (BuNo 57391)[27] would never fly again—both were complete losses.

The next several days were the same: convoy duty, combat patrols, dawn to dusk patrols. One sweep—consisting of Jennings, Erdmann, Warren and Wolf—was flown over Mindanao to detect any Japanese activity near Diklom and Tagaloan airfields in the northwest part of the island. No activity was detected so they flew to Carmen where they shot up three barges along the east bank of the Mindanao River.

By 6 February, MAG-14 supplies had built up to the point where the squadron could begin carrying bombs on its missions. Targets in Cebu, Negros, Mindanao and the northern section of Samar would occupy squadron pilots for the remainder of the month. On the same day, pilots from VMF-251 began their run of fighter bomber attacks for the month by striking a group of 46 buildings about a mile southwest of Carolina Airfield on the northwest shore of Negros. It would prove to be a very successful strike.

Two missions were flown against the target during the day; the first from 0800 to 1010 and the second from 1340 to 1610. The attacks were flown by divisions led by Bacheler, Schroeder, Smith (with Henley in Rosellen's place) and Cunningham. For both attacks each Corsair carried two 500 pounders.

The first attack commenced at 0850, with the Corsairs approaching the target from east to west. They nosed over at 10,500 feet, making 70 degree dives with wheels down. By the time the third division commenced its attack, the western portion of the target was covered in black smoke from a large gasoline or oil fire. A column of smoke from the massive fire extended nearly 2,000 feet into the air. After the third and fourth divisions delivered their strike, the planes formed up to drop their second 500 pound bomb in another run on the target. By the time the bomb runs were finished, the buildings appeared to be consumed in a mass of flames. As if that wasn't enough, three strafing runs were made on what few buildings were left standing. Two P-38 Lightnings flying in the area observed the attack and broke in on the radio frequency remarking "the Navy's doing a good job down there." One of the squadron pilots was quick to reply, "Navy, hell, it's Marines."[28]

The afternoon strike was accompanied by Colonel Zebulon C. Hopkins, commander of MAG-14, flying a SBD. In the back seat was squadron intelligence officer 1Lt. Henry B. Welch. The sixteen Corsairs picked up where they left off in the morning, destroying all but two of the buildings still standing from the first strike.

The Japanese kept their guns silent, offering no resistance. None of the Corsairs received any damage during the strikes. Photographs taken the following day showed that 39 of the 46 buildings would no longer render any service to the Japanese—they were obliterated.

The squadron followed its success the next day with two coordinated strikes against Japanese barracks and administrative offices in the town of Mandaue, located north of Cebu City on the island of Cebu. Participating in the morning strike were four divisions of VMF-251—led by Humberd, Hart, Henley and Jennings—12 Corsairs of MAG-12's VMF-115 out of Tanauan, Leyte Island, and three other aircraft[29] out of Tacloban, Leyte Island.

The first attack commenced at 0845 with the three aircraft out of Tacloban dropping 100 pounders from 10,000 feet. Humberd observed the strike and could only shake his head in disgust as the bombs did little damage.

Following the ineffective opening move, Humberd led his divisions in the attack. Fourteen of the 16 Corsairs were able to drop their 1,000 pounders in the target area. Only seven of those appeared to detonate; the rest were duds. Despite the defective bombs, the squadron set many fires, sending much smoke into the air. VMF-115 Corsairs finished out the attack, dropping all their bombs on target. As the strike force departed, the target area was burning fiercely with smoke extending 2,000 feet.

Both squadrons, less the three aircraft from Tacloban, returned to hit Mandaue in the afternoon. VMF-115 was the first to hit the target and thoroughly devastated what remained of the buildings from the morning strike. One 1,000 pounder hit a church which was torn apart by a powerful explosion, indicating the Japanese may have been using

Two unnamed squadron maintenance men work on a F4U-1D late 1944 or 1945 (courtesy Madden Family).

it as an ammunition storage facility.[30] VMF-251 commenced their attack at 1600 and their 1,000 pounders, landing in the target area, added to the devastation. Army reconnaissance flights sent over Mandaue the day after the strike revealed the entire area was flattened, with most of the larger buildings a pile of rubble.

As for the squadron's duds encountered during the morning mission, an exact cause could not be determined. Ordnance personnel suspected defective detonators.

No missions were flown on 8 February, giving the maintenance men time to work on their aircraft. However, divisions led by Bacheler and Smith stood scramble alert the entire day. While the two divisions waited out the day on alert, an unusual request came to the squadron via the 5th Fighter Command's intelligence officer and representatives from DuPont Chemical Company. They wanted someone to give a demonstration on the use of napalm in a bombing attack. According to Bacheler, they asked him. A few hundred yards off the beach in full view of the squadron's and the 93rd Seabees' camp, Bacheler "dropped down to about 50 feet altitude while heading north,"[31] passed the end of the runway and dropped the napalm canister. "Banking vertically in my pull-up, I looked back to see the results of this experiment, which were spectacular. A sheet of flame covered the water behind me about 50 yards wide and 300 yards long...," wrote Bacheler.[32]

Heavy rain scrubbed all missions on 9 February, but combat operations resumed on 10 February with strikes on Negros and Cebu, and convoy patrols near Panay. Three divisions took off at 0730 to hit airfields on the nearby islands; Jennings, Erdmann, Kammeyer and Robinson were assigned to hit Mologo Airfield on Negros; Schroeder, Evans, Daigle, and Jernigan hit Silay Airfield on Negros; Smith, Neilson, Henley and MacLachlan

Control tower at Guiuan Airfield on Samar, Philippine Islands, 1945 (courtesy Madden Family).

flew to Talisay Airfield on Negros. On all missions, each Corsair carried two 1,000 pound bombs.

As Jennings' division approached their target, they saw that the runway was pitted with hundreds of bomb craters. Having been pounded repeatedly by other squadrons over the last several months, nothing was left to be hit at the airfield. They did find some buildings off the east end of the runway and planted their 1,000 pounders there, scoring a damaging hit.

Schroeder's division ran into the same situation at Silay; the airfield and nearby facilities were bombed out. Nothing was left standing that could be called a target but they dropped their bombs on the airfield none the less. Jernigan and Daigle did find a 35-foot barge running along the coast and after two strafing runs, they left it on fire.

Talisay Airfield was also unserviceable but Smith's division dropped their bombs anyway, causing no damage. Low on fuel, the four Corsairs landed at Tanuan to gas up before returning to Guiuan.

None of the patrols encountered any Japanese resistance.

At 1445, Schroeder's division took off to hit Carolina Airfield on Negros but Schroeder was unable to take off to fly with them due to a locked brake on his Corsair. Daigle took over as lead and the remaining three Corsairs ended up dropping three of their half-tonners on a red-roofed building southwest of the runway. The remaining three bombs were dropped on another building located on the south side of a main highway running east to west south of the airfield. Results of the bombings went unobserved.

Smith's division took off at 1500 to strike Opon Airfield on Mactan Island, located off the coast from Cebu City. MacLachlan had to stay behind due to a mechanical problem with his Corsair. Smith, Neilson and Henley dropped their 1,000 pounders on a group of buildings just west of the southwest end of the airfield. Whether the buildings remained standing or were blown to bits is unknown; results of their strike could not be observed.

Bacheler's division drew patrol duty, protecting a convoy west of Panay Island. Irwin, flying as section leader, had to abort the mission early due to a fuel leak. The others remained over the convoy from 1300 to 1415, encountering no Japanese.

In an administrative move, the squadron lost the man who had guided them through training and led it during its second tour of combat—commanding officer Major William C. Humberd. Humberd moved on to MAG-14 Headquarters, becoming the Assistant Operations Officer.[33] Taking over from Humberd was Bacheler, the squadron's executive officer. During a short change of command ceremony, the new commanding officer remarked to the assembled squadron that "it was the proudest day"[34] of his life.

The first target assigned to the squadron under Bacheler's command was the suspected Japanese held town of Surigao, Mindanao Island. The town was to be hit twice: once in the morning and once in the afternoon. Sixteen Corsairs, armed with two 1,000 pound general purpose bombs each, took off at 0845 on 11 February. As the four divisions made their way to Surigao the weather deteriorated, eventually forcing Major Thomas W. Furlow—the squadron executive officer—to abort the strike and return to Guiuan. The weather gradually worsened, forcing a halt to operations for the rest of the day.

On 12 February, the squadron tried once again to strike Surigao. Furlow led the flight of sixteen Corsairs, each armed with two 1,000 pound bombs. Philippine guerrillas had reported the town recently evacuated by the Japanese but brass at the 85th Fighter Wing wanted the town hit to prevent the Japanese from reoccupying it.

The pilots attacked the eastern end of the town during the morning strike which occurred at 0930. Many hits were scored and several fires were started. One fire continued to burn as the Corsairs returned to Guiuan to prepare for the afternoon strike.

At 1540, the same 16 pilots returned to attack the western portion of the town. Along to observe the attack were 1Lt. John W. Irwin—squadron engineering officer, the mess officer, Welch—squadron intelligence officer, and Lt. John P. Gallagher, USN, Flight Surgeon, all flying in a borrowed TBM Avenger. The TBM was the General Motors built version of the Grumman TBF Avenger. It was designed to carry a crew of three, so for the four Marines inside the borrowed TBM, space must have been at a premium.

Sixteen tons of bombs devastated the target. Some buildings were pulverized; many were reduced to piles of rubble. Explosions sent dust columns nearly 1,000 feet into the air. The observers in the TBM were very satisfied with the results. The guerrillas on the ground—led by Lt. Colonel Wendell Fertig—had a slightly different opinion of the strike, and said so in a radio message sent days after the strike: "U.S. planes struck—burning all houses center sector, lasting two days. Few supplies burned. Both raids few casualties."[35]

Liloan, on the eastern shore of Cebu, was the target of a 16 plane strike on 13 February. Located north of the city of Cebu, it was the last Japanese stronghold on the island. Four divisions, led by Bacheler, flew both the morning and afternoon strikes; the first occurred at 0825 and the next one at 1620. Other divisions included ones led by Jennings, Schroeder and Smith. Each Corsair carried two 1,000 pound bombs for both strikes.

The morning strike was successful. Two explosions sent sheets of flames nearly 200 feet into the air. What may have been in the buildings that ignited is unknown. Several buildings were demolished, and many were severely damaged. When the bomb run was complete, the Corsairs made strafing runs, putting thousands of rounds into the target area.

The afternoon strike destroyed three more buildings, and left two smoking. Strafing runs followed, holing more buildings. In their efforts to make Liloan untenable for the Japanese, the Corsairs dropped 32 tons of ordnance and expended 14,000 rounds of .50 caliber ammunition.

Despite previous strikes rendering Surigao pretty much useless to the Japanese, VMF-251 Corsairs were called on once again to hit the Mindanao town. The attack on 14 February centered on the few remaining buildings left standing in the western part of the town. The town was hit twice—at 1020 and 1550—by the same 16 pilots consisting of divisions led by Furlow, Garrett, Henley and Inglehart. As in the previous day's mission, each Corsair carried two 1,000 pounders for each strike.

The two strikes pulverized the area, flattening buildings and starting many fires. The Japanese did put up intense machine gun fire during the afternoon strike, but no Corsairs were hit. Upon their return to Guiuan, the afternoon pilots reported that "not one good building left standing in this town." Fertig's 10th Military District guerrillas watching the attack from hills near the town confirmed the results, with additional good news: "Houses NW section totally burned; high school damaged. Surigao city now vacated by Nips."[36]

Squadron Corsairs returned to Mindanao on 15 February, with two strikes delivered on the town of Butuan. Bacheler led the two strikes which consisted of his division and those led by Schroeder, Smith, and Jennings. They destroyed several buildings during the attacks, dropping 32 tons of bombs and expending 17,000 rounds of ammo to do so. The pilots felt they didn't do much damage but guerrillas reported that evening that the "results were good, specific results not available yet...."[37] Jennings' Corsair was damaged during the attacks when shrapnel from the explosions penetrated his engine cowling, severing a couple of spark plug leads. He was able to bring his plane back to Guiuan safely.

During the period of the strikes, Cunningham's division flew two reconnaissance missions to observe any Japanese activity over a number of airfields in the northwest coast of Mindanao. They found no signs of Japanese activity.

The squadron caught a break from strikes on 16 February, performing patrols over Leyte Gulf all day. One section during one of the patrols broke off to intercept a suspected Japanese aircraft but could not find the enemy airplane. The break continued the next day with the squadron getting the day off from flying combat operations. Twelve planes did fly to Leyte during the day to pick up belly tanks and returned.

It was back to Mindanao on 18 February with strikes on Surigao and Licanan Airfield, Mindanao. For unknown reasons, the 85th Fighter Wing wanted another strike on Surigao, despite the fact the Japanese had been reported to be no longer present in the town.

With each Corsair carrying a payload of three 1,000 pounders, Furlow led his and three other divisions for the morning strike on Surigao, commencing the attack at 0900 with only 13 of the 16 Corsairs assigned to the mission. Two of the Corsairs developed hydraulic problems preventing them from participating in the strike, and one was late taking off but never rejoined the squadron for the attack. With very little left standing in the town, Furlow's Corsairs managed to start two fires. The Japanese offered no resistance and the Corsairs arrived back at Guiuan at 0925.

The same divisions that participated in the morning strike—led by Furlow, Hart, Henley and Inglehart—flew the afternoon strike. Their target was a group of buildings near Licanan Airfield located north of Davao. This time each Corsair carried two 1,000 pound bombs and a centerline belly tank. Only 13 of the 16 Corsairs took off at 1300; three of the Corsairs suffered a blowout on one of the tires of their main landing gear while taxiing.

The flight received moderate AA fire during the attack and once again no Corsairs were hit. The bombs were dropped in the target area but results went unobserved, perhaps because of solid overcast over the target. After spending four hours in the air, they were back on the ground at Guiuan at 1700.

The squadron returned to Licanan on 19 February, this time with Bacheler leading his division and divisions led by Schroeder, Smith and Jennings. They were to hit the same group of buildings Furlow's flight tried to destroy the previous day. For the strike, each Corsair carried two 1,000 pounders and a belly tank. The planes departed at 0845, but two of them had to return to base due to hydraulic problems.

The planned route was designed to avoid known—and active—Japanese AA positions. They approached the target from the east and south to put the sun behind them and to the south to avoid the AA gun positions to the north of the field.

Bacheler pushed over at 10,000 feet, commencing the attack at 1025 and the first to release his bombs at 2,000 feet. The others followed, with MacLachlan being hit in the wing by AA fire despite the best of plans to avoid it. The target area was covered by the bombs, but results went unobserved. The pilots did not stick around to see what they had done and rendezvoused at Samal Island, about five miles to the east of their target, and returned home with wheels down at 1205.

During the afternoon, Hart led a four plane strike—consisting of his and planes flown by Wyatt, Garrett and Robinson—to hit a group of buildings on the Japanese held island of Capul in the San Bernadino Strait, off the northwest coast of Samar. It was a preliminary strike ahead of the upcoming landing on the island, and Biri Island, by elements of the 23rd Infantry Division (also known as the Americal Division).

Following a 50 minute flight, the Corsairs were over the target at 1355. The pilots nosed over at 6,000 feet, entered a 60 degree dive and lowered their wheels before letting loose their 1,000 pounders at 2,000 feet. After making six runs on the target area and dropping eight bombs, the pilots succeeded in demolishing a barracks building, and possibly damaged other buildings in the area. By 1500, the planes were back at Guiuan.

Soon after the squadron Corsairs hit the island, the First Battalion of the 182nd Infantry Regiment set foot on Capul. On 25 February, at a cost of 5 men killed and 10 wounded, the battalion wrestled the island from the Japanese, who lost 75 men defending the island.[38]

It was a busy day for the squadron on 20 February, putting up 26 Corsairs over the course of the day to hit targets on Negros, Mindanao and Biri Island. First up were three different airfields on Negros: Fabrica, La Carlota and Lahug. Hart, Wyatt, Garrett and Poor were assigned to hit Fabrica; Henley, Barton, Jennings and Schoetz were given La Carlotta; and Inglehart, Scott, and Lingenfelter had La Hug. The three divisions took off at 0800, and each plane carried two 1,000 pounders. All three airfields had been previously hit by other squadrons in the past few months, leaving nothing that could be called a target for the 251 pilots. Each dropped their bombs on their assigned airfields anyway, pummeling what may have been left of any buildings standing.

Also taking off at 0800 were Furlow, Scoville, Cunningham and Sandbach. Sandbach blew a tire while rolling down the runway, and failed to get into the air. With each Corsair carrying a one ton bomb load, they were assigned to strike Lumbia Airfield on Mindanao after guerrillas reported three operational Mitsubishi A6Ms (Allied code name Zeke) hidden there. When the Corsairs arrived over the target, the Japanese put up meager AA fire hitting none of the planes. The flight could not find the hidden Zekes so the planes dropped their bombs on dispersal areas, concentrating on a clump of trees where the planes could have been hidden. After dropping their 1,000 pounders they strafed a building off the south end of the runway, pumping over 2,500 rounds of ammo into the structure. For their efforts the runway was cratered and plenty of trees were shredded.

While 251 was busy hitting airfields on Negros and Mindano, elements of the 182nd Infantry Regiment assaulted Biri Island, located off the northwest coast of Samar. LCMs carried one infantry company assigned to attack the island. For support there were four PT Boats and a lone P-38, which strafed the beach prior to the assault. As they made their approach to the beach, the four LCMs struck a reef, and at the same time Japanese defenders opened up with heavy machine gun fire. Many of the LCM crewmen were killed or wounded. Infantrymen, some of whom were experienced in amphibious assaults and had received training on LCMs, backed the ships off the beach and away from the machine gun fire.[39]

At some point during this disastrous turn of events, MAG-14 received a call to put all available planes in the air to provide help for the amphibious force. VMF-251 supplied 10 Corsairs: Smith's division, Inglehart's division and pilots Daigle and Jernigan. VMF-212 and VMF-223 each put up four Corsairs.

VMF-251's Corsairs were advised by the PT Boats off Biri to spray the beach with machine gun fire. They expended over 6,000 rounds of ammo while strafing the beach,

Six. Guiuan Field, Samar, Philippine Islands, and Deactivation

and the village of Biri. As they retired back to Guiuan, one hut was on fire and many were left smoldering.

The assault force was able to regroup, and landed at a different beach during the afternoon. After three days of fighting, the Americal Division declared Biri secured on 23 February. Around 70 Japanese were killed at the cost of five Americans killed and 50 wounded.[40]

Fourteen Corsairs, flying in two plane sections throughout the day, covered two convoys in the Mindanao Sea on 21 February. Two other Corsairs flew a three hour patrol over Leyte Gulf, and two others were sent to look for a reported downed pilot in Davao Gulf. Unfortunately the pilot was not located.

Two strikes led by Furlow were the order of the day on 22 February. The target for each strike was the town of Iloilo on the island of Panay. In addition to Furlow's division, divisions led by Hart, Henley and Inglehart participated in both missions. The Corsairs carried two 500 pounders for each mission.

The first strike occurred at 0950 with 15 Corsairs, after squadrons from MAG-12 finished with their strikes. The fires they started marked the target for the VMF-251 Corsairs, making it easy to find. Unfortunately a strong wind out of the north made putting the bombs on target difficult; most of the bombs missed and damage was slight. The afternoon strike at 1445 with 16 Corsairs wasn't much better. Three of the bombs scored hits, causing several fires in the western portion of the town. Due to thick smoke over the town, Furlow cancelled all strafing runs. During both strikes the Japanese offered no resistance and all Corsairs returned to Guiuan without any damage.

On February 23, the squadron commander, Bacheler, led two attacks on the village of Kabacan on Mindanao. Flying with Bacheler's division for both attacks were divisions led by Schroeder, Smith and Jennings. Each of the Corsairs involved in the attacks carried two 500 pounders.

The town lay at the juncture of the Kabacan and Pulangi Rivers and was believed to be occupied by the Japanese. The morning attack began at 0950 with the 16 Corsairs entering their dive bombing runs from 10,000 feet and at a 70 degree dive angle. Bombs were released between 2,500 and 3,000 feet. After dropping 16,000 pounds of ordnance, the only damage that could be confirmed was one fire putting up a huge column of white smoke. The afternoon strike at 1510 fared no better: two damaging hits and no fires with no specific damage observed. Despite the poor results, guerrillas in the area reported that the attacks did a lot to raise their morale.

The following morning Furlow, Scoville, Cunningham and Frank, each carrying two 1,000 bombs, departed Guiuan at 0735 for Cebu to strike Lahug Airfield. The four pilots arrived to commence their attack at 0815, along with seven Corsairs from VMF-218. The 251 Corsairs were the first to attack. They dropped their bombs on the runway and buildings along the west side of the runway, but scored no hits. When the Corsairs from VMF-218 began their attack, the Japanese opened up on them with machine gun, 20MM and 40MM anti-aircraft fire. VMF-218 planes managed to score a direct hit on an ammunition dump which disappeared in an intense explosion, but a Corsair flown by 2Lt. Frank Harriman was hit by AA fire during the attack.

As his plane began to smoke, he turned for home—Tanuan, Leyte Island. Unable to keep his plane in the air, he ditched it about 15 miles northeast of Maston Island. Harriman scrambled out of his cockpit, deployed his raft and lifted himself into it. The four VMF-251 pilots, along with VMF-218 pilot 2Lt. Walter Bean, remained over Harriman for two hours until he was rescued by Dumbo. Once Harriman was safe, Furlow led his Corsairs back to Guiuan, landing at 1115.[41]

With their Corsairs armed with two 1,000 pounds each, Inglehart's division departed Guiuan at 1400 with orders to deliver them to Silay Airfield on Negros. Like many of the airfields in the Philippine Islands, there wasn't much left to bomb at Silay. So the four pilots dropped their ordnance on the strip but no results were observed. They were back at Guiuan by 1600.

The squadron also supplied eight planes to fly combat air patrols over Leyte Gulf throughout the day. Nothing was seen by the patrols.

Japanese occupied Buena Vista on Mindanao was the target for two squadron attacks on 25 February. Each of the Corsairs in both attacks carried the same ordnance: two 1,000 pound bombs armed with delay fuses. Divisions led by Bacheler and Jennings flew the morning mission, taking off at 0815. Jennings developed mechanical problems and ended up staying at Guiuan so Erdmann took over as division leader for the mission.

Reaching the target 50 minutes later, Bacheler led the attack by diving from 7,000 feet at a 40 degree dive angle. At around 2,000 feet he triggered his bomb release but both of the 1,000 pounders hung up. The misfire continued with Harris, one of his bombs hung and had to be jettisoned later. Pirages was able to drop his two, scoring two area hits. Irwin had one his bombs hang up and it too had to be jettisoned. Erdmann's three Corsairs were next, scoring five area hits.

Following the disappointing bomb run, the seven Corsairs followed a road from Butuan to Surigao looking for any strafing targets. None were found so Bacheler's Corsairs retired empty-handed to Guiuan, pancaking at 1010.

The afternoon strike fared much better. Divisions led by Schroeder and Smith dropped seven of eight bombs in the target area, demolishing one building and starting several fires. They also flew over the road from Butuan to Surigao looking for targets to strafe and apparently found a few but no damage was recorded.

La Paz, Panay was hit twice by the squadron on 26 February. Several large buildings, with large white crosses painted on the roofs to mark their humanitarian intent, were the primary target for each attack with known warehouses as secondary targets. Intelligence was received that indicated the primary target buildings were being used to house Japanese troops and supplies.

Furlow led both attacks that included his division and those led by Hart, Henley and Inglehart. The morning attack occurred at 0925 and the afternoon attack at 1320. After dropping a total of 32 1,000 pound bombs and making several strafing runs, only one building was left burning. One Corsair was damaged during the attacks, receiving a couple of holes in one of its wings.

The squadron got a break from operations on 27 February as the squadron stood down to allow ground crews to catch up on maintenance.

Bacheler's and Jennings' divisions left Guiuan at 0700 on 28 February to hit Parang, Mindanao. A front over northern Mindanao, which extended to 25,000 feet, blocked their route to the target. Bacheler led the flight in trying to find a hole in the front in order to fly through it but was unsuccessful. The squadron commander called off the mission and returned to Guiuan, landing at 0900. Attacks for the afternoon, directed at the same location, were also cancelled due to the weather.

In addition to the aborted strike on Parang, the squadron provided two aircraft to protect a convoy moving through the waters south of Negros Island. No Japanese appeared to challenge the convoy.

March 1945

With the weather now clear over Mindanao, the squadron opened up the month of March by sending sixteen Corsairs to hit several buildings along the shore at Parang. Furlow led the morning attack with Scoville, Cunningham, and Frank; and Inglehart, Scott, Kammeyer, and Lingenfelter. With each Corsair loaded with one 1,000 pounder each, Furlow's division took off at 0715, followed by Inglehart's division at 0830. Only two damaging hits were scored, but no fires were started and specific damage was not observed. However, when the afternoon flight arrived over the target, it reported that many buildings were seriously damaged by the morning attack.

Hart led the afternoon strike, which consisted of his division (with Wyatt, Garrett and Poor) and Henley's division (with Barton, Schoetz and Ward). Their target was three large warehouses located two miles inland from Parang. The attack was delivered at 1420; Wyatt and Barton both scored direct hits on a large building, demolishing it, while damaging hits were scored by other pilots in the flight. Both flights strafed their targets, expending over 13,000 rounds .50 caliber ammunition.

While the squadron was busy attacking Parang, six other Corsairs of the squadron flew cover for a convoy in the Mindanao Sea, and four others flew combat air patrols over Leyte Gulf without seeing any Japanese.

Fifteen Corsairs from the squadron, along with eight Corsairs from VMF-223, flew an early morning strike to San Jose,[42] Panay on 2 March. Unlike previous missions where all planes attacked an area target, each division of the squadron had a specific target to hit in and around the town. Bacheler's division consisting of himself, Beattie, Pirages and Irwin were assigned to hit the radio station and air raid shelter in the town; Schroeder, Evans, Daigle, and Jernigan were given the task of hitting the radar station; Smith, Neilson, Rosellen, and MacLachlan were to hit a pillbox; and Jennings, Erdman and Wolf were assigned to strike a large H-shaped building.

The 15 VMF-251 Corsairs, armed with one 1,000 pound bomb each, took off from Guiuan at 0645. Thirty minutes later, the eight Corsairs from VMF-223—loaded with same payload—left Guiuan.[43] VMF-223's Corsairs were assigned to hit a supply and personnel area.

As the squadron's Corsairs made for San Jose, Smith's engine began to develop problems and he was unable to get the Pratt & Whitney radial functioning correctly. Smith jettisoned his bomb and turned for home, escorted by Neilson, who also jettisoned his bomb.

Bacheler and his fellow pilots arrived to commence their attack at 0800. The pilots found the targets nearly impossible to locate, and dropped their bombs on what they thought were their targets. No fires were started, and apparently none of the targeted buildings were hit.

Fifty minutes later, seven Corsairs from VMF-223 arrived to start their attack. One of the planes that left Guiuan had to return early after developing an oil leak. Much to the chagrin of the VMF-251 pilots—who stayed to observe the attack—the "Bulldogs" of VMF-223 scored a direct hit on their target, blasting apart one of the buildings. The

Bulldogs regrouped for a strafing run and were successful in igniting a nearby fuel dump, sending a column of black smoke several thousand feet into the air.[44]

Japanese AA guns were silent, and the Corsairs from both squadrons returned to Guiuan unscathed.

Two attacks were made against the Japanese held town of Cotabato, situated near the Kabacan Delta in west central Mindanao on 3 March. The first flight, carrying 1,000 pounders, consisting of Furlow (flight leader), Scoville, Cunningham, Frank and Henley (division leader) along with Barton, Schoetz, and Ward, took off from Guiuan at 0705. Following an 85 minute flight, the Corsairs delivered their attack. The results were slight: two small fires started at the northwest end of the town.

Hart led the second attack which consisted of his division and Inglehart's division. Carrying the same ordnance, the eight Corsairs took off 1215. They were over the target at 1340. They nosed over from 10,000 feet, extended their landing gear and released their 1,000 pounders at 2,000 feet scoring several direct hits, one of which caused a large explosion. By the time the Corsairs regrouped to head back to Guiuan, smoke over the town had dissipated revealing several buildings had been destroyed.

Guerillas near the town who had observed the attack sent a radio report indicating the attacks killed or wounded an estimated 150 Japanese troops.

Also on the same day, the squadron greeted three new pilots: 2Lt. Benjamin L. Dudley, 1Lt. Lynford S. Walters, and Major Howard E. King. King, from MAG-14 Headquarters Squadron, was temporarily attached to the squadron.[45] Colonel Zebulon Hopkins, the MAG-14 commanding officer, wanted King to get more combat time with VMF-251 with the aim of having him take over the squadron from Bacheler at a later date. Bacheler was soon due to be rotated back to the states after spending slightly over a year in combat.

The squadron returned to hit San Jose, Panay on 4 March. Sixteen Corsairs led by Bacheler, loaded with one 1,000 pound bomb each, left Guiuan at 0700 to hit a fortified hill east of the town. Following a 75 minute flight, the Corsairs dropped their bombs amid light AA fire. No Corsairs were hit and all the bombs struck the hill. Despite all the bombs being on target, no specific damage could be seen by the pilots. After letting loose their ordnance, the Corsairs regrouped and strafed the hill twice before returning home.

The Japanese held village of Pikit, Mindanao was the target for two planned strikes on 5 March. Pikit, on the Kabacan Delta, was located about 30 miles from Cotabato. Furlow led the 12 plane strike consisting of himself, Scoville, Neilson and MacLachlan, and Hart's and Inglehart's divisions. The flight took off at 0720, with each Corsair armed with two 500 pounders each.

Soon after reaching cruising altitude, the flight ran into bad weather, which delayed their arrival over the target. After spending nearly two hours in the air, they finally reached Pikit at 0920 to find clear skies. From 13,000 feet the Corsairs went into their dives and all but one released their bombs at 2500 feet. Nearly all the bombs scored direct hits, thoroughly demolishing the town. Furlow reformed his Corsairs, lining up to strafe the town. Dropping below 1,000 feet, each Corsair strafed Pikit three times.

One of Hart's bombs hung up during the dive and as the Corsairs were heading home, the bomb's tail fin dropped off. He tried shaking the bomb loose but it would not budge. His wingman flew under him to inspect his plane and found the arming vane had unwound and dropped off. Hart was now flying with a live 500-pounder. He tried again to shake the bomb loose to no avail.

Hart pleaded with anyone who would listen to stay with the formation and land at Guiuan. He was perfectly within his rights to do so since, according to Bacheler, it was standard operating procedure to allow a plane to land with a hung bomb.[46] In this case, it was decided it would be too risky for Hart to land his plane with a live bomb. As the flight approached Guiuan, Furlow ordered Hart to abandon his plane. Dropping to 7,000 feet, Hart bailed out and floated safely into the waters of Leyte Gulf. He was quickly rescued and brought back to base.[47]

Furlow was scheduled to lead another strike to Pikit in the afternoon, but they had done such an outstanding job during the morning strike that operations cancelled the afternoon mission to the town. Instead, Furlow led eight Corsairs to Cebu where they were to contact the guerrilla fighter director on the island to see what they could hit.

Armed with two 500-pounders, seven of the eight Corsairs took off at 1420. Furlow's Corsair blew a tire while taxiing, forcing him to stay behind. Inglehart, leading the second division, became the flight leader.

Arriving over Cebu at 1615, Inglehart contacted the guerrillas asking for a target. He was directed to hit buildings in Cebu City, just south of the racetrack. Inglehart led his seven Corsairs to the target, where they placed all their bombs in the target area—four of which scored direct hits. As they pulled away to head home, four fires were burning fiercely.

In addition to the strikes on Pikit and Cebu City, squadron planes flew cover for a convoy, and like the morning and afternoon mission, encountered no Japanese.

Malabang and Parang, both located on the island of Mindanao, were the targets for two strikes flown by squadron pilots on 6 March. For the morning strike to Malabang, Bacheler led his division, Smith's and Wolf's. Each division had a specific target to attack: Bacheler's division was to hit a fortified outpost, Smith's division was assigned a radio station and personnel area just outside of town, and Wolf's division was given the assignment of hitting Fort Carouera. In order to successfully complete their tasks, each Corsair was loaded with two 500 pounders.

Bacheler's 12 Corsairs took off at 0730. It took about 90 minutes to travel the 260 miles to the Japanese held coastal town in west central Mindanao. They arrived over the target area at 12,000 feet, pushed over into 80 degree dives, and let loose their 500 pounders at 2,000 feet. Sixteen of the 24 bombs were misses. Wolf's division was able to place their bombs on several buildings, damaging a few. The planes regrouped for a strafing run before returning to Guiuan, smoking an outpost after pumping nearly 7,000 rounds of ammo into the structure.

Once again Bacheler was the flight leader for the afternoon strike on Parang. Along with his division were divisions led by Smith and Schroeder. As in the morning strike, each Corsair was armed with two 500 pounders.

The 12 Corsairs left Guiuan at 1320. No problems were encountered along the way to Parang and when they arrived a few clouds hung over the target at around 5,000 feet, but otherwise the pilots had a clear view of the town for their strike. They pushed over at 9,500 feet into 60 degree dives and released their 500 pounders at 2,000 feet, scoring several hits and starting nearly a half-dozen fires. Harris, flying in Bacheler's division, was hit either by AA fire or debris from a bomb explosion during his pullout, forcing him to jettison his fuel tank. It exploded on impact, causing a large grass fire. The pilots then circled around and executed two strafing runs, expending close to 6,000 rounds of .50 caliber ammunition, to no apparent effect.

In addition to the strikes on Malabang and Parang, eight planes from the squadron flew patrols over Leyte Gulf. In what was becoming routine for these patrols, no Japanese were spotted.

VMF-251 Corsairs returned to hit the coastal town of Malabang on 7 March. Two strikes were launched: one in the morning, utilizing 1,000 pound bombs with instantaneous fuses in a medium altitude dive bombing attack, and one in the afternoon using bombs armed with 8 second delay fuses dropped at tree-top level.

Furlow led both attacks. Accompanying him for the morning strike were Scoville, Frank, Poor, Henley, Barton, Ward and Scott. Their target was a group of buildings at the fork of the Malabang-Tubok River and a tributary running along the coast. They arrived over the target at 0820 after a 70 minute flight. No clouds were over the target and visibility was unlimited. They entered their dives at 12,000 feet and released their 1,000 pounders at 2,200 feet. Out of the eight bombs released one was seen to be a hit, one was a miss and the rest went unobserved. The eight Corsairs also strafed the town with no obvious results.

For the afternoon strike Scoville, Frank and Poor once again accompanied Furlow, along with pilots Inglehart, Scott, Henley and Barton. This time the Corsairs went into a shallow dive from 5,000 feet and released their bombs at 100 feet. The eight second delay allowed the planes to turn and view the results of their attack: two direct hits on a fort, turning it into a pile of rubble and two direct hits on a nearby mansion, obliterating the center section of the building and leaving the wings on each side with blown out walls. The results of a strafing run following the attack went unobserved.

The Japanese, if they were even capable of doing so, put up no resistance during both attacks.

To round out the day, four pilots provided escort for a convoy while Kammeyer and Lingenfelter flew two escort missions to protect a C-46 carrying supplies for guerrillas on Negros and Cebu Islands. While waiting for supplies to be off-loaded at Tuburan, Cebu Island, Kammeyer and Lingenfelter were treated to a meal of fried chicken and fresh bananas by the guerrillas. When they returned to Guiuan, they reported the meal "tasted mighty good."[48]

The next day the squadron once again launched two strikes, this time to the Mindanao town of Cotabato. The morning strike was led by Bacheler with fellow pilots Harris, Irwin, Robinson, Schroeder, Beattie, Daigle, and Jernigan. The Corsairs, armed with 1,000 pounders with delay fuses, took off from Guiuan at 0645. Arriving over the target at 0805, Bacheler entered into a shallow dive from 7,000 feet, lined up on a group of buildings along Manpay Creek in the town and hit his bomb release switch. His bomb released but so did his centerline fuel tank. The fuel tank struck the bomb, causing a premature explosion and swallowing up Bacheler's plane in smoke and flame. His wingman thought Bacheler was killed and his Corsair destroyed but breathed a sigh of relief when he emerged unscathed from the explosion.

The others continued with their attacks, destroying one building and damaging several others. A strafing run following the initial strike left several more buildings smoking.

It was back to the same target in the afternoon. Bacheler once again led the strike with pilots Harris, Irwin and Jennings in his division and Neilson leading the second division composed of pilots Smith, MacLachlan, and Wyatt. Attacking the buildings on Manpay Creek, Bachler's division scored one direct hit, burning a hut to the ground and damaging several others. Neilson's division released their bombs on a group of trees suspected of hiding an enemy bivouac with unobserved results. After spending three hours in the air, they were back at Guiuan at 1530.

The last remaining Japanese airfield, located near Dumaguete on southeast Negros was the assigned target on 9 March. Furlow, leading the morning mission, had with him the rest of his division and divisions led by Poor, Henley and Inglehart. Taking off at 0650, it wasn't long into their flight when, west of Leyte, the 16 Corsairs ran into a solid front with clouds extending from 2,500 feet to 10,000 feet. The divisions lost sight of each other as they penetrated the thick clouds. Eight planes jettisoned their bombs and returned to Guiuan. Five more planes also jettisoned their bombs and ended up landing at Dipolog, Mindanao—an airfield held by guerrillas. All but one of these planes returned to Samar later in the day.

Poor, Wyatt and Sandbach pushed on to Dumaguete. As they approached the Zamboanga Peninsula, they sighted a bogey to the northwest. The three Corsairs were at 7,000 feet and heading almost due north and still had their 1,000 pound bombs and belly tank. The bogey—identified as a possible Zeke—was slightly over 2,000 feet above the Corsairs and heading in the opposite direction. The pilots did not chase the bogey and it quickly disappeared in thick clouds.

The three pilots finally arrived over Dumaguete at around 9:30 only to find the skies over the town socked in with clouds above 2,500 feet. Poor, Wyatt and Sandbach commenced their attacks at 2,500 feet and dropped their 1,000 pounders at 2,000 feet. For their efforts they missed the airfield but cratered a nearby road. They didn't waste any time over the target and turned for home, arriving at Guiuan at 1045.

After the weather cleared out in the afternoon, Furlow led the same pilots back to Dumaguete, leaving Guiuan at 1515. Arriving over the target at 1625, they found clear skies over the airfield and took advantage of the opportunity. Fifteen of the sixteen bombs hit the target area, destroying one building. A strafing run following the attack set off several fires among huts located at the northern end of the airfield.

By this time the squadron had been in theater for a year, and a slate of transfers soon began. Joining the squadron were 37 enlisted men and 17 pilots, all second lieutenants: James I. Ellis, Henry Fink, Martin H. Kalvelage, Orville S. Kemp, Ernest A. LaMarre, David W. Lindner, Roy A. McAlister, Mahlon Morris, Thomas K. Peterson, Douglas D. Petty, Robert Rause, Paul F. Romberg, Howard W. Schewe, Samuel R. Smith, Joseph G. Wagner, Thomas H. Walsh and Robert N. Welch.

Weather curtailed combat operations on 10 March. However Furlow and Scoville flew to Dipolog to carry a starter cord to a pilot who remained there following the bout with nasty weather the previous day. The three pilots returned to Guiuan later in the day.[49]

The target on 11 March was a new one for the squadron. A morning and afternoon attack were planned with Furlow leading both. They were to bomb and strafe a stretch of road along the eastern shore of Lake Mainit, leading from San Roque to Kitchararao, in northeast Mindanao. Flying with Furlow's division for the morning strike was Garrett's division. The eight Corsairs were armed with 1,000 pound bombs and took off at 0740. Upon reaching the target area, Furlow could not locate the assigned target. Apparently the thick jungle growth and lack of features made spotting the stretch of road impossible.

Undeterred, Furlow led his eight Corsairs to Cebu. As he approached the island, he contacted guerrilla leaders to get a target to attack. They advised Furlow to strike a ridge about two miles north of Cebu City where the Japanese were suspected of having dug tunnels to house supplies.

Arriving over the target area at around 0930, and just before they commenced their attacks, the Japanese opened up with light AA fire. Furlow broke for the AA position while the remaining Corsairs lined up to attack the ridge. Furlow planted his bomb very near the AA position, silencing the guns. The remaining seven Corsairs struck the ridge, with guerrillas reporting "all bombs on target"[50] but failing to report any specific damage.

At 1515, Furlow led eight more Corsairs back to the road on Mindanao. This time he located the target, and after spending an hour over the road section they dropped 16 500 pounders. No results were seen for their efforts.

Four planes also flew escort duty for convoys and the 17 new pilots who joined the squadron on 10 March flew familiarization flights to get them acquainted with the area.

Combat operations were not flown on 12 March. However, eight planes flew air patrols over Leyte Gulf and two others flew convoy cover. The Japanese made no effort to put up a fight, leaving the Corsairs unmolested.

Lousy weather moved in during the overnight hours of 12/13 March, forcing operations to cancel all combat missions for the next three days. The only incident of flying occurred on 14 March when Barton and Kemp, on standby, were scrambled to intercept a reported bogey but they were unable to make their way through the weather to intercept.

The weather finally cleared out on 16 March allowing missions to resume. Ward, Kemp, Lingenfelter and Morris, carrying 1,000 pound bombs, took off at 1430 to provide guerrillas on Cebu ground support. The guerrilla fighter director identified the target as a clump of trees near a road fork, approximately 18 miles north and east of Tuburan Airfield. After some difficulty finding the assigned target, two of the Corsairs put their bombs in the trees but results went unobserved. The other two Corsairs hit a road junction to the east of Tuburan Airfield, again with results unobserved.

To conclude the day, the squadron also provided four flights, each with two Corsairs, to fly patrols over Leyte Gulf while Neilson and MacLachlan escorted a C-46 on a supply run to guerrillas on Cebu and Mindanao. Apparently the two pilots were treated like royalty by the guerrillas at Tuburan, Cebu. On departing the airfield, they were driven to their planes in a Packard sedan, apparently hidden away in a cave since the Japanese occupied the island in 1942.

One officer and four enlisted men joined the squadron on the 16th. The officer was 2Lt. Danny W. Johnson, the Marine who designed the Lucifer's Messengers patch.

Striking several locations on Cebu kept the squadron busy on 17 March. Carrying 1,000 pounders, six divisions flew throughout the day hitting targets provided by the guerrilla flight director on the island. Some of the targets hit included houses near Cebu City suspected of harboring Japanese soldiers, the villages of Maya and Medillin, and enemy troop concentrations south of Ilihan. Cloud cover over the island, extending from 2,500 feet to 6,500 feet, did not aid the pilots with their accuracy. The results of all attacks went unobserved.

During one of the morning raids, Schroeder was requested by the guerrillas to land at Tuburan. Upon arrival, he was given a packet of leaflets and instructed that they be given to a later flight so that they could be dropped along the main highway north and south of Cebu City.

When Bacheler's division flew its mission, it was Bacheler who dropped the leaflets. The leaflets instructed all Filipinos to avoid the main roads and towns so that they would not be injured in future attacks.

On top of the missions to Cebu, eight Corsairs also provided cover for convoys; some of which may have been on their way to Panay.

Once all the pilots were back safely at Guiuan, they were ordered to the squadron intelligence tent. There, the MAG-14 intelligence officer briefed the pilots on the upcoming landing of Army troops on the island of Panay to be executed on 18 March. Until the operation was complete, the squadron would be providing air support for the operation.

Sometime in March, the 40th Infantry Division was withdrawn from Luzon and attached to the Eighth Army. The division, less the 108th Regimental Combat Team (RCT), was assigned to lead the assault on Panay. Leaving Luzon on 15 March, they arrived off Panay early in the morning of 18 March. The landing at Tigbauan was unopposed and they were met by Filipino guerrillas as they waded ashore.[51]

Air support provided by VMF-251 started early that morning and continued through the day. First, 20 Corsairs, in two plane flights, provided cover for the convoy as it made its last leg to Panay. When they returned, six of them were loaded with ordnance and refueled. During the course of the afternoon the six Corsairs—in two plane flights and carrying two 500 pounders each—coordinated with PT boats of Motor Torpedo Squadron 33, commanded by Lt. A. Murray Preston, operating in the Guimaras Straight near the invasion point south of Iloilo, to hit targets in the area. Since there was no Japanese opposition and the invasion troops seemed to be advancing unopposed, the PT boats could not provide any targets for the squadron Corsairs. With no targets to hit, and no requests from Army troops on the ground, they turned for home.

On the way back to Guiuan, one flight—consisting of Furlow and Poor—checked in with guerrillas on Cebu asking if they wanted anything hit on the island. The guerrillas were happy to provide one and requested that the Corsairs hit a grove of trees near Sac Sac suspected of harboring Japanese troops. Three of the four bombs hit the clump of trees but no obvious results were seen.

Support operations continued on 19 March with the squadron providing 24 aircraft (six divisions) to provide continuous combat air patrol over Panay. No Japanese planes came up to challenge the Corsairs at any time during the course of the day.

In addition to the Panay patrols, 12 Corsairs flew combat air patrols over Leyte Gulf and again met no Japanese.

Forces on Panay launched an attack on Iloilo on 20 March and quickly took the city. The Japanese had withdrawn from Iloilo overnight and retreated to the north, leaving most of the city in ruins.[52] The squadron supported the operations by providing five divisions (20 Corsairs) during the day, as well as flying patrols over Negros and Cebu. As for Panay, no targets were found but one flight did receive orders from Army ground controllers to hit a suspected enemy troop concentration in a wooded area north of Iloilo. The area was strafed but results were not visible to the pilots, nor could ground forces confirm anything was hit. On their way home, several of the flights strafed villages on Negros and Cebu, expending nearly 20 thousand rounds of ammo during the attacks only to set one hut on fire and possibly damaging a few others.

On 21 March, the 40th Infantry Division and Filipino guerrillas methodically eliminated pockets of Japanese resistance on Panay. VMF-251 provided six divisions during the day, ready to provide any assistance. None was needed by the Army.

Three of the flights, as they made their way home, struck targets in Cebu and Negros. Divisions led by King and Warren shot up a grove of trees just north of Sagay, Cebu, suspected of hiding an enemy bivouac. The results of both attacks went unobserved.

Wolf's division—consisting of McAlister, Robinson and Walsh scored big while flying over Negros. They spotted two vessels—a boat with a length of about 45 feet and a barge, approximately 30 feet long—off the northwest shore of the island. Wolf got on his radio and contacted guerrilla headquarters at Tuburan, securing permission to hit the boats.[53] The four Corsairs riddled the boats in several strafing runs, ensuring the vessels would not sail again.

Wolf regrouped his division and set a course for Daga. When they reached the town, they spotted a train with 15 cars and two engines: one in front and one in back. It wasn't moving but both engines were shrouded in steam. Two army P-38s in the vicinity saw the Marines and joined in the attack. Diving to nearly tree-top level, they put thousands of rounds into the train with several passes, exploding one of the engines and damaging all the cars.

Eighth Army declared Panay secure on 22 March, relieving VMF-251 from their support operations over the island. With the help of guerrillas, elements of the 40th Infantry hunted down the remaining Japanese on the island. For the rest of the day, the squadron flew cover for convoys and patrols over Leyte Gulf. Other missions scheduled to be flown were canceled as bad weather moved in, grounding the planes.

The tropical weather grounded all planes on 23 March. However, at around 1545, the squadron put four planes in the air at the request of units on Panay. Wolf, McAlister, Robinson and Irwin flew the patrol, which turned up nothing. They were back at Guiuan by 1900.

The squadron continued to see a change in personnel. First Lieutenant Dewitt C. Fisher and 44 enlisted men checked in, while 80 enlisted men were transferred out. For a few of the enlisted men leaving the squadron, it was their lucky day; they would be returning to the United States.

The squadron flew cover for two convoys on 24 March, launching 20 Corsairs in 10 two plane flights from 0700 to 1800. None of the patrols saw any sign of the Japanese. During the evening, all pilots were ordered to the intelligence tent. The MAG-14 intelligence officer, as well as the Army liaison officer attached to the group, briefed the men on the upcoming amphibious landing on Cebu scheduled to be executed within 48 hours. As it did for the army at Panay, it would support army operations as it wrestled the island from the Japanese.

The Americal Division was busy fighting the Japanese on Leyte when it received word it would also be responsible for liberating Cebu and several other islands in the Southern Visayas. The island was already being hammered from above as part of a five day pre-invasion air bombardment on suspected enemy positions. The division, less its 164th RCT, was to enter the island at Talisay, five miles southwest of Cebu City.[54]

The squadron began its work supporting the army on 25 March, providing four divisions for air cover as the convoys made way to Cebu. The Japanese did not attempt to interfere with the convoy.

On the same day, the squadron detached 11 of its most experienced officers: Hart, Cunningham, Erdmann, Garrett, Henley, Jennings, Neilson, Scoville, Howard F. Smith, Daigle and Lindsey. Most were sent to other squadrons but a few earned a ticket back to the U.S.A.

At 0730 on 26 March, cruisers and destroyers of Admiral Russell H. Berkey's Task Force 74 commenced its bombardment of Talisay. High above the invasion force, Furlow, along with pilots Rause, Poor and Welch watched the spectacle. Against the noise of their engines, they could not hear the report of the guns, nor the explosions covering the invasion area. After nearly an hour, the guns ceased fire and dark specks trailing white made their way towards the beach. These were the LTVs (landing vehicle tracked) carrying the leading waves of 132nd and 182nd Infantry Regiments. They landed unopposed at Talisay, and to the north of the city. To the flyers above, it appeared all was going well.

Things went awry for the invasion troops soon after landing. Several of the LVTs struck mines offshore, killing and wounding nearly two dozen men. Invasion troops from the first two assault waves stayed put on the beach and as more vehicles and men came ashore, it quickly became crowded. The off shore bombardment, while effective, did not destroy all of the Japanese defensive positions or all the mines planted in the area. Had the enemy opened up on the crowded beach, it could have been a disaster.

The Americal Division's assistant division commander, Brigadier General Eugene W. Ridings, got men of the 132nd Infantry Regiment moving. With teams leading the way clearing the mines that extended inland from the shore, the soldiers advanced toward Cebu City to the north. The Japanese had withdrawn from the beach area to defensive positions further north, and in the process lost a chance to push the Americans off the beach.[55]

Furlow's four Corsairs saw no Japanese in the air nor received any requests from flight controllers on the ground to hit Japanese positions. He turned his Corsairs around and flew back to Guiuan. His was the first of six divisions the squadron supplied to fly cover for the army during the day. With the Japanese retreating to the north, four of the remaining five divisions got a chance to hit the Japanese on the ground.

Barton's division, which flew twice during the day, attacked ten trucks and other vehicles parked near a jetty at Cebu City, setting fire to two of them and damaging the remaining eight. Barton's plane was hit by AA fire but the damage was light. During the afternoon, the division spotted a large vehicle near Lahug Airfield, north of Cebu City, and attacked it. As the planes lined up to shoot it up, six to eight Japanese were seen running from the truck to seek cover as the Corsairs let loose with their machine guns. The truck was peppered full of holes, and the soldiers seen running from the truck may have been killed.

Capt. Francis E. Doughty's division was directed by the fighter director to hit a suspected enemy position north of Lahug Airfield. Doughty, Schewe, Wyatt and 2Lt. David W. Lindner, approached from the east just north of Opon Airfield on Mactan Island, taking anti-aircraft fire as they flew past the airfield. No one was hit. Quickly crossing Cebu Harbor they soon were making strafing runs on the concealed position. After each plane made several strafing runs with unobserved results, they turned for home.

Frank's division also hit Lahug Airfield. Spotting several trucks on a road leading to the hills west of the airfield as the enemy fled Cebu City, they quickly lined up the vehicles in their sites and let loose with thousands of rounds of .50 caliber ammunition. One truck exploded in flames, another was set on fire, and several others were damaged.

The Americal Division made good progress against the Japanese on 27 March. The squadron continued its aerial support, providing 12 Corsairs over the course of the day. In all cases, the planes found nothing to attack and all returned safely to Guiuan.

Bad weather moved in 28 March, curtailing operations for the rest of the month.

The only missions flown were on 29 March; two two-plane patrols over Leyte Gulf and one division sent to Cebu to cover the army. None of the patrols spotted the enemy.

On the same day the patrols were sent to Leyte Gulf and Cebu, Bacheler was summoned to see the MAG-14 commanding officer, Colonel Zebulon Hopkins. When Bacheler arrived at his tent, Hopkins offered him a chair. He wanted to know when King would be ready to take over the squadron. Hopkins assured Bacheler that he had done a fine job with VMF-251; instead he would be heading back to the states for a new assignment. But there was a hitch. He would go home only when he pronounced King ready to take over.

Bacheler felt King was not ready, having only been with an active combat squadron for two months prior to joining the squadron. Furlow, his exec, was the man for the job. Despite his misgivings he told Hopkins King would be ready in a week. Apparently that was all Hopkins wanted to hear. He informed Bacheler that he was being assigned to Marine Corps Schools at Quantico, Virginia to attend the Marine Air-Infantry School.[56]

The turn in the weather came as a blessing in disguise for the squadron. The torrid pace of operations while covering Army operations over Panay and Cebu and the numerous patrols over Leyte Gulf seriously taxed the maintenance section's ability to keep the Corsairs operational. By the end of March, of the 21 Corsairs assigned to the squadron, only 11 were fit to fly. During the last days of March, maintenance men took advantage of the down time and worked furiously to increase the number of operational planes. If the last three months were any indication, there would be no let up for the squadron during the month of April.

April 1945

With their missions over Panay and Cebu in support of army operations in the islands, the squadron was finally supporting ground troops—though not Marines. In January 1938, the Secretary of the Navy issued a directive which established the mission for Marine aviation. It stated that "Marine Corps aviation is to be equipped, organized and trained primarily for the support of the Fleet Marine Force in landing operations and in support of troop activities in the field; and secondarily as replacement squadrons for carrier-based naval aircraft...."[57] It was envisioned that Marines would operate from carriers when land bases were not available to support ground troops. While it gave the Marines direction, the directive did not spell out "how" to do it. It took several years for the Marines to fulfill this directive; it wasn't until March 1944 that Marine air units directly supported Marine ground units.

The Marine Corps cannot be faulted for this delay. Projection of airpower was of utmost importance. Operations in the Pacific were often planned with the acquisition of airfields in mind, especially for the use of aircraft by the USAAF. In the early years of the war, air power was used in a defensive role. It came to a head at Guadalcanal; after seven months of brutal combat the United States gained foothold in the Solomon Islands and halted the Japanese juggernaut. After Guadalcanal was secured, airpower carried the fight to the Japanese by being used to isolate key Japanese strongholds—most notably Rabaul. As these strongholds were isolated and bypassed, allied airpower—especially New Zealand—took up the job of continuing these types of missions, allowing Marine air to focus on ground support operations and to carry the fight closer to Japan.

Six. Guiuan Field, Samar, Philippine Islands, and Deactivation

The control of ground support operations in the Pacific went through numerous changes during the course of the war. By the time VMF-251 was flying close air support for the army, divisions in the Philippines had assigned to them Air Liaison Parties (ALP's), who were trained to quickly transmit requests from front line personnel for strikes to Support Air Parties (SAP's), who then transmitted the requests to the pilots.

Since 26 March the pilots of VMF-251, while flying support missions for army ground forces over Cebu, had to assist them an airborne fighter director. Circling the target area in a B-24 and carrying the latest intelligence concerning the situation on the ground, the airborne director aided the pilots in locating requested targets. In most cases, targets were usually marked by phosphorous shells fired by divisional artillery or heavy weapons support companies. Many of the targets in the coming days consisted of area targets occupied by Japanese troops, gun positions and entrenchments. Despite the help from the air, assessment of damage proved difficult for the squadron.

By 1 April, the 5th Air Force had passed responsibility of the coordination of strikes in the southern Philippines to the 13th Air Force. The area of responsibility for the 13th AF included the islands of Samar, Leyte, Panay, and Mindanao. With the change, squadrons of MAG-14 would now be getting their strike orders through the 13th AF.[58]

On the ground, the Americal Division had captured Lahug Airfield, located north of Cebu City. The Japanese had been pushed back into the hills to the northwest and west of the airfield. The hills were the target of two missions flown by the squadron on April Fools' Day. Furlow, Rause, Poor and Welch flew the morning mission while Barton, Kemp, Sandbach and Morris flew the afternoon mission. Fourteen 1,000 pound bombs were dropped on targets consisting of AA positions, troops and vehicles. Damage was hard to assess but the fighter director, flying over the area in a B-24, reported the bombs appeared to be on target. A few strafing runs were flown before low clouds blanketed the area. Despite AA guns in the area they remained silent, allowing the Corsairs to return home unscathed.

Squadron Corsairs returned to Cebu on 2 April. Flying throughout the day, sixteen Corsairs in four-plane flights attacked an enemy command post three miles northwest of Lahug Airfield; a concentration of enemy troops north of Tuburan, huts in a valley 10 miles north of Kahug Airfield, and a Japanese communication center in the hills to the west of Lahug. Thirteen 1,000 pound bombs were dropped on the targets but no damage was observed by the pilots. The airborne flight director reported bombs dropped on the command post and communication center were right on target and damage was believed to have occurred. Once again the Japanese guns remained silent; all the Corsairs returned home without a scratch.

It was back to Cebu the next day. Taking off at 0730 and arriving over the target 45 minutes later, eight Corsairs with only four of them carrying two 1,000 pound bombs each, attacked a school building in Consolacion suspected of housing Japanese troops and equipment. All the bombs overshot the target but landed close enough to do some damage. The area was also thoroughly strafed. Following the attack on the school building, the Corsairs strafed buildings at Liloan and a wooded area near Silay Airfield suspected of concealing Japanese troops and equipment. The strafing at Silay started a gasoline fire, most likely from a burning truck. The fighter pilots met no enemy opposition and were back at Guiuan by 0930.

Taking advantage of the air support, army units on Cebu once again called on VMF-251 to strike enemy strongholds. On 4 April, six divisions flew at different times during the day to hit targets in the vicinity of Lahug Airfield, Silut Lagoon, Tuburan, and Liloan. Each of the 23 Corsairs carried two 1,000 pound bombs and hit targets that included pillboxes, Japanese troop concentrations and buildings. Numerous fires were started, buildings destroyed and a 20MM AA gun was knocked out despite intense AA fire offered by the Japanese. Slightly over 40,000 pounds of ordnance and over 19,000 rounds of .50 caliber ammunition were expended to render the targets useless to the Japanese.

More experienced pilots left the squadron the same day. Inglehart, McLachlan, Pirages, Rosellen, Schoetz, and Archibald A. Harris were all detached for reassignment.

Cebu received more attacks from the squadron on 5 April, as did Negros. Doughty—who recently joined the squadron—led Schewe, Wyatt and Lindner to Cebu where the flight controller directed them to plant four 1,000 pound bombs in a group of buildings at Liloan suspected of being used by the Japanese. The bombs and several strafing runs may have caused some damage to the buildings, but nothing specific was seen by the pilots.

Twelve Corsairs, in flights of two, struck targets in northwest Negros at various times during the day. The enemy was seen moving north and west on roads in the area. One road, leading east from the capital city of Bacolod, was packed full of trucks. The trucks bore the brunt of strafing attacks by all the pilots; 10 trucks were seen on fire or destroyed, and five were left smoking, In addition, two buildings were destroyed by fire and one pilot set off a huge explosion. What he may have hit was never determined.

Two pilots joined the squadron—2Lt. Nathaniel L. Whisenhant and 2Lt. Lehn J. Potter—making up for some of the losses of the previous day.

Northwest Negros continued to receive attacks from squadron pilots on 6 April. The first attack was delivered by King, Beattie, Irwin and Johnson. Their target marked by a phosphorous shell, they dropped their 1,000 pounders and strafed a truck park and Japanese troops concentrations in hills 10 miles east of Dos Hermanos, setting fire to a truck and a house.

Also loaded with 1,000 pounders, the next three divisions took off at varying times during the day to hit AA guns and a supply area north of Mt. Mandalagan—also marked by phosphorous shells. They smothered the target, destroying one truck and setting fire to three others.

The next two days would be rough for the squadron; one pilot was killed and another escaped with his life. The 7th of April started off well enough. Twenty-two Corsairs, flying in pairs and carrying two 1,000 pounders each, flew at different times during the day to hit gun positions, trenches, supply dumps and camouflaged trucks in the hills northwest of Lahug Airfield on Cebu. The first two flights hit AA gun positions but no damage could be ascertained. The third flight, led by Doughty, hit a large Japanese supply area. His four Corsairs started a large fire, destroyed a hut, and burned up at least five supply dumps. After his attack, Doughty spotted a large group of trucks in a nearby ravine. When his division returned to Guiuan, he sought and received permission to go back and hit the trucks. After two Corsairs were fueled up and rearmed, he and Schewe took off.

They easily found the trucks. Doughty made his attack run, followed by Schewe. Their 1,000 pounders destroyed three trucks and may have damaged several others. The Japanese opened up with AA fire. Both turned around to strafe the exposed gun position. Soon after Doughty finished his run, Schewe could only watch helplessly as Doughty's Corsair (BuNo 57512) crashed and exploded approximately three miles northwest of Lahug Airfield. Whether Doughty was hit by the AA fire or failed to pull out of his strafing

Six. Guiuan Field, Samar, Philippine Islands, and Deactivation

run was never determined. His remains were recovered and eventually interred at Robstown Cemetery in Robstown, Texas. He was 23 years old.

All but one of the remaining flights hit the previously mentioned targets again, but no results could be seen. Wolf's flight missed all the action, having been assigned to drop leaflets for the guerrillas along roads near Tabogon, Pogo, and Sagay. Doughty was the only casualty for the day; none of the other Corsairs sustained any damage.

On 8 April, 20 Corsairs, each carrying two 500 pounders, returned to attack supply dumps, guns and entrenchments in hills near Cebu City, and one flight struck buildings at Sac Sac. While the bomb runs in the hills proved ineffective, strafing runs set off an oil or gas fire which eventually sparked an ammo dump explosion, followed by multiple explosions. In Sac Sac, a direct hit by a 500 pounder destroyed two buildings.

Defective bombs may have had a lot to do with the poor results. Of the 40 bombs carried by the Corsairs, 17 bombs hung up and were either shaken loose or brought back to Guiuan and seven were duds. What caused this massive failure of ordnance is not known. It certainly wasn't a good day for the bomb boys, and for Hugh "Yogi" Irwin his hung bomb nearly cost him his life.

"...I was unable to release one of the two 500 pound general purpose bombs carried under the body of my Corsair," wrote Irwin. "After completing our strafing runs as directed by the Forward Air Control overlooking the city, my wingman (Johnson) and I headed for our home strip on Samar. En route, violent maneuvers to try to shake loose my 500 pound extra cargo met with no success. After radioing for a straight-in approach—to avoid an accidental drop in bivouac areas—I proceeded with what I expected to be an otherwise normal landing. I had no qualms about such a procedure since several months earlier when landing at Green Island after a strike on Rabaul a 1,000 pounder dropped from my plane and rolled harmlessly onto the runway.

"But that was hardly the case this time when, on contact with the ground, the 500 pounder jettisoned and in rolling under the plane, it's nose fuse was chewed off leaving it fully armed and with one more skip detonated. The result was half an airplane with only bits and pieces of the tail section remaining aft of the cockpit and shredded wings and cowling forward."[59]

Irwin's plane, practically torn in half by the explosion, skidded off the runway, jumped a ditch and came to a halt; the plane's nose buried into the ground.

"I recognized immediately what had happened and after realizing that I was still in this world, scrambled from what was left of my Corsair fearing that fire might follow the explosion. It did not, but I was left alone with my wreckage while the strip ambulance crews, thinking I could never survive such a blast, drove instead to three ground personnel who had been struck by some of my bomb's shrapnel and transported them to the base's Navy hospital.

"Stumbling around in my tattered parachute and flight suit (which as I remember consisted of mostly a zipper down the front) and doing considerable yelling, I finally aroused some attention from the tower area, but when an operations jeep finally arrived, the driver got out and in awe, walked all around what was left of old number 22 (BuNo 57518) before taking me back to where our own squadron flight surgeon was on duty. After the usual shots following such an incident and temporary patching of major bleeding areas he assured me that I was intact and sent me to the hospital, the ambulance now having returned from their regular run. I was to learn later that an Army Air Corps doctor also on duty at the time remarked that although I had walked away from the crash site it was doubtful I would survive the proximity to such an explosion. Praise God he was wrong.

"Although I had several cuts to my arms and legs where small bits of shrapnel had passed through or lodged superficially, I suffered only one major laceration to my left shoulder and was released from the hospital after several days of observation on April 11 ... given the choice of returning to the U.S. or staying with my squadron, I chose the latter and enjoyed some "hammock duty" while my buddies continued to help clean up the Philippine liberation. Because my shoulder wound proved slow to heal and right where parachute straps made contact, it was two months before I resumed flying, by which time MAG-14 had moved to Okinawa."[60]

Irwin was lucky to escape with his life. There can be no doubt that the thick armor plating behind the cockpit seat deflected most of the blast away from Irwin, allowing him to walk away from the wreck.

The squadron's ordnance department, as well as MAG-14's Bomb Disposal Technician, agreed with Irwin's cause of the explosion. Both determined that the arming vane and the bomb's nose fuse were sheared away, arming the bomb. A few weeks after Irwin's incident, policy changes went into effect. No longer would pilots be allowed to land with a hung bomb. They were ordered to jettison their bombs over water; if they couldn't, they were to bail out.[61]

Irwin's Corsair following a bomb explosion during a landing at Guiuan Field, Samar, Philippines on April 8, 1945 (courtesy Hugh E. "Yogi" Irwin).

Hung bombs were a continuing thorn in the side for MAG-14. The group was aware of the problem and the B-10 shackles that secured the bombs to the Corsairs. The group ordnance section was getting an earful from the pilots, claiming the bombs hung upon release anywhere from "split seconds to five minutes" and as seen above remained stuck, unable to be jettisoned. Group ordnance men tried to get a handle on the problem: filing lugs on the bombs, checking the method of suspension, and an inspection of each plane after a mission for problems failed to get 100 percent bomb drops on missions.[62]

The incessant pounding of Cebu continued on 9 April. Eight Corsairs carried two 500 pounders each, while 12 Corsairs each carried one 260 pound fragmentation bomb. The attacks by the five divisions occurred throughout the day, targeting gun positions and enemy trenches three miles northwest of Lahug Airfield and troop concentrations near Tabuelan, located on the northwest coast of the island. The bombing and strafing of the assigned targets produced no observable results and came at cost of one Corsair damaged; Wolf's Corsair was hit by enemy AA fire, nearly severing the aileron control cable and leaving a large dent in the pilot's armor plating behind his seat.

The next five days saw the squadron pound the same area near Lahug Airfield. Japanese pillboxes, trenches and gun positions were repeatedly hit; over the five days 58 tons of ordnance was unloaded on the Japanese. In all cases, the effectiveness of the bombs could not be observed, not even by the Support Air Party. Strafing after the bomb runs was somewhat effective, setting fire to several huts. The Japanese did put up sporadic AA fire, damaging one Corsair.

The squadron received a respite from bombing attacks by flying patrol duty over Leyte Gulf on 15 April. Four two-plane flights flew at different times during the day as they searched in vain for any signs of the enemy. In addition, three two-plane flights flew from 0730 to 1235 to cover a south bound convoy.

Bacheler was officially relieved of duty as commanding officer of the squadron. King, the Marine groomed by Hopkins to take over, did not get the assignment. Instead the job went to the squadron's exec, Major Thomas W. Furlow, the man Bacheler wanted for the job. Furlow's reign would not last long since word came down—unofficially—that the squadron was selected to be deactivated.

Having reached a peak strength of 145 squadrons[63] by September 1944, Marine Air began to downsize. The strategic situation had radically changed since the dark days of 1942. Japanese held islands had been recaptured or isolated over the last three years, reducing the area defended by the Japanese. No longer was it necessary to maintain squadrons to keep isolated Japanese positions in check, that job was taken over by allied air forces—all that remained was Japan. Squadrons would soon be flying out of Okinawa and carriers off Japan's shores. By 30 June 1945, 14 squadrons had been deactivated—VMF-251 among them.

Until the day of deactivation came, the squadron continued its ground support role for the Army. Due to weather, attacks on Negros and Cebu were cancelled on 16 April. The next day, the support missions to Cebu resumed. Three flights, each consisting of six Corsairs carrying a 1,000 pound bomb, dropped the nine tons and expended all their .50 caliber ammunition attacking gun positions, trenches and fortifications near Liloan. While the pilots could not see any specific damage, the Support Air Party reported the target areas were well covered and that two AA guns were knocked out.

Eighteen squadron Corsairs in three six plane flights returned to Cebu on 18 April. Evans, leading Romberg, La Marre, Peterson, Fink, and Potter, took to the air at 0645 to plant their 1,000 pounders on enemy trenches west of Liloan. Along the way, Fink's plane developed hydraulic trouble. Fink and his wingman, Potter, jettisoned their bombs and returned to Guiuan. The remaining four Corsairs arrived over the target at 0730. For the next 35 minutes they dropped their four 1,000-pounders and strafed the target area. One bomb did cause a landslide which may have rendered some of the trenches useless. Other than the landslide, no other damage was observed.

The next flight of Corsairs took off at 1100 carrying the same bomb load as the first flight. Jernigan led fellow pilots Petty, Robinson, Whisenhant, Walters, and Ellis to Cebu where they attacked enemy installations to west of the village of Consolacion. Greeted by moderate 20MM AA fire, the Corsairs let loose their 1,000 pounders. The accompanying Support Air Party saw four direct hits on pillboxes, destroying all of them. The following strafing runs set two huts burning. After spending 30 minutes attacking the area, the Corsairs turned for home.

The last six Corsairs left Guiuan at 1630 with orders to attack enemy troops along a ridge in north central Cebu. Wyatt, McAlister, Fink, Potter, Robinson and Whisenhant, each carrying a 500-pounder, arrived over the target area at 1725 and for the next 45 minutes pounded the Japanese. The ridge was strafed by all the planes but no one could tell if any troops had been killed. Bombs were dropped along the nearby main east-west road, destroying one building. With their munitions expended the Corsairs turned for home, touching down at 1845.

Targets near Liloan, Cebu City and Danao were the focal points of attacks conducted by the squadron on 19 April. Carrying 500 pounders, CPT. Norman O'Bryan, who joined the squadron on 2 April, led five pilots to hit buildings along the main north-south road just north of Liloan. Soon after they took off at 0815, Welch had to turn back due to an oil leak. He jettisoned his bomb and landed safely at Guiuan. The others continued to their target and arrived at 0855. Following two area hits with their bombs and five strafing passes, the pilots could not confirm any damage for their efforts.

VMF-251's Nat Whisenhant flying an F4U-1D over the Philippines, possibly April 1945. Note the insignia on the engine cowling (courtesy Jack Cook).

At 1245, Wolf led Schewe, Scott, Lindner, Rause and Lingenfelter to hit enemy troop concentrations northwest of Cebu City. Following a 45 minute flight, the five Marines planted five of their six 500-pounders right on target. With the enemy troops hiding under a grove of palm trees, it was impossible to see the results of their bombings but no doubt a few of the Japanese soldiers felt the sting of shrapnel tearing into their bodies.

The last flight of the day was flown by Poor, Kemp, Rhodes, Morris, Scott and Lindner. Taking off at 1645, the six pilots were assigned to strike the village of Danao. Kemp returned to Guiuan soon after takeoff, his plane developing a hydraulic problem. Scott's plane blew a tail wheel on takeoff but he managed to get his plane in the air and join up with his flight. Arriving over Danao at 1735, they spent the next 10 minutes dropping their bombs and strafing the village resulting in a series of huts set on fire.

They turned for home, arriving at Guiuan 1830. Scott's flat tail wheel came back to haunt him. When he touched down, Scott lost control of his Corsair. The Corsair ran off the runway and flipped over on its back. Scott survived the ordeal but his plane (BuNo 57456) was damaged beyond repair.

On 20 April two six-plane flights attacked suspected troop concentrations in northwest Negros, about seven miles east of Concepcion. The first flight, led by Evans, took off at 0640, followed by O'Bryan leading the second flight at 0715. Each Corsair carried one 500-pounder. With friendly forces approximately 100 yards from the target, the two flights had to be precise with their strikes. Fortunately, the target area was marked by phosphorous shells fired by nearby artillery. Ten of the 12 bombs were planted in the target area—one was a dud and one hung up and later jettisoned. Again, the results of the attack went unobserved.

Four targets were hit by the squadron on 21 April; two on Cebu and two on Negros. Each of the 16 Corsairs involved in the day's attacks carried one 500 pound bomb. Over Cebu, one division hit gun positions northwest of Silut Lagoon in the morning, and the second division hit enemy occupied caves to the west of Liloan during the afternoon. All eight bombs may have scored damaging hits. Even though the pilots could not see any results of their attacks, the nearby Support Air Party reported all were right on target.

While Silut Lagoon was under attack, another division was pounding enemy troops and pillboxes between Canlaon Volcano and the Bago River on Negros. The bombs were dropped on target and the accompanying Air Support Party reported the attack was "very good."[64] During the afternoon attack on Negros, the Corsairs planted their 500-pounders on an enemy occupied ridge northwest of the target hit during the morning with unknown results. All Corsairs involved in the day's attacks made it back safely despite meager AA fire put up by the Japanese.

At varying times during 22 April, the squadron hit several enemy ground positions on Cebu, and two attacks against pinned down Japanese troops in northwest Leyte. Walters, with Ellis, Beattie and Johnson, struck first. Dropping four 1,000 pounders and then followed by several strafing runs, they smoked one house containing a 20MM AA gun. Jernigan's division struck next, attacking a knoll with caves and pillboxes four miles north of Cebu City with no observed results.

During the afternoon, Jernigan again led his division back to Cebu, attacking buildings near a coconut grove 2 miles west of Tabogon. They dropped four 500 pounders, scoring direct hits on two buildings, demolishing both of them. The Japanese opened up with light, intense AA fire. Jernigan regrouped his Corsairs to attack the coconut grove which was where the AA fire appeared to be originating. They planted their remaining 500-pounders in the grove, apparently silencing the gun. Walter's division was the last to hit Cebu, dropping four 1,000-pounders and repeatedly strafing a bomb shelter near Liloan. The strafing may have ignited a nearby fuel dump; several fires were started which put up a column of black smoke.

By late April, elements of the Americal Division and the 1st Filipino Infantry Regiment, both under the Eighth Army Area Command, had many Japanese stragglers hemmed up in northwest Leyte.[65] Air support strikes were made to hit two pockets of Japanese troops, each containing about 1,000 soldiers.[66] O'Bryan was tapped to lead the attacks against the pockets. Each Corsair participating in the strikes carried three 500 pound bombs. The first flight of seven Corsairs took off at 0612. Evans remained behind, unable to get his Corsair started due to magneto problems. The remaining six Corsairs arrived over the first pocket at 0655 and found it marked by artillery smoke shells. For the next half hour they pummeled the Japanese. Results of the attack were obscured by the jungle but all bombs were placed in the pocket, likely killing and wounding many Japanese.

O'Bryan had his Corsairs home by 0800. Within an hour and half, he and his seven pilots were heading back to Leyte to attack the second pocket. They found it marked by smoke when they arrived at 1015. After 35 minutes, 24 500-pounders tore up the target area and several strafing runs caused a good sized explosion, sparking a fierce fire. As the Corsairs left the target area behind the fire was still burning, putting up a dark column of smoke.

F4U Corsairs prepare to fly a mission from Guiuan Airfield, Samar, Philippines. Note VMF-251 Corsair second from right (courtesy Jack Cook).

The squadron launched two attacks on 23 April, each attack consisting on four Corsairs each carrying two 500-pounders. Wolf and Scott led the divisions, attacking enemy positions and installations near Silut Lagoon and Sacsac. Eight 500-pounders were placed on each target and nearly 10,000 rounds of .50 caliber ammunition were expended in several strafing runs. One direct hit was scored and several huts were left smoking. The enemy put up light AA fire but no Corsairs were hit. All returned safely to Guiuan.

The squadron got a break from combat operations on 24 April by flying practice gunnery missions. The break was short-lived since combat operations resumed the following day with strikes delivered to Cebu and Negros. At various times during the day, four divisions hit enemy concentrations near Sac Sac, a road halfway between Tabogon and Bogo, and Medillin Airfield, all on Cebu. Sixteen 500-pounders hit all the target areas; while direct damage could not be observed, hits no doubt damaged equipment and hit Japanese personnel. Strafing left a pair of huts smoking.

On Negros, one division hit trenches and gun positions near Cuimbalaon, another hit an enemy occupied hill 15 miles from Bacolod, and a third division hit Japanese troop concentrations southeast of Buena Vista. Twelve 500 pound bombs were placed in the target areas but no damage was observed.

The two islands received the attention of the squadron for the next two days. On 26 April three divisions, flying at various times during the day, attacked enemy troops near Mt. Mandalagan and Bacolod on Negros. After dropping 11 500-pounders and strafing each target area, all they had to show for their efforts were two burning huts.

Three divisions were also sent to Cebu during the day, the first two carrying a 100 pound napalm bomb along with one 500-pounder. The first flight planted their bombs and strafed a coconut grove—suspected of housing enemy troops—along a road south of Sogod, starting two large fires. The second flight hit enemy troops in another coconut grove south of Bogo, setting a hut on fire. Enemy occupied caves were hit by the third division west of Ilihan. Once the smoke cleared from the bombs runs and the strafing, smoke was seen pouring from a cave.

The Japanese offered no resistance on either island, allowing all the Corsairs to return to Guiuan unscathed.

On 27 April, Wolf led two 12-plane ground support strikes in northwest Negros. The first flight was over the target at 0745 and dropped 11 500-pounders on an enemy held knoll about 12 miles east of Bacolod. The target area was thickly covered in smoke from friendly artillery as well as the bombs that damage could not be assessed. During the attack, Scott's plane suffered a bad oil leak as he approached the knoll. Quickly losing oil pressure Scott notified Wolf, jettisoned his bomb and headed for Bacolod Airfield, recently taken from the Japanese. The field was in no condition to receive a Corsair. On the advice of the fighter director on the ground, Scott made a wheels-up landing just as his oil pressure hit zero.

Scott escaped injury and the plane was lightly damaged. However, because there were no repair facilities at the airfield, getting it airworthy was out of the question. The plane (BuNo 57383) was written off. The squadron's engineering officer, 1Lt. John Irwin, made a trip to the field the next day and arranged to have all serviceable parts stripped from the plane and brought back to Guiuan.

The afternoon strike concentrated on Japanese troops along the right bank of a river about five miles southeast of Concepcion. Thick smoke from artillery and the 500 pounders once again ruled out any assessment of damage. The ground controller notified Wolf that his planes "must have killed lots of Japs ... as the bombs all hit in the assigned target."[67]

O'Bryan and Jernigan led two eight plane flights to Negros on 28 April to attack enemy troops in the hills east of Bacolod. Also participating in the strike were eight Corsairs from VMF-212. The planes were without .50 caliber ammunition due to a shortage of .50 caliber ammunition, recently announced by the 13th Air Force. Sixteen 500-pounders and four 100 pound napalm bombs were planted on top of the enemy by the squadron but debris and fires created by the blasts prevented any chance of determining any damage.

The next day, 24 Corsairs, flying in two 12-plane flights during the day, dropped 44 napalm clusters on enemy troops in a ravine northwest of Canlaon Volcano. Assisting in the strikes were four Corsairs from VMF-223. The fighter director reported that the area was thick with Japanese, and that many must have been killed since the target area was well covered by the attack. It was impossible to confirm any direct damage from the strike since thick fire and smoke from the strike covered the ravine.

The last day of April brought news of the squadron's demise. By the end of the day pilots, enlisted personnel and Corsairs would be transferred to other squadrons or sent home, if they had enough time overseas. Until that happened the strikes on Negros and Cebu continued.

The first strike of the day was delivered at 0720 by 12 squadron Corsairs carrying two 260 pound fragmentation bombs each. The recipient of these fragmentation bombs was Japanese troops located in a valley 7 to 8 miles east and north-northeast of Tuburan,

Cebu. The squadron placed their bombs right on target but results could not be determined with any certainty.

Four squadron Corsairs carrying a 500-pounder each, along with seven Corsairs from VMF-212, returned to hit the same target at 1210. Once again, results went unobserved for the squadron. VMF-212 pilots claimed seven hits, damaging six Japanese occupied houses near Tabuelan, just south of VMF-251's target.[68]

At 1530, the last flight of eight Corsairs, along with eight Corsairs from VMF-222, delivered more than a dozen 500-pounders on Japanese troops located in a ravine 3,000 yards east of the army's front line north of Mt. Mandalagan on Negros. For both squadrons, the results went unobserved.

Once the squadron's Corsairs returned, the breakup of the squadron began. One hundred nine enlisted men and two navy enlisted men were transferred. Eight Corsairs were transferred to VMF-223 and seven transferred to VMF-222. Twelve pilots were transferred to VMF-212, 12 to VMF-222 and 13 to VMF-223. A dozen pilots, a few ground officers and Corsairs remained with the squadron, along with an unknown number of enlisted personnel.

The squadron officially flew its last mission on the first day of May, sending 12 Corsairs to Leyte in support of ground forces near Sulpa. The assigned target area was in the path of advancing Philippine ground units and the Corsairs placed their bombs right on the money, prompting the commander of the ground forces to report the target area was well covered.

During the course of the month, the remaining men of the squadron were transferred or sent home. Furlow relinquished command to 1Lt. Glen F. Keithley on 21 May. With First Marine Air Wing General Order number 14–1945, dated 24 May, the squadron was deactivated effective 1 June. All TOE gear, as well as recreational items, was turned in to MAG-14.

When the first day of June came, the last three officers with the squadron—Keithley, 1Lt. John J. McCaskill, and Warrant Officer Andy J. Wiart—closed the books on VMF-251. The squadron's World War II days were over.

Epilogue

The Marines of VMO/VMF-251 worked hard and long to accomplish all that it was asked to do. Pilots often spent anywhere from three to seven hours in the air, sometimes flying missions three times a day. Ground crew personnel spent countless hours performing maintenance to keep the planes flying, often starting before daybreak and extending into the late evening. Sleep was at a premium. An examination of the number of hours the squadron flew during the period of June 1944 through May 1945 shows just how hard the squadron was utilized—especially in the Philippines (January through May 1945). The hours flown during the critical days of Guadalcanal cannot be determined due lack of records and the way the pilots were utilized during that campaign.

Hours Flown by VMO/VMF-251 June 1944–May 1945[1]

Month	Squadron Hours	Individual Combat Missions
June 1944	1,408.5	200
July 1944	1,368.2	517
August 1944	1,241.9	487
September 1944	797.0	387
October 1944	969.6	307
November 1944	821.3	363
December 1944	378.2	124
January 1945	2,409.2	626
February 1945	1,653.5	576
March 1945	1,847.9	519
April 1945	1,632.3	588
May 1945	23.1	N/A

The low hours of December 1944 and May 1945 are due to the squadron's move to Guiuan and its deactivation. Combat operations ceased for the squadron in these months, accounting for the low numbers. It must be noted that the squadron was not forced to cancel any of its missions due to lack of aircraft; the maintenance crews of the squadron kept more than 90 percent of its aircraft operational throughout its second tour of combat. The recommendation for the Navy Unit Commendation Award, written by Hopkins in February 1945 (Appendix 9), is well-deserved.

Just as they were at the start of World War II, the islands where the squadron served remain unknown to most of today's generation. Within a decade, those veterans remaining who participated in the largest war yet seen by man will no longer be with us. There will be no more eyewitnesses to the great battles: Pearl Harbor, Guadalcanal, Midway, the Normandy invasion, the Battle of the Bulge to name a few of the many battles where young men sacrificed their lives. It will be up to future generations to ensure that their deeds live on.

Some of the airfields where the squadron operated during World War II continue to function today; others are slowly disappearing or have disappeared. Tontouta Airfield survived to become the main airport of New Caledonia. Bomber Field No. 1 on Espiritu Santo is in disuse as is the former fighter strip at Turtle Bay. The New Hebrides, of which Espiritu Santo is one of its islands, is now known as Vanuatu. Henderson Field, the sight of so many desperate struggles, was closed after the war. At the end of the 1960s it was reopened and today serves as the main airport for flights in the Solomon Islands region—Honiara International Airport/Henderson Field. Nature has reclaimed the airfields at Piva on Bougainville; the north and south runways are barely discernable in satellite photos. Guiuan Airfield was used as an emergency landing strip after Typhoon Haiyan devastated the area in late 2013. It remains in operation, serving as a waypoint for other destinations in the Philippines. The fields remain accessible, but require many hours of travel due to the remoteness of the locations. There are organizations that offer tours to Pacific battle sites and prices vary.

Appendices

Containing **1.** *Commanding Officers;* **2.** *Assignments 1941–1945;* **3.** *Casualties, 1 December 1941–1 June 1945;* **4.** *Roster of Personnel, August 1942;* **5.** *Roster of Personnel, March 1945;* **6.** *Number of Japanese Planes Shot Down by 251 Pilots;* **7.** *Aircraft Markings;* **8.** *Squadron Awards;* **9.** *Citations for Recommended Awards*

1. Commanding Officers

VMO-251 and VMF-251
December 1, 1941—June 1, 1945

Name	Date	Squadron Designation
Capt. Elliot E. Bard	1 Dec 1941–11 Dec 1941	VMO-251
Maj. John N. Hart	12 Dec 1941–29 Oct 1942	VMO-251
Lt. Col. Charles H. Hayes[1]	30 Oct 1942–30 Nov 1942	VMO-251
Capt. Ralph Yeaman	1 Dec 1942–7 Dec 1942	VMO-251
Maj. William R. Campbell	8 Dec 1942–10 Dec 1942	VMO-251
Maj. Joseph N. Renner	11 Dec 1942–12 Mar 1943	VMO-251
Capt. Claude H. Welch	13 Mar 1943–21 May 1943	VMO-251
Capt. Michael R. Yunck	22 May 1943–3 Jun 1943	VMO-251
Maj. Carl M. Longley	4 Jun 1943–31 Oct 1943	VMO-251
Capt. Robert W. Teller	1 Nov 1943–5 Nov 1943	VMO-251
Maj. William C. Humberd[2]	6 Nov 1943–9 Feb 1945	VMO-251, VMF-251
Maj. William Bacheler	10 Feb 1945–14 Apr 1945	VMF-251
Maj. Thomas W. Furlow	16 Apr 1945–20 May 1945	VMF-251
1stLt. Glen Keithley	21 May 1945–1 Jun 1945	VMF-251

2. Assignments, 1941–1945

Assignment	Date
MAG-21, 2nd MAW	1 December 1941
1st Marine Division	May 1942
1st MAW	22 August 1942
MAG-11	1 December 1942
MAG-14 (TAD)	17 January 1943
MAG-12	8 April 1943
MAG-11	14 May 1943
Service Group, Marine Fleet Air West Coast	2 June 1943
Marine Base, Defense Aircraft Group 44, MCAS Mojave, Ca.	15 July 1943
MBDAG-41 at El Toro (TAD Camp Pendleton Air Field, Oceanside, Ca.)	22 November 1943

Assignment	Date
Detached from Marine Fleet Air West Coast for overseas duty	20 Feb 1944
1st MAW	10 Mar 1944
MAG-11	25 Apr 1944
1st MAW	15 June 1944
MAG-24	23 July 1944
MAG-14 until deactivation	1 October 1944

Abbreviations:
MAG—Marine Air Group
MAW—Marine Air Wing
TAD—Temporary Additional Duty or Temporary Assigned Duty
MBDAG—Marine Base Defense Air Group

3. Casualties, 1 December 1941–1 June 1945

Alphabetical Listing

Name	Date	Rank	Status	Location
Anderson, Emmett L.	21 October 1942	SSGT (NAP)	KIA	Solomon Islands
Andrews, Robert L., Jr.	10 May 1943	TSGT	AD	Guadalcanal
Baer, Paul D.	26 September 1942	PVT	INJ	Guadalcanal
Baird, Richard E.	27 or 28 September 1942	PVT	INJ	Guadalcanal
Batistich, Dennis	22 January 1943	PVT	KIA	Guadalcanal
Booth, Roy L.	21 December 1942	2LT.	AD	Espiritu Santo
Brooks, Clifford E.	23 February 1943	PVT.	WIA	Guadalcanal
Campbell, William R.	13 November 1942	Major	WIA	Guadalcanal
Christian, Wayne W.	30 January 1943	1LT.	KIA	Guadalcanal
Doughty, Francis E.	7 April 1945	CAPT.	KIA	Cebu, Philippines
Ernst, John G.	January 1943	SGT.	WIA	Guadalcanal
Erwin, Paul V.B.	23 January 1943	2LT.	KIA	Solomon Islands
Foley, James A., Jr.	31 August 1944	1LT.	KIA	New Britain
Glenn, Joseph N.	19 June 1944	1LT.	AD	Green Island
Gray, Roy C., Jr.	9 January 1945	1LT.	WIA	Philippines
Hathaway, Mortimer D.	6 June 1944	1LT.	AD	Solomon Islands
Kirby, William P.	9 August 1942	2LT.	KIA	Detached Duty, USS *Vincennes*, Savo Island
Kobler, George S.	8 December 1942	1LT.	KIA	Guadalcanal
Leeds, Phillip J.	23 January 1943	2LT.	WIA	Guadalcanal
Loban, Glen A.	30 January 1943	1LT.	KIA	Guadalcanal
Lorch, Orville F.S.	3 August 1944	1LT.	KIA	New Britain
Lucero, Ralph A.	9 February 1943	PFC.	AD	Guadalcanal
McMasters, John C.	18 August 1944	1LT.	WIA	New Britain
Merkel, Galen K.	16 November 1943	2LT.	AD	MCAS Mojave
Moynihan, Michael H.	28 January 1945	1LT.	MIA/KIA	Philippines
Neal, Lawrence L.	3 July 1944	1LT.	AD	Bougainville
O'Harra, Lee E.	1 November 1943	1LT.	AD	MCAS Mojave
Osterlund, John F.	9 October 1943	2LT.	AD	MCAS Mojave
Robinson, Max K.	12 September 1944	1LT.	MIA/KIA	Cape Gazelle
Rutledge, Oscar P.	13 September 1942	2LT.	WIA	Solomon Islands
Scheussler, Carl	9 August 1942	2LT.	KIA	Detached Duty, USS *Vincennes*, Savo Island

3. Casualties

Name	Date	Rank	Status	Location
Schoetz, David J.	11 August 1944	1LT.	WIA	Bougainville
Sigan, Nick A., Jr.	20 January 1945	1LT.	KIA	Philippines
Sturgis, James B.	20 January 1945	1LT.	KIA	Philippines
Swick, Orville F.	29 August 1944	1LT.	WIA	New Britain
Wallace, Harold C.	28 January 1945	CAPT.	MIA/KIA	Philippines
Watson, Robert T., Jr.	? January 1943	CPL.	WIA	Guadalcanal
Whitten, Robert T.	13 September 1942	2LT.	WIA	Solomon Islands
Willey, Howard T.	16 November 1943	2LT.	AD	MCAS Mojave

Listing by Date

Name	Date	Rank	Status	Location
Kirby, William P.	9 August 1942	2LT.	KIA	Detached Duty, USS *Vincennes*, Savo Island
Scheussler, Carl	9 August 1942	2LT.	KIA	Detached Duty, USS *Vincennes*, Savo Island
Rutledge, Oscar P.	13 September 1942	2LT.	WIA	Solomon Islands
Whitten, Robert T.	13 September 1942	2LT.	WIA	Solomon Islands
Baer, Paul D.	26 September 1942	PVT	INJ	Guadalcanal
Anderson, Emmett L.	21 October 1942	SSGT (NAP)	KIA	Solomon Islands
Baird, Richard E.	27/28 November 1942	PVT	INJ	Guadalcanal
Campbell, William R.	13 November 1942	Major	WIA	Guadalcanal
Kobler, George S.	8 December 1942	1LT.	KIA	Guadalcanal
Booth, Roy L.	21 December 1942	2LT.	AD	Espiritu Santo
Batistich, Dennis	22 January 1943	PVT	KIA	Guadalcanal
Erwin, Paul V.B.	23 January 1943	2LT.	KIA	Solomon Islands
Leeds, Phillip J.	23 January 1943	2LT.	WIA	Guadalcanal
Loban, Glen A.	29 January 1943	1LT.	KIA	Guadalcanal
Christian, Wayne W.	29 January 1943	1LT.	KIA	Guadalcanal
Ernst, John G.	? January 1943	SGT.	WIA	Guadalcanal
Watson, Robert T., Jr.	? January 1943	CPL.	WIA	Guadalcanal
Lucero, Ralph A.	9 February 1943	PFC.	AD	Guadalcanal
Brooks, Clifford E.	23 February 1943	PVT.	WIA	Guadalcanal
Andrews, Robert L., Jr.	10 May 1943	TSGT	AD	Guadalcanal
Osterlund, John F.	9 October 1943	2LT.	AD	MCAS Mojave
O'Harra, Lee E.	1 November 1943	1LT.	AD	MCAS Mojave
Merkel, Galen K.	16 November 1943	2LT.	AD	MCAS Mojave
Willey, Howard T.	16 November 1943	2LT.	AD	MCAS Mojave
Hathaway, Mortimer D.	6 June 1944	1LT.	AD	Solomon Islands
Glenn, Joseph N.	19 June 1944	1LT.	AD	Green Island
Neal, Lawrence L.	3 July 1944	1LT.	AD	Bougainville
Lorch, Orville F.S.	3 August 1944	1LT.	KIA	New Britain
Schoetz, David J.	11 August 1944	1LT.	WIA	Bougainville
McMasters, John C.	18 August 1944	1LT.	WIA	New Britain
Swick, Orville F.	29 August 1944	1LT.	WIA	New Britain
Foley, James A., Jr.	31 August 1944	1LT.	KIA	New Britain
Robinson, Max K.	12 September 1944	1LT.	MIA/KIA	Cape Gazelle
Gray, Roy C., Jr.	9 January 1945	1LT.	WIA	Philippines
Sigan, Nick A., Jr.	20 January 1945	1LT.	KIA	Philippines
Sturgis, James B.	20 January 1945	1LT.	KIA	Philippines
Moynihan, Michael H.	28 January 1945	1LT.	MIA/KIA	Philippines

Name	Date	Rank	Status	Location
Wallace, Harold C.	28 January 1945	CAPT.	MIA/KIA	Philippines
Doughty, Francis E.	7 April 1945	CAPT.	KIA	Philippines

Notes: The listing was tabulated using available VMO/VMF-251 War Diaries, Muster Rolls, Aircraft Action Reports, Aircraft Accident Reports and USMC casualty cards posted on the USMC History Division website. Where there were discrepancies in sources, I used the casualty cards as the primary source. The bodies of the pilots lost during combat, in some cases, were not recovered. Many went down in the vast expanse of the Pacific waters, never to be seen again. Three pilots are listed as missing in action, presumed dead. In a few instances dates could not be ascertained especially when it came to enlisted personnel. Unless killed, their names were rarely published in war diaries. Even those who may have been wounded in action were not mentioned.

Key: KIA—Killed in Action; WIA—Wounded in Action; AD—Accidental Death; INJ—Injured (non-battle); MIA—Missing in Action.

4. Roster of Personnel, August 1942

United States Marine Corps

Name	Rank	Notes
Hart, John N.	Lieutenant Colonel	Commanding Officer, Naval Aviator
Hayes, Charles H.	Lieutenant Colonel	Executive Officer, Naval Aviator
Campbell, William R.	Major	Naval Aviator
Longley, Carl M.	Captain	Naval Aviator
Welch, Claude H.	Captain	Naval Aviator
Yeaman, Ralph R.	Captain	Naval Aviator
Pardee, Walter W.	2nd Lieutenant	
Straine, Robert G.	2nd Lieutenant	
Gilmore, Richard E.	Marine Gunner	
Witt, Lowell M.	Marine Gunner	
Musaschia, Seraphin G.	Quartermaster Clerk	
Davis, Merle C.	Sergeant Major	Squadron Sergeant Major
Bailey, Howard A.	Master Technical Sergeant	
Bunker, George P.	Master Technical Sergeant	
Farmer, Claude U.	Master Technical Sergeant	
Ryder, Roger F.	Master Technical Sergeant	
DeJong, Hans	Technical Sergeant	
Garton, Wendell P.	Technical Sergeant	NAP—Enlisted Pilot
Harper, Marcus N.	Technical Sergeant	
Knight, John Z.	Technical Sergeant	
Morris, Jay W.	Technical Sergeant	
Myers, Kenneth D.	Technical Sergeant	
Rosenthal, Philip	Platoon Sergeant	AA Crew Chief
Adams, Chester	Staff Sergeant	
Anderson, Emmett L.	Staff Sergeant	NAP—Enlisted Pilot
Baker, Harold B.	Staff Sergeant	
Cignotti, Louis J.	Staff Sergeant	
Collier, Homer E., Jr.	Staff Sergeant	
Hoffman, Albert	Staff Sergeant	
Irwin, John W.	Staff Sergeant	
Owen, Robert L.	Staff Sergeant	
Stewart, Warren L.	Staff Sergeant	
Sullivan, Timothy D.	Staff Sergeant	

4. Roster of Personnel, August 1942

Name	Rank	Notes
Waggoner, David H.	Staff Sergeant	
Cloud, Noah F.	Sergeant	
Cosner, James J.	Sergeant	
Foley, William H.	Sergeant	
Greene, Vernell L.	Sergeant	
Holms, William C.	Sergeant	
Irons, Don A.	Sergeant	
Kozlowski, Stanley, Jr.	Sergeant	
Kraushur, Raymond J.	Sergeant	
Mathews, William A.	Sergeant	
Moody, Howard C.	Sergeant	
Murgolo, Vito L.	Sergeant	
Nichols, William	Sergeant	
Rees, David C.	Sergeant	
Siep, Charles A., Jr.	Sergeant	
Summerville, Luther E.	Sergeant	
Taylor, Robert F.	Sergeant	
Vowels, John F.	Sergeant	
Grabowski, Harley A.		Mess Sergeant
Teague, Wayne H.		Chief Cook
Barkman, Jonathan J.	Corporal	
Blehm, Raymond E.	Corporal	
Booker, Dewey P., Jr.	Corporal	
Felt, Kenneth Leroy	Corporal	
Frosh, Lloyd J.	Corporal	
Husted, Leon J.	Corporal	
Jones, Charles	Corporal	
Karnowski, Harold E.	Corporal	
Kisielewski, Casimir R.	Corporal	
Macek, Robert C.	Corporal	
Miezwa, Frank B.	Corporal	
Moody, Howard R.	Corporal	
Pesch, William P.	Corporal	
Robinson, Cyrus B.	Corporal	
Ryan, Norman	Corporal	
Sarris, Chris J.	Corporal	
Schanen, George W.	Corporal	
Stachura, Theodore E.	Corporal	
Wakefield, William G.	Corporal	
Watson, Robert T., Jr.	Corporal	
Wood, Richard E.	Corporal	
Davis, Jimmie V.		Field Cook
Abrams, Dan C.	Private First Class	
Ainsworth, Clarence Leroy	Private First Class	
Aker, Dan R.	Private First Class	
Alexander, Donald N.	Private First Class	
Anderson, James L.	Private First Class	
Barreras, Miguel P., Jr.	Private First Class	
Berry, Fred	Private First Class	
Bisol, Angelo J.	Private First Class	
Bledsoe, Steve	Private First Class	
Bond, George M.	Private First Class	

Name	Rank	Notes
Buhrmester, Charles	Private First Class	
Canaan, Melvin J.	Private First Class	
Carpenter, Arthur J.	Private First Class	
Cayce, Robert D., Jr.	Private First Class	
Christiansen, Jack S.	Private First Class	
Cole, Daniel O.	Private First Class	
Cook, Deward	Private First Class	
Costiloe, Ottis L.	Private First Class	
Cowley, John W.	Private First Class	
Dolan, Donald J.	Private First Class	
Donahoo, Charles W., Jr.	Private First Class	
Easter, Charles H.	Private First Class	
Gentry, James A.	Private First Class	
Graulich, Herbert L.	Private First Class	
Hass, Fred O.	Private First Class	
Hall, Jack D.	Private First Class	
Hayward, John C.	Private First Class	
Hines, Vern U.	Private First Class	
Jackson, Thomas A.	Private First Class	
Johnson, Raymond O.	Private First Class	
Lackey, Cecil E.	Private First Class	
Leyba, George J.	Private First Class	
Lowery, Richard W.	Private First Class	
McCoy, Clarence L.	Private First Class	
Miller, William F.	Private First Class	
Montgomery, Kenneth C.	Private First Class	
Mulligan, Albert F.	Private First Class	
O'Neall, Robert E.	Private First Class	
Patrick, Otha D.	Private First Class	
Peterson, Raymond H.	Private First Class	
Pieper, Raymond A.	Private First Class	
Porter, Harold B.	Private First Class	
Pruett, Truman L.	Private First Class	
Reynolds, Norman E.	Private First Class	
Richison, Donald T.	Private First Class	
Rider, Joel T.	Private First Class	
Sharpe, Stanley H., Jr.	Private First Class	
Simkins, Wyman R.	Private First Class	
Smith, James A.	Private First Class	
Staggs, Lloyd M.	Private First Class	
Steenbock, Gordon K.	Private First Class	
Taylor, Harry A.	Private First Class	
Thompson, Edward	Private First Class	
Trask, Vernon A.	Private First Class	
Tuttle, Louis P.	Private First Class	
Tyler, William E.	Private First Class	
Vinson, Verne E.	Private First Class	
Vogel, Marvin K.	Private First Class	
Webster, Richard M.	Private First Class	
Whiteshield, Charles W., Jr.	Private First Class	
Williamson, Ivan J.	Private First Class	
Wills, Donald L.	Private First Class	

4. Roster of Personnel, August 1942

Name	Rank	Notes
Martin, Howard W.		Assistant Cook
Moore, James D.		Assistant Cook
Ruiz, Michael A., Jr.		Assistant Cook
Evans, Harold O.		Field Music First Class
Alderson, James R.	Private	
Ashley, William H., Jr.	Private	
Baer, Paul D.	Private	
Bailey, Ferris A.	Private	
Batistich, Dennis	Private	
Balducci, Louis	Private	
Barbarigos, John J.	Private	
Blake, Louis G.	Private	
Bogard, Charles E.	Private	
Brown, Burnett L.	Private	
Burke, James W.	Private	
Chmiel, Leo F.	Private	
Clark, Cleo j.	Private	
Dwyer, Edward W.	Private	
Fahy, William C.	Private	
Ferrazzoli, Patsy F.	Private	
Field, Arthur E.	Private	
Fields, Willis E.	Private	
Fleck, Eugene R.	Private	
Fraser, Francis D.	Private	
Greeley, Ralph G.	Private	
Grimes, Paul R.	Private	
Gustafson, Leonard E.	Private	
Justis, James H.	Private	
Karlovich, Robert J.	Private	
Kimler, Aubrey R.	Private	
Kinard, Samuel M.	Private	
La Bree, Royal M.	Private	
Lis, Stanley J.	Private	
Lucero, Ralph A	Private	
Matthews, James N.	Private	
McCraw, Howard E.	Private	
Miller, Lester R.	Private	
Nichols, Jack C.	Private	
Peck, Myron W.	Private	
Perkins, Fines J.	Private	
Peterson, Robert A.	Private	
Poore, James A., Jr.	Private	
Prendergast, Frederick P.	Private	
Rice, Dan V.	Private	
Robbins, Charles A.	Private	
Rose, Vernon V.	Private	
Rosenthal, Jack	Private	
Shaffer, Stanley C.	Private	
Shoemaker, George H.	Private	
Slack, George G.	Private	
Smith, Malcom V.	Private	
Stottlemyre, Jay R.	Private	

Name	Rank	Notes
Szafranski, Leonard A.	Private	
Tucker, Seibert B.	Private	
Uram, John R.	Private	
Warren, Cecil O.	Private	
Warren, Charles C.	Private	
Wells, Thomas H.	Private	
Wigney, James G.	Private	
Wlostowski, John	Private	
Zellmer, Dale LeRoy	Private	
Baird, Richard E.	Private	Transferred, sick
Layton, George B.	Private	Transferred, classified

United States Marine Corps Reserve

Name	Rank	Notes
Adams, James P.	Captain	
Collins, John V.	First Lieutenant	

United States Marine Corps Reserve (AVC)

Name	Rank	Notes
Weiland, Charles P.	First Lieutenant	Naval Aviator
Baessler, Blaine H.	Second Lieutenant	Naval Aviator
Kirby, William P.	Second Lieutenant	Naval Aviator
Kirk, Kenneth J., Jr.	Second Lieutenant	Naval Aviator
Kobler, George S.	Second Lieutenant	Naval Aviator
Livingston, Robert M.	Second Lieutenant	Naval Aviator
McGlothlin, Joe H., Jr.	Second Lieutenant	Naval Aviator
Peters, Herbert A.	Second Lieutenant	Naval Aviator
Railsback, Eldon H.	Second Lieutenant	Naval Aviator
Rutledge, Oscar P., Jr.	Second Lieutenant	Naval Aviator
Schuessler, Carl I.	Second Lieutenant	Naval Aviator
Schwetheim, Harry F.	Second Lieutenant	Naval Aviator
Spurlock, Roy T.	Second Lieutenant	Naval Aviator
Whitten, Robert T.	Second Lieutenant	Naval Aviator
Wojcik, Thaddeus	Second Lieutenant	Naval Aviator
Yunck, Michael R.	Second Lieutenant	Naval Aviator

United States Marine Corps Reserve (AAQM)

Name	Rank	Notes
Platt, Frank M.	Second Lieutenant	Quartermaster

Class I(e)

Name	Rank	Notes
Lee, Chester F.	Sergeant	

Class III(b)

Name	Rank	Notes
Kaelin, Louis	Technical Sergeant	NCOiC Metal Shop
Haverkamp, Joseph R.	Staff Sergeant	
Peak, Wilbur L.	Staff Sergeant	
Tanner, Clifford A.	Staff Sergeant	
Ernst, John G.	Sergeant	
Greenwood, Robert W.	Sergeant	
Hill, Rawley R., Jr.	Sergeant	
Keithley, Glen F.	Sergeant	
Plaskett, Arthur L.	Sergeant	
White, John J.	Sergeant	
Woten, Carlton S.	Sergeant	
Smith, Thomas H.		Chief Cook

4. Roster of Personnel, August 1942

Name	Rank	Notes
Andrews, Robert L., Jr.	Corporal	
Arnholt, Richard A.	Corporal	
Campbell, James J.	Corporal	
Green, Lloyd G.	Corporal	
Holcomb, John A.	Corporal	
Mulry, Edward J.	Corporal	
Olson, Thrace B.	Corporal	
Richers, George J.	Corporal	
Whitaker, James W.	Corporal	
Black, Elton T.	Private First Class	
Bourgaux, Henry H.	Private First Class	
Constantin, Armand J., Jr.	Private First Class	
Cox, Alvin E.	Private First Class	
Jeffries, Robert P.	Private First Class	
Killingsworth, William l.	Private First Class	
Lucke, Arthur E.	Private First Class	
Madden, Albert	Private First Class	
Madden, John V.	Private First Class	
Nessler, Carl, Jr.	Private First Class	
O'Reilly, John D.	Private First Class	
Ory, Joseph Z.	Private First Class	
Otis, Edward F.	Private First Class	
Rubenstein, Abraham	Private First Class	
Shepard, Joseph L.	Private First Class	
Vincent, John E.	Private First Class	
Waite, Edward	Private First Class	
Omernik, Edwin P.		Field Music First Class
Barber, William L.	Private	
Beveridge, Theodore H.	Private	
Burt, Allen C.	Private	
Clary, Willard M.	Private	
Craik, Arthur H.	Private	
Cronin, Thomas F.	Private	
Demoret, Casady A.	Private	
Fauteck, Robert L., Jr.	Private	
Frank, Wilbur L.	Private	
Gates, Raymond H.	Private	
Granier, Irving J.	Private	
Hood, Tyrus O.	Private	
James, Karl D.	Private	
Jeffrey, William G.	Private	
Kay, Joseph E.	Private	
Kile, Paul D.	Private	
Lehman, William L.	Private	
Madden, Walter F.	Private	
Meyers, Joseph N.	Private	
Miller, William H.	Private	
Miranda, Tony	Private	
Neuhauser, David A., Jr.	Private	
Newtown, Ralph D. O.	Private	
Ordway, William C.	Private	
Owen, Estil	Private	

Name	Rank	Notes
Redabaugh, Harold W.	Private	
Reed, Arthur B., Jr.	Private	
Robinson, Jesse W.	Private	
Schneider, Frank C.	Private	
Scholz, Robert W.	Private	
Smith, Ralph E.	Private	
Stuemky, William R.	Private	
Williams Loyal D.	Private	

U.S. Navy

Name	Rank	Notes
Holewinski, Joseph J.	Pharmacist Mate First Class	
Christy, J. D.	Pharmacist Mate Second Class	
Dougherty, James F.	Pharmacist Mate Second Class	
Switzer, Robert N.	Pharmacist Mate Second Class	

U.S. Naval Reserve

Name	Rank	Notes
Kalez, Marion M.	Lieutenant Commander	Medical Officer
Wallenborn, Ramon J.	Lieutenant	
Hurlbut, Charles R.	Pharmacist Mate Third Class	
Peterson, Frank R.	Pharmacist Mate Third Class	
Finger, Arthur J.	Hospital Apprentice First Class	

Temporarily Attached

Name	Rank	Notes
Kelly K. E.	Staff Sergeant	New Zealand Army
Lipanovic, R. A.	Corporal	New Zealand Army

5. Roster of Personnel, March 1945

United States Marine Corps

Name	Rank	Notes
Furlow, Thomas W.	Major	Executive Officer, Naval Aviator
Fisher, Dewitt C.	1st Lieutenant	
Irwin, John W.	1st Lieutenant	Engineering Officer
Wiart, Andy J	Warrant Officer	Asst. Engineering Officer
Cignotti, Louis J.	Warrant Officer	
Robinson, Cyrus B.	Warrant Officer	
Jones, Dallas P.	Master Technical Sergeant	
Martin, Frederic C.	Master Technical Sergeant	
McCoy, Clarence L.	Master Technical Sergeant	
Reynolds, Norman E.	Master Technical Sergeant	
Robbins, Charles A.	Master Technical Sergeant	
Stoflet, Harold N.	Master Technical Sergeant	
Tuttle, Louis P.	Master Technical Sergeant	
Blake, Granville B.	Technical Sergeant	
Caperton, Buel H.	Technical Sergeant	
Hanson, John C.	Technical Sergeant	
Jones, Morelle W.	Technical Sergeant	
Pecorella, Joseph A.	Technical Sergeant	
Perkins, Fines J.	Technical Sergeant	
Whitekeller, William	Technical Sergeant	
Garan, Mike	Staff Sergeant	
Monsen, Arnold J.	Staff Sergeant	
Ogden, Victor P.	Staff Sergeant	

5. Roster of Personnel, March 1945

Name	Rank	Notes
Thibodeau, Louis T.	Staff Sergeant	
Wood, Charlie H.	Staff Sergeant	
Burczynski, Joseph E.	Sergeant	
Herman, Kenneth E.	Sergeant	
Hershon, Edwin A.	Sergeant	
Somdahl, Carlton P.	Sergeant	
Swierczek, Frederic L.	Sergeant	
Vest, Thomas E.	Sergeant	
Wilson, Clarence T.	Sergeant	
Van Dorp, Maurice J., Jr.	Sergeant	Field Cook
Barton, Edmund L.	Corporal	
Bell, Jack T.	Corporal	
Counselor, William W.	Corporal	
King, James C.	Corporal	
Malcom, Chester H.	Corporal	
Meyers, Calvin F.	Corporal	
Mitchell, Edmund S.	Corporal	
Pena, Pater D.	Corporal	
Pineo, Russell H.	Corporal	
Schroeder, Robert W.	Corporal	
Smith, Byron M.	Corporal	
Stacy, James C.	Corporal	
Thomas, Lemuel J., Jr.	Corporal	
Crisp, Robert S.	Corporal	Assistant Cook
Barzyk, Edward F.	Private First Class	
Becker, Gerald A.	Private First Class	
Hilow, Abraham	Private First Class	
Scitar, Rudolph S.	Private First Class	
Zell, Robert J.	Private	

Temporarily Attached

Name	Rank	Notes
King, Howard E.	Major	TAD in connection with ferrying aircraft

Transferred

Name	Rank	Notes
Blehm, Richard E.	Master Technical Sergeant	to SMS-14, MAG-14, 1st MAW
Kraushur, Raymond J.	Master Technical Sergeant	to SMS-14, MAG-14, 1st MAW
Peterson, Robert A.	Master Technical Sergeant	to SMS-14, MAG-14, 1st MAW
Wood, Carl L.	Master Technical Sergeant	to SMS-14, MAG-14, 1st MAW
Bisol, Angelo J.	Technical Sergeant	to SMS-14, MAG-14, 1st MAW
Gruntner, Mathew j.	Technical Sergeant	to SMS-14, MAG-14, 1st MAW
Kinard, Samuel M.	Technical Sergeant	to SMS-14, MAG-14, 1st MAW
Rosenthal, Jack	Technical Sergeant	to SMS-14, MAG-14, 1st MAW
Viaclovsky, Jerome J.	Technical Sergeant	to SMS-14, MAG-14, 1st MAW
Yarbrough, Theodore R.	Technical Sergeant	to SMS-14, MAG-14, 1st MAW
Fleckenstein, Henry A.	Staff Sergeant	to SMS-14, MAG-14, 1st MAW
Hightower, Jack L.	Staff Sergeant	to SMS-14, MAG-14, 1st MAW
Lachetta, Frank	Staff Sergeant	to SMS-14, MAG-14, 1st MAW
Kasper, Melvin J.	Staff Sergeant	to SMS-14, MAG-14, 1st MAW
Buczynski, Michael A.	Staff Sergeant	to SMS-14, MAG-14, 1st MAW
Benson, Edmund K.	Sergeant	to SMS-14, MAG-14, 1st MAW
Blaszczyk, Joseph R.	Sergeant	to SMS-14, MAG-14, 1st MAW
Howard, Burdell C.	Sergeant	to SMS-14, MAG-14, 1st MAW

Name	Rank	Notes
Wros, Edward B.	Sergeant	to SMS-14, MAG-14, 1st MAW
Graham, Harris E.	Corporal	to SMS-14, MAG-14, 1st MAW
Heckman, William O.	Corporal	to SMS-14, MAG-14, 1st MAW
Kelly, Thaddeus J.	Corporal	to SMS-14, MAG-14, 1st MAW
Pensyl, Russell L.	Corporal	to SMS-14, MAG-14, 1st MAW
Smith, Lewis E.	Corporal	to SMS-14, MAG-14, 1st MAW
Core, Walter L.	Private First Class	to SMS-14, MAG-14, 1st MAW
Hester, Randolph L.	Private First Class	to SMS-14, MAG-14, 1st MAW
Hunter, John E.	Private First Class	to SMS-14, MAG-14, 1st MAW
Juarez, Benito	Private First Class	to SMS-14, MAG-14, 1st MAW
Robbins, Alfred A.	Private First Class	to SMS-14, MAG-14, 1st MAW
Sedlak, William T.	Private First Class	to SMS-14, MAG-14, 1st MAW
Smith, Thomas E.	Private First Class	to SMS-14, MAG-14, 1st MAW
Vis, Wesley P.	Private First Class	to SMS-14, MAG-14, 1st MAW
Wright, Jack D.	Private First Class	to SMS-14, MAG-14, 1st MAW

United States Marine Corps Reserve

Name	Rank	Notes
Bacheler, William L.	Major	Naval Aviator, Commanding Officer
Doughty, Francis E.	Captain	Naval Aviator
Schroeder, Frank A	Captain	Naval Aviator
Frank, Lewis C.	1st Lieutenant	Naval Aviator
Inglehart, George G.	1st Lieutenant	Naval Aviator
Keithley, Glen F.	1st Lieutenant	Naval Aviator
Maclachlan, Archibald W.	1st Lieutenant	Naval Aviator
McCaskill, John J.	1st Lieutenant	
Pirages, William J.	1st Lieutenant	Naval Aviator
Rosellen, Robert R.	1st Lieutenant	Naval Aviator
Schoetz, David J.	1st Lieutenant	Naval Aviator
Thomas, Lewis P.	1st Lieutenant	Naval Aviator
Walters, Lynford S., Jr.	1st Lieutenant	Naval Aviator
Warren, Walter J., Jr.	1st Lieutenant	Naval Aviator
Welch, Henry B.	1st Lieutenant	
Barton, Wilson G.	2nd Lieutenant	Naval Aviator
Beattie, Alexander L.	2nd Lieutenant	Naval Aviator
Collins, James S.	2nd Lieutenant	
Dudley, Benjamin A.	2nd Lieutenant	Naval Aviator
Ellis, James I.	2nd Lieutenant	Naval Aviator
Irwin, Hugh E.	2nd Lieutenant	Naval Aviator
Jernigan, Curtis D.	2nd Lieutenant	Naval Aviator
Johnson, Danny W.	2nd Lieutenant	Naval Aviator
Kavelage, Martin H.	2nd Lieutenant	Naval Aviator
Kammeyer, Preston L.	2nd Lieutenant	Naval Aviator
Kemp, Orvil S.	2nd Lieutenant	Naval Aviator
Lamarre, Ernest A.	2nd Lieutenant	Naval Aviator
Lindner, David W.	2nd Lieutenant	Naval Aviator
Lingenfelter, Virgil A.	2nd Lieutenant	Naval Aviator
McAllister, Roy A., Jr.	2nd Lieutenant	Naval Aviator
Morris, Mahlon	2nd Lieutenant	Naval Aviator
Peterson, Thomas K.	2nd Lieutenant	Naval Aviator
Petty, Douglas D., Jr.	2nd Lieutenant	Naval Aviator
Poor, Ernest R.	2nd Lieutenant	Naval Aviator
Rause, Robert	2nd Lieutenant	Naval Aviator

5. Roster of Personnel, March 1945

Name	Rank	Notes
Rhodes, Frank J.	2nd Lieutenant	Naval Aviator
Robinson, James W.	2nd Lieutenant	Naval Aviator
Romberg, Paul F.	2nd Lieutenant	Naval Aviator
Sandbach, Harold G.	2nd Lieutenant	Naval Aviator
Schewe, Howard W. F.	2nd Lieutenant	Naval Aviator
Scott, Charles W.	2nd Lieutenant	Naval Aviator
Smith, Samuel R.	2nd Lieutenant	Naval Aviator
Wagner, Joseph G.	2nd Lieutenant	Naval Aviator
Walsh, Thomas H.	2nd Lieutenant	Naval Aviator
Ward, Ray G.	2nd Lieutenant	Naval Aviator
Welch, Robert M.	2nd Lieutenant	Naval Aviator
Wolf, John C.	2nd Lieutenant	Naval Aviator
Wyatt, John W.	2nd Lieutenant	Naval Aviator
Anderson, Joseph H.	Master Technical Sergeant	
Burns, Jessie M.	Master Technical Sergeant	
Conroy, Robert E.	Master Technical Sergeant	
Ernst, John G.	Master Technical Sergeant	
James, Karl D.	Master Technical Sergeant	
Madden, Albert	Master Technical Sergeant	
Madden, John V.	Master Technical Sergeant	
Madden, Walter F.	Master Technical Sergeant	
Marine, Noel G.	Master Technical Sergeant	
Roessler, Wilbur W.	Master Technical Sergeant	
Sanker, John T.	Master Technical Sergeant	
Whitaker, James W.	Master Technical Sergeant	
Bujnowski, George	Technical Sergeant	
Elliott, Roy V.	Technical Sergeant	
Johnson, Donald L.	Technical Sergeant	
Lannom, Robert L.	Technical Sergeant	
Le Barron, Lawrence C.	Technical Sergeant	
Maxson, Stanley W.	Technical Sergeant	
Pappas, Nickolas	Technical Sergeant	
Powers, Joseph P.	Technical Sergeant	
Reichler, Alfred O., Jr.	Technical Sergeant	
Riddell, Francis A.	Technical Sergeant	
Robinson, William, Jr.	Technical Sergeant	
Scott, Cecil H.	Technical Sergeant	
Silke, Henry V.	Technical Sergeant	
Smith, Paul E.	Technical Sergeant	
Sustman, Edward F.	Technical Sergeant	
Massel, Walter B.	Technical Sergeant	
Webeer, Royal S.	Technical Sergeant	
Weems, Robert P.	Technical Sergeant	
Arrick, Lowell E.	Staff Sergeant	
Barrett, Charles R.	Staff Sergeant	
Burns, James W.	Staff Sergeant	
Coughlin, John R., Jr.	Staff Sergeant	
De Suiter, Richard L.	Staff Sergeant	
Docy, Glenn R.	Staff Sergeant	
Douglas, Erwin L.	Staff Sergeant	
Finn, Raymond J.	Staff Sergeant	
Cecan, Valentine P.	Staff Sergeant	

Name	Rank	Notes
McNicoll, Joseph F.	Staff Sergeant	
Meroski, Frank P.	Staff Sergeant	
Miller, Verlin C.	Staff Sergeant	
Newell, Carlton R.	Staff Sergeant	
Platek, John E.	Staff Sergeant	
Potter, Lewis M., Jr.	Staff Sergeant	
Schutt, Alvin H.	Staff Sergeant	
Socha, Edward F.	Staff Sergeant	
Stark, Ralph C.	Staff Sergeant	
Stenier, Earl F.	Staff Sergeant	
Stennick, William E.	Staff Sergeant	
White, Vernis R.	Staff Sergeant	
Yaccarino, Edmund C.	Staff Sergeant	
Smith, Thomas B.	Staff Sergeant	Chief Cook
Andersen, Arland R.	Sergeant	
Ballard, Richard C.	Sergeant	
Cerovski, George S.	Sergeant	
Criswell, Robert E.	Sergeant	
Devitt, Francis J.	Sergeant	
Doyle, Arthur R., Jr.	Sergeant	
Dunaway, Paul B.	Sergeant	
Flynn, Daniel J.	Sergeant	
Henderson, Keith W.	Sergeant	
Huffman, Harvey R.	Sergeant	
Lowe, Clarence R.	Sergeant	
Rolan, Richard L.	Sergeant	
Schuler, Frederick D.	Sergeant	
Thompson, Johnny M.	Sergeant	
Tiede, Fred R.	Sergeant	
Urban, William J.	Sergeant	
Williams, Bennett J.	Sergeant	
Zonta, Leo A.	Sergeant	
Watson, Roy L., Jr.	Sergeant	Field Cook
Atwood, Charles S.	Corporal	
Baker, Merle G.	Corporal	
Behling, Roland H.	Corporal	
Brunegraff, Wilson R.	Corporal	
Clements, Bille M.	Corporal	
Denmark, Richard S.	Corporal	
Duncan, Jack D.	Corporal	
Dunfee, William G.	Corporal	
Everhart, Donald D.	Corporal	
Fellows, Hobart A., Jr.	Corporal	
Hume, George W.	Corporal	
Jackson, Mitchell F.	Corporal	
Knight, Willard H.	Corporal	
Langenfeld, Richard C.	Corporal	
Leone, Joseph	Corporal	
Metivier, Roland A.	Corporal	
Miller, Windell H.	Corporal	
Odum, Meredith L.	Corporal	
Robson, Lee J.	Corporal	

Name	Rank	Notes
Schoelch, Richard W.	Corporal	
Sepik, John M.	Corporal	
Waddell, Owen A.	Corporal	
Zugger, Henry L.	Corporal	
Calzone, Joseph A.	Corporal	Assistant Cook
Cihak, Rudolph S.	Corporal	Assistant Cook
Dixon, Earnie N.	Corporal	Assistant Cook
Gilbert, Louis H.	Corporal	Assistant Cook
Hand, Norman C.	Corporal	Assistant Cook
Kemner, William J.	Corporal	Assistant Cook
Thompson, Tummie J.	Corporal	Assistant Cook
Aguirre, Amando C.	Private First Class	
Burgett, Dorr G., Jr.	Private First Class	
Chakleski, John A.	Private First Class	
DeVito, Americo J.	Private First Class	Cook
Emley, William	Private First Class	
Esterby, Owen A.	Private First Class	
Fettes, Robert G.	Private First Class	
Frost, Dainer	Private First Class	
Henderson, Quinton J.	Private First Class	
Jackson, John W.	Private First Class	
Karnowski, James W.	Private First Class	
Kazane, Peter	Private First Class	
Kidd, Laurence D.	Private First Class	
Lee, Floyd T.	Private First Class	
Leute, Howard A.	Private First Class	
Long, Carl W.	Private First Class	
Lynn, Ralph C.	Private First Class	
Machupa, Rudolph	Private First Class	
Moore, Paul A.	Private First Class	
Odachowski, Florian S.	Private First Class	
Oliver, Henry J.	Private First Class	
Osborn, Eugene A.	Private First Class	
Porter, Robert C.	Private First Class	
Pezenitski, John J.	Private First Class	
Ratta, Joseph	Private First Class	
Requardt, Howard A.	Private First Class	
Ribiero, Edward	Private First Class	
Sheppard, John H.	Private First Class	
Simpson, Donald E.	Private First Class	
Slezak, George F.	Private First Class	
Terrone, Joseph J.	Private First Class	
Thompson, Robert L.	Private First Class	
Tickhill, Walter H.	Private First Class	
Timko, Eugene W.	Private First Class	
Trakewski, John H.	Private First Class	
Adkinson, John I.	Private	
Brent, Gerald M.	Private	
Christie, Richard H.	Private	
Frazier, John F.	Private	
Frishee, Seymour P.	Private	
Garrett, Hubert L.	Private	

Name	Rank	Notes
Gentry, Thomas C.	Private	
Gilham, Henry M., Jr.	Private	
Gilliam, Herschel T.	Private	
Gorman, John M.	Private	
Hume, Lionel R.	Private	
Lucero, Leonardo T.	Private	
Macusza, Walter	Private	
Mast, Robert E.	Private	
McGinnis, Edward E.	Private	
Monihon, Maurice V.	Private	
Ortel, Alan R.	Private	
Pitts, William C.	Private	
Purcell, Lee W.	Private	
Reinhart, Richard V.	Private	
Riley, Hugh C.	Private	
Ritchey, Charles B.	Private	
Roberts, William H.	Private	
Ross, Matthew W.	Private	
Rudakewiz, Russell	Private	
Rudakewiz, William	Private	
Ruetz, Charles W.	Private	
Spence, William J.	Private	

Detached

Name	Rank	Notes
Hart, Joseph P.	Captain	to MCAD Miramar
Cunningham, Russell F.	1st Lieutenant	to MCAD Miramar
Erdman, William A.	1st Lieutenant	to MCAD Miramar
Garrett, James D.	1st Lieutenant	to MCAD Miramar
Henley, Paul B.	1st Lieutenant	to MCAD Miramar
Jennings, Francis C.	1st Lieutenant	to MCAD Miramar
Neilson, Russell H.	1st Lieutenant	to MCAD Miramar
Scoville, William H. II	1st Lieutenant	to MCAD Miramar
Smith, Howard F., Jr.	1st Lieutenant	to MCAD Miramar
Daigle, Bernadin J.	2nd Lieutenant	to MCAD Miramar
Lindsey, Robert E.	2nd Lieutenant	to MCAD Miramar

Transferred

Name	Rank	Notes
Greenwood, Robert W.	Master Technical Sergeant	to SMS-14, MAG-14, 1st MAW
Jeffery, William C.	Master Technical Sergeant	to SMS-14, MAG-14, 1st MAW
Klamm, William E., Jr.	Technical Sergeant	to SMS-14, MAG-14, 1st MAW
Meyers, Joseph N.	Technical Sergeant	to SMS-14, MAG-14, 1st MAW
Nicotra, Ignazio	Technical Sergeant	to SMS-14, MAG-14, 1st MAW
Ordway, William C.	Technical Sergeant	to SMS-14, MAG-14, 1st MAW
Poprawski, William J.	Technical Sergeant	to SMS-14, MAG-14, 1st MAW
Race, Denver D., Jr.	Technical Sergeant	to SMS-14, MAG-14, 1st MAW
Schwenk, Herman E.	Technical Sergeant	to SMS-14, MAG-14, 1st MAW
Zedrick, Louis M.	Technical Sergeant	to SMS-14, MAG-14, 1st MAW
Henson, Edgar, Jr.	Staff Sergeant	to SMS-14, MAG-14, 1st MAW
Chambers, Donald M.	Staff Sergeant	to SMS-14, MAG-14, 1st MAW
Davis, Calvin C.	Staff Sergeant	to SMS-14, MAG-14, 1st MAW
Macioge, Henry M.	Staff Sergeant	to SMS-14, MAG-14, 1st MAW
Siegler, Walter D.	Staff Sergeant	to SMS-14, MAG-14, 1st MAW
Stewart, James T.	Staff Sergeant	to SMS-14, MAG-14, 1st MAW

6. Number of Japanese Planes Shot Down by 251 Pilots

Name	Rank	Notes
Tebelak, Andrew	Staff Sergeant	to SMS-14, MAG-14, 1st MAW
Trimble, Prentice E.	Staff Sergeant	to SMS-14, MAG-14, 1st MAW
Vauter, Paul B.	Staff Sergeant	to SMS-14, MAG-14, 1st MAW
Walch, Stanley J.	Staff Sergeant	to SMS-14, MAG-14, 1st MAW
Alexander, John W.	Sergeant	to SMS-14, MAG-14, 1st MAW
Crocker, William E.	Sergeant	to SMS-14, MAG-14, 1st MAW
Lombardi, Luca J.	Sergeant	to SMS-14, MAG-14, 1st MAW
Svob, Paul J.	Sergeant	to SMS-14, MAG-14, 1st MAW
Szegeti, Frank	Sergeant	to SMS-14, MAG-14, 1st MAW
Calicchio, Lawrence F.	Sergeant	to SMS-14, MAG-14, 1st MAW
Cole, Ralph E.	Sergeant	to SMS-14, MAG-14, 1st MAW
Lester, Claude H.	Sergeant	to SMS-14, MAG-14, 1st MAW
Czapar, Michael G.	Corporal	to SMS-14, MAG-14, 1st MAW
Fellows, Harlan K.	Corporal	to SMS-14, MAG-14, 1st MAW
Grunklee, Maynard C.	Corporal	to SMS-14, MAG-14, 1st MAW
Kissenberger, William A.	Corporal	to SMS-14, MAG-14, 1st MAW
Leopard, Frank M.	Corporal	to SMS-14, MAG-14, 1st MAW
Linebarger, Oscar L.	Corporal	to SMS-14, MAG-14, 1st MAW
Longo, Anthony S.	Corporal	to SMS-14, MAG-14, 1st MAW
Lynch, Lawrence G.	Corporal	to SMS-14, MAG-14, 1st MAW
Markey, Richard P.	Corporal	to SMS-14, MAG-14, 1st MAW
Morgan, Arnold L.	Corporal	to SMS-14, MAG-14, 1st MAW
Quinn, Graham S., Jr.	Corporal	to SMS-14, MAG-14, 1st MAW
Rowenhorst, Wesley R.	Corporal	to SMS-14, MAG-14, 1st MAW
Suez, Paul A.	Corporal	to SMS-14, MAG-14, 1st MAW
Burgess, Arlie D.	Private First Class	to SMS-14, MAG-14, 1st MAW
Donnelly, William J.	Private First Class	to SMS-14, MAG-14, 1st MAW
Kurzweil, Robert	Private First Class	to SMS-14, MAG-14, 1st MAW
Laughlin, Hoyle S.	Private First Class	to SMS-14, MAG-14, 1st MAW
MacMurray, Harold L.	Private First Class	to SMS-14, MAG-14, 1st MAW
McCloskey, Thomas D.	Private First Class	to SMS-14, MAG-14, 1st MAW
McGeehan, Eugene P.	Private First Class	to SMS-14, MAG-14, 1st MAW
Kershaw, Charles W.	Private	to SMS-14, MAG-14, 1st MAW

U.S. Navy Medical Detachment

Name	Rank	Notes
Gallagher, John P.	Lieutenant	Flight Surgeon
Parish, Richard T.	Pharmacist Mate 1st Class	
Rodriguez, Joe, Jr.	Pharmacist Mate 2nd Class	
Provance, Donald E.	Pharmacist Mate 3rd Class	
Rist, James O.	Pharmacist Mate 3rd Class	
Ragland, William B.	Hospital Apprentice 1st Class	
Smith, Samuel W.	Hospital Apprentice 1st Class	
Treesgar, George C.	Hospital Apprentice 1st Class	

6.[1] Number of Japanese Planes Shot Down per 251 Pilot

Credited by date of action:

Date	Type	Pilot	Location
11 Nov. 1942	Fighter	Maj. William Campbell	Guadalcanal
11 Nov. 1942	Bomber	2Lt. Herbert Peters	Guadalcanal
12 Nov. 1942	Fighter	Maj. William Campbell	Guadalcanal
13 Nov. 1942	Fighter	2Lt. Herbert Peters	Guadalcanal

Date	Type	Pilot	Location
Dec. 1942	A/C	1Lt. Joe McGlothlin, Jr.	Solomon Islands
3 Dec. 1942	Float Biplanes x3	1Lt Michael Yunck	Ramada Bay, New Georgia
24 Dec. 1942	Fighter x3	1Lt. Kenneth Kirk, Jr.	Munda Pt.
27 Dec. 1942	Fighter	1Lt. Roy Spurlock	Munda Pt. Airfield
27 Dec. 1942	Fighter	Capt. Charles Weiland	Munda Pt. Airfield
15 Jan. 1943	Fighter	1Lt. Walter Baran	Guadalcanal
15 Jan. 1943	Fighter	Maj. Joseph Renner	Guadalcanal
15 Jan. 1943	Fighter x2	Capt. Jack Moore	Vella Lavella Island
15 Jan. 1943	Fighter x2	1Lt. Glen Loban	Vella Lavella Island
23 Jan. 1943	Fighter	Maj. Joseph Renner	Guadalcanal
23 Jan. 1943	Fighter	2Lt. Paul Erwin	Guadalcanal
23 Jan. 1943	Fighter	1Lt. Glen Loban	Guadalcanal
25 Jan. 1943	Fighter x2	2Lt. Herbert Peters	Guadalcanal
25 Jan. 1943	Fighter	1Lt. Henry Sabatier	Guadalcanal
25 Jan. 1943	Fighter	Maj. Ray Vroome	Guadalcanal
27 Jan. 1943	Biplane	Capt. Henry Sabatier	Solomon Islands
1 Feb. 1943	Fighter x2	1Lt. William Whitaker	Solomon Islands
1 Feb. 1943	Bomber	Capt. Walter Baran	Guadalcanal
1 Feb. 1943	Fighter	Capt. James Anderson	Guadalcanal
1 Feb. 1943	Bomber	2Lt. Henry McCartney	Rendova

Probables by date of action:

Date	Type	Pilot	Location
13 Nov. 1942	Fighter	2Lt. Robert Livingston	Guadalcanal
15 Jan. 1943	Fighter x2	1Lt. Walter Baran	Guadalcanal
25 Jan. 1943	Fighter x2	2Lt. Herbert Peters	Guadalcanal
25 Jan. 1943	Fighter	Maj. Ray Vroome	Guadalcanal
1 Feb. 1943	Fighter	Capt. Walter Baran	Guadalcanal

Squadron totals:

32 credited—24 fighters, 3 bombers, 4 biplanes, 1 unknown type
7 Probables—7 fighters

Rankings by credited kills:

Name	Credited Kills	Probables
Herbert Peters	4	2
Michael Yunck	3	0
Kenneth Kirk, Jr.	3	0
Glenn Loban	3	0
William Campbell	2	0
Walter Baran	2	3
Joseph Renner	2	0
Jack Moore	2	0
Henry Sabatier	2	0
William Whitaker	2	0
Joe McGlothlin	1	0
Roy Spurlock	1	0
Charles Weiland	1	0
Paul Erwin	1	0
Ray Vroome	1	1
James Anderson	1	0
Henry McCartney	1	0

Name	Credited Kills	Probables
Robert Livingston	0	1
Total	**Total**	
32	7	

7.¹ Aircraft Markings

U.S. Naval aircraft went through a rapid series of paint schemes and identification regulations during World War II. By the time VMO-251 was sent to the South Pacific in 1942, the Wildcats were sporting a two tone paint scheme of Blue Gray on surfaces not seen from the ground and a Light Gray on surfaces not seen from above the plane. The national insignia on the fuselage between the cockpit and the tail section was a white five-pointed star against a circular Insignia Blue background. The squadron was identified by block letters located between the cockpit and the wing root: the squadron number followed by the last two letters of the squadron designation, in this case MO, followed by the squadron designated plane number. An example would be 251MO11: 251—the squadron number; MO—the last two letters of the squadron designation; 11 being plane number 11 of the squadron.

Identification went through a change prior to VMO-251 shipping overseas, eliminating the squadron number and designation. Only the squadron plane number remained. The number was placed next to the national insignia or the engine cowling. By January 1943, VMO-251 Wildcats were displaying the new identification. The elimination of the squadron number and designation makes it nearly impossible to identify squadron planes in photographs.

While the above regulations came directly from the Navy, local squadron commanders had some leeway when it came to local insignia and identification. VMO-251 painted the squadron insignia on their planes forward of the cockpit on the fuselage. Some pilots named their aircraft, and were allowed to display the name on the aircraft as long as it did not interfere with official markings.

When VMO-251 returned overseas in June 1944, the F4U-1 Corsairs were painted an overall Sea Blue. Plane identification was by squadron plane number or the last three digits of the aircraft bureau number or a combination of the two. In some cases the bureau number ID was applied to the front wheel cover (which also acted as a dive brake) on the main landing gear struts. The national insignia was redesigned with a rectangle on each side of the star. After the squadron was established in the Philippines, the "Lucifer's Messengers" squadron insignia was applied to both sides of the engine cowling on some of its Corsairs.

8.¹ World War II Squadron Awards

Award	Date	Remarks
American Defense Service Streamer	1 Dec. 1941–7 Dec. 1941	
Presidential Unit Citation	19 Aug. 1942–9 Dec. 1942	Guadalcanal Campaign
American Campaign Streamer	7 Dec 1941–18 Jun 1942 31 May 1943–29 Feb 1944	
Asiatic-Pacific Campaign Streamer	Capture and Defense of Guadalcanal 19 Aug 1942–8 Feb 1943	1 Silver and 1 Bronze Star

Award	Date	Remarks
	Consolidation of Southern Solomon Is. 9 Feb 1943–11 May 1943	
	Santa Cruz 26 Oct 1942	
	Consolidation of Northern Solomon Is. 18 Jun 1944–30 Dec 1944	
	Luzon Operation 3 Jan 1945–1 April 1945	
	Southern Philippines 2 April 1945–1 May 1945	
World War II Victory Streamer	7 Dec 1941–1 June 1945	
Philippine Liberation Streamer	2 Jan 1945–2 Jun 1945	1 Bronze Star
Philippine Presidential Unit Citation	2 Jan 1945–2 Jun 1945	

Recommendations

Award	Date	Remarks
Navy Unit Commendation	21 Feb 1945	The recommendation for this award was discovered in the VMO-251 files held at the National Archives. The final disposition of this award is not known.
Distinguished Unit Citation (Army)	6 Jun 1946	The recommendation for this award was discovered in the VMO-251 files held at the National Archives. The final disposition of this award is not known.

9.[1] Citations for Recommended Awards

Navy Unit Commendation Award

21 February 1945:

"For outstanding performance in combat made possible by outstanding performance and cooperation of both flight and ground personnel from 23 July, 1944 to 15 February, 1945. Pounding the NORTHERN SOLOMONS and BISMARCK ARCHIPELAGO AREAS with maximum, continuous, accurate bombing and strafing attacks during the period of 23 July, 1944 to 8 December, 1944, Marine Fighting Squadron Two Hundred Fifty One aided materially in the destruction and complete neutralization of the enemy in these areas. Being the first squadron in its group ready for a forward move, it advanced by air over a distance of twenty-two hundred miles, most of which distance was over open expanse of water, without the loss or delay of a single aircraft. The day following its late afternoon arrival in this new area, the PHILIPPINE ISLANDS, on 2 January, 1945, the squadron resumed its steady pounding of enemy defenses with ninety-five percent of its aircraft. During the month of January 1945, in spite of adverse weather and very poor operation conditions, this squadron flew six hundred twenty-six (626) combat flights totaling two thousand four hundred and three (2,403) hours, a record made possible only by the high spirit, untiring and relentless efforts of the personnel as a unit. In ten days from 6 February to 15 February, 1945, this squadron carried one hundred and fifty-two tons of bombs in accurate, telling attacks upon strongly defended enemy [positions]. Efficient, dependable, skillful operation against the enemy was the result of a unit spirit and performance of duty which is in keeping with the highest traditions of the United States Naval Service."

Z.C. Hopkins

U.S. Army Distinguished Unit Citation

6 June 1946

1. In accordance with the provisions of paragraph 2g, Section 4, War Department Circular 333, 1943, it is requested that the personnel attached to Marine Observation Squadron VMO-251 during the period 31 July to 30 November 1942 be authorized to wear the Distinguished Unit Badge.

2. The personnel of the above mentioned squadron, listed in Inclosure, serviced with the 11th Bombardment Group, United States Army Air Forces, in the South Pacific during the period of 31 July to 30 November 1942. This unit, which was operating obsolete type fighter aircraft with only 27 officers and 271 enlisted men, performed a multitude of missions in connection with this operation. Their primary mission as stated in the operation plan was: "Provide all possible service to bombardment aviation temporarily based at Bomber One on Espiritu Santo. Also in conjunction with Task Group 63.6 operate in defense of Efate and Espiritu Santo under Commanding General Rose." During the initial phase, this island was the advanced base and this squadron (the only other squadron besides units of the 11th Bombardment Group on this single landing strip and island) maintained continuous fighter patrol. In addition to the above this squadron set up two SCR-270 radar installations, established and maintained this one landing strip, assisted in the service of bombs, oxygen, and ammunition on a 24 hour schedule to all B-17's of the Bombardment Group and many other Army and Navy transient aircraft. Most of the fuel servicing was done from drums and loading of bombs was done by hand, taking all night to allow early take-offs and continuous operations. The squadron furnished photographic reconnaissance personnel and some ordnancemen for the strike and search missions. These photographers and ordnancemen were bonafide combat crew members. For its work during this period, the 11th Bombardment Group was cited in General Orders No. 4, War Department, 1943, for outstanding performance of duty in action against the enemy.

3. For the outstanding manner in which this single Marine Squadron on independent duty, performed its mission in support of our operations and, in addition, supplement the personnel of the 11th Bombardment Group in combat conditions and thereby materially and effectively aided in the successful completion of this operation to secure a foothold in the Solomon Islands—our first offensive mission and the turning point in the war in the Pacific, it is recommended that General Orders No. 4 be amended to include Marine Observation Squadron Two Fifty-One and that the personnel attached during the above period be authorized to wear as a permanent part of their uniform, the Distinguished Unit Badge.

4. As a former commanding officer of the 11th Bombardment Group I have full and complete knowledge of the acts performed by this squadron while it served with me during the period which this award is recommended. To my knowledge, all subsequent service of this squadron and of the individuals whose names are listed in Inclosure 1 has been ascertained to have been honorable and no reason exists to prevent such an award.

Laverne G. Saunders, Brigadier General

Chapter Notes

Preface

1. Hugh Irwin letter to author, 30 September 2014.
2. VMO-251 Operational Records, Letter to Commanding General, Marine Aircraft Wings, Pacific, 28 August 1943. National Archives.

Chapter One

1. Wendell Garton Papers, Wendell Garton Family.
2. Author phone interview with Vito Murgolo, 21 April 2014.
3. MAG-21 Group Transfer Order No. 44, 26 November 1941. Wendell Garton Papers.
4. Dan Abrams Interview, Voices of Veterans Oral History Project, Texas General Land Office. Accessed 9 May, 2014. URL: http://www.glo.texas.gov/voices-of-veterans/interviews/assets/abrams-d/danabrams.pdf
5. Major John N. Hart Citation for the Distinguished Flying Cross accessed 14 April 2014. URL: http://valor.militarytimes.com/recipient.php?recipientid=42326
6. Wendell Garton Papers.
7. Roy Spurlock, "Savo Island—The Lost Battle," personal memoir, unpublished.
8. Wendell Garton Papers.
9. VMO-251 Historical Narrative, 1 December 1941–30 October 1942. USMC History Division.
10. Richard S. Dann, *F4F Wildcat in Action* (Carrollton, TX: Squadron/Signal Publications, 2004), pp. 4–5.
11. Dann, p. 7.
12. Chris Bishop, editor, *The Encyclopedia of Weapons of World War II* (New York, NY: Barnes & Noble, 1998), p. 398.
13. Enzo Angelucci and Peter Bowers, *The American Fighter* (New York, NY: Random House, 1987), p. 226.
14. Interview with Major J. N. Renner, USMC, conducted at the Bureau of Aeronautics in Washington, D.C. 17 July 1943. National Archives.
15. Location of U.S. Naval Aircraft, 15 April 1942. Accessed 3 March 2014. http://www.history.navy.mil/research/histories/naval-aviation-history/location-of-us-naval-aircraft-world-war-ii.html
16. Dann, p. 16.
17. F4F-3P, Marine Corps Aviation Reconnaissance Association. accessed 9 May 2014. URL: http://www.mcara.us/F4F-3P.php
18. Charles Patrick Weiland, *Above and Beyond* (Pacifica, CA: Pacifica Press, 1997), p. 16.
19. Wendell Garton Papers.
20. Paramount Notes, Main Title Billing dated 5 June 1942. Academy of Motion Pictures Arts and Sciences, Margaret Herrick Library.
21. Paramount Notes dated 25 March 1942. Academy of Motion Pictures Arts and Sciences, Margaret Herrick Library.
22. Bevy was the actual code name for Guadalcanal. The main objectives, the airfield on Guadalcanal and Tulagi, Florida Island, were designated Cactus.
23. VMO-251 Operational Records, Letter to Commanding General, Marine Aircraft Wings, Pacific, 28 August 1943. National Archives.
24. Location of U.S. Naval Aircraft, 25 June 1942. http://www.history.navy.mil/a-record/ww-ii/loc-ac/loc-ac.htm, accessed 16 March 2014.
25. Wendell Garton Papers.
26. The name of the ship is not known. The USS *Alcyone* eventually delivered these supplies but was not at San Diego on 15 June 1942.
27. VMO-251 Operational Records, Letter to Commanding General, Marine Aircraft Wings, Pacific, 28 August 1943. National Archives.

Chapter Two

1. VMO-251 War Diary, July-August 1942, National Archives and VMO-251 Historical Narrative, 1 Dec. 1941–30 Oct. 1942, USMC History Division.
2. War Diary, USS Heywood, June-July, 1942, National Archives.
3. Charles P. Weiland, *Manuscript Found in Battle* (Cavu Press, 1991), pp. 7–11.
4. VMO-251 War Diary, July 1942, National Archives. Baird would suffer the same type of wound in Sept. 1942, taking him out of the war.
5. Gordon L. Rottman, *World War II Pacific Island Guide* (Westport, CT: Greenwood Press, 2002), pp. 66–69.

6. "Al Hoffman's War Experiences in the Pacific," Personal account courtesy of Briana Madden.
7. Wendell Garton Papers.
8. VMO-251 History, 1 December 1941 to 30 October 1942, USMC History Division, p. 6.
9. Wendell Garton Papers.
10. This is the official story. Unofficially it appears Kobler flew underneath a bridge and unknown to him, damaged his tail wheel during the stunt. When he tried to land back at the field, the damaged tail wheel threw his plane around, leading to the crash.
11. VMO-251 War Diary, July 1942, National Archives.
12. VMO-251 History, 1 December 1941 to 30 October 1942, USMC History Division, p. 7.
13. Statement of Major C. H. Welch, VMO-251 Operational Records, National Archives.
14. VMO-251 Operational Records, December 1941–June 1945, National Archives.
15. John B. Lundstrom, *The First Team and the Guadalcanal Campaign* (Annapolis, MD: Naval Institute Press, 2005), p. 29.
16. Statement of Major C. H. Welch, VMO-251 Operational Records, National Archives and VMO-251 War Diaries for August–September 1942, National Archives.
17. VMO-251 Operational Records, Extract from letter written by BG Laverne G. Saunders, National Archives. See Appendix 9 for the complete write up.
18. Ibid.
19. Roy Spurlock, "Savo Island—The Lost Battle," personal memoir, unpublished p. 12.
20. Charles P. Weiland, *Manuscript Found in Battle* (Cavu Press, 1991), p. 30.
21. Ibid, pp. 30–31.
22. Spurlock, p. 13.
23. Force consisted of the Chokai, Aoba, Furutaka, Kako, Kinugasa (all heavy cruisers), Tenryu, Yubari (both light cruisers), and the destroyer Yunagi.
24. Charles P. Weiland, *Manuscript Found in Battle* (Cavu Press, 1991), p. 31. Note: Spurlock had these events occurring on the 7 August when they actually occurred on 8 August.
25. LtCol. Frank O. Hough, Major Verle E. Ludwig and Henry Shaw, Jr., *Pearl Harbor to Guadalcanal* (Washington DC: U.S. Government Printing Office, 1958), pp. 258–259.
26. Spurlock, p. 23.
27. Ibid, p. 25.
28. James D. Hornfischer, *Neptune's Inferno* (New York, NY: Random House, 2011), pp. 66–70.
29. Charles P. Weiland, *Manuscript Found in Battle* (Cavu Press, 1991), p. 32.
30. VMO-251 War Diary, August 1942, National Archives.
31. "Capt. Whitten is Commended," *Wilmington Delaware Journal*, 10 May 1943.
32. Information from All Things Quackenbush, url http://allthingsquackenbush.weebly.com/quackenbushs-gypsies.html, accessed 2 June 2014; and MCARA Notables, url http://www.mcara.us/notables_photo_pioneers.php, accessed 2 June 2014.
33. History of the 42nd Bombardment Squadron, Air Force Historical Association, IRIS No. 44028, p. 11.
34. All Things Quackenbush, p. 3.
35. Extra Activities Performed in the Field, Operational Records of VMO-251, 2 November 1942, National Archives.
36. USS Curtiss War Diary, August 1942, National Archives.
37. USS Alcyone War Diary, August 1942, pp. 9–12. National Archives; VMO-251 Historical Narrative, 1 December 1941–30 October, 1942, USMC History Center, pp. 10–11.
38. Hoffman, personal account.

Chapter Three

1. Spam, rice, dehydrated potatoes, carrots and cabbage, hardtack, captured Japanese food items, and the occasional local wild animal to name a few items.
2. Barry Craig, *Marine Corps Aviation Chronolog* (Paducah, KY: Turner Publishing Company, 1989), p. 22.
3. Rottman, pp. 73–78.
4. Rottman, pp. 97–108.
5. "Capt. Kenneth J. Kirk of Barre, Marine Flyer, Gets 3 Jap Planes," *Burlington Free Press*, 15 February 1943.
6. VMO-251 Historical Narrative, 1 December 1941–30 October 1942, USMC History Center, p.12.
7. VMO-251 War Diary, 24 September 1942, National Archives.
8. In official documents, it is spelled as Palikulo or Pallikulo.
9. Jeff Millstein, *US Marine Corps Aviation Unit Insignia 1941–1946* (Paducah, KY: Turner Publishing Company, 1995), pp. 67–68.
10. Extra Activities Performed in the Field. VMO-251 Operational Records, 2 November, 1942, National Archives, p. 23.
11. Muster Roll for VMO-251, August 1942. USMC History Center.
12. VMO-251 War Diary, September 1942. National Archives.
13. Norman Polmar and Thomas B. Allen, *WWII: The Encyclopedia of the War Years, 1941–1945* (Mineola, NY: Dover Publications, 2012), p. 623.
14. Abrams interview, Texas General Land Office, February 2008. URL: http://www.glo.texas.gov/voices-of-veterans/interviews/abrams.html accessed December 2014.
15. *Pearl Harbor to Guadalcanal*, p. 276.
16. Eric Hammel, *Carrier Clash* (Pacifica, CA: Pacifica Military History, 2009), p.132.
17. Ibid.
18. Gerald Astor, *Semper Fi in the Sky* (New York, NY: Ballantine Books, 2005), p. 60.
19. Millstein, pp. 67–68.
20. Dann, p. 17.
21. Wendell Garton Papers.
22. VMO-251 War Diary, September 1942. National Archives; Wendell Garton Papers.
23. Wendel Garton Papers.

24. Weiland, *Manuscript*, p. 56.
25. Barrett Tillman, *Wildcat: The F4F in WW II* (Annapolis, MD: Naval Institute Press, 1990), p. 82.
26. VMO-251 War Diary, 12 September 1942, National Archives.
27. Lundstrom, p. 202.
28. Weiland, *Manuscript*, p. 45.
29. VMO-251 War Diary, 12 September 1942, National Archives.
30. Lundstrom, p. 182–183.
31. Weiland, *Manuscript*, p. 48.
32. Lundstrom, p. 203.
33. Weiland's and Garton's account differ in how they reached Rutledge. Garton recalls that they ran from a field artillery position. Weiland writes they hopped in a jeep driven by Longley.
34. Weiland, *Manuscript*, p. 48
35. Lundstrom, p. 206.
36. Tillman, p. 84.
37. Wendell Garton Papers.
38. Weiland, *Manuscript*, p. 56.
39. "Malaria, Not Japs, Sends Guadalcanal Flier Home," *Wilmington Delaware Journal*, 17 April 1943.
40. WW2 USMC Casualty Card. Baer, Paul David. USMC History Division.
41. MAG-23 War Diary, 23 September, 1942. National Archives.
42. Wendell Garton Papers.
43. VMO-251 War Diary, September 1942. National Archives.
44. WW2 USMC Casualty Card. Baird, Richard E. USMC History Division.
45. *Pearl Harbor to Guadalcanal*, p. 310–327.
46. Murgolo. Phone interview with author, 21 April 2014.
47. *Pearl Harbor to Guadalcanal*, p. 327; Weiland, *Manuscript*, p. 60.
48. *Pearl Harbor to Guadalcanal*, p. 328.
49. Hoffman, personal account.
50. Murgolo. Phone interview with author, 21 April 2014.
51. Hoffman, personal account. Hoffman identified the crewmen by last name only: Cram, Metz, Anderson, Kirby, Horton, Hoffman and Mason.
52. WW2 USMC Casualty Card. Anderson, Emmett Lawrence. USMC Historical Division.
53. Weiland, *Manuscript*, p. 70.
54. Walter Lord, *Lonely Vigil* (New York, NY: The Viking Press, 1977), p. 165.
55. Lundstrom, p. 470.
56. VMF-112 and MAG 23 War Diary dated 7 November, 1942, National Archives. The number of dive bombers participating in the attack varies depending on the report consulted. VT-8's war diary for 7 Nov. states 12 SBDs took off but 3 never made contact with the ships. The MAG 14 report for the same date states 7, and also mentions VMSB-141 participating in the attack.
57. VMF-112 War Diary Pilots Record accounting for enemy planes, dated 10 Oct. 1942–2 Feb. 1943. National Archives.
58. VT-8 War Diary dated 7 Nov. 1942, National Archives.
59. MAG-14 Record of Events 16 Oct. 1942–16 Dec. 1942, page 3, National Archives.
60. VMF-112 War Diary dated 7 November 1942, National Archives.
61. Japanese Naval and Merchant Shipping Losses during World War II By All Causes prepared by the Joint Army-Navy Assessment Committee, February 1947. http://www.history.navy.mil/library/online/japaneseshiploss.htm accessed on 22 November 2014.
62. In January 1944, VMO-251 Guadalcanal veterans held a get together at the Desert Room in Glendale, California. The poem appeared in the program guide. Dated 2 November 1942, the poem was forwarded to Lt. Col. P.O. Parmelee by 251's executive officer, Charles Hayes.
63. Lundstrom, p. 472; MAG-23 War Diary, Nov. 11, 1942, p. 133. National Archives
64. Lundstrom, p. 473.
65. Lundstrom, p. 474.
66. *Pearl Harbor to Guadalcanal*, p. 354.
67. VMO-251 War Diary, December 1942, pp. 1–2, National Archives.
68. Dennis and Roger Latourneau, *Operation KE* (Annapolis, MD: Naval Institute Press, 2012), p. 44.
69. Statement by Lt. Colonel William Campbell, pp. 1–2. VMO-251 squadron records, National Archives. It is noted on the statement that the comments are from memory and that there could be errors.
70. Latourneau, p. 45.
71. Weiland, *Manuscript*, 72–73. The exact cause of Kobler's crash has never been determined. Weiland does not state that the strip was No. 2. Since Fighter Strip 1 was in operation in September, and Weiland mentions a newly cleared runway. I am assuming it was Fighter Strip 2.
72. Latourneau, p. 60–61; Date of return based on WW2 Casualty Card for Andre on file at USMC History Division.
73. Ibid, p. 67–68
74. Weiland, *Manuscript*, p. 81–82.
75. Letourneau, p. 69.
76. Ibid, p. 71.
77. USS Crescent City War Diary, January 1943, pp. 17–24, National Archives; VMO-251 War Diary, January 1943, pg. 2. National Archives. Also on board were elements of VMF-122, the 69th Signal Company and an Army B-17 squadron.
78. Statement by Lt. Colonel William Campbell, pg. 2. VMO-251 squadron records, National Archives.
79. VMO-251 war diary for January 1943 has the squadron as 122 when it should be 112. The typo appears to have been corrected by hand.
80. Letourneau, pp. 110–112.
81. VMO-251 War Diary, January 1943, pg. 3, National Archives.
82. Lord, pp. 154–155.
83. VMO-251 War Diary, January 1943, p. 2. National Archives.
84. Abrams interview, Texas General Land Office, February 2008. URL: http://www.glo.texas.gov/voices-of-veterans/interviews/abrams.html accessed December 2014.

85. Letourneau, pp. 93–94.
86. USMC Casualty Cards for Leeds and Erwin, USMC History Division.
87. Letourneau, pp. 122–124; VMO-251 War Diary, January 1943, p. 3, National Archives.
88. Letourneau, 130–142; VMO-251 War Diary, January 1943, pg. 3, National Archives.
89. Letourneau, p. 154; VMO-251 War Diary, January 1943, pg. 2, National Archives; WW2 USMC Casualty Cards for Loban and Christian, USMC History Division.
90. Letourneau, pp. 162–163.
91. Moss's rank determined by listing on the Defense Prisoner of War/Missing Personnel Office (DPMO) site accessed 6 December 2014. http://www.dtic.mil/dpmo/wwii/reports/mar_m_m.htm.
92. Letourneau, pp. 177–178.
93. Letourneau, pp. 180–182; Olynyk, pp. 113–114.
94. Letourneau, pp. 198–205.
95. Abrams interview, Texas General Land Office, February 2008. URL: http://www.glo.texas.gov/voices-of-veterans/interviews/abrams.html accessed December 2014.
96. USMC Casualty Card for Clifford Edward Brooks, USMC History Division.
97. USMC Casualty Card for Robert L. Andrews, Jr., USMC History Division.

Chapter Four

1. USS Kitty Hawk War Diary, 29 May 1943, p. 74. National Archives.
2. USS Kitty Hawk War Diary, 31 May–June 2, 1943, pp. 3–4. National Archives.
3. VMO-251 War Diary, July 1943, p. 1. National Archives.
4. The California State Military Museum, http://californiamilitaryhistory.org/MCASMojave.html accessed February 9, 2015.
5. Sherrod, pp. 434–435.
6. VMO-251 War Diaries, August–October 1943. National Archives.
7. Angelucci and Bowers, pp. 436–444.
8. VMO-251 War Diary, September 1943. National Archives.
9. Osterlund is interned in Section 8, Grave 5406-EH. Arlington National Cemetery (http://www.arlingtoncemetery.mil/Explore-the-Cemetery/Find-a-Grave) accessed 27 January 2015.
10. VMO-251 War Diary, October 1943. National Archives.
11. Capt. Oscar M. Bate, Jr. pilot statement on Report of Accident, 2 November, 1943. VMO-251 Operational Records. National Archives.
12. 2Lt. Nick A. Sagan pilot statement on Report of Accident, 2 November, 1943. VMO-251 Operational Records. National Archives.
13. Report of Accident and Statements, VMO-251 Operational Records, 7 November, 1943. National Archives.
14. Report of Accident, VMO-251 Operational Records, dated 7 November, 1943. National Archives.
15. Report of Accident and Statements, VMO-251 Operational Records, 8 November, 1943. National Archives.
16. Report of Accident and Statement, VMO-251 Operational Records, 10 November, 1943. National Archives.
17. Report of Accident and Pilot Statement (Inglehart), VMO-251 Operational Records, 13 November, 1943. National Archives.
18. Report of Accident and Pilot Statement (McMasters) VMO-251 Operational Records, 13 November, 1943. National Archives.
19. Report of Accident and Pilot Statement (McMasters and Condon) VMO-251 Operational Records, 14 November, 1943. National Archives.
20. Report of Accident and Pilot Statements (Goldstein, Willey and Furlow) VMO-251 Operational Records, 16 November, 1943. National Archives.
21. Report of Accident and Pilot Statement (Merkel, Robinson and Schoetz) VMO-251 Operational Records, 14 November, 1943. National Archives.
22. VMO-251 War Diaries for December 1943 and January 1944. National Archives.
23. Report of Accident (Neilson), VMO-251 Operational Records, 6 December, 1943. National Archives.
24. Report of Accident (Scoville), VMO-251 Operational Records, 12 December, 1943. National Archives.
25. Report of Accident (Wilson), VMO-251 Operational Records, 12 December, 1943. National Archives.
26. Report of Accident (Hathaway), VMO-251 Operational Records, 13 December, 1943. National Archives.
27. Report of Accident (Rancourt), VMO-251 Operational Records, 18 December, 1943. National Archives.
28. Report of Accident (Holiday), VMO-251 Operational Records, 21 December, 1943. National Archives.
29. Report of Accident (Kane), VMO-251 Operational Records, 23 December, 1943. National Archives.
30. Report of Accident (Jennings), VMO-251 Operational Records, 31 January, 1944. National Archives.
31. Report of Accident (Erdmann), VMO-251 Operational Records, 31 January, 1944. National Archives.
32. VMO-251 War Diary, February 1944. National Archives.
33. USS Tangier War Diary, February 1944. National Archives.

Chapter Five

1. USS Tangier Way Diary, March 1944. National Archives.
2. *Reports of General MacArthur: Japanese Operations in the Southwest Pacific Area, Volume II—Part 1, 2nd ed.* (Washington DC: U.S. Government Printing Office, 1994), p. 244.

3. Rottman, pp. 78–79.
4. MAG-11 War Diary, May 1944. National Archives.
5. VMO-251 War Diary, June 1944, National Archives.
6. MAG-11 War Diary, June 1944, National Archives.
7. VMO-251 War Diary, June 1944, National Archives.
8. Hugh "Yogi" Irwin, letter to author, 30 September, 2014.
9. VMO-251 War Diary, June 1944, National Archives, pp. 4–9.
10. SCAT—South Pacific Combat Air Transport Command.
11. Rabaul, Pacific Wrecks website, http://www.pacificwrecks.com/provinces/png_rabaul.html, accessed 27 Feb. 2015.
12. A Kawanishi H8K, given the code name Emily by the Allies. An Emily was a large 4-engine Japanese float plane used for maritime patrol duty.
13. Sources include VMO-251 War Diaries of Jun-Dec 1944, ComairPiva War Diaries for Jun–Nov 1944, available VMO-251 Mission Reports and Aircraft Action Reports for the period July–Dec. 1944, and available MAG-24 War Diaries for the period of Jun-Dec. 1944.
14. Irwin Letter to author, 30 September, 2014.
15. VMSB-235 War Diary, July 1944, page 6. National Archives.
16. VMSB-235 War Diary, July 1944, page 7 and VMSB-235 Mission Report for 5 July, 1944, National Archives.
17. VMO-251 Mission Report, 10 July 1944, National Archives.
18. Ibid.
19. There is no mention of this sighting in available VMO-251 reports.
20. War Diary, USS Alnitah, July 1944, National Archives.
21. The pilot would set his dive brake switch to "on." Depending on the speed of the aircraft, the landing gear would partially extend or fully extend. In the -1 model, if speeds were greater than 380 knots the gear would partially extend. Below that speed, the gear would fully extend. In the -1D model the speed was 260 knots. Information from *Pilot's Handbook of Flight Operating Instruction Navy Models F4U-1, F3A-1, FG-1, F4U-1C, F3A-1D, FG-1D, and F4U-1D Airplanes* (Washington DC: Bureau of Aeronautics, 15 March 1945), p. 41.
22. VMSB-235 War Diary, July 1944 and Mission Report, 17 July 1944, National Archives.
23. VMO-251 Mission Report, 17 July, 1944. National Archives.
24. ComAirPiva War Diary, 20 July 1944, p. 27. National Archives.
25. The mission report and the war diary differ as to who turned back. The mission report for 22 July states his wingman, while VMO-251's War Diary for July 1944 states it was Teller who turned back.
26. War Diary, *USS Alnitah*, July 1944. National Archives.
27. William L. Bacheler, *Brave, Splendid Fools: A Life in Aviation* (CreateSpace Independent Publishing Platform, 2014), p. 74.
28. It is unclear if the squadron flew the photo mission.
29. RNZAF 19 Squadron Diary, 15 August, 1944. RNZAF Archives. No records could be located for 21 Squadron.
30. VMF-223 Mission Report, 15 August 1944. National Archives.
31. VMF-115 Mission Report, 15 August 1944. National Archives.
32. VMF-211 Mission Report, 15 August 1944. National Archives.
33. VMF-215 Mission Report, 15 August 1944. National Archives.
34. Air Command Northern Solomons Intelligence Summary, 16 August 1944. National Archives.
35. It is not clear if this is a code word for a location or if it refers to an island in the Treasury Islands group.
36. Bacheler, p. 73.
37. Ibid, p. 73
38. Ibid, pp.73–74. Note: Based on documents from participating squadrons, there were 93 aircraft involved in the strike. As for the number of squadrons forming up over Bougainville for the strike, there were two—VMF-223 and VMO-251. It does not appear Torokina's RNZAF 21 Squadron formed up with them.
39. VMF-223 Aircraft Action Report, 18 August 1944. National Archives.
40. VMF-215 War Diary, August 1944, p. 10. National Archives.
41. Commander Aircraft Northern Solomons Intelligence Summary, 19 August 1944, p. 626. National Archives.
42. VMF-115 Mission Report, 18 August 1944. National Archives.
43. VMF-211 Mission Report, 18 August 1944. National Archives.
44. VMSB-243 Mission Report, 18 August 1944. National Archives.
45. VMO-251's War Diary entry of the date indicates 12 VMF-223 Corsairs participated in the attack, as well as 10 VMO-251 Corsairs.
46. Bacheler, p. 74–75.
47. Commander Aircraft Northern Solomons Intelligence Summary, 24 August 1944, p. 668. National Archives.
48. VMSB-236 Aircraft Action Report #3, 25 August 1944. National Archives.
49. VMF-223 Aircraft Action Report #16, 25 August 1944. National Archives; Commander Aircraft Northern Solomons Intelligence Summary, 26 August 1944, p. 687. National Archives.
50. VMO-251 War Diary, 25 August 1944. National Archives; VMO-251 Aircraft Action Report #2, 25 August 1944. National Archives; Commander Aircraft Northern Solomons Intelligence Summary, 26 August 1944, p. 687. National Archives.
51. Commander Aircraft Northern Solomons Intelligence Summary, 27 August 1944, p. 698. National

Archives. In the summary the squadron was not named.

52. Commander Aircraft Northern Solomons Intelligence Summary, 26 August 1944, p. 699. National Archives.

53. VMSB-236 Aircraft Action Report, 26 August 1944. National Archives; Commander Aircraft Northern Solomons Intelligence Summary, 26 August 1944, p. 699. National Archives.

54. Results of VMF-223's attack are not available.

55. Commander Aircraft Northern Solomons Intelligence Summary, 29 August 1944, p. 718. National Archives; VMO-251 Aircraft Action Report, 28 August 1944. National Archives.

56. Commander Aircraft Northern Solomons Intelligence Summary, 30 August 1944, p. 726–727. National Archives.

57. Douglas E. Campbell, *Volume II: US Navy, US Marine Corps and US Coast Guard Aircraft Lost During World War II* (Lulu.com, 2011), p. 191.

58. Commander Aircraft Northern Solomons Intelligence Summary, 23 September 1944, p. 1006–1008. National Archives.

59. VMSB-133 War Diary and Aircraft Action Report, 22 September 1944. National Archives; VMSB-236 War Diary and Aircraft Action Report, 22 September 1944. National Archives.

60. VMF-223 War Diary, 22 September 1944. National Archives.

61. Commander Aircraft Northern Solomons Intelligence Summary, 23 September 1944, p. 1006. National Archives.

62. Commander Aircraft Northern Solomons Intelligence Summary, 25 September 1944, pp. 1027–1029 National Archives.

63. Campbell, p. 191. VMO-251's Aircraft Action Report for the period reports the incident but it does not state if the plane was written off nor the specific date. MAG-14 reports also do not account for the incident. Irwin's maintenance notes indicate the plane lost on 9 October.

64. The next four divisions were added on 21 November 1944.

65. VMO-251 War Diary, November 1944, pp-19–20, National Archives.

66. ComAirPiva War Diary, November 1944, p. 11. National Archives.

67. The available documents do not make it clear when the planes were hit. The damage is noted but the date is not given. Based on the documentation available, this is a best guess by the author.

68. ComAirPiva War Diary, November 1944, pg. 13, National Archives. VMO-251 documents for the strike state that RNZAF 19 Squadron participated in the attack instead of 15. It is not clear where the RNZAF squadrons were stationed at the time of the attack.

69. VMF-212 Aircraft Action Report No. 62, 16 November 1944. National Archives.

70. VMF-223 Aircraft Action Report No. 71, 16 November 1944. National Archives.

71. VMSB-236 War Diary, 20 November 1944, National Archives.

72. VMSB-133 War Diary, 20 November 1944, National Archives.

73. VMF-212 War Diary, 22 November 1944. NationalArchives.

74. ComAirPiva War Diary, 22 November 1944, pp. 21–22, National Archives.

75. VMF-223 War Diary, 22 November 1944, National Archives.

76. VMF-212 War Diary, 22 November 1944, National Archives.

77. VMF-223 Aircraft Action Report No. 77, 24 November 1944, National Archives.

78. VMF-223 War Diary, 24 November 1944, National Archives.

79. VMF-212 War Diary, 25 November 1944, National Archives.

80. VMF-212 Aircraft Action Report No. 68, 25 November 1944, National Archives.

81. VMF-212 Aircraft Action Report No. 70, 26 November 1944, National Archives.

82. MAG-14 War Diary, December 1944, National Archives.

83. Major Charles W. Boggs, Jr., *Marine Aviation in the Philippines* (Washington DC: U.S. Government Printing Office, 1951), p. 49.

84. Ibid, p. 50.

Chapter Six

1. Bacheler, William. Brave, Splendid Fools, p. 81.

2. Irwin Letter to author, September 30, 2014. Bacheler's wingman had to abort his approach, moving Irwin to the No. 2 position for landing.

3. Boggs, p. 50. Squadron documents seem to indicate some planes landed at Guiuan on 30 December and the rest on 9 January (History, VMO/VMF-251 #5743, VMO-251 Operational Records, National Archives.). No mention of this is made in the AARs for the squadron nor is not entirely clear if the RFDs followed the same route as the Corsairs.

4. Boggs, pp. 52–53.

5. Irwin Letter to author, September 30, 2014.

6. Irwin Letter to author, September 30, 2014. "Surveyed" is a term meaning written off, no good. "Meat ball" is slang for the red sun in the center of the Japanese flag.

7. The 85th FW was responsible for setting up and maintaining a series of radar installations in and around Leyte. With the adoption of a map grid system, it could vector aircraft to various target areas. While VMO/VMF-251 reports do not mention this process; other units under MAG-14 did.

8. Bacheler, p. 81.

9. Dale Andrade, *Luzon: The U.S. Army Campaigns of World War II* (Washington DC: U.S. Government Printing Office, 1995), p. 9.

10. His body was recovered sometime after the collision, but was buried as an unknown at Batangas #1 USAF Cemetery. His remains were identified in 1946 and interred at the Manila American Cemetery in 1948. Information from the casualty card of Nick Sigan, USMC History Division.

11. American Battle Monuments Commission, www.abmc.gov, accessed 26 July 2015.
12. VMO-251 Aircraft Action Report No. 63, 14–20 January 1945, National Archives.
13. MAG-14 Headquarters War Diary, January 1945, National Archives, p. 4. Total combat hours flown: 5,440. VMO-251 accounted for 2,404 of them.
14. Irwin Letter to author, 30 September 2014.
15. Ibid.
16. Don Evans, Walter Gaylor, Harry Nelson, and Lawrence Hickey, *Revenge of the Red Raiders: The Illustrated History of the 22nd Bombardment Group During World War II* (Boulder, CO: International Research and Publishing Corporation, 2006), pp. 1557–1559.
17. Bacheler, p. 86.
18. Budy survived the impact but lost both of his legs. Irish and the Filipino were killed; VMF-222 War Diary, January 1945, pp. 6–7. National Archives.
19. VMF-212 War Diary, January 1945, pp. 15–16. National Archives.
20. The VMF-223 War Diary for January 1945 makes no mention of any pilots flying over Cebu. According to the diary, missions were flown over Mindanao.
21. American Battle Monuments Commission, www.abmc.gov, accessed July 27, 2015 and Casualty Card for Harold C. Wallace, USMC History Division.
22. VMO-251 War Diary, January 1945, p. 16, National Archives.
23. David W. Hogan, Jr., *US Army Special Operations in World War II* (Washington DC: U.S. Government Printing Office, 1992), p. 80.
24. Reports of General MacArthur, p. 319.
25. Irwin Letter to author, September 30, 2014. According to Irwin, Johnson was a Disney illustrator in civilian life. However, Disney Studios could not find any record of a Danny W. Johnson employed as an illustrator.
26. VMF-223 Aircraft Action Report #85, 28 January–3 Feb. 1945. National Archives.
27. John Irwin Papers.
28. VMF-251 War Diary, 6 February 1945, p. 4, National Archives.
29. VMF-251's War Diary for 7 Feb 1945 states B-24s but Aircraft Action Report #67 for the mission states PB4Y. The PB4Y was the navy version of the B-24.
30. MAG-12 War Diary, February 1945. National Archives; VMF-115 War Diary, February 1945. National Archives.
31. Bacheler, p. 87. The squadron's war diary for Feb. 1945 states Humberd flew the demo. This may be a misidentification. Bacheler's description of the event is very precise.
32. Ibid, p. 87.
33. MAG-14 War Diary, February 1945, National Archives.
34. Bacheler, p. 90.
35. VMF-251 War Diary, February 1945, p. 7, National Archives.
36. VMF-251 War Diary, February 1945, p. 8, National Archives.
37. Ibid, pp. 8–9.
38. Robert Ross Smith, *Triumph in the Philippines* (Harrisburg, PA: National Historical Society, 1994), p. 436.
39. Ibid, p. 436.
40. Ibid, p. 437.
41. VMF-251 War Diary, February 1945, p. 13, and Aircraft Action Report No. 82, National Archives; VMF-218 War Diary, February 1945, p. 7. National Archives.
42. Also known as San Jose De Buenavista.
43. VMF-223 Aircraft Action Report No. 93, 2 March 1945, National Archives.
44. VMF-223 War Diary, March 1945, National Archives.
45. Muster Roll for VMF-251, March 1945, USMC History Division.
46. Bacheler, p. 89.
47. Ibid, p. 90.
48. VMF-251 War Diary, March 1945, p. 6. National Archives.
49. The squadron's war diary states it was Neilson who remained at Dipolog. However he did not fly on that particular mission based on the Aircraft Action Report for 9 March.
50. VMF-251 Aircraft Action Report No. 94, 11 March 1945. National Archives.
51. Reports of General MacArthur, p. 339–340.
52. Ibid, pp. 341–342.
53. Boggs, p. 118.
54. Ibid, pp. 343–344.
55. Smith, pp. 610–613.
56. Bacheler, pp. 92–93.
57. Gordon L. Rottman, *U.S. Marine Corps World War II Order of Battle* (Westport, CT: Greenwood Press, 2002), p. 393.
58. Wesley Frank Craven and James Lea Cate, *The Army Air Forces in World War II: Volume Five, The Pacific: Matterhorn to Nagasaki, June 1944 to August 1945* (Washington DC: U.S. Government Printing Office, 1983), pp. 456–457.
59. Irwin letter to author, 30 September 2014.
60. Irwin letter to author, dated September 30, 2014.
61. Bacheler, p. 90.
62. MAG-14 War Diary, May 1945, p. 8. National Archives.
63. Robert Sherrod, *History of Marine Corps Aviation in World War II* (Washington DC: Combat Forces Press, 1952), p. 434.
64. VMF-251 ACA No. 121, 21 April 1945. National Archives.
65. M. Hamlin Cannon, *Leyte: The Return to the Philippines* (Harrisburg, PA: National Historical Society, 1994), p. 365.
66. VMF-251 War Diary, April 1945, p. 13. National Archives.
67. VMF-251 Aircraft Action Report No. 129, 27 April 1945, National Archives.
68. VMF-212 Aircraft Action Report No. 041-45, 30 April 1945, National Archives.

Epilogue

1. Hours from squadron war diaries for each month listed.

Appendix 1

1. Later became Assistant Commandant of the Marine Corps, April 1963–June 1965. Lt. Gen. Hayes passed away on 3 April 1995.
2. Humberd flew with VMF-221 during the battle of Midway in June 1942.

Appendix 6

1. Frank J. Olynyk, *USMC Credits for the Destruction of Enemy Aircraft in Air-to-Air Combat World War 2* (self-published, 1982), pp 113 and 114.

Appendix 7

1. John M. Elliott, *The Official Monogram, US Navy & Marine Corps Aircraft Color Guide, Vol. 2, 1940–1949* (Sturbridge, MA: Monogram Aviation, Second Edition, 1998), pp. 28–115.

Appendix 8

1. Awards verified by the USMC History Division and NAVMC 9211 (updated February 2010).

Appendix 9

1. Copies of these citations were located in the records of VMO/VMF-251 held at the National Archives. RG 127 Records of the United States Marine Corps, U.S. Marine Corps Aviation Unit War Diaries and Unit Histories 1941–1949: Squadrons VMO-251 to VMF-251, BOX 47.

Bibliography

Books

Angelucci, Enzo. *American Fighter*. New York, NY: Random House, 1987.

Astor, Gerald. *Semper Fi in the Sky*. New York, NY: Ballantine Books, 2005.

Bacheler, William L. *Brave, Splendid Fools: A Life in Aviation*. CreateSpace Independent Publishing Platform, 2014.

Bishop, Chris. *The Encyclopedia of Weapons of World War II*. New York, NY: Barnes & Noble, 1998.

Campbell, Douglas E. *Volume II: US Navy, US Marine Corps and US Coast Guard Aircraft Lost During World War II*. Lulu.com, 2011.

Craig, Barry. *Marine Corps Aviation Chronolog*. Paducah, KY: Turner Publishing Company, 1989.

Dann, Richard. *F4F Wildcat in Action*. Carrollton, TX: Squadron/Signal Publications, 2004.

Evans, Don; Gaylor, Walter; Nelson, Harry; Hickey, Lawrence. *Revenge of the Red Raiders: The Illustrated History of the 22nd Bombardment Group During World War II*. Boulder, CO: International Research and Publishing Corporation, 2006.

Gamble, Bruce. *Target Rabaul*. Minneapolis, MN: Zenith Press, 2013.

Hammel, Eric. *Carrier Clash*. Pacifica, CA: Pacifica Military History, 2009.

Hornfischer, James D. *Neptune's Inferno*. New York, NY: Random House 2011.

Latourneau, Dennis and Roger. *Operation KE*. Annapolis, MD: Naval Institute Press, 2012.

Lord, Walter, *Lonely Vigil*. New York, NY: The Viking Press, 1977.

Lundstrom, John B. *The First Team and the Guadalcanal Campaign*. Annapolis, MD: Naval Institute Press, 2005.

Millstein, Jeff. *US Marine Corps Aviation Unit Insignia (1941–1946)*. Paducah, KY: Turner Publishing Company, 1995.

Mrazek, Robert J. *A Dawn Like Thunder*. New York, NY: Bay Back Books, 2008.

Olynyk, Frank. *USMC Credits for the Destruction of Enemy Aircraft in Air-to-Air Combat World War 2*. Self-Published, 1982.

Polmar, Norman and Thomas B. Allen. *WWII: The Encyclopedia of the War Years, 1941–1945*. Mineola, NY: Dover Publications, 2012.

Rottman, Gordon L. *U.S. Marine Corps World War II Order of Battle*. Westport, CT: Greenwood Press, 2002.

_____. *World War II Pacific Island Guide*. Westport, CT: Greenwood Press, 2002.

Sherrod, Robert. *History of Marine Corps Aviation in World War II*. Washington, D.C.: Combat Forces Press, 1952.

Tillman, Barrett. *Wildcat: The F4F in WW II*. Annapolis, MD: Naval Institute Press, 1990.

Weiland, Charles Patrick. *Above and Beyond*. Pacifica, CA: Pacifica Press, 1997.

_____. *Manuscript Found in Battle*. Cavu Press, 1991.

Interviews

Vito Murgolo, 21 April 2014. Phone interview with author.

Libraries

Paramount Notes pertaining to the filming of *Wake Island*. Academy of Motion Pictures Arts and Sciences, Margaret Herrick Library. Beverly Hills, California.

Newspapers

"Capt. Kenneth J. Kirk of Barre, Marine Flyer, Gets 3 Jap Planes." *Burlington Free Press*, 15 February 1943.

"Capt. Whitten is Commended." *Wilmington Delaware Journal*, 10 May 1943.

"Malaria, Not Japs, Sends Marine Flyer, Home." *Wilmington Delaware Journal*, 17 April 1943.

Official Documents

ComAirNorSols War Diary and Intelligence Summaries. August–November 1944. National Archives.

ComAirPiva War Diaries. June–November 1944. National Archives.

History of the 42nd Bombardment Squadron. Air Force Historical Association, Maxwell Air Force Base. IRIS No. 44028, Maxwell Air Force Base.

Interview with Major Joseph N. Renner. Bureau of Aeronautics, 1943. National Archives.

MAG-11 War Diaries. May-June 1944. National Archives.

MAG-12 War Diary. February 1945. National Archives.

MAG-14 Record of Events. 16 October 1942–16 December 1942. National Archives.

MAG-14 War Diary. November 1944, January–February, May 1945. National Archives.

MAG-23 War Diary. September–November 1942. National Archives.

MAG-24 War Diaries. June–October 1944. National Archives.

Pilot's Handbook of Flight Operating Instruction Navy Models F4U-1, F3A-1, FG-1, F4U-1C, F3A-1D, FG-1D, and F4U-1D Airplanes. Bureau of Aeronautics, 15 March 1945.

RNZAF 19 Squadron Diary. 15 August 1944. RNZAF Archives.

USS Alcyone War Diary. August 1942, National Archives.

USS Alnitah War Diary. July 1944. National Archives.

USS Curtiss War Diary. August 1942. National Archives.

USS Crescent City War Diary. January 1943. National Archives.

USS Heywood War Diaries. June–July 1942. National Archives.

USS Kitty Hawk War Diaries. May–June 1943. National Archives.

USS Tangier War Diary. February 1944. National Archives.

VMF-112 War Diary. November 1942. National Archives.

VMF-115 Mission Report. August 1944, February 1945. National Archives.

VMF-211 Mission Report. August 1944. National Archives.

VMF-212 War Diary and Aircraft Action Reports. November 1944, January 1945. National Archives.

VMF-215 War Diary. August 1944. National Archives.

VMF-218 War Diary. February 1945. National Archives.

VMF-222 War Diary. January 1945. National Archives.

VMF-223 War Diary and Aircraft Action Reports. August, November 1944, January–March 1945. National Archives.

VMO-251 Historical Narrative. December 1941–October, 1942. USMC History Division.

VMO/VMF-251 Muster Rolls. USMC History Division.

VMO/VMF-251 Squadron records. 1941–1945. National Archives.

VMSB-133 War Diary and Aircraft Action Reports. September, November 1944. National Archives.

VMSB-235 War Diary and Aircraft Action Reports. July 1944. National Archives.

VMSB-236 War Diary and Aircraft Action Reports. August–September, November 1944. National Archives.

VMSB-243 Mission Reports. August 1944. National Archives.

VT-8 War Diary. November 1942. National Archives.

Official Histories

Andrade, Dale. *Luzon, The U.S. Army Campaigns of World War II*. Washington, D.C.: US Government Printing Office, 1995.

Craven, Wesley Frank and Cate, James Lea. *The Army Air Forces in World War II: Volume Five, The Pacific: Matterhorn to Nagasaki, June 1944 to August 1945*. Washington, D.C.: US Government Printing Office, 1983.

Cannon, M. Hamlin. *Leyte: The Return to the Philippines*. Washington, D.C.: US Government Printing Office, 1994.

Hogan, David W., Jr. *US Army Special Operations in World War II*. Washington, D.C.: US Government Printing Office, 1992.

Lt. Col. Hough, Frank O., Major Ludwig, Verle E. and Shaw, Jr., Henry I. *Pearl Harbor to Guadalcanal*. Washington, D.C.: US Government Printing Office, 1958.

Major Boggs, Jr., Charles W. *Marine Aviation in the Philippines*. Washington, D.C.: US Government Printing Office, 1951.

Major Zimmerman, John L. *The Guadalcanal Campaign*. Washington, D.C.: US Government Printing Office, 1949.

Smith, Robert Ross. *Triumph in the Philippines*. Washington, D.C.: US Government Printing Office, 1994.

The Reports of General MacArthur: The Campaigns of MacArthur in the Pacific, Volume 1. Washington, D.C.: US Government Printing Office, 1994.

The Reports of General MacArthur: Japanese Operations in the Southwest Pacific Area, Volume II-Part 1. Washington, D.C.: US Government Printing Office, 1994.

Bibliography

Personal Histories

Albert Hoffman—Command Museum, MCRD San Diego
Dan Abrams—Voices of Veterans Oral History Project, Texas General Land Office
Hugh "Yogi" Irwin—Correspondence with Author

Personal Papers

Wendall Garton Papers, Garton family.
John Irwin Papers, Irwin family
Roy Spurlock Papers, Kristine Whitten and the Spurlock family.
Robert Whitten Papers, Whitten family.

Unpublished

Major McFadden, Brian S. *Marine Close Air Support in World War II*. Fort Leavenworth, KS: Command and General Staff College, 1989.

Websites

All Things Quackenbush, http://allthingsquackenbush.weebly.com/quackenbushs-gypsies.html
American Battle Monuments Commission, www.abmc.gov
California State Military Museum http://californiamilitaryhistory.org/MCASMojave.html
Defense Prisoner of War/Missing Personnel Office (DPMO) http://www.dtic.mil/dpmo/wwii/reports/mar_m_m.htm
F4F-3P, Marine Corps Aviation Reconnaissance Association. URL: http://www.mcara.us/F4F-3P.php
Japanese Naval and Merchant Shipping Losses during World War II By All Causes prepared by the Joint Army-Navy Assessment Committee, February 1947. http://www.history.navy.mil/library/online/japaneseshiploss.htm
Naval History and Heritage Command—Location of Naval Aircraft, http://www.history.navy.mil/research/histories/naval-aviation-history/location-of-us-naval-aircraft-world-war-ii.html
Rabaul, Pacific Wrecks, http://www.pacificwrecks.com/provinces/png_rabaul.html
United States Marine Corps History Division—World War II Casualty Cards, https://www.mcu.usmc.mil/historydivision/cc_ww2/SitePages/Home.aspx
Voices of Veterans Oral History Project, Texas General Land Office, http://www.glo.texas.gov/voices-of-veterans/interviews/abrams.html

Index

Page numbers in **_bold italics_** indicate pages with illustrations.

Able Charlie Search 101–104
Abrams, Dan 8, 35, 63, 66
Adams, James D. 46
Advanced Carrier Training Group 8
Air Liaison Party 191
Aircraft:
 Allied:
  B-17—18–19, 29–30, 33, 38, 40
  B-24—9, 47, 165–166, 191
  B-25—83
  B-26—31
  C-46—184, 186
  C-47—161, 166–167
  F2F—73
  F4F see Grumman Wildcat
  F4U Corsair see Chance-Vought Corsair
  J2F Duck—8, 21, 40–41
  LB-30 see Aircraft, B-24
  Lockheed Hudson—31
  OS2 Kingfisher—8
  P-38—172, 178, 188
  P-39—51, 54, 59, 61
  P-47—163
  PBJ-1—156
  PB4Y-1 see Aircraft, B-24
  PBY Catalina—9, 29, 30–31, 33, 40–41, 47, 49, 59, 65, 83–84, 87, 89, 101, 105, 109–110, 116, 137, 162, 180
  R4D—46, 155–156
  RD-1—41
  SNJ-3—8, 41–42, 47
  SBD Dauntless—9, 25, 33, 43, 51 64, 91–92, 98, 112, 114, 117, 119, 120, 127–128, 168, 173
  XFL-1—70
  XF5F-1—70
 Japanese:
  A6M (Zero)—9, 26, 30, 45, 54–55, 60, 63, 178, 185
  A6M2-N (Rufe)—30
  G4M (Betty)—63–64
  H8K (Emily)—87
  Ki-48 (Lily)—66
Aitapa 153
Akron, Ohio 70

Alicante 168
Alitagtag 170
Anasugaro 128
Anderson, Emmett 42, 49–**_50_**
Andre, David 59
Andrews, Robert Lowell, Jr. 67
Annapolis, Maryland 10
Arakawaun 128
Arara 141
Arawa Bay 110–111, 117, 136, 139
Arlington National Cemetery 73
Army Navy Training School 70
Ataliklikun 106, 140, 142, 149
Auda 128
Australia 11–12, 14, 32, 39, 43, 97, 124, 143, 145, 147
HMAS _Australia_ 26
Austria Sound 51

B-10 Bomb Shackles 194
Bacheler, William 102–105, 107–108, 110, 112, 114–115, 117–119, 122–124, 127, 129, 130–131, 134–140, 142–148, 150–152, 154, 156, 162–164, 166–170, 172, 174–177, 179–184, 187, 190, 194–195
Baer, Paul D. 46
Baesler, Blaine H. **_12_**, 43, 46, **_54_**, 56, **_58_**–**_59_**
Bago 161, 197
Bailey, Howard W. 21–22
Baird, Richard E. 14, 47
Baker, Robert M. 56
Ballale Island 150
Balu Plantation 130
Baniu Plantation 127
Banpfragwerk Plantation 149
Baran, Walter A. 57, 62, 66
Bard, Elliot 5, 7
Barnard Plantation 125
Barton, Wilson G. 112, 120–122, 131, 135, 137–139, 143, 145, 147, 151, 153–154, 169, 172, 178, 181–182, 184, 186, 189, 191
Basiad Bay 163
Bate, Oscar M., Jr. 74, 81–85, 89–90, 92, 93–94, 96–97, 105
Batistich, Dennis 35, 63

Battle of the Bulge 201
Bauer, Harold W. 18, 20–21
Bean, Walter 179
Beattie, Alexander D. 136, 138, **_141_**, 143, 147, 149–150, 152, 158, 160–162, 166, 171, 181, 184, 192, 197
Becker, Edward J. 91
Bellona Island 30
Berkey, Russell H. 189
Berteling, John B. 57, 66
Biesel, Rex 70
Binalbigan 161
Biri 178–179
Bismarck Archipelago 128
Bismarck Sea 110
Bitagalip 96
Blanche Bay 91, 96, 104, 149
Bogo 198–199
Bohang 107
Bohol 161, 167
Bomamu 133
Bomber Field #1 31, 33, 38, 41–42, 47, 202
Bonis 95
Booth, Roy L. 56–57
Borpop 100, 116
Bougainville 62, 79, 81, 87–90, 92, 94–96, 98, 101, 103–104, 107, 110–112, 114, 116–118, 120–121, 123–125, 127–132, 135–136, 138–142, 144–147, -149–151, 153, 155, 202
Bovo River 99–110, 117, 136
Bowers, Glenn L. 104, 109, 115, 128–129
Britain 32
Brooks Clifford E. 67
Bryson, Robert L. 57
Budy, D.M. 167
Buena Vista 180, 198
Buka 81, 90, 94–95, 101, 103–104, 109, 119–125, 129, 132, 135, 139–142, 145–146, 148, 150, 151
Bulan 171
Bulbuk 83
Bureau of Aeronautics 70
Butchkombo 131
Butuan 162, 168–169, 176, 180

235

Index

Cactus Air Force 18–19, 36, 39–40, 43–44, 46–47, 49–51, 55, 58, 60–61, 63–66
Calamia Island 162
California City, California 72
Callaghan, Daniel J. 18
Caluaung 167
Camang 168
Camotes Sea 167, 169–170
Camp Pendleton 76
Campbell, William R. 15, 18, 22, 24–25, 29, 32, 40–41, 43, 50, 53, **54**–57, 61
HMAS *Canberra* 26–27
Canloan Volcano 197, 199
Cape Archway 146–147, 149, 152, 154
Cape Cumberland 20–21
Cape Esperance 56, 63–65
Cape Friendship 140
Cape Gazelle 96, 101, 107, 124–125, 127, 129, 130–131, 134–135, 137, 139–143
Cape Lalahan 140
Cape Lambert 105–113, 122–123, 125, 130–131, 134, 139–140, 142–143, 146–147, 149, 152, 155
Cape Liguan 121, 123, 146
Cape Namaroda 99–101
Cape Pomas 141
Cape Quiros 40
Cape Roloss 84
Cape St. George 83, 92, 99, 102, 105, 111
Cape Senna 83, 109
Cape Tawii 102
Cape Torokina 101
Cape Tosahui 140
Capul 178
Carmen 169, 172
Carolina 172, 175
Caroline Islands 138
Carter, Irwin 59
Castillo 164
Catabagan 164
Cebu 160–161, 167–169, 172–174, 176, 179, 182, 184–192, 195, 197–200
Cebu City 161, 168, 173, 175–176, 182, 185–186, 188–189, 191, 193, 195–196
Cebu Harbor 189
Chabai 125
Chaitin, Herbert L. 117
Chance-Vought F4U Corsair 37–38, 61–62, 67, 69, 70–71, 73, 75–200
Cherry Point, North Carolina 73
China 5
Chivorante 128
Choiseul Island 151
Christian, Wayne W. 57, 64
Collier, Homer E. 30
Commander Air Piva (COMAIRPIVA) 147
Commander Air Solomon Islands (COMAIRSOL) 96
Commander Air Southern Pacific (COMAIRSOPAC) 33

Commander Aircraft Northern Solomons (COMAIRNORSOL) 114, 118–119, 121, 127–128, 147
Commander in Chief (COMINCH) 171
Concepcion 196, 199
Condon, Joseph A. 73, 75, 82, 89, 94–95, 97, 105
Conroy, Joseph A. 127, 131, 135, 138, 145
Conroy, Robert E. 158
Consolacion 191
Cook, James 32
Coral Sea 11
Corman, Ned J. 104–105, 109, 115, 117, 129
Cosner, James A. 22
Cotabato 182, 184
Cram, Jack 31, 47, 49
Credner Islands 97
Crutcher, Ernest R. 81, 90, 100–101, 105, 112, 129, 130, 135, 138, *141*, 147, 150, 153, 161–162, 168
Cuimbalaon 198
Cunningham, Russell F. 81–82, 84–85, 94, 96, 100, 110, 113, 117, 131, 133, 136, 138–140, 151–**154**, 162, 164, 168–172, 177–179, 181–182, 188

Daigle, Bernadine J. 125, 129, 131–133, 138, 140–141, 147, 151, 154, 161, 163, 170, 174–175, 178, 184, 188
Danao 195–196
Davao 168–169, 177
Davao Gulf 179
Delmonte 192, 168–169
De Neyra, Alvaro de Mendaña 32
De Queros, Pedro Fernandez 32
Desert Room 78
Diklom 172
Diplog 188
Distinguished Unit Citation 23
Donlevy, Brian 11
Dos Hermanos 192
Doughty, Francis E. 189, 192–193
Doyle, G.B. 56
Drucker, Dave 112–118
Dudly, Benjamin L. 182
Duke of York Islands 83, 97, 105–113, 120–121, 125, 130, 134–135, 137, 139–142, 146–147, 149, 152, 154
Dumaguete 168, 185
Dumbo *see* Aircraft, PBY
Dunn, John T. 56
Dupont Chemical Company 174
Dutch East Indies 5
Duvall, E.E. 68

Edson, Merritt 45
Efate 18–21, 45, 57
Erdmann, William A. 78, 81, 83, 87, 93, 97, 10–101, 103, 131, 135, 138, 144, 146–149, 151–152, 161, 167, 170, 174, 180–181, 188
Erwin, Paul V.B. 57, 63
Espiritu Santo 18–21, 23, 29–33,

35, 39–41, 43, 45–47, 49, 56–57, 61, 66–67, 78–79, 81, 83, 96–97
Evans, Arthur C., Jr. 136, 138, 143, 145, 151–152, 163–164, 168, 174, 181, 195–197

F4F-3P *see* Grumman Wildcat
F4F-4 *see* Grumman Wildcat
F4F-7 *see* Grumman Wildcat
F4U-1 *see* Chance-Vought F4U Corsair
F4U-1D *see* Chance-Vought F4U Corsair
Fabrica 178
Fairchild F-56 Camera 10
Faisi Island 143, 150
Farrell, W.G. 11
Feni Island 101
Fertig, Wendell 176
Fighter Strip #1 44, 49, 54–55
Fighter Strip #2 57, 61
Fiji Islands 23, 47
Fink, Henry 185, 195
Fisher, Dewitt C. 188
Fletcher, Frank Jack 18, 26
Flickenger, Judson 105, 107–108, 112, 123, 134–136, 138
Florida Islands 24, 51, 54
Foley, James A., Jr. 81, 84, 97, 108, 111–112, 114–117, 121–122
Fontaine 29
Formosa 165, 167
Fort Carovera 183
Foss, Joe 31
Fowler, Millard F. 104–115, 117, 119, 122, 124, 129
France 32
Frank, Lewis C 108, 111–112, 114–115, 121, 129–130, 134–135, 137–138, 140, 147, 149, 151–152, 160, 166, 168, 171, 179, 181–182, 184, 189
Fremont Valley, California 72
French Indo-China 5
Furlow, Thomas W. 73, 76, 81–85, 87, 89, 92, 96–97, 100, 104, 106–108, 110–111, 113–114, 117, 124–126, 128–130, 134–139, 175–185, 187, 189, 191, 195

Gallagher, John P. 81, 87, 176
Garreer Bay 108
Garrett, James B. 81, 87, 96–97, 100, 110, 113, 129–130, 134–138, 153, 167, 172, 176, 178, 181, 185, 188
Garton, Wendell P. 7–8, 10, 13, 16, **40**–41, 43–47, **50**, **54**, 56, **58**
Gavit Plantation 106
Gazelle Peninsula 122, 129, 143, 152–155
Geiger, Roy L. 31, 49
Georgia Islands 57
Gerety, Edward J. 81, 83, 89, 95–100, 103
Ghormley, Robert L. 18, 29, 35
Gilbert Islands 79, 138
Giles, Walt 31
Gilmore, Richard E. 46

Index

Glendale, California 78
Glenn, Joseph N. 82
Goldstein, Sydney 76
Goodyear Aircraft Corporation 70
Gorman, James M. 125, 131, 134–135, 137–138, 142, 152, 155
Gray, Roy C. 125, 131, 134–136, 138–140, 144–152, 154, 161–163, 167, 170
Greater East Asia Co-Prosperity Sphere 5
Green Island 81–85, 87, 90–92, 98, 101, 103, 105, 110, 118–124, 127, 129, 149, 154–155
Ground Defense Bill 138
Grumman Wildcat 9, 10, 13, 16–19, 31, 33, 37–38, 40–41, 43–51, 53–66, 68, 71–76
Guadalcanal 11–13, 17–19, 23–26, 29–33, 35–36, 39–40, 43–44, 46–53, 55–57, 61–66, 69, 78, 81, 138, 190, 201
Guerrillas 175–176, 179, 182–188, 192
Guimaras Straight 187
Guiuan 155, 156, 158–199, 201, 202

Haberman, Roger 49, 75
Haleha 148
Halsey, William F. 31
Hamilton Standard 70, 166
Hanson, Howard L. 138, 140–141, 145
Hapan 119
Hari 151–152, 154
Harlan, William B. 56
Harper, Marius N., Jr. 29
Harriman, Frank 179–180
Harring, Richard A. 51
Harris, Archibald A. 125, 129–130, 132, 137–140, 161, 166, 168–169, 171, 180, 183–184, 192
Hart, John P. 10–*12*, 14–15, 17–18, 29, 31, 33, ***39***, 43–44, 50
Hart, Joseph P. 81–84, 87, 89–90, 97–104, 117, 119–124, 129, 131, 134, 153, 177–178, 180–183, 188
Haruna 48
Hathaway, Mortimer D. 74, 77, 79–80
Hawaii 7
Hayes, Charles *12*, 36, 50, ***54***, 56
Hearn, Alex 60
Heisel, Thomas B. 125, 130, 132, 135, 137–139, 143, 146–147, 152
Heito 165
Hellerrde, Arthur O. 56
Henderson Field 35–36, 44, 47–50, 53–55, 57, 61–64, 66, 202
Henley, Paul B. 81–84, 89–90, 98–99, 101–106, 108–110, 112–113, 125, 129–130, 132, 134–136, 138–139, 150–154, 162–163, 167, 169, 170–182, 184–185, 188
Henze, Gil 65
Hero, C. 168
Hiei 53, 55
Hildebrand, Richard W. 72–73, 81, 84, 89, 90, 97, 105

Hitokappu Bay 5
Holderer, George M. 138, 140–141, 145
Holiday, Robert C. 77, 81, 92–93, 97, 101–103
Hollandia 155–156
Homes, William C. 41
Hongarai River 114
Honiara International Airport 202
Hopkins, Zebulon 155, 173, 182, 189, 194, 201
Hospital Ridge 85, 119–120
Humberd, William C. 73, 81–84, 87–92, 94–104, 106, 109–114, 117, 124–125, 127–131, 130–131, 134–139, 155, 159, 161–163, 165, 167, 173, 175
Hume, James C. 165–166
Hyakuyake, Harukoshi 51

Ilihan 186, 199
Iloilo 179, 187
Ilu River 48
Inglehart, George C. 75, 81, 92, 96, 99–100, 103, 110–111, 117, 131, 133–135, 137–139, 151, 160–162, 165, 167, 169–170, 172, 176–178, 180–185, 192
Irish, P.E. 167
Irwin, Hugh E. 89, ***141***, 143–***144***, 152–153, 158–***159***, 161, 166, 171, 174, 180–181, 184, 188, 192–194
Irwin, John W. 7, ***50***, 61–62, ***67***, ***93***, 176, 199
Iula 145
Iwo Jima 138

Jaba River 107
James Karl D. 47
Japan:
  Air Units:
    Tainan Air Group—44
  Ground Units:
    3rd Company—136
    12th Company—136
    17th Army—51, 56
    35th Brigade—44
    38th Division—53, 55
  Navy Units:
    3rd Battleship Division—48
    8th Fleet—26, 51
Jennings, Francis C. 74–75, 78, 81–83, 87, 89, 96–97, 104, 106, 108–109, 112, 114–116, 120–124, 129, 131, 138, 140–143, 149–150, 152–153, ***159***, 161–163, 167, 169, 172–181, 184, 188
Jernigan, Curtis D. 138, 143, 147, 151–152, 160, 162, 166, 171, 174–175, 178, 181, 184, 195, 197, 199
Johns, Quentin R. 136, 138–139, 141, 143
Johnson, Alfred L. 104, 108, 112–113, 115, 129
Johnson, Danny W. 172, 186, 192, 197
Johnson, Harry C. 104, 106, 112, 115, 129
Jolink, Albert 104–107, 109–110,

112–115, 117, 119, 122, 123–124, 127, 129
Jones, Ollie O. 127, 129, 131, 134–138, 140, 142, 144, 146, 149, 155, 161–162, 164, 165, 168
Jugban 162

Kabacan 179, 182
Kabagada Point 94
Kabakan 121
Kabanga Bay 96, 112, 130, 137
Kabanga Plantation 130
Kabanga Point 131
Kahili 63, 108–109, 124, 129, 131, 133, 135, 147–148, 150–151, 153–154
Kahug 191
Kaino-Kupai 132
Kakada 113
Kakurai 153
Kalez, Marion M. 32
Kalvelage, Martin H. 185, 189
Kamanakam 152
Kamar 143
Kamdaru River 99
Kamiraba Plantation 100
Kammeyer, Preston L. 125, 129, 138, 140–141, 152, 161–163, 169–170, 174, 181, 184
Kanakdraw 135
Kanam River 99
Kandau 109
Kane, John R. 75, 78, 82, 90, 93, 97, 100–103
Kangu Hill 133, 150
Kapauinaui Stockade 142
Kapui 133
Kara 116, 135, 139, 150, 151, 153
Kara Plantation 116
Karavia Bay 94–95, 97, 102
Karsorilau 120
Kaukaui 129
Kawaguchi, Kiyotake 44–45, 47
Kearny Mesa, California 69
Keithley, Glen F. ***39***, 200
Kemp, Orville S. 185–186, 191, 196
Kennicott, John A. 125, 129, 135, 138–139, 145, 152–153
Keravat 82–83, 85, 105–114, 117, 122–125, 129–130, 133–135, 137, 139–143, 152
Kiano 124
Kieta 99, 107, 112, 114, 128–133, 135, 139
King, Howard E. 182, 188–189, 192, 194
Kirby, William P. 18, 23–24, 26
Kiriwana 130
Kirk, Kenneth *12*, 32, 40, 42, ***54***, 56, 59, ***60***
Kitchararao 185
Klas, Donald L. 57
Kleiner Island 117
Kobler, George S. 16–17, 36, 47, ***54***, 56–58
Koehn Dry Lake, California 72
Kokomira 135
Kokopo 87, 90, 96
Kokumbona 49, 52

Index

Koliai 150
Kolobangara 64
Kongo 48
Korea 5
Koro 24
Koromira 128, 130, 132, 140, 142–143, 151
Krueger, Walter 164
Kukugai 135
Kukum 25, 57
Kulkil 143
Kulon Plantation 90, 127
Kupai 133
Kuper, Geoffrey 51
Kurakakul 145
Kurrajong Plantation 130
Kwajalein 79

La Carlota 168, 178
La Paz 180
Laginda Plantation 152
Lagogon Bay 100
Laguna de Bay 169–170
Lahug 168, 178–179, 189, 191–192, 194
Lake Lahala 135, 140
Lake Mainit 185
Lakunai Airfield 82, 120
LaMarre, Ernest A. 185, 195
Lassul Bay 137
LCM 178
Leaf, Munro (*The Story of Ferdinand*) 40
Leeds, Phillip 56, 63
Lemingi 124, 129, 130–131, 134, 137, 139–143
Letronico, Joseph 117
Leyte 138, 157, 161, 165–167, 173, 177, 179–180, 185, 191, 197, 200
Leyte Gulf 159, 161–163, 167–170, 177, 179, 181, 183–184, 186–190, 194
Libmanan 164
Licanan 177
Liguan Bay 93–94
Lilinakala Plantation 137
Liloan 161, 172, 176, 191–192, 195, 197
Lindner, David W. 185, 189, 196
Lindsey, Robert E. 143, 147, 152, 156, 163–164, 166–167, 188
Lingayen Gulf 160, 163
Lingenfelter, Virgil A. 138, 147, 150, 153, 167, 170, 178, 181, 184, 186, 195–196
Livuan Plantation 110, 143
Loban, Glen A. 57, 62–**65**
Lonahan 140
Longley, Carl **12**, 29, 43, 46, **54**, 69, 73
Lorch, Orville F. **72**–73, 81, 83, 94, 99, 101–102, **105**
LTV 189
Lucena 164, 171
Lucero, Ralph Abel 66
Lucifer's Messengers **38**, **171**–172, 186
Luganville Bomber Field 79, 81, 83
Luluai 129, 151

Lumbia 178
Lunga Point 12, 24–25, 54
Luzon 157, 160, 162–165, 167, 169, 170–171, 187
Lynch, Joe 64

Mabio Point 169
Mabiri Plantation 128
MacArthur, Douglas 79, 138, 156, 159
Mackenzie, Hugh 36
MacLachlan, Archibald W. 82–84, 87, 95–97, 100, 103–104, 114–115, 119–121, 125, 130, 133–135, 138, 140–141, 147, 149–150, 152, 162, 166, 174–175, 177, 181–182, 184, 186, 192
Mactan Island 175, 189
Madden, Albert **41**–42, 52–**53**, **93**, **132**
Madden, John **41**, **53**, **93**, **132**
Madden, Walter **41**, **53**, **93**
Maitairuitap Plantation 149
Makada Island 106
Makiki 128
Makurapau Plantation 127, 131
Malabang 183–184
Malabeta Hill 123
Malaboa Plantation 152
Malabunga 105–106, 108–110, 112–114, 130, 134
Malaysia 5
Manatai Mission 111
Manchuria 5
Mandave 173–174
Mandras Plantation 143
Mandras Sawmill 112
Manila 165, 169, 171
Manila American Cemetery 165, 170
Manpay Creek 184
Marine Air Infantry School 190
Marshall Islands 79, 138
Maston Island 179
Matchin Bay 145, 147
SS *Matsonia* 47
Matupi 83, 119–121
Maya 186
Maya, Waldemar D. 81, 84, 101–103
McAllister, Roy A. 185, 187–188, 195
McCabe, Earl W. 103, 105, 108, 112, 114–115, 121, 129
McCain, John 14–15, 17–18, 20, 35–36
McCartney, Henry A. 56, **66**
McCaskill John A. 200
McGlothlin, Joe H., Jr. **12**, 16, 40–41, 43, 47, **54**, 56, **58**–**59**
McMasters, John J. **72**–73, 75–76, 81, 90, 95, 97, 108–109, 111, 114–116, 129
Medillin 186
Merkel, Galen K. 72, 76
Meton River 128
Metong Point 125
Micko Islands 113
Midway Island 8, 11, 73, 201

Mikawa, Gunichi 26
Miller, William H. 41
Mindanao 162, 168–169, 172, 175–186, 191
Mindoro 157, 161–162, 166–167
Moila Point 120, 150
Moisuru 150, 153
Mologo 174
Monuito Mission 151, 154
Moore, Jack R. 57, 62–63
Moro 133, 153
Morone 153
Morotai 79
Morris, Jay W. 30
Morris, Mahlon 185–186, 191, 196
Mosiga 150
Moss, Abraham 65
Motupena Point 112, 114, 139, 151
Mt. Bai 150
Mt. Lawernz 133
Mt. Mandalagan 192, 198
Mt. Senfft 132, 153
Mt. Varzin 112, 114
Moynihan, Michael E. 80–81, 89, 101, 125, 131, 134–135, 138, 146–149, 151–152, 153, 161, 167, 170
Mugai Mission 153
Munda 58–59, 61, 64–65, 138
Muntinglupa 165
Murgolo, Vito 7, **12**, 48–49
Mussman, William E., Jr. 125, 131, 134–135, 138, 151–152, 161, 163

Naga 163, 170–171
Nagumo, Chuichi 5
Naliwan 139
Namatanai 100, 109, 141
Nambung River 130
Narangoi River 135
Naval Air Station North Island 5, 8, 31, 78
Naval Air Station San Diego 5
Navigation School 10
Navy Unit Commendation 101, 201
Neal, Lawrence L. 71, 82–84, 90–92
Neefus, Jim 96
Negritos Camp 167
Negros 160–161, 163, 167–169, 172, 174–175, 178, 180–181, 184–185, 187–188, 192, 195–200
Neilson, Russell H. 73, 77, 82, 90, 92, 94, 96, 100–101, 120–121, 125, 130, 134–135, 138, 140–143, 149, 152–153, 168–169, 171, 174–175, 181, 182, 184–186, 188
Neinduk Plantation 87, 108
New Britain 79, 82–83, 90, 97, 103–104, 109–110, 118, 122–123, 125, 127–130, 133–135, 137, 139–145, 147–149
New Caledonia 13–15, 18, 23, 30, 32–33, 47, 202
New Georgia 58, 61–62
New Guinea 11, 79, 138
New Hebrides 20, 26, 32, 78, 202
New Ireland 81–84, 94, 99–100, 111, 116, 118, 120, 128, 141, 154

New Mobisberg Plantation 149
New Zealand 11, 13–14, 29, 83, 112, 119, 149, 189
New Zealand Squadrons:
 RNZAF 15 Squadron—142, 147
 RNZAF 19 Squadron—112, 118
 RNZAF 21 Squadron—112, 114–117
 RNZAF 23 Squadron—142
 RNZAF 31 Squadron—99
Nichols Field 170
Nielson Auxiliary Field 170
Nimitz, Chester W. 31, 79, 138
Nissan Island *see* Green Island
Nordup 103
Normandy 201
North Africa 9
North Patrol Force 26–27
Noumea 14–15, 30, 31
Numa Numa 129, 135, 140
Nupapar 143

Oas 163
O'Bryan, Norman 195–197, 199
Oerth, Karl 167
O'Harra, Lee E. 73–74
Olmstead, J.H. 74
Open Bay 143, 148
Operation Ke-Go 56
Operation Watchtower 12, 27
Opon 175, 189
Osterlund, John Frederick 73
Owi Island 155–156
Oxygen Equipment School 70

Pal Pal Plantation 149
Palangumar Bay 137
Pallikulo Bay 21, 33, 43, 47, 61, 79, 96
Palompan 165
Pamplopa 163
Panay 160–161, 168, 174–175, 179–192, 187–188, 190
Pandi River 143–145, 147
Paramount Pictures 11
Parang 180–181, 183–184
Pasley, Ralph L. 119
Patch, Alexander 56, 65
Patrol Torpedo Boats (PT) 51, 62, 167, 178, 187
Payne, F.R. 20–21
Peak, Wilbur L. 30
Pearl Harbor 5, 8, 19, 46, 154, 201
Peleliu 155, 156
Pendergrast, Frederick R. 30
Pensacola, Florida 29
Persons, W.D. 92
Peters, Herbert A. 43, 50, **54**, 55, 63, **64**
Petersen Plantation 22
Peterson, Thomas K. 185, 195
Petty, Douglas D. 185, 195
Philippine Islands (Philippines) 5, 79, 81, 155–157, 161, 165, 180, 191, 200–202
Philippine Islands Ground Units:
 1st Filipino Infantry—197
 10th Military District—176
 44th "Hunters" Division—171

45th Infantry Regiment—171
 Hunters ROTC—171
 President Quezon's Own Guerillas (PCOG)—171
Pierce, Francis E. 11
Pikit 182–183
Pirages, William J. 73, 82–83, 90, 101, 103, 105, 108, 110, 115, 129–130, 135, 138, 150–151, 153, 162, 166, 171, 181, 192
Piva Airfield 81, 87–156, 158, 202
Plaines des Gaiacs 15
Plano Mission 153
Platt, Frank 18
Poehlman Arthur W. 125, 130, 132, 137–138, 142, 147, 151–152, 155, 161, 165
Pogo 193
Point Pussei 41
Pokolomo Point 147
Pondo 121, 134, 137, 139, 140–143, 146, 149, 154
Poor, Ernest E. 167, 169, 178, 181, 184–185, 187, 189, 191, 196
Popatala Island 153
Poporang 144
Porton Plantation 127
Potter, Lehn J. 192, 195
Praed Point 104, 116, 124
Pratt and Whitney 70, 181
Prescans, Nicholas 11
Preston, A. Murray 187
Propeller School at Hamilton Standard 70
Proulx, Eugene F. 172
Puk Puk Island 128, 131
Pulangi River 179
Puriatia Island 123
Purita River 151
Purple Heart 129
Puruata Island 101, 123
Put Put 105–114, 116, 123–124, 129–131, 133–135, 137, 140–143

Quackenbush, Robert S., Jr. 29–30
Quantico 190

Rabaul 44, 47, 54, 63, 79, 81–85, 87, 90, 93–95, 98–99, 102, 104, 108, 110, 117–118, 121, 124, 127, 146, 152, 190
Raganga Plantation 141
Railsback, Eldon H. **37**, 40, 43, **54**, 56, 61
Ralabang Plantation 131, 137, 141
Raluana Point 94, 101, 108, 121, 126–127, 150
Ralum Supply Dump 87, 89–91, 101–103, 127–128
Rancourt, Louis W. 77–78
Rangarere 140
Rapopo Airfield 82, 84, 87, 92, 96, 101–103, 143
Rataval 102, 104, 117, 118, 121–123
Ratsoa 140
Rause, Robert 185, 189, 191, 196
Raviola 143
Reit 142
Rekata Bay 50, 51

Renee River 79
Rennell Island 30
Renner, Joseph N. 9, 56, 61–63, 66
Reusser, Kenneth L. 56
Rhodes, Frank J. 159, 162, 167, 196
Rhodes, Richard M. 56
Ridings, Eugen W. 189
Rigu Mission 151
Robinson, Frank A. 136
Robinson, James W. **159**, 162–164, 166, 168–169, 174, 178, 188, 195
Robinson, Max K. 76, 82–84, 87, 96–98, 102, 118, 119, 120, 125
Robinson, Richard W. 165
Robstown, Texas 193
Rokunda Plantation 107
Romberg, Paul F. 185, 195
Rosario 164
Rose, William I. 18
Rosellen, Robert R. 71, 81, 83, 95, 97, 100, 104, 114–115, 119, 123, 130, 134–135, 138, 140–141, 149, 150, 152, 162, 166, 168, 172, 181, 192
Roviana Lagoon 59
Rowan, W.H. 168
Rowell, Ross E. 11
Royal New Zealand Air Force (RNZAF) 47, 112
Ruby Bay 140
Rumba 99, 134, 140
Ruri Bay 136
Russell Islands 138
Rutledge, Oscar P. 36, 43–45

Sabatier, Henry S. 57, 63
Sac Sac 187, 198
Sae River 99
Sagay 188, 193
St. George Channel 83, 87
St. George Channel 98, 105
St. Johns 149
St. Paul 108
Salt Lake City, Utah 11
Salton Sea, California 11
Samal Island 177
Samar 62, 89, 155–161, 169, 172, 178, 185, 191
Samiepan 164
Samoa 14
San Bernadino Straight 178
San Diego, California 11–12, 16, 31, 69–70, 72, 78
San Erique 161
San Francisco, California 69
San Jose 160–161, 163–164, 181–182
San Roque 185
Sandbach, Harold G. 159, 162, 165, 178, 191, 195
Santa Cruz 53
Santa Isabel 50–51, 57, 63
Saunders, Laverne G. 23
Savo Island 26
Scheussler, Carl I. 18, 23–24, 26, **28**
Schewe, Howard W. 185, 189, 192, 196
Schoetz, David J. 76, 80–81, 84, 89–90, 97, 109, 129–130, 138,

140–141, 152, 154, 169, 178, 181–182, 192
Schroeder, Frank A. 138, **141**–143, 145–148, 151–152, 154, 160–164, 166, 168–169, 172, 174–177, 179, 180–181, 183–184, 186
Schwethelm, Harry F. 41, 43, **54**, 56, **58**
Scott, Charles 159, 162, 167, 169–170, 178, 181, 184, 196, 198–199
Scoville, William H. 77, 81, 84, 87, 96–97, 99–100, 106, 110, 114, 117, 130, 134–135, 137–139, 151–152, 160, 162, 166, 178–179, 181–182, 184–185, 188
SCR-270 Radar Set 20–21, 23
Seabees 155
Sealark Channel 26
Secrest J.L. 51
Segond Channel 29, 41, 79, 81
Selik River 99
Seragi 137, 141
Serekata River 79
Sergai 149
Seventh Day Mission 134
Sharp, George E. 166
Shively, R.L. 51
Shortland Islands 144, 150
Sigan, Nick A. 74, 81, 83, 87, 91, 96–97, 99–100, 107, 110, 117, 131, 133–134, 137–139, 152, 162, 165
Silut Lagoon 192, 197–198
Simpson Harbor 82–83, 87, 119–120
Smith, Howard E., Jr. 82–85, 87, 100–104, 117, 120–123, 125, 129, 130, 135, 138, 140–141, 143, 146–153, 161–162, 166, 168–170, 172, 174–181, 183–184, 188
Smith, Samuel R. 159, 162, 165, 178, 185, 191, 195
Sogod 199
Sohana Island 94, 99, 104
Solomon Island 11–12, 29, 32, 52, 55, 58, 66, 79, 128, 138, 190, 202
Soragon Bay 167
Soraken Plantation 141, 143, 145–146
South Patrol Force 26–27
Spindler, Thornton F. 104–105, 108, 115, 129
Sprenger, Robert F. 81, 94, 101
Spurlock, Roy T. 8, **12**, 18, 24–**25**, 27–29, 43, 45, **54**, 56, **58**, 59, 60–61
STAD (Special Temporary Aviation Duty) 33, 81, 101
Sterling 114
Stiles, W.H. 10
Stockholm Plantation 137
Stout, Robert F. 50
Sturgis, James B. 81–82, 95–96, 99–100, 103, 107, 110, 117, 131, 133–134, 137–139, 151, 161–162, 165
Sulpa 200
Support Air Party 191, 194–195, 197
Surigao 162, 168, 175–177, 180

Suva 47
Swick, Orville R. 104–105, 108, 115, 129
Sydney, Australia 97, 104, 127

Tabago 101
Tabogon 193, 197–198
Tabuelan 194, 200
Tabut 142
Tacloban 173
Tagoloan 168, 172
Takasago Farm 108–109
Takis Plantation 123
Talisay 175, 188–189
Tamalili Plantation 130
Tanjay 168
Tanner, Grover K. 81, 87, 101–102, 125, 129, 138, 140, 147–148
Tanuan 170, 175, 179
Tassafaronga 52
Tautaua River 129
Tawara 79
Tawui Point 102, 122
Tay Tay 169
Taylor, Robert W. 73
Teller, Robert W. 79–83, 85, 89, 90, 94, 97–104, 117, 120–121, 123–125, 131, 134–135
Teop Island 151
Thatch Weave 9, 42, 57
Thornton, Powell D. 82, 85, 97, 100, 102–103
Three Oaks Restaurant 78
Tigbauan 187
Timputd Mission 153
Tobera Airfield 82–83, 89–92, 95–98, 103–107, 113, 115, 137, 149, 152, 155
Toberei Plantation 99
Toboi 121
Toburai 107
TOE (Table of Equipment) 200
Tokyo Express 47, 56, 66
Toma 107–108, 134
Tomavatur Radar Station 148
Tonga 46–47
Tonolei 117, 134, 142, 150, 153
Tontouta Airfield 15, 18, 20, 23, 201
Toriu 121–122, 134, 149
Torokina 87–88, 112, 114–115, 117, 121–123, 130, 145, 149
Totavi 133
Towannmaronga 139
Trenchard, Harold R. 57
Trihup 140
Truk 79, 82
Tsimba Plantation 153
Tubok 184
Tuburan 184, 186, 188, 191–192, 199
Tugui 135
Tulagi 23–26, 30, 51
Turner, Richmond K. 11
Turtle Bay 22, 47, 83, 202
Tuttle, Louis P. 48–49
Typhoon Haiyan 202

Ulagun 143
Ulamona 147

Ulaveo Plantation 56
Ulu Plantation 149
United States 5, 11, 14, 67
United States Army:
 Air Corps Units:
  5th Air Force—158–159, 191
  5th Fighter Command—174
  11th Bombardment Group—15, 18, 23, 38, 40
  13th Air Force—199
  22nd Bomb Group—165
  42nd Bomb Squadron—29
  85th Fighter Wing—159, 175, 177
  98th Bomb Squadron—29
 Ground Units:
  4th Defense Battalion—20, 23
  Sixth Army—160, 164
  Eighth Army—197
  XIV Corps—88
  23rd Infantry Division (Americal)—88, 139, 178–179, 188–189, 191, 197
  25th Infantry Division—55
  37th Infantry Division—88
  52nd Army Hospital—90–91
  76th Coast Artillery—33
  132nd Infantry Regiment—65, 189
  164th Infantry Regiment—48, 139, 188
  182nd Infantry Regiment—33, 178, 189
United States Marine Corps:
 Air Groups and Ground Units:
  1st Marine Air Wing (MAW)—31, 33, 50, 53, 153, 155, 166, 200
  I Marine Amphibious Corps—88
  1st Marine Division—11, 13, 18
  1st Marine Raider Battalion—12, 15, 23, 25
  3rd Marine Division—88
  4th MBDAW—56
  5th Marines—26
  7th Marines—47
  22nd Marines—12
  Marine Air Group (MAG)-11—79, 83
  Marine Air Group (MAG)-12—173, 179
  Marine Air Group (MAG)-14—81, 84, 103, 129, 143, 155–156, 158–159, 164–165, 170, 172–173, 175, 178, 182, 187–188, 190–191, 194, 200
  Marine Air Group (MAG)-23—19, 44, 46
  Marine Air Group (MAG)-24—89, 101, 129
  MBDAG-44—69
 Squadrons:
  VMB-154—8, 30
  VMF-112—51, 61, 65
  VMF-115—103, 112–116, 173
  VMF-121—49–51, 54, 58–59
  VMF-122—61, 66
  VMF-124—67
  VMF-211—11, 51, 112–117
  VMF-212—18, 19, 33, 40, 43, 45,

Index

51, 143–144, 147–149, 165, 167–168, 178, 200
VMF-215—112–114, 116
VMF-218—71, 178
VMF-221—73
VMF-222—165, 167, 200
VMF-223—19, 37, 110–114, 116–121, 127–128, 143–144, 147–148, 165, 169, 172, 178, 181, 199–200
VMF-224—19, 38, 40
VMF-225—69, 71
VMJ-2—7
VMJ-253—33, 41
VMO-151—56
VMSB-131—63, 66
VMSB-132—51
VMSB-133—127–128, 145–146
VMSB-141—51
VMSB-142—56-57
VMSB-231—7, 19, 38
VMSB-232—19, 37
VMSB-233—63, 65
VMSB-234—63, 66
VMSB-235—91–92, 94, 98
VMSB-236—69, 119–121, 127–128, 145–146
VMSB-243—112–114, 117
VMSB-341—92
United States Naval Academy 8, 11
United States Navy:
  Ground Units
    7th Construction Battalion—33
    61st Construction Battalion—158
    91st Construction Battalion—158, 174
    CUB-1—33, 36
  Ships:
    USS *Alnitah*—96, 101
    USS *Astoria*—23–28
    USS *Bagley*—28
    USS *Chicago*—26–27
    USS *Colhoun*—23
    USS *Crescent City*—61
    USS *Curtiss*—14, 17, 29–31, 33, 42
    USS *Elliot*—26
    USS *Enterprise*—53
    USS *George Clymer*—67
    USS *Heywood*—12–15, 31
    USS *Hornet*—8, 43
    USS *Jarvis*—26
    USS *Kitty Hawk*—67, 68
    USS *Long Island*—19, 37
    USS *Maryland*—31
    USS *Mugford*—26
    USS *President Jackson*—28
    USS *Quincy*—26–28
    USS *Refuge*—168
    USS *Saratoga*—46
    USS *Tangier*—78, 79
    USS *Tippercanoe*—7
    USS *Vincennes*—23, 26–28
    USS *Wasp*—43
  Squadrons:
    VB-6—33
    VF-5—33, 44
    VF-71—33
    VS-3—33
    VT-8—33, 51
  Task Forces and Task Groups"
    Task Force 61—18, 24
    Task Force 62—24
    Task Force 63—24
    Task Group 63.6—18
    Task Force 65—47
    Task Force 74—189
    Task Group X-ray—24
    Task Group Yoke—24
  United States Navy Photograqhic School 29
Uri 137
Urukuk 131, 137
USAF Cemetery Manila #1 170
Utuan 113

Vandegrift, Alexander 18, 24, 26, 30–31, 47, 56
Van der Haeghen, Robert F. 91
Vanderpool, Jay D. 171
Vangunu 66
Vanuatu 202
Varzin Plantation 110
Verahue 65
Vila 65
Visayan Islands 161, 188
Vroome, Ray L. 56, 63, 65
Vulanlama Coffee Plantation 141
Vulcan Crater 97, 119–121
Vunabal Plantation 125, 130
Vunagalip 109
Vunakanau Airfield 82–85, 87, 102, 106–107, 108–109, 112–114, 116, 133, 141, 148, 149
Vunalama Plantation 108, 149
Vunapaldig 114, 143
Vunapope 85, 96, 102
Vunipa 140

Wagner, Joseph G. 185, 195
Waitavalo 129, 135
Wake Island (Film) 10–11
Walaur 120
Wallace, Harold C. 81, 145, 152–153, 159–160, 162–163, 165, 167, 169–170
Walsh, Thomas W. 185, 188
Walters, Lynford S. 182, 197

Warangoi River 105–107, 113, 130–131, 142, 152
Ward, Ray G. 136, 138–139, 141, 151–152, 154, 170, 181–182, 184, 186
Warren, Arthur J., Jr. 125, 131, 138–140, 144, 150–152, 161, 163, 169, 170, 172, 188
Wat Wat Plantation 129–131, 141, 143
Waterhouse Cove 131
Watom Island 105, 112, 123, 130, 137, 146, 149, 155
Webber, William G. 81–82, 84, 94–95, 97–98, 100, 103
Weems, Philip Van Horn 10
Weiland, Pat *10*, 43–45, *54*, 56–*58*, 59–61
Welch, Claude H. 19, *20*–23, *54*, 66
Welch, Henry B. 87, 148, 173, 176
Welch, Robert W. 185, 189, 191, 195
Whisenhant, Nathaniel L. 192, 195
Whitaker, William H. 57, 66
Whitten, Robert T. 18, 24–26, *27*–29, 43, 45, *54*
Wiart, Andy 200
Wickham Bay 61
Wide Bay 104, 135
Willard, Edward C. 98
Willey, Howard T. 73, 76
Wilson, Cecil M. 77, 81, 84, 94, 97, 105
Wirawir Point 143
Wisner Ben 59
Wojcik, Thaddeus 43, *54*, 56
Wolf, John C. 138, 141, 145, 147, 151–152, 160–161, 167, 170–172, 181, 183, 188, 193–194, 196, 198–199
Wubber, Hazlett H. 81, 87, 96–97, 102–103
Wunataishi River 139
Wunawatung 121
Wurawunurur 143
Wyatt, John W. *159*, 161, 168–169, 178, 181, 184, 198, 195

Yamamoto, Isoroku 5
Yeaman, Ralph *12*, 16–17, 40–42, *54*, 56
Yunck, Michael R. 40, 43, 50–*52*, 53, 57, 66
Yost, Don 58–59

Zero *see* Aircraft: Japanese
Zamboanga Peninsula 185
Zeke *see* Aircraft: Japanese